BLACK TRIALS

BLACK TRIALS

Citizenship from
the Beginnings of Slavery to the End of Caste

Mark S. Weiner

ALFRED A. KNOPF   NEW YORK 2004

THIS IS A BORZOI BOOK
PUBLISHED BY ALFRED A. KNOPF

Copyright © 2004 by Mark S. Weiner

All rights reserved under International and Pan-American
Copyright Conventions. Published in the United States by
Alfred A. Knopf, a division of Random House, Inc., New York,
and simultaneously in Canada by Alfred A. Knopf Canada, a division
of Random House of Canada Limited, Toronto. Distributed by
Random House, Inc., New York.

www.aaknopf.com

Knopf, Borzoi Books, and the colophon are registered trademarks
of Random House, Inc.

Library of Congress Cataloging-in-Publication Data

Weiner, Mark Stuart
Black trials : citizenship from the beginnings of slavery to the end of caste /
Mark S. Weiner—1st ed.
p.   cm.
"Published simultaneously in Canada"—T.p. verso
Includes bibliographical references.
ISBN 0-375-40981-5
1. African Americans—Legal status, laws, etc.—United States—History.   I. Title.

KF4757.W45 2004
342.7308'73—dc22   2004040860

Manufactured in the United States of America
First Edition

For Stephanie

Love and harmony combine,
And around our souls intwine,
While thy branches mix with mine,
And our roots together join.

Out of the cradle endlessly rocking

—WALT WHITMAN

Contents

Preface

This book tells a story about American citizenship by telling a series of stories about American law. By examining a group of prominent legal cases that I call "black trials," I aim to depict the changing status of black Americans within American national identity, and in so doing to reveal a central feature of that national identity itself. While the full meaning of the term "black trials" as I use it here will be developed in the following chapters, for now suffice it to say that black trials are legal events that figure symbolically and dramatically in American culture by making public certain basic ideological conflicts about race and civic life. They are legal dramas of citizenship, civic rituals through which we have come to know ourselves as a people. The grand jury investigations of the "Great Negro Plot," a slave conspiracy to burn down Manhattan in 1741. The hanging of the abolitionist John Brown for his raid on Harpers Ferry in 1859. The Supreme Court decisions of the *Amistad* in 1841, and *Dred Scott* in 1857, and *Plessy v. Ferguson* in 1896. The prosecution of Huey Newton, cofounder of the Black Panther Party, for killing a police officer in 1968. The televised charges and countercharges of Anita Hill and Clarence Thomas in 1991. All are part of a continuing narrative in our national life and cultural history.

The changes and continuities in this narrative have much to teach us. For the purposes of this book, the story of black trials sheds light on the vital issue often posed as "what it means to be an American."[1] Black trials can help us appreciate what our civic ideals have become—what we stand for as a society—as well as some of the obstacles that prevent us from achieving those ideals more completely. In the pages ahead, I depict a series of legal cases that allow us to peer into a history of resistance to principles of racial exclusion that, for centuries, were central to American conceptions of national identity. The struggle of Afro-Americans for individual and social justice forcefully challenged those principles and helped to fashion a more inclusive, liberal culture of citizenship in our country. The United States has now entered a decisive stage in the history of this effort, and if we are finally to see its success—the *full* inclusion of black Americans in civic life—we would be well served to clarify our common ideals and refresh the language in which we speak about them. I believe that studying the history of black trials can assist us in this process.

The cases I discuss are a blend of the famous and the forgotten. Many readers will have heard of the trials of the Scottsboro Boys or John Brown from their studies of American history, though they may not recall the details. Many will also have heard of some of the Supreme Court decisions I examine, such as *Plessy v. Ferguson* or *Brown v. Board of Education*. Some may know generally about Huey Newton's trial, a relatively recent event, or the case of the revolt aboard the slave ship *Amistad*, about which there was a Hollywood film a few years ago. It would be surprising, however, if more than a handful knew the names Joseph Hanno or Prudence Crandall, or had heard of the 1883 Supreme Court decision in *The Civil Rights Cases* or the prosecution of members of the Ku Klux Klan in up-country South Carolina after the Civil War. Some of these cases bear on great constitutional questions; most do not. But all were well known in their day—they were causes célèbres with a prominent presence in American culture.

It should be said that these cases have inspired a good deal of existing scholarship, on which I have gratefully relied. This book could not have been written without the venerable traditions of historical work on American slavery and American constitutional history, as well as the many excellent specific studies of the trials I examine, referenced in the notes. *Black Trials* differs from these studies in weaving the stories of individual cases into a single narrative within a particular interpretive frame. This book, however, is not a comprehensive survey of black trials; it rather is a selective rendering of their meaning as a tradition. There are a great many legal cases not examined here that would have been suitable for my analysis.

Much of my research for this book involved the recovery of biographical details from archives and primary documents. This was the sort of work common to many kinds of history, but in connection with this subject, I wish to make special note of an unfortunate reality: the lives of many black Americans involved in legal battles central to our national history, even the most famous and carefully studied cases, remain largely unexamined, even by professional historians. Many scholars who have written about the most influential legal decisions concerning slavery, for instance, have at times failed to mention even the names of the black men and women caught up in these proceedings. This neglect has unwittingly exacerbated the condition the historian E. P. Thompson, writing of the eighteenth-century English poor, called "the crime of anonymity."[2] It also has circumscribed our understanding of the past, concealing some of what its particularity might have to tell us.

This failing is not primarily the result of racial prejudice, though that played a part at one time. Historians of two or three generations ago were surely guilty of malign neglect of black history, but today the field is one of the most vibrant in the historical profession, and Afro-American issues figure prominently in many branches of university teaching and research. A more persistent and immediate cause of neglect may be found in the peculiar nature of legal history as a field. The work demands specialized academic training in both history and law, and the time and cost of such training ensures that its practitioners are relatively few. And owing to legal history's strong affiliation with law schools, as opposed to history departments, most legal historians have been concerned with issues significant primarily to the legal profession; the investigation of obscure past lives, whether of blacks or whites, has been far from the main line of their interests.

Whatever its cause, the lack of knowledge about the litigants in the cases I examine represented one of the great challenges in writing this book. The stories I tell are thus exercises not only in narrative history, but also in painstaking historical recovery, though for the most part the fact of that recovery will be apparent only to specialists. This is particularly so for the stories of Joseph Hanno, *Somerset's Case*, *Jones v. Van Zandt*, and *The Civil Rights Cases*, many of whose biographical features have been unknown until now.

As historians can best appreciate, such work is not only labor-intensive, but also one whose triumphs are occasioned by minute discoveries. For example, in Chapter 3, I discuss the life of James Somerset, a Virginia slave whose legal case against his master was long said to have "ended slavery in England." To learn simply that Somerset had been given a variety of expensive gifts by his master, an indication of his social status, took a month of full-time research into old account records, on microfilm, filled mostly with documentation about the price of molasses and indigo in the 1760s. That James Somerset was given half a yard of silk ribbon in 1765 may seem a small revelation, and yet I consider it to be a highly meaningful discovery, in fact one of the more significant of my career as a historian. Likewise, to learn that the foreman of the jury that convicted Joseph Hanno of murder in 1721 was related to the minister who gave his execution sermon required me to compare half of the illegible signature that remained on a poor microfilm copy of a weathered piece of colonial parchment to facsimiles of hundreds of signatures of prominent Bostonians of the early eighteenth century. A perfect match eventually appeared from behind the flashlight I brought into the stacks of Yale's Sterling Memorial Library, as I knelt on its dusty floor—a thrilling moment on whose memory I still draw in times of frustration.

In addition to the ethical importance of such recovery work, I have been motivated especially by its conceptual value. Specifically, as I discuss in the Introduction, I believe that issues of broad jurisprudential significance can be read in the most minute social and cultural phenomena of human experience: that in the slightest facts of cultural life, such as the gift of half a yard of silk ribbon by a master to his slave, or the shape of an individual's life or the contours of his or her personality, we can see a jurisprudence of race—a vision of race, law, and the social order. I also like to think of my historical method as essentially literary. My goal is to portray the past from an interpretative perspective rooted in the present, strongly guided by my own individual consciousness, sensitive to the subtleties of language, and ultimately grounded in particulars.

My hope is that this book will appeal to both the scholar and the general reader of serious nonfiction. The Introduction provides a theoretical framework for the remainder of the volume, but while necessary to professionals, it may not be for everyone. Those whose interest primarily lies in reading the stories of the trials may prefer to begin with Chapter 1. In any event, the framework made explicit in the Introduction is to be found implicitly in the succeeding chapters.

No book is an author's own singular achievement, and this is particularly the case for a book of history. The number of people I have to thank for their assistance is extensive. A few individuals, however, deserve special mention for their help. I wish to thank my students in "Major Trials in African-American History," taught in the American Studies Program at Stanford University during the winter term of the 1997–98 academic year, who have been a continuing source of inspiration. Mitchell Orenstein of the Maxwell School at Syracuse University not only was a great personal support, but also influenced my ideas on American history through his own work on the rule of law in Eastern Europe. My friend and agent, Tina Bennett, believed in this project from the start. My editor, George Andreou, provided support and exceptional expertise.

A number of friends, colleagues, and mentors were particularly encouraging or helpful at various points during the years this project developed. They include Jean-Christophe Agnew, Enrique Aguado-Asenjo, Amy Bach, Sarah Bilston, Donald Braman, John Brigham, Lincoln Caplan, Moises Castillo, Lois Chiang, Charleton Copeland, Joseph Corn, Prudence Cumberbatch, Deven Desai, Joel Fetzer, William Forbath, Jock Friedly, Richard Gillam, Robert Gordon, Ulrich Haltern, Christine Harrington, Thomas Hilbink, Allegra Hogan, Anthony Kronman, Chris Kubiak, David and Cathy Kuduk, Mark Lawrence, Brian Leiter, Catherine Lhamon, Daniel Markovits, Sean McCann, Andrea McDowell, Diarra McKinney, Carmen Moreno-Nuño, William Nelson, John Pollack, Robin Reardon, Joe Reed, Stephen Rich, Shelly Rosenblum, Chris Shannon, Ori Simchen, Rogers Smith, Kevin Stack, Michelle Stephens, Kate Stith, Holly Thomas, Karin Thomas, Trysh Travis, and Torben and Kristin von Staden. I have been grateful for the support of my students and colleagues at Rutgers School of Law–Newark, and I am proud to have joined the community of scholars and teachers there. I am especially indebted for the support of Stuart Deutsch, who twice provided the sponsorship of the Dean's Research Fund for my work, as well as Claire Dickerson, Charles Jones, John Leubsdorf, Greg Mark, Keith Sharfman, and George Thomas. I also wish to extend a special thanks to my parents, Bernard and Marijana Weiner.

I gratefully acknowledge the assistance of the National Endowment for the Humanities, which provided a year-long fellowship without which it would have been impossible for this book to have been written. Henry Abelove provided a warm welcome at the Center for the Humanities at

Wesleyan University during much of my fellowship term as an independent scholar in 2000–2001, and I am grateful to both him and the other residents of the Center.

The librarians and staff at the Yale Law School, Sterling Memorial Library, Stanford University, New York University, Wesleyan University, Columbia University, Temple University, Rutgers School of Law–Newark, Amherst College, the Library of Virginia, Colonial Williamsburg, the Library of Congress, the National Library of Scotland, the British Public Record Office, the Scottish National Portrait Gallery, the Massachusetts State Archives, the New York State Archives, the U.S. National Archives and the National Archives-Central Plains, -Great Lakes, -Northeast, -Pacific, and -Southeast, the American Antiquarian Society, the Supreme Court Historical Society, the Kentucky Historical Society, the Ohio Historical Society, the New Haven Historical Society, and many other smaller institutions were invaluable. Jon Butler and Harry Stout of the Institute for the Advanced Study of Religion at Yale were generous in acknowledging and encouraging my work on Joseph Hanno at an awards dinner in 2000, and the journal *Slavery & Abolition* provided similar support by publishing my research on James Somerset in April 2002. I was also greatly assisted by the opportunity to present my work at the Legal History Colloquium at New York University School of Law and at faculty colloquia at Cardozo and the University of Texas schools of law. The Center for Interdisciplinary Research (ZiF) in Bielefeld, Germany, similarly provided a lively forum for presenting some of my work on the Civil Rights Movement in April 2003, as did the German-American Lawyers' Association (DAJV) in October of that year in Berlin.

Finally, I wish to thank my wife, Stephanie, with whom I share both an intellectual and a personal partnership, and for whom words are not enough. We met the day I arrived at Stanford to teach the seminar that was to become this book, and she has been by my side ever since. My gratitude for the gifts she has given me in the course of our lives together is approximated by the words of William Blake on the dedication page to this volume, which Stephanie helped see through many months of trial and delight.

A note on historical editing. As this is a volume intended in part for the general reader, I have sometimes imposed contemporary form on older styles of spelling, punctuation, and typeface. It has never been my intention to alter the meaning of the original words quoted, only to change their appearance on the page.

A note on usage. Throughout this volume, I generally use the terms "Afro-American" and "black," though I occasionally use the terms "African-American" and "Negro," depending on the context. The appropriateness of these terms—and of using any one of them to describe people who would not have described themselves as such—is the subject of intense debate. I agree with the Harvard sociologist Orlando Patterson that "Afro-American" is a more accurate term than "African-American" in acknowledging but not overstating a connection with the culture of Africa and in denoting an ethnicity rather than a race. I disagree, however, that the term "black" carries unavoidably negative connotations rooted in Western and, especially, American history and that it should be avoided. I use the terms "colored" and "negro," with a lowercase *n*, only when quoting directly from older sources.

BLACK TRIALS

Introduction:
Rituals of Citizenship

▲

On June 7, 1892, in New Orleans, a young black man stepped on board a train and into American history. His name was Homer Adolph Plessy, and though born and raised in Louisiana, the thirty-year-old shoemaker must have looked uncomfortable in the summer heat clutching a first-class ticket to Covington. After all, he knew he was about to be arrested. Plessy boarded the East Louisiana Railroad with no other purpose, and he probably wasted no time carrying it out: he walked into one of the coaches reserved for whites, and he sat down. Plessy himself could "pass" for white (he was an "octoroon," as a person with "one-eighth African blood" would have been known at the time), but it was not his intention to pass here. When the conductor saw Plessy and asked about his race, he readily admitted he was "colored," but he refused to move to one of the Jim Crow cars set aside for blacks. Plessy's challenge did not go unanswered. He was quickly arrested by detective Chris C. Cain. The next day, he was released on a $500 bond, posted by a small but influential political group of blacks and Creoles, but the matter hardly ended there. Homer Plessy had set off on a legal odyssey that would not conclude until a full four years later, in 1896, with the Supreme Court opinion in *Plessy v. Ferguson*, one of the most notorious cases about race in American constitutional law, and one of the best-known examples of what I call "black trials."

Over one hundred years later, on June 17, 1994, in Los Angeles, another black trial would begin as a middle-aged black man stepped into his white Ford Bronco. His name was Orenthal James Simpson, and unlike Homer Plessy, he was already famous: he had achieved lasting celebrity as a football star, admired especially for his ability to run. Throughout America, he was known simply as "O. J." Five days earlier, Simpson's former wife, a blond white woman, had been found brutally murdered in front of her Brentwood apartment, along with a white male friend. Both had been stabbed repeatedly by a man of great strength. O. J. had physically abused his wife in the past, and Los Angeles police quickly gathered evidence to suggest he was the killer. After writing an ambiguous farewell note to family and friends, O. J. stepped into the passenger seat of his car, in his bag a disguise kit, $8,000 in cash, and a .357 Magnum revolver. His former teammate Al Cowlings then drove him north on Interstate 5. When they were intercepted by police, Cowlings slowed to forty miles per hour and called 911 to negotiate how O. J. would be taken into custody. News helicopters buzzed overhead, broadcasting the scene live across the nation. For the next year and a half, Americans seemed to follow every detail of a dramatic trial that, despite its lack of constitutional significance, would be a momentous event in Afro-American legal history.

Two hundred years earlier, in 1771, a well-dressed black man walked through the streets of London. His name was James Somerset, and he was on his way to meet an antislavery activist named Granville Sharp. Somerset would tell Sharp that he had run away from his master, Charles Steuart, a Virginia merchant and high-ranking official in the British colonial customs. Steuart owned a number of slaves, but his records indicate that Somerset was his favorite. Steuart even took Somerset with him as his personal manservant during travels along the North American coast; he had every indication that "able" Somerset was a loyal slave, a willing participant in the ordered world in which whites ruled and blacks served. But after the two sailed together for England, where slavery had not been formally recognized by Parliament, their relationship quickly changed. Somerset was baptized, taking the name James (many slaves believed baptism would advance their quest for freedom), and he ran away; to the chagrin of his stunned and irate master, Somerset disappeared into the London black underground. Soon afterward, Somerset appeared at Sharp's door seeking advice and support, and he was not disappointed. A year later, James Somerset would have his freedom, and the Court of King's Bench would issue an opinion in *Somerset's Case*, one of the great black trials of the eighteenth century. The court's declaration that slavery found no support in natural law would nourish antislavery activism in both Britain and America for decades to come.

In describing the cases of Homer Plessy, O. J. Simpson, and James Somerset as "black trials," I have used the term with a specific meaning in mind. Black trials are legal events that by their dramatic quality have symbolically defined the status of blacks in American civic life. That act of definition centers on a vital but unexamined issue in the history of American citizenship: the relationship of Afro-Americans to the concept of law. Put another way, black trials have determined the civic status of Afro-Americans by defining their status within the very idea of legality—by addressing whether they are "a people of law." And because the spirit of American law has been a subject of dispute among ordinary people of all races, black trials have also carried a larger significance, serving as public occasions in which Americans have fought to define the nature of their collective identity. Black trials have unfolded, in particular, against a backdrop of three contending traditions of popular legal and political thought: a liberal jurisprudence based on individual rights, a Christian tradition rooted in the Old and New Testaments, and a caste vision founded on principles of racial purity and pollution. The struggles among the advocates of these three civic traditions over the legal stakes in individual black trials, I will explain, has also been a struggle about the civic meaning of America.

My interpretative framework is based on a distinctively cultural approach to Afro-American legal history. In taking this approach, I draw on ideas from diverse academic fields, from legal studies to anthropology, and illustrations from other lands and other times. This method is intended above all to highlight phenomena often intuitively understood but rarely discussed and, in turn, to suggest how the stories and figures I describe are endowed with a larger historical meaning.

THE CULTURE OF CIVIC BELONGING

American identity, the culture and values that hold us together as a nation: if newspapers are any indication, Americans are becoming increasingly interested in the subject. In the *New York Times*, the phrase "American identity" appeared 14 times from 1980 to 1984; 17 from

1985 to 1989; 47 from 1990 to 1994; 104 from 1995 to 1999, a jump of more than 100 percent; and already has appeared 98 times in the less than four years between 2000 and the time of this writing. In the "Major Papers" file of the Lexis database (which includes newspapers such as the *Los Angeles Times* and the *Washington Post*), there is an even more marked increase. Or take the career of the related phrase "what it means to be an American." It appeared in the "Major Papers" file 16 times from 1980 to 1984; 72 times from 1985 to 1989; 230 from 1990 to 1994; 409 from 1995 to 1999; and already has appeared 522 times from 2000 through May 2004. The reasons behind this trend are complex, and while we cannot exclude the tenacity of cant, at the very least the numbers would seem to suggest the beginning of a gradual but building process of national self-examination. Academic scholarship seems to confirm this development. A wide array of recent books about issues of national identity has been produced by young and more established scholars alike.[1]

The word "citizenship" is the drumbeat of this intellectual process, the meter to which it keeps time. The word itself has rich and diverse meanings, yet we tend to use it with little awareness of that complexity. For instance, by one convention the term means something rather like "civilian," a person not employed as a professional by the state; by another etymology, now largely obsolete, citizen is synonymous with "city dweller." A more common usage, though one that seems slowly and sadly to be losing currency, refers to a state of active political participation and community involvement, a way of speaking about citizenship associated with those high school civics classes that once sought to instill "good citizenship" (an effort derived from conceptions of "civic virtue" central to the thought of ancient Rome). Other contemporary meanings are purely formal and refer to the official grant or recognition of an individual's national affiliation. This last is a distinctly modern sense of the term, a product of the development of the nation-state in the wake of the European Renaissance. This concept of citizenship has become indispensable to a world in which state bureaucracies are responsible for providing a wide range of goods and services, and its value is never more evident than when it is absent, as in the case of stateless peoples such as Palestinian refugees; its significance has been heightened in recent decades by greater global migration.

Despite this diversity of meaning, there is a tendency in American public and scholarly debate today to think about citizenship in connection specifically with the civic status of groups, especially minority groups. The roots of the trend reach especially to the "multiculturalism" and "identity" debates of the 1980s, aspects of the cultural legacy of the Civil Rights Movement, whose success inspired many minorities to demand greater public acknowledgment of their place in the fabric of American life.[2] The issues associated with citizenship now typically cause us to consider the civic status of a wide variety of individual communities that make up our larger national community—from women who wish to serve in the armed forces, to gay men who wish to marry, to Latin American migrants who have settled in the United States. Will these groups be granted "full citizenship," the question is put, or will their members instead be forced to remain "second-class citizens" because of some distinctive trait, belief, or practice that cuts against the American grain? Among scholars, this idea of citizenship often goes under the name of "group inclusion," and a large body of literature speaks to its underlying assumption: that most Americans judge their nation in part by the place minorities hold in our civic life; the way we treat minority groups is a reflection of who we are. The story of black trials concerns an especially vital aspect of the history of group inclusion, because the minority community whose status has been of the greatest consequence for the development of our society as a whole—whose particular fate has been most closely bound with the meaning of our nation—has been Afro-Americans.

Group inclusion involves two distinct notions of citizenship itself. The first, explicitly legal, often coincides with the idea of civil or political rights.[3] To be considered a citizen in this sense, at least in a democratic society, one must not only possess formal citizenship, but also enjoy the rights to vote and participate in the process of government (for instance, by sitting on juries), as well as the freedom to go about one's life in "the pursuit of happiness." Absent the legal guarantee of such rights, one is at best only a partial member of the community. Throughout American history, a great many have lived in this civic shadow land, a status that was the direct result of belonging to some disqualified group as defined by the state. For instance, such was long the case for women, who won the federal right to vote only in 1920, and though we tend to overlook the fact because it somehow seems justified, it is still the case for many felons and for children, who are citizens in the formal sense of the term but typically cannot vote and are denied a wide range of legal protections of their liberties. In the Jim Crow era of which the decision *Plessy v. Ferguson* stood as an icon—having advanced the principle of "separate but equal" at the heart of southern segregation—Afro-Americans were relegated to an even more limited civic status. They may have had the formal standing of American nationals, but they were denied fundamental civil and political rights. They were a subjugated, disenfranchised class of partial citizens living under the power of the American government but denied many of its protections.

The second notion of group citizenship is a cultural one. For a group to enjoy full citizenship in a cultural sense, the civic majority must recognize that the group "belongs," that it shares certain basic characteristics with the community, a principle scholars sometimes call "community solidarity."[4] This is a subtle phenomenon—it is usually much less tangible than, say, a statute denying women the right to vote—but it is partly the intangibility of this aspect of citizenship that makes it so important. The value we place on community solidarity in America owes much to our history as a nation of immigrants, but its importance can be seen with special clarity when we look beyond our own borders. The Federal Republic of Germany, for instance, with one of the largest immigrant populations in Europe, is home to over 2 million people of Turkish descent. About a half million of those hold German citizenship, which grants them the right to vote in federal elections, so long as they surrender their Turkish passports. Yet all the political rights in the world have not made these Turks full members of their country, insofar as Germans, like other Europeans—and Americans through most of our history—have customarily defined their national identity in terms of racial descent. The children of Turkish immigrants may be legal citizens of the state and entitled to its benefits, but as the recent effort to ban the wearing of headscarves in German schools suggests, the majority would balk at calling these citizens fully "German" (a view just now beginning to shift, especially among younger Germans, as the third generation of Turkish immigrants comes of age). Similarly, we might consider the restricted status of Asian immigrants in Japan, a society still more evidently devoted to ideals of ethnic purity, where one can find signs reading NO FOREIGNERS ALLOWED at private clubs and businesses. Even after having lived for generations in the country, mastered its language and culture, and taken Japanese names, descendants of immigrants from Vietnam, Korea, or China are generally not considered "real" Japanese—they are deemed to be outsiders, despite the nation's pressing need to attract immigrant labor, and are subject to a range of social and economic discriminations.[5] Afro-Americans in the time of Homer Plessy faced a comparable cultural barrier; it provided the basis for W. E. B. Du Bois to observe, in *The Souls of Black Folk*, that being "an American" and being "a Negro" were "two warring ideals."[6] In the eyes of the majority, to be fully American was to be white, a view that went far in determining the scope of black civil and political rights as well.

Rogers M. Smith, a political scientist and historian, recently coined a useful term for explaining the link between the legal and cultural aspects of citizenship: "civic myths" or "myths of civic identity."[7] A civic myth, he explains, is a widely shared story that serves as the basis of national identity. It is an underlying civic principle that describes why a group of people constitutes a nation, who can belong to the nation and who cannot, and what the nation's values and aims are; the myth informs not only law and legal decisions but also social and cultural life. A good example can be found in South Africa under apartheid. There, one dominant civic myth—not only enshrined in the constitution, but also manifest in even the smallest social interactions across the lines of race—described the nation as a gift from God to whites, whose ancestors had made an arduous, Exodus-like trek across the continent. The civic myths of a number of other countries are similarly grounded in racial descent (in the United States, this obtains for Native American nations), but civic myths may also encompass religion, language, and historical struggles for principles of all kinds, including those strongly opposed to racial hierarchy. The guiding civic myth of the former Soviet Union, for instance, described its citizens as participating in an ongoing historical struggle that would create a global classless society—an ideal embodied in cultural and legal forms throughout Soviet life, from the use of the term "comrade" to laws mandating highly centralized social welfare.

Smith's notion of "civic myth" expresses an assumption that informs my approach to the stories in this book: that the identity of any nation, the way it draws its circle of civic belonging, is defined by a set of sometimes unarticulated core ideas that can be discovered through reflection and inquiry. From the colonial era to our own time, the history of black trials has centered on one such core idea: the need for groups seeking full civic membership in the United States to be widely perceived as being "a people of law." In turning to this concept now, I wish to peer beneath the surface of our national identity to describe the conceptual machinery at work in the American culture of citizenship.

BECOMING A PEOPLE OF LAW

The concept of "a people of law" has deep roots in the Judeo-Christian tradition. It is associated most closely with the Hebrews of the ancient Near East, who, the Bible records, entered into a covenant, or contract, with their one God and pledged to obey his strict, complex system of rules. Scholars believe that this commitment to the law of a monotheistic God dramatically distinguished the Hebrews from the peoples around them, who believed their fate to be governed by the host of capricious deities to whom they paid tribute (the Babylonians, for instance, worshiped Anu, the sky god; Enlil, the storm god; and Ea, the water god, among others). Moreover, it was by accepting the Law as their measure of moral aspiration that the Hebrews were transformed from a collection of seminomadic tribes into a people and, ultimately, a nation. This transformation is the subject of copious discussion among religious and secular scholars alike. For our purposes, though, we need only bear in mind that adherence to the Mosaic Code was the prerequisite for true membership in the community the Law defined. To live within the nation of Israel was to observe the Law, and thus to be a part of a people of law. This notion of group identity based on common legal commitment has been central to the civic and religious life of the West, as well as to Islamic nations. While the distinction was later made in the Christian tradition, especially by Martin Luther interpreting the writings of Paul, between a people of law and a people of grace (between those who were justified by strict adherence to prescribed rules and those justified by faith), Christians would nevertheless see themselves, too, as a people of law, pledging devotion to a new covenant growing out of the Old Testament while at the same time transforming and superseding it. Muslims have a related term: *ahl al-kitab*, usually translated as "people of the book," a concept that includes Jews and Christians.

Today, the condition denoted by the phrase "a people of law" is an unspoken but prevailing requirement for civic membership within multiethnic, constitutional democracies. In such societies—the United States and Great Britain are good examples, and Europe will become one as its political integration proceeds—full civic membership is based not on racial descent, but on allegiance to the state. For this reason, their citizens are described as "a people" only for rhetorical effect (when politicians speak of the American people, it is a very different matter from speaking about the German *Volk*); they instead are described as "a nation," a community defined by shared legal values. The civic glue of these communities is a commitment to law and the constitution, just as Islamic societies have traditionally welcomed all peoples of the book. Conversely—and here lies a key issue for the history of Afro-American citizenship—those groups thought to lack a capacity for law are typically viewed as internal exiles, a people apart. Minority groups collectively seeking "full citizenship" in the United States have thus usually been obliged to struggle in diverse ways to overcome a perception of their legal incapacity. This effort has been an important aspect of the fight for civic assimilation by American Indians, Catholics, Jews, Latinos, and Asians—and it is the animating force behind the history of black trials as a legal and cultural tradition.

The specific requirements incumbent on a minority group aiming to establish its qualification as a people of law have varied from one group to another, but in general they may be arranged into three irreducible criteria. First, a people of law has an inherent *capacity* to honor the most fundamental legal principles of the nation. In a liberal legal order, for instance, where property rights are fundamental, no group could achieve full citizenship if it were thought to reject the concept of private property. In the late nineteenth century, an alliance of white reformers thus sought to "save" American Indians by destroying systems of Indian tribal governance and settling natives on individual plots of land. This twin effort to undermine Indian law and promote white conceptions of property was motivated by the hope that, once taught the distinction between "mine and thine," natives could become full Americans. Oppressive though this campaign was, the dominant alternative vision against which its supporters fought was far worse: that Indians, deemed inherently incapable of such a conceptual conversion, could never join the circle of American civic life, probably would "disappear" as a people, and perhaps should be liquidated. Despite its brutal consequences, the reformers' faith that Indians could learn to live by the principles of American legality—that they were able to conform to liberal legal standards and thereby become a people of law—was in their eyes an advocacy of Indian welfare. By contrast, those who thought natives incapable of upholding white legal norms were resigned to the view of Indians as irredeemable outcasts.[8]

Second, to become a people of law requires that a group be deemed *worthy* of the law and its protection. In other words, the values underlying the law must be consistent with the notion that the group in question is entitled to enjoy the benefits of the law. If a nation lives under a law whose animating purpose is to distribute goods according to race, for instance, then low-status racial groups can never hope to achieve full civic membership. The traditional Indian caste system, to take a prominent though not exclusive example, was based on a rigid hierarchy governed by notions of religious purity and pollution that corresponded roughly to occupation. The society was divided into four main groups, or *varnas*, each a hereditary status: Brahmans (priests), Kshatriyas (warriors), Vaisyas (merchants), and Shudras (peasants).[9] While individual members of these groups could experience temporary forms of impurity, a large class, known in English by the catch-all term "untouchables," was branded permanently impure and relegated to the lowest forms of work, traditionally the tanning of hides. Indeed, untouchables were formally outside the caste system itself—literally they were people of no caste—and as such were unworthy even to enter Hindu temples. The religious principles at the heart of Indian society forever confined them to the role of outsider. A similarly severe instance can be found in the case of the Japanese *burakumin* (hamlet people) or *eta* ("full of filth"), descendants of peoples who through their occupations bore the stigma of Buddhist and Shinto ritual pollution. A much less extreme example exists in Islamic societies, where the hospitality for which they are historically renowned is extended to all peoples of the book, but not beyond.

Finally, to be a people of law requires that a group demonstrate a commitment to the law in its *culture* and everyday practices. Here, we might consider again the ancient Hebrews. Jewish law does not merely proscribe the most egregious lapses of human conduct, such as murder and adultery. Beyond the Ten Commandments, the Law also governs a wide array of minute aspects of daily life, with hundreds of codes, the ones encompassing dietary rules being only the most famous; some censure misdeeds, others compel positive acts such as charity. The regulation of everyday life by the Mosaic Code is so particular, in fact, that the most routine daily tasks and habits become to a degree sacred performances—all actions pointing toward the Law and its demands. (The Law is so demanding that one fine Talmudic story describes how, when God offered it to other nations, each refused upon learning of its requirements.[10]) Today if a minority group is to achieve full civic membership, its commitment to the law of the larger community must, similarly, be revealed in both large and small acts. The power of such minute cultural practices to define a minority group as being within or without the larger community can be glimpsed in the skepticism with which many Americans view Muslim immigrant women who wear the *hijab*, which many non-Muslims perceive as an icon of inherited, group oppression contrary to American national principles, however willingly the putative victims submit. Similarly, Catholics, especially the Irish, long faced a marked skepticism of their loyalty to America in light of their concurrent loyalty to the Vatican. In American literature of the early nineteenth century, the black robe of a priest was often a symbol of "Popish" political subversion.

All minority groups that have sought to achieve full civic membership in the United States have struggled to be seen as a people of law, but this struggle has been uniquely important for Afro-Americans. More than for any other racial or ethnic minority, the life and identity of black Americans have for centuries been inextricable from law and legal ideals. The ancestors of most people of African descent arrived in North America as slaves; that status was a creation of the law, and in its various legal mutations it continued to influence black life for over a hundred years after slavery was formally abolished. As the literary scholar Jon-Christian Suggs notes, Afro-American culture has as a result been veritably preoccupied with law, and many of the high achievements of Afro-American literature take legality as a central topic, from the slave narratives of the antebellum years through the writings of Richard Wright during World War II (and even, ignominiously, the "gangster rap" of today).[11] One cannot fully appreciate the nature of Afro-American identity, in the past or in our own time, without extended reference to the character of American law. It is for this reason that the history of black trials so closely traces the history of black civic inclusion in general. For it has been primarily in the context of these legal cases that we have rendered cultural judgment as to the status of Afro-Americans in relation to the law—our sacred text.

RITUALS OF CITIZENSHIP

To understand why, it is helpful to think of black trials as performing the function of a *civic ritual*—and thus to turn to the work of anthropologists, for whom the study of ritual was a founding concern of their discipline.[12] In anthropology, the term "ritual" generally refers to symbolic actions undertaken in relation to basic social values and status relationships (or, more broadly, "in relation to the sacred"). Rituals are divided into two general types, acts and events. Ritual acts express the underlying principles of a community through discrete behaviors, such as shaking hands or saying "Bless you" when someone sneezes. Significantly, they must be performed according to precise rules or conventions. If a man reaches for a hammer, for instance, he is probably performing a purely utilitarian act: he wishes to drive a nail. Because the act does not speak to his society or its values, there is no rule dictating how he should reach for the tool. But if the same man reaches to tip his hat when he encounters a woman of equal or higher social rank, he is performing a deeply symbolic function. The man is not simply tipping his hat for the sake of repositioning it on his head, he is acknowledging the respect and deference men are asked to accord to women of the same or higher class. And unlike reaching for a hammer, this act must be executed in a specific way if it is to have the intended meaning. For instance, if a man encountering a lady were to slide his hat off his head and onto the ground, she might think he had dropped it inadvertently or were otherwise in the throes of some spasm. If a construction worker passing a woman in a grandly attired evening gown were to reach out his arm in a broad circular motion, take his hard hat gingerly between two fingers, and dip it forward to his waist, the lady might rightly assume the man was mocking her and her class.

Ritual events are ritual actions on a much larger scale. In everyday speech, they are often referred to as ceremonies. They include rites of passage from youth to adulthood in Nigeria, Ash Wednesday services in Spain, Hindu pageants in India, the taking of communion in various Christian churches, as well as a great variety of secular public occasions, from graduations to state dinners. In ritual events, members of a community come together to depict the values that structure their lives, typically presenting those beliefs in the form of a shared narrative. The involvement of community members in ritual events, as either participants or spectators, enables them not only to acknowledge but also actively to affirm and define the character of the community. Ritual events thereby are not merely passive representations: they are performances that establish an individual's status in relation to basic social principles. By reenacting the biblical story of the Last Supper, for instance, the celebration of the Eucharist affirms that the members of a church are one in Christ. A graduation ceremony is a ritual that reinforces a change in status between youth and maturity; it typically concludes with a speech that instructs graduates on the responsibilities of the new role they will assume and commends those members of the community who are ready to uphold its values as adults. A wedding joins an unrelated man and woman together as kin, giving separate individuals a new social status that draws its meaning from the basic values our society holds about men, women, and children.

Ritual events "work" because they follow a conventional structure. They achieve symbolic power because they proceed according to a predetermined set of rules, just as a man must tip his hat in a particular way for the action to have the meaning he intends. For it is only by following a predictable form—proceeding according to a narrative structure—that rituals transform their actors into representative figures whose actions embody general social meanings. Consider the typical American wedding, a highly structured affair involving a prescribed set of actions and a rigid standard of dress. The bride, for instance, usually walks down the middle of the aisle rather than snaking through the chairs of the assembled guests or entering through a more convenient side door—that would seem absurd. Similarly, on this most nervous-making of days she wears a white gown rather than jeans, which would doubtless be more comfortable, and she appears last in the procession. The bridesmaids who precede the bride dress alike, in uniforms inferior in their finery to that of the bride, and they carry bouquets of flowers, as opposed to any other objects, however lovely, of their own choosing. One can easily predict that the groom will wear a dark suit or tuxedo, and that he will wait for his fiancée as she walks toward him down the bedecked aisle, as often as not to be "given" by her father. The participants in such an event are not simply themselves. They represent social roles—the cherished bride, the supportive female friends, the supplicant and petitioning groom—and by upholding the conventions of the ceremony, they invoke and affirm the ideas behind those roles. The wedding is a performance whose themes are gender and family.

Significantly, in the United States, our most important public rituals, those we share as a society, concern not religion or the family but rather law and national identity. Our public rituals affirm the legal values by which we conduct our civic life. These rituals come in various forms. Many take place on the same day of every year: for instance, the laying of a wreath at the Tomb of the Unknowns on Memorial Day or the celebration of the Declaration of Independence on the Fourth of July. Other civic rituals may take place more frequently or in connection with specific occasions. Standing for "The Star Spangled Banner" before a sporting event is a ritual of this type, affirming the collective values of patriotism and sacrifice, and has become only more solemn since the events of September 11, 2001. These rituals are no less powerful for being occasional: if you care to test their power, you might try gathering with a group of distinctively dressed friends near the front rows of a stadium when the anthem begins and not standing.

As rituals go, black trials have an unusual origin: They begin as legal cases, discrete events whose purpose is to sanctify decisions in civil suits or criminal prosecutions. The defining quality of black trials as I use the term is that a local ritual event—a legal case—is transformed into a ritual with significance for the larger American community. Legal cases have a number of characteristics that permit this symbolic transformation, this broadening of meaning and implication from a trial into a black trial. First, they are public, potentially open to a large audience—indeed, Americans today can watch many trials, like that of O. J. Simpson, in real time. Second, legal cases are always in some measure self-referential: the abstract concept of legality and the distinctive ideals of a particular body of law are present throughout the proceedings. Most important to the symbolic transformative power of a trial is the more literal transformation it affects on the parties to the case: the ultimate result of a trial is the declaration that its parties stand in a new relation not simply to a specific rule, but to the law as a general ideal. A civil trial determines whether a given plaintiff's claims will be recognized and supported by legal authority, potentially transforming a defendant into an individual liable for damages. A murder trial can turn the accused into a criminal. As it transforms an individual's status in the particular, a legal case takes us from the realm of largely discrete events with specific meanings to the realm of ideals with communal importance.

Finally, most legal cases are highly conventional. They are conducted according to a traditional order, with a standard set of characters as familiar to us as those in a wedding or a detective novel or a classical tragedy. The very predictability by which the resolution of a dispute is achieved compels us to view the individual participants as representative of basic social and institutional relationships. When the State of California prosecuted the police officers who assaulted Rodney King on a Los Angeles freeway, for instance, King transcended his individuality as the alleged victim: he became a symbol of black men and their troubled relation to the institutions of law enforcement. Similarly, the acquittal of his attackers became more than a judgment of the actions of the officers, a fact made clear by the widespread distress and riots that followed. Thus a specific, local legal ritual taking place in a Los Angeles courtroom, and its central question—whether the police who attacked King had violated his civil rights, thereby becoming not upstanding agents of the law but criminals themselves—became a civic ritual with national symbolic force. It spoke to the relation of Afro-Americans to the law and, by extension, to the degree of their inclusion in the civic community that the law defines. Like a character in a novel or a participant in a wedding, Rodney King came to stand, in the eyes of an entire community, for a set of abstract status relationships.

Individual cases become black trials for a variety of reasons: the fame or social standing of their participants, as with O. J. Simpson; the importance of the legal questions they raise, as with *Plessy v. Ferguson* or *Somerset's Case*; the drama of the crime, as with Rodney King; or the particular social context in which they take place. At times, it might be said, a community *needs* a black trial: it may seize on a local event and imbue it with larger significance as a means of working through its underlying social tensions. The case of Emmett Till, a black boy brutally murdered in Mississippi in 1955, which I discuss briefly in Part Four, may to some degree be understood in this way. Whatever the cause, the importance of black trials lies ultimately in their symbolism, as judgments about the status of blacks within the values that define American national identity, as ritual events that determine the place of Afro-Americans within the idea of law itself. When we say that a case like that of O. J. Simpson is important for being "about race," despite its lack of constitutional meaning, I believe we are referring to this symbolic significance. A constitutional case like *Plessy v. Ferguson* attains its symbolic importance both through its role in popular culture and through its technical implications for legal doctrine.

To say that black trials are civic rituals that concern the relation of Afro-Americans and the law, however, is to describe only part of their symbolic weight. It would be quite another matter if, like most ritual events, their outcome were inevitable. In a wedding, for example, a couple always is married, or else a wedding has not taken place. In communion, a church always becomes one in Christ. Within the ritual form of the trial, however, the legal and civic status of Afro-Americans is open to debate, subject to the contestation inherent in our adversarial system of justice. Trials also invite a special type of community participation: actual (for the jurors) and more vicarious (for every onlooker coming to his or her own conclusions). Black trials, in other words, are dynamic rituals whose ending, and thus whose *meaning*, is uncertain at the outset, and which invite competing points of view.

THREE VISIONS OF LAW AND CIVIC LIFE

In America, law has never been a single, undisputed idea. Throughout our history, Americans have differed dramatically not only in how they understand particular laws but also in how they understand the nature of law itself—the broad legal principles they believe should define the essence of our national identity. Significantly, these competing views of law have been embraced not simply by intellectuals or those whose lives are devoted to thinking about ideas. As the historian Robert Westbrook has written, political theory is not the province only of professional thinkers.[13] Every day people express theoretical and philosophical positions about society in what they say and, even more important, in the way they live and the culture they produce. In the songs we sing, the films we watch and images we love, in the way we lead our lives day to day, and in our explicit social commitments, all Americans hold "popular political theories" about how society should be organized and how people should live within it. Apropos of black trials, we can add that these popular theories express a jurisprudence, a vision of law, no less meaningful for being conceptually unarticulated.[14] This popular jurisprudential pluralism is central to the way black trials exercise their symbolic power.

American views of law have fallen into three broad traditions (at times overlapping, and always evolving), each of which has spoken in its own way to the question of black legal capacity. The first, well known because it accords with the dominant conception of American civic life today, is the rich, historically varied philosophy of political liberalism or, more specifically, liberal individualism. Proponents of this view, drawn ultimately from the ideas of philosophers such as John Locke and John Stuart Mill, consider the protection of individual freedom a preeminent good. As individualists, they view the United States as a nation dedicated to principles directly contrary to racial hierarchy and civic exclusion based on race.[15] This tradition began its modern career during the great Western revolutions of the seventeenth and eighteenth centuries, when its commitment to individual rights extended mainly to white men, and today it is embodied in the universalism of the human rights movement, which seeks to extend the protections of individual rights around the globe. Notably, until the Civil War, an important constituency of liberalism stood opposed to the civic interests of Afro-Americans as a group; dedicated to the sanctity of private property as a foundation of individual liberty, some liberals supported the property interests of slaveholders in their slaves. But it is the racially inclusive tendency of the liberal tradition, developed over the last three centuries—the assertion that a person's race should never in itself put them beyond the protections of law or outside the circle of civic life—that most concerns me here.

The second tradition of civic jurisprudence is that of racial caste, whose proponents view society not as a gathering of individuals, but rather as a community of stratified groups. Despite the vast differences between the United States and the social order of traditional India, essential features of the caste vision of civic life—no less than the liberal tradition—have been central to American history and formed a basic part of how we have viewed the nature and purpose of law. Indeed, from the start of our history as a nation, the great majority of Americans believed that our nation was intended to protect white racial dominance and "honor"—ours was "a white man's country," a community of groups, with whites firmly on the top, a view by no means confined to uneducated, poor whites (nor, it should be said, limited to educated, wealthy ones). This vision is not uniquely American, of course; Europe, too, had a well-honed, mainstream intellectual tradition that considered social questions in terms of racial hierarchy. In fact, some of the same men who created modern liberal philosophy in the eighteenth century were also the founders of modern scientific racism—most notably Thomas Jefferson—and were deeply engaged with European thought in both endeavors.[16]

The third popular tradition of American jurisprudence is that of Christianity. Proponents of this tradition view the United States as a Christian nation, and believe that the law its citizens are morally bound to follow—their true law—is embodied in the works and teachings of Jesus, or in the codes of the Old Testament as recast by the New. The Christian vision of society and politics, the relation of any present historical moment to the future Kingdom of God, is enormously diverse, and thus Christians have spoken in a range of voices about the civic status of blacks. For hundreds of years, for instance, many Christians believed blacks should not receive baptism or become full church members; many also believed Africans were the descendants of Ham, cursed by his father, Noah, to perpetual servitude.[17] Even in the twentieth century, under Jim Crow, while Afro-Americans were accepted as Christians, blacks and whites not only worshiped separately by social custom, but were even asked in court to swear on separate Bibles. On the other hand, Christian social activists played a central role in some of the most important drives toward civic egalitarianism and reform in American history, and it was their opposition to racial hierarchy—based on the principle that all are one in the body of Christ—that was to transform the modern Christian outlook on matters of race and ethnicity.[18] This egalitarian Christian vision achieved recent prominence after World War II, during the Civil Rights Movement, and it is this vision on which I focus attention in this book.

Liberal, caste, Christian: the diversity of American views of law has given black trials a quality we might describe as dialectical, as something changed by what it changes. For in the context of American juris-prudential pluralism, the central symbolic question of black trials—whether Afro-Americans are a people of law—has been inseparable from the question of what law is. To ask one question has been, necessarily, to ask the other. In the trial stories I shall tell, I therefore also follow the rise and fall of these three competing traditions of American jurisprudence. The story is complex, and not without its surprising turns. During the course of American history, advocates of black civic inclusion have used the rhetorical weapons of Christian and liberal jurisprudence to oppose the caste vision of black legal incapacity born of American slavery. Over centuries, Afro-Americans and their allies won this fight, destroying caste theories of citizenship, a victory of which our society can justly be proud. The terms of the victory, however, were not only to draw a liberal notion of citizenship more deeply into the heart of American national identity, but also to marginalize the Christian legal vision long central to the fight against caste. Moreover, the victory gave rise, ironically, to new sources of the popular perceptions that Afro-Americans as a group exist outside the law—perceptions that arise from tensions within liberalism itself.

NARRATIVE AND THE CULTURAL HISTORY OF LAW

This is a book of narratives, a work of stories, but it is not a traditional narrative history. I believe that narratives are not merely one way of describing past events; rather, there are essential aspects of the past that can best be recovered through storytelling and literary interpretation. Those features of history available by such an approach are the symbolic meanings embedded in culture, including the culture of citizenship. "The concept of culture I espouse," writes Clifford Geertz in a famous passage in *The Interpretation of Cultures* that has been a particular influence on my approach, "is essentially a semiotic one. Believing . . . that man is an animal suspended in webs of significance he himself has spun, I take culture to be those webs, and the analysis of it to be therefore not an experimental science in search of law, but an interpretive one in search of meaning."[19] Like the Geertzian ethnographer, the cultural historian of law must, I believe, enter the "webs of significance" in which humans were once "suspended," and all at once recover, interpret, and represent the complex meanings of past legal lives and events.

In making narratives of the details I have collected from the past, my goal has been to portray the webs of significance surrounding black trials through a process Geertz called "thick description," in which description and interpretation blend into one. In this process, I consider black trials at three primary levels of meaning. These levels are the doctrinal, the social and biographical, and the symbolic. The first level, the doctrinal, is the most familiar within the circles of legal history. From a purely doctrinal perspective, for instance, the case of *Plessy v. Ferguson* is a milestone in the history of the Supreme Court's interpretation of the Equal Protection Clause of the Fourteenth Amendment. In its decision in *Plessy*, the Court asserted that laws requiring separate facilities for whites and blacks on intrastate passenger trains did not violate the principles of equal protection, and it thereby gave judicial blessing to the practice of racial segregation—an interpretation that would be overturned by the Court more than fifty years later, in the landmark case of *Brown v. Board of Education*. The doctrinal story of Afro-American citizenship is a traditional and essential one, but only part of this study has an explicitly doctrinal focus. Many of the black trials I examine indeed have no doctrinal importance at all.

To fully appreciate the meaning of black trials, we thus also need to attend to their social and biographical features. From this perspective, for instance, the story of *Plessy v. Ferguson* begins not with the transformation of Fourteenth Amendment jurisprudence after Reconstruction, but rather with the racial history of New Orleans, where the case was brought. Most important, the city had a long history of intermarriage between blacks and whites, and was home to French-speaking Creoles and mulattoes who held substantial positions in urban society. These light-skinned residents felt a particular oppression from the racial restrictions increasingly imposed on blacks throughout the South. In the wake of the passage of Jim Crow train legislation in 1890, a group of these residents formed the Citizens' Committee to Test the Constitutionality of the Separate Car Law (their efforts also seem to have been supported by railroad transportation companies, for whom maintaining separate car facilities had been an economic burden). With the cooperation of the East Louisiana Railroad, the Citizens' Committee and its attorney, Albion Tourgée, worked to create a "test case" through which they could challenge the law. That case began when light-skinned Homer Plessy, his very name a marker of the history of French-black intermarriage in New Orleans (his birth record reads "Homere Patris Plessy"), boarded a train car in June 1892.

The third level of historical meaning in black trials and, for me as a cultural historian, the most interesting, is the symbolic level. A symbolic approach to black trials is based on the perception that the rich, individual details of a legal case, including those taken from their doctrinal and biographical features, may resonate far beyond their literal significance, that they may become symbols in the classic literary sense, standing in for ideas they do not themselves immediately portray (with the same sort of force as, say, a cross, a red rose, or a white whale). In black trials, I believe, it is minute details that have had the ultimate power to denote, to make concrete, the conceptions of race, law, and civic belonging around which the trials revolve—and to give effect to their ritual process. To retrieve the symbolic aspect of black trials demands their history be told in a particular way, for symbols carry meanings that can be best apprehended within the form of a narrative, meanings apt to be lost in the isolation wrought by other kinds of analysis. Symbols form through juxtaposition and repetition, through the weaving of webs of significance within the larger web of culture, and the meanings of those symbols are largely irreducible; they generally are not subject to paraphrase and cannot be separated from their representation.

We might in this context return for a moment to the *Plessy* case. Among the important symbols of the case, for instance, are trains—recall that the dispute concerns Jim Crow on the East Louisiana Railroad. In the 1890s, trains were icons of social and economic progress whose praises were sung by politicians and poets alike. They were symbols of speed and modernity, engines of geographical and political consolidation and the glories of national economic expansion. Railroad construction was to the nineteenth century something of what the space race was to the twentieth. To attack Jim Crow on a train thus was to attack segregation at the symbolic heart of America itself. Conversely, racial segregation on trains reduced the status of blacks in the public space that most represented the promise of national life. All black trials rest on a foundation of such symbols: from the tremendous, flowing white beard with which the abolitionist John Brown is often portrayed at the time of his execution (an image crafted by those who would see him squarely as an Old Testament prophet, an exponent of biblical law) to the dreadlocks of the black radical Mumia Abu-Jamal (a hairstyle that is the physical expression of his commitment to what his MOVE compatriots call "natural law").

My narrative method is alert to motif, the creation of patterns of words and images across time, some of which speak with force, but most of which are meant only to whisper. More specifically, I have worked to identify motifs whose meaning issues from the basic social tension at the heart of black trials, that between the reality of black civic exclusion and the desire for Afro-American citizenship. This opposition, we shall see, is very often symbolized by images of stasis and of motion, as for instance encapsulated in the Jim Crow imperative that blacks remain "in their place," or the description of the civil rights struggle as the Movement. Such opposing images correspond to an essential conflict, as well, between physical, even spiritual, life and death—a tension that forms the basis for my concern, present throughout this book, with an ideal central to Afro-American history: the principle of hope and its reality in social struggle and civic aspiration.

PART ONE

Colonial Visions,

1619–1773

The Birth of Black Trials

The origins of black trials and of America are entirely intertwined; both coincide with a revolution in the history of modern slavery. In that revolution, which took place in the late seventeenth and early eighteenth centuries, African bondage became the most important institution of North American society, the foundation of economic and cultural life. The British colonies, in particular, changed from societies in which slavery played only a minor role to ones in which slavery was the institution on which all communal life depended. To understand how black trials were born during this historic shift, it is important first to consider the years just before it occurred: the early decades of English colonization, over one hundred years before the trials I examine took place. How were blacks viewed by whites during this early period of settlement? What was their place within colonial society? What was their status with respect to the concept of law? Paradoxically, it is the very ambiguity of the answers that can shed light on the birth of black trials.

Blacks first arrived on North American shores in the early 1600s, stolen from Africa and held in bondage. Wolof, Fante, Ngongo; Mende, Bakongo, Yoruba—they were peoples of the western coast. Their numbers were very small. Although slavery would come to touch every aspect of our national life, it began slowly, gradually.[1] The case of Virginia is typical in this respect. Africans were first brought there in 1619, when a Dutch warship anchored near Jamestown and unloaded about twenty "negers." From that day until the late 1600s, however, blacks never amounted to more than 7 percent of the total population (by contrast, in 1770, they were over 40 percent).[2] Virginia was not anomalous. From Catholic Florida to Puritan Massachusetts, black slavery in the early seventeenth century was slight in demographic terms and limited in economic significance. Generally, it was intended merely to supplement a far more substantial system of white indentured labor, in which whites were contractually bound to work for extended periods, often in exchange for passage to the New World. Among the hardscrabble poor who worked the soil for others, blacks were a minority.

What did the English think of these first Africans in their midst? There is ample evidence that at least some saw them as loathsome simply for being black. It would be surprising had it been otherwise: it would be centuries before "racism" was to be widely viewed as a repugnant attitude, centuries before the term was even invented, and the English were renowned for their sense of national superiority, even over other Europeans. Many English held their Irish, Welsh, and Scots neighbors in complete disdain, viewing them as backward peoples fit only for subjugation. Africans seemed even more different and lower still. They had ebony-dark skin, which the English commonly attributed to descent from Ham and Canaan, marking them as the rightful inheritors of Noah's curse. Their hair, too, was different—a potent symbol of human variation. Their music was unfamiliar, and included rhythmic patterns and dance movements whose complexity the English could not appreciate, finding them simply barbaric. Their homelands were filled with strange beasts, including apes and monkeys, a fact that gave rise to theories that blacks were the close cousins of these primates. They were not Christian, and indeed appeared to have no religion at all.[3]

The first known legal proceeding involving blacks in North America suggests that such differences bred contempt. All that remains of the case is a single sentence indicating that, in 1630, a white Virginian named Hugh Davis was to be "soundly whipt before an assembly of negroes & others."[4] The crime? He had had—in the parlance of the day—conjugal relations with a black woman, "abusing himself to the dishonor of God and the shame of Christianity by defiling his body in lying with a negro." Naturally, the colony disapproved of fornication in general; this was a highly religious age. But the case suggests that physical relations between whites and Africans were cause for special reproach. Davis was punished for violating the taboos of racial caste—his crime "defil[ed] his body"—according to which many whites, and evidently those in power, saw blacks as clearly outside the circle of their community.

But race relations in the early colonies were not quite so simple. Until the 1670s, for instance, a significant number of slaves were released from bondage—in Virginia, at times one out of three blacks was free—and once released, they were not prevented from assuming stable, even respected, positions in society. They owned property, raised families, worked their own land, and engaged in trade. Some lived amid whites and themselves owned black slaves. And they were energetically involved in the legal system, exhibiting a practical knowledge of English law, taking part in civil suits as both defendants and plaintiffs, often "adept at challenging the law on its own terms."[5] In eastern Virginia, free blacks fared just as well before courts as small white planters of the same economic class, an indication of a status that has moved some historians to describe colonial blacks as "black Englishmen." One Anthony Johnson, who had arrived in Virginia a penniless slave in 1621, was by 1651 a free man with 250 acres of farmland to his name. One of his sons, John Johnson, owned 550.[6]

And so where did blacks stand in the early seventeenth century? As slaves, blacks were clearly pariahs, the lowest members of the society. But as blacks? On this point, the evidence is more ambiguous. The stories of Hugh Davis, whipped for lying with a Negro, and of Anthony Johnson, the black landowner, suggest two different realities, the reconciliation of which leads us to the birth of black trials.

Though hardly mitigating, it is a truth often ignored in discussions of American race relations that slavery has existed throughout human history and taken root across the globe. It seems that no region of the world has been without slaveholding at some point in its development. Europe, Africa, Asia; Christian, Muslim, Hindu; all at some time have been slaves and have held others in bondage. Slaves have toiled, laughed and bled, yearned and taken flight, under a Senegalese as well as a Georgian or Turkish sun, suffered under a Celtic as well as a Korean lash. The very term "slave" derives from "Slav," because for years Slavic peoples, not Africans, were the bondsmen of Europe. Slavery is a basic experience of nearly all human societies.[7]

But it must also be said that slavery has had many faces. The society of ancient Rome, in which slaves could rise to become great statesmen, was different from that of Aristotle's Greece, in which they could not.

And so scholars make a distinction between "societies with slaves" and "genuine slaveholding societies."[8] In the former, slavery is only marginal to economic life, with other types of servile labor (such as serfs, vassals, or indentured servants) predominating. As a result, slavery is also marginal to cultural life, and does not affect the character of social experience so deeply or personally as in a "genuine slaveholding society," in which the opposite is true. There, slavery is the foundation of the entire economy, and cultural life is fundamentally affected by it. The presence of slavery is implicit in almost everything people do, say, or think. Even individual social roles and outward characteristics are understood in terms of their correspondence to or bearing upon the master-slave relationship, whether it be "wife" or "worker," "Christian" or "heathen," "child" or "adult"—and in the case of North America, "white" or "black."

In the early seventeenth century, the American colonies were societies with slaves, not slaveholding societies. Settlers who needed labor relied less on slaves than on indentured servants, tens of thousands of whom immigrated to New England, the Chesapeake region, and the lower South from northern Europe, far outstripping the slave workforce in colonial agriculture. As historians have noted, British America could have survived for many years without slaves. It could not have functioned for a moment without the system of indenture, and its culture reflected this fact. Colonial society did not fundamentally equate blackness with bondage, servitude with darkness. There was certainly racial mistrust and animus, as the fate of Hugh Davis attests. But unbridgeable barriers of racial caste did not yet exist, because the colonial economy could afford blacks a certain social fluidity; it could afford them movement. One might say that in this respect the colonies were not yet *America*, not yet the society that produced the fundamental moral and political issue that would help define our national history up to the present day, that of black citizenship. It was not yet the society economically dependent on a substantial population of adults who, nevertheless, were defined as permanent, degraded outsiders.

But that society was not long in coming. During the last quarter of the seventeenth century, economic and political life in the colonies began to change.[9] As land became scarcer, indentured servants had less incentive to emigrate from Europe, and white labor became more expensive. New crops boomed on the transatlantic market, especially tobacco and rice, demanding a larger labor force. At the same time, the international price of slaves dropped, making the substitution of slave labor for indentured labor financially attractive. After Bacon's Rebellion in 1676, when poor whites and black slaves formed an armed alliance against wealthy elites, that substitution became politically attractive as well.[10] Slave labor was on the rise. In New York and Pennsylvania as in Maryland and the Carolinas, the numbers rose steadily and often dramatically. In the North, the population jumped from about 1,900 in 1680 to almost 48,000 in 1770. In the South, the change was even more dramatic: in Virginia alone the black population climbed from 3,000 in 1680 to over 187,000 in 1770, in percentage terms from 7 percent of the population to 42 percent (blacks in the low country and lower South during the same years grew from 17 percent of the population to 58 percent).[11] America was becoming a genuine slaveholding society. The change was noticed but, in a world whose defining theme was hierarchy, its essentials were hardly questioned, at least not by whites. Every aspect of colonial life, from the goods people traded to how they understood their own social relationships, from the power civic leaders wielded within representative bodies to the private sexual fantasies of ordinary citizens, was to be touched by slavery's rule.

Throughout this transformation, law played many important roles. As an instrument of commerce, law rationalized relations between buyers and sellers, enabling the trade in human beings to become mundane transactions; it allowed, most simply, one person to purchase another. It governed the relations between masters and servants, giving slaves just enough rights to mitigate the basic moral contradiction of treating humans as things. And law drew stark formal lines between whites and blacks, between those who could become members of the civic community and those who were viewed by definition as external to its increasingly strict new boundaries of citizenship.

Law played, too, a cultural role in this respect. As the more supple racial norms of a society with slaves were challenged by the caste vision of a slaveholding society, the status of blacks became an increasingly charged public issue. There was a need in colonial America for a laboring class, and that need was to be met by a people permanently exiled from the community and its law while still living within it. Public trials involving blacks provided an important forum in which colonists implicitly confronted and worked through this need, in which they could debate, solidify, or challenge the fundamental racial and legal banishment taking place around them. The legal cases I examine in this chapter reflect three different jurisprudential visions within which that cultural process took place. These visions, those of Christianity, racial caste, and a nascent vision of individual rights, would define the basic terms of debate in the black trials of the early republic, and they would long remain central to our national political life.

The first case is that of Joseph Hanno, a black man put on trial for murdering his wife in early eighteenth-century Boston. Before his execution, Hanno was interviewed by the great Puritan minister Cotton Mather, who gave a sermon before Hanno's death, just as a smallpox epidemic was descending upon the town. Lecturing to a large, frightened congregation, Mather presented a striking vision of spiritual egalitarianism and, at the same time, forcefully justified the earthly institution of slavery. In doing so, he revealed the complexities and contradictions of Christian racial jurisprudence in the colonial Northeast. The second case is that of the New York Conspiracy of 1741, a series of legal proceedings that took place in the wake of white fears that blacks had conspired to burn down New York City and kill its white masters. Those fears led to a wave of legally sanctioned violence in which 13 blacks were burned alive and scores were deported to the West Indies. I discuss the case as a way to explore the function of public punishment in enforcing a civic vision of caste. Finally, I tell the story of James Somerset, the young black man who, in 1771, ran away from his master into the London black underground, initiating a case that long was said to have "ended slavery in England." While the judicial opinion in what became known as *Somerset's Case* did not, in fact, end English bondage, its liberal spirit would give heart to antislavery reformers throughout Anglo-America.

1

Let Us Make a Tryal

▲

On May 2, 1721, in Boston, Massachusetts, with New England still contentedly oblivious to the smallpox epidemic that was about to descend, a free black man went on trial for murder. His name was Joseph Hanno, and he was "distinguished from the most of his Complexion" by the breadth of his Christian learning and knowledge of the Bible.[1] The victim was Hanno's wife, a prominent free woman named Nanny Negro. Authorities accused Hanno of beating Nanny over the head with the blunt edge of an ax as she was preparing to go to bed and then slitting her throat with a razor—a "barbarous" and "uncommon" act that struck at one of the central institutions of Puritan society, the holy covenant of marriage.[2] Two months later, as the first red blotches of the pox began to appear on town residents, Joseph Hanno was hanged. Within a year, over 800 Bostonians would succumb to plague and be buried near the town common. It is uncertain how Hanno's executioners disposed of his remains, but they probably did so with little ceremony. They may have given his corpse to a group of slaves and freemen to inter near Copp's Hill, in Boston's North End.

In life, Joseph Hanno was a man of no special consequence. But his crime made him notorious, and to the anxious Puritan mind, which believed that individual crimes reflected the moral state of society as a whole, the outbreak of pox just before his execution must have seemed like a divine punishment visited on a community of sinners. Indeed, Cotton Mather, who was deeply concerned with the spiritual welfare of blacks—he was something of a spiritual egalitarian—had ministered to Hanno in prison, and accused him of bringing "plagues upon all about you." Mather also gave a fire-and-brimstone sermon just before Hanno's execution, drawing a "vast assembly" into the Old North Church as scores of colonists came to gaze upon the doomed ex-slave and consider how the evil deeds of this "miserable African" reflected on their newly afflicted town. Sin. Sickness. Slavery. Law. Hanno's case had illuminated the racial tensions that lay at the heart of Puritan society and spiritual life.[3]

In this story of a poor black criminal brought face-to-face with one of the most prominent divines of the English colonies, we find a question at the dramatic center of American history: what place could blacks have within a civic order defined by a commitment to Christian principles? Cotton Mather had one answer, far more complex than we might expect. In the antebellum South, many Christian slaveholders would hold another view. In the fire of the Harpers Ferry raid of 1859, John Brown, an inheritor of Mather's Puritan tradition, would claim yet another. And in the Civil Rights Movement of the 1950s and 1960s, Martin Luther King, Jr., would offer one more still. The tensions within Mather's answer suggested some of these possible futures.

It was wintertime in New England the night Joseph Hanno killed his wife, when the sun sinks quickly on the horizon. It was a Thursday, and perhaps Nanny felt grateful to be home after a strenuous day of cooking, cleaning, and other chores for some local white family. She had Sunday to look forward to, the Christian day of rest. Or she may have sat at the edge of a bed in a small house in the North End, filled with resentment at her lot in the world, cursing her god or gods, or the man she married.

The two certainly did not get along. Months later, while languishing in prison, Hanno would complain that his wife was ill-tempered and treated him poorly, making his life miserable. Did the two have a fight when Hanno came in late? Did Hanno provoke a confrontation? All we know is that Nanny ended up lying on the bed with her head bashed and throat cut. We also know that after killing her, Hanno rushed outside, exclaiming that his wife had committed suicide, and awakened his neighbors.

Hanno's neighbors probably were some of Boston's small but

vibrant community of free blacks, which clustered near the Charles Town ferry in a neighborhood then called New Guinea. They might have been married couples, to judge from obscure colonial records with references to Josiah and Jane, Sebastian and Elizabeth, or Mingo and Sarah. Others probably were some of the men whose full names we can still retrieve from the past: Peter Quaquo, Dick Dudley, Exeter Foxcroft, and Ephraim Boyser. The black population of Massachusetts as a whole was not large, only 2 percent just before the Revolution, but blacks were a significant presence in the port and urban center of Boston. The year Nanny died, blacks there probably numbered between 700 and 1,000 out of a total of 12,000 residents. As Joseph Hanno opened the door and stepped into the street, he probably looked upon rows of houses sheltering scores of former slaves and their descendants.[4]

Hanno had lived in the colonies a long time, forty-four years, having arrived as a child around 1677, in the grim wake of the destruction brought by King Philip's War.[5] He likely came from Madagascar and perhaps had been sold by Muslim traders.[6] We know little specifically about his life, but we do know something of the lives of slaves in New England, which were unlike those in other British colonies. Among other differences, most masters used slaves on small farms, holding only one or two at a time. In accordance with the Old Testament, New England slaves also were typically lodged in their masters' homes, taking meals with them under a common roof. And that intimacy often had an evangelical component.[7] Joseph Hanno's masters "brought [him] up in the Christian Faith," and Hanno, baptized and literate, came to be known in Boston for frequently citing scriptures. In the scornful words of Cotton Mather, he was "always vaingloriously *Quoting* of Sentences from them wherever [he] came."[8]

The lot of slaves in New England was also unique in one other, critical respect: they were more frequently set free, as Joseph Hanno was in about 1707. A Boston law of that same year required Hanno at times to participate in the "repairing of the highways, cleansing of the streets, or other service, for the common benefit," but otherwise, he was at liberty. By then, he had been in America for about thirty years, and may have been known to the blacks of Boston as a kind of elder, a man rich in hard-earned experience navigating a foreign white land.[9]

Just who Nanny was remains a mystery, though there are some tantalizing clues. She may have been a woman of some standing: in the various directives obliging free black men to do road repair, Hanno is listed consistently as "Jo. Black Nann^s husb^d" or "Jo Nanney^s husb^d," the only black man identified in relation to his wife. Perhaps she had been a servant to a prominent white family, or maybe she owned a small business, a rare though not entirely unknown status for free blacks at the time. She may also have been married before. Cotton Mather joined "Anthony Negro & Nannee free negros" in holy union on September 5, 1706. And she may have had at least one child, possibly Joseph's. On August 12, 1715, three days after Hanno had been impressed into roadwork as "Jo. Black Nann^s husb^d," town records indicated a "Nanney Negro" had given birth to a daughter named Hagar (in Genesis, the Egyptian mother of Ishmael).[10]

After Hanno announced his wife's suicide to his neighbors, someone alerted the town authorities.

Jonathan Pollard, the coroner, arrived from his home on Brattle Street. He brought with him fourteen other men from Boston, a coroner's inquest charged to determine how Nanny had died. We know some of their names (the others are illegible on worn colonial parchment): Samuel Maxwell, Thomas Townsend, John Peake, Mathew Barnot, John Goldthwait, Joshua Kent, William Pitts, and Elias Parkman. Their foreman was Joshua Gee, a famous shipbuilder whose yards lay near Copp's Hill and whose son, the Reverend Joshua Gee, received his Christian upbringing in the Old North Church and later preached there with Cotton Mather. Standing together around the light of lanterns in the cold North End, speaking pointedly with people in the neighborhood, they must have seemed an ominous assembly.[11]

Once each had examined the body, Pollard gathered the group and asked them to explain for the record what had happened. After the men conferred, Pollard produced a form used to document investigations of suspicious deaths in Boston. In a small, even hand, Pollard wrote that Nanny "was murdered by her husband Joseph free Negro of Boston aforesaid by giving her a blow on the back part of the head with an ax & with a repeated blow on the right side of the head as she was going into bed it being then from the instant about ten at the clock at night."

The killing of a man's own wife. The technical term is uxoricide. It not only was a sin, like all other murders, but one that struck deeply at the heart of the Puritan vision of a society of saints: the marital bond, the covenant of husband and wife, and the benevolent exercise of paternal authority, lay at the center of the holy community Puritans were struggling to build in America. To break that bond through *adultery* was a capital offense, but to break it by murder was unspeakable.[12]

The men each signed their names, and affixed seals next to them in bright red wax.

Hanno was lodged in the town prison on Queen Street, in the center of Boston, where he would await trial. The Superior Court of Judicature, sitting as the "Court of Assize and General Gaol Delivery," would not convene until May. Though some politicians in the Massachusetts House of Representatives, outraged at Hanno's crime and concerned about the cost of keeping him in jail, tried to bend judicial procedure to hasten his execution, justice was not to be rushed. Hanno would have to wait five months before he stood before the law.[13]

In colonial Boston, the philosophy of criminal law was a religious one, derived from the Old Testament and Puritan theology.[14] The stern folk who settled Massachusetts saw themselves as reenacting the biblical story of Exodus, and considered it their duty to enforce God's commands in their new colonial world. Hanno's case would publicly dramatize the place of blacks in relation to this religious conception of law, but even more, it would lay bare social tensions and reveal the possibilities of racial inclusion in a Christian community that supported racial slavery. And no one understood this better than Cotton Mather.

For Mather, New England was one of the central battlegrounds in the great struggle between God and the Devil, a war Satan was winning.[15] Born in 1663, he was the eldest son of Increase Mather, who was one of the most prominent ministers of Massachusetts Bay, and the grandson of two other equally renowned church leaders. Driven by strictly orthodox views, he worked tirelessly with his father in the Old North Church to rein in the deviations from hard-line Puritanism that had begun to surface in the colony in the late seventeenth century, and he poured forth a seemingly endless flow of devotional and other writings in service of the Lord (including, though we tend to forget the fact, works on science and medicine, in which he maintained a lively interest). Today, he is best known for his prominent role in the Salem witch trials.[16]

In 1721, Mather was fifty-seven years old, and deeply dissatisfied. It was the sunset of his life, yet his days seemed filled with ceaseless difficulty and conflict. His revered father's health was failing; Increase would suffer a stroke in 1722 and die the following year. The prospect of the Old North Church without Increase's towering presence was sorrowful to imagine. Then there was his wife. Lydia was subject to fits of nearly pathological rage against her husband, followed by equally disturbing periods of wild admiration and erotic desire. Try though he might to see

Lydia's behavior as one more trial to be endured as a Christian, it caused him frustration and grief. And professionally, Mather's spiritual power over Massachusetts had waned considerably since his youth. In April and early May, for instance, a number of his flock, "vain, proud, foolish People," had left the Old North for the recently erected "New Brick Church" two blocks away. Mather felt increasingly alienated from a society that seemed heedless of his theological warnings. Everywhere, the souls of New England were in jeopardy. He felt certain the Lord soon would smite the sinful community of Boston with the "speedy approach of the destroying angel."[17]

The angel descended in 1721. Immediately after Hanno's trial, smallpox was reported on board the man-o'-war *Sea-horse*, spotted on a "Negro man" who came with the ship from Salt Tortuga, off the coast of Venezuela. In Puritan thought, a community could be held accountable for the sins of its individual members, and Hanno's barbaric murder suggested just how sinful Boston had become. When the terrifying plague was discovered, Mather felt his apocalyptic admonitions had been vindicated, and he even took such satisfaction in the fulfillment of his prediction that he feared God would rebuke him for his vanity. But for Mather, the very horror of Hanno's crime and the wrath it precipitated could be the seeds of the regrowth of a righteous society. For one, it was a staple of Puritan theology that redemption required a candid acknowledgment that one had sinned. The harsh light of terror might encourage self-examination and with it the seeking of God's forgiveness. And more important, Hanno's murder allowed, even forced, Mather to reassert his complex vision of the place of blacks in a Christian world, and this reassertion furthered the orthodox social and theological ideals he believed were so at risk in the waning years of his life. Hanno's crime was Mather's homiletic opportunity.[18]

To the modern ear, Mather's views on race and law sound contradictory. On one hand, Mather expressed a strong commitment to the possibility of black spiritual equality. For many Christians of the day, blacks were by nature incapable of obeying the commandments of divine law or achieving a state of grace. Some thought they even might not possess souls. Mather vigorously disputed this view—this *"Brutish* insinuation," he wrote with disgust, should be "never Whispered any more." As an orthodox Calvinist, he believed that no person ever could be certain who belonged to the elect and that God's saints could be found among all peoples. He thus advocated a vigorous campaign of proselytizing among blacks and argued that they should be given no less a chance than whites enjoyed to show themselves to be true Christians. "Suppose these wretched Negroes to be the offspring of Ham (which yet is not so very certain)," wrote Mather, "yet let us make a tryal, whether the Christ who *dwelt in the tents of Shem* have not some of His Chosen among them." For Mather, to do otherwise was contrary to faith.[19]

Mather enthusiastically practiced what he preached, devoting his time, energy, and money to the cause of black spiritual welfare. He invited black parishioners to his home for Christian discussion. He helped found a Religious Society for Negroes. At his own expense, he created a school to teach them to read the Bible, a school Hanno may have attended. And in 1706, he distributed his pamphlet *The Negro Christianized* to convince masters to apply themselves to black religious instruction. "Let not this opportunity be lost," he admonished, "if you have any concern for *souls*, your own or others." As a practical guide, Mather's pamphlet included sample prayers for beginning black Christians; a list of biblical verses that slaves could commit to memory; and two catechisms, one with three simple questions and another, longer and more complex, "for the *Negroes* of a bigger Capacity."[20]

For all this, however, Mather believed, like other Christians of his time, that equality before God did not entail equality on Earth. While he thought blacks capable of salvation, he also considered them generally degenerate and untrustworthy. Moreover, Mather himself owned slaves, and apparently without remorse or doubt. When members of his church bought him a black servant as a gift, he joyfully called the act "a mighty smile of Heaven upon my family." And, most strikingly, with the same vigor that he asserted blacks should be granted the opportunity for baptism, Mather also insisted that the conversion of slaves did not render them free—a fear that prevented some colonists from giving their slaves religious instruction. "What law is it," he wrote in the same pamphlet in which he advocated black Christianity, "that sets the baptized slave at liberty? Not the law of Christianity: that allows of slavery. . . . Will the civil law do it? No: Tell, if you can, any part of Christendom, wherein slaves are not frequently to be met withal. But is not freedom to be claimed for a baptized slave by the English constitution? The English laws . . . will not say so." For Mather, slavery was wholly compatible with Puritan society.[21]

Indeed, the two were not just compatible, they were symbiotic. Slavery brought Christianity to heathen Africans and Christianity, in turn, made slavery more effective by rendering slaves more pliant. To owners diffident about black conversion, Mather argued that religion would teach blacks to know their place as part of a well-ordered Christian world. Accordingly, Mather counseled blacks that submitting to their white masters was an essential component of spiritual obedience to Christ. To the question "If you serve Jesus Christ, what must you do?" the Christianized Negro was to answer, in a catechism, "I must love all men, and never quarrel, nor be drunk, nor be unchaste, nor steal, nor tell a lie, nor be discontent with my condition."[22]

Although Joseph Hanno was known to go about town declaiming scripture, he was hardly the kind of pupil for whom Mather hoped. Orthodox Puritanism demanded slave conversion. Yet masters would allow conversion to take place only if it were beneficial, or at least not harmful, to black discipline. How, then, to bring Hanno back within the fold of Puritan orthodoxy and show that, despite this particular brutal act, blacks in general should still be deemed potential members of the Puritan community, balancing their religious capacity and their social subordination? The conundrum must have passed through Mather's mind: here was the most knowledgeable of black Christians who also was the worst of criminals.

On Tuesday, May 2, 1721, the superior court met in the Town House in the center of Boston. Presiding was Chief Justice Samuel Sewall, a large, dignified man in a black silk robe with white bands, who was customarily greeted on the opening day of court by the salute of a cannon. He always began court sessions with a prayer.[23]

Could Hanno expect a fair trial in a Massachusetts court? In general, free black men received rather even treatment in the New England judicial system, at least at this period. In civil matters, free blacks could actively use the law to their economic advantage. With a practical knowledge of jurisprudence, they sued for debts and collected money, for instance. In criminal matters, too, free blacks were treated similarly to, if not the same as, whites. They were entitled to the full range of legal rights, with the important exception of the ability to serve on juries. There also was no marked inequality between the punishments they received and those of white convicts.[24] And though Hanno, in particular, certainly faced hostility and anger in the courtroom, in Sewall, he was facing no irredeemably biased magistrate; in fact, years earlier, Sewall had written the first antislavery pamphlet published in the American Northeast (a pamphlet coincidentally titled *The Selling of Joseph*, after the story in Genesis).[25]

We know little of the proceedings.[26] When officially accused of murder, Hanno was asked how he wanted his case to be determined. He could have given only one answer, putting himself on "god and the Country" and asking in effect for a jury trial. The petit jury consisted of twelve "good and lawful" local men: Samuel Barret, John Roberts, Joseph Scarborough, Jonathan Capen, Thomas Johnson, Samuel French, William Greenleaf, Jeremiah Belknap, Charles Davenport, Benjamin Owen, Samuel Gulliver, and Nathaniel Tate. A prosecutor laid out the case against Hanno, using as evidence the findings of the coroner. Hanno had no defense counsel, for at the time the institution was almost unknown. From the record, it is clear that Hanno had at some point denied his guilt, or at least did not concede it directly. He seems to have thought he stood some chance of regaining his freedom because of the lack of an eyewitness to the crime, or perhaps he was hoping for a reprieve or pardon. But in this he was disappointed. After the jury deliberated, Judge Sewall turned to Barret, the foreman, who pronounced the verdict onlookers surely had expected, that Hanno was guilty. The court recorder entered the story into his ledger.[27]

Justice Sewall ruled that the defendant was to "suffer the pains of Death." Hanno was "to go from hence to the place from whence you came"—that is, to the jail—"and from thence to the place of execution"—to the gallows—"and there to be hanged by the neck until you are dead." Puritans hardly took executions lightly, and the mood must have been one of anger, terror, compassion, grief, and righteousness. Justice Sewall's customary parting words were heavy with meaning: "Lord have mercy on your soul." Hanno was led out, scheduled to die in twenty-three days.

The next afternoon, Cotton Mather visited Hanno in prison. He had been informed of Hanno's need for spiritual counsel the week before, the day after the pox had been found on board the *Sea-horse* (on hearing of the coming pox, Mather asked that a new edition of one of his essays be printed and "scattered thro town and country" to provide solace to "them who are expecting an hour of travail, to quicken their preparation for death"). Arriving at the jail with scribe in tow, Mather hoped to lead Hanno through a series of theologically prescribed steps toward salvation, a kind of Puritan script by which sinners showed their repentance and perhaps approached grace—after which, Mather hoped, he could publish his interview as an object lesson for others. The script began with the minister's stern admonitions concerning a wrathful God. Then, the prisoner was to recognize the depth of his sin and confess his depravity, fly toward Christ, and express doubt as to his worthiness of divine forgiveness. Finally, he was to accept that he was entirely in the hands of God's inscrutable will and glorify Christ through this personal subjection to the wonders of His sacrifice.[28]

Mather began with a few pious words of greeting. "The report of your sad condition, Joseph, has brought me to visit you, and advise you."[29] His speech was deliberate and forceful, a consequence of his having overcome a youthful stutter. "I know not how better to express an obedience and conformity to the glorious Christ, who came down to seek and to save that which was lost, and who had a wonderful compassion on us, when we were shut up in sin and unbelief." All was not lost, Mather counseled. "That which yet more encouraged me," he said earnestly, "is the encouragement which I have to bring unto *you*. That is, that this glorious Christ is a savior, whom *Negro's* themselves, yea, the worst of sinners among those poor Black Outcasts"—Hanno himself—"may be welcome to. Ethiopians will be found by His grace, in His fulfilling that word, *He shall sprinkle many nations.*"

Hanno is reported to have replied simply, "I thank you, Sir, I'm glad to see you, Sir."

Mather began the task of scrutinizing Hanno's soul. "You have been many months in the prison," he asked, leadingly. "I pray, how have you spent your time hitherto? I hope they have not all been months of vanity."

Hanno knew the response he must give: "In reading and praying, Sir."

Mather was incredulous, for he knew, from what source is uncertain, that Hanno had lacked a Bible. "In *reading!*" he exclaimed. "Of what, I pray? I know that within these few days, a gentleman, who heard you had no Bible with you, sent a Bible to you. You lived many months without reading a word in that most necessary book, the Bible." Then with cutting understatement, Mather suggested, "It has, I must plainly tell you, a very uncomfortable aspect on you; it looks very strangely, very oddly, how you could live quietly so long, and have no *Bible* with you."

To this, Hanno offered a simple excuse. "I had no Bible," he stated, "and I knew not where to get one."

"*Not where to get one!*" Mather cried. "There are more than twice five hundred Christians in the town that would have helped you to a Bible, if you had asked for it." Even Hanno's pious jailer was incredulous, chiming in, "And, Joseph, I would have helped you to one at the first word, if you had asked for it."

"Your neglect of the Holy Scriptures at such a time," Mather admonished, "and this after you have been a great pretender to the reading of them, and were always vaingloriously *Quoting* of Sentences from them wherever you came—it looks very suspiciously. It confirms my fear of a reigning *hypocrisy*, under all the noisy profession of religion you have made among us."

Mather prepared to lead Hanno to Christ. "Give me your best attention," he exclaimed, "as one within a few hours of an awful eternity!"

"You are now to dy," he said simply. "The land where you now live would be polluted if you should be spared from death—for a horrible murder.

"The murder of any person," he declared, "is a crime which forfeits the life of him that commits it. And, you know very well"—here, Mather referred to Hanno's religious education—"that no murderer has eternal life. But the Murder that you have been guilty of, is a very uncommon one, one so barbarous as rarely to be known among the children of men."

Mather was outraged. "To *murder* one[']s *wife!*" he cried. "How inhumane! How hideous! How monstrous the wickedness! To murder where the greatest love that is possible is called for! I know, you have gone to extenuate your crime, with grievous accounts of the base humor and vile carriages in her that should have been a wife unto you. And I do believe she was a very insupportable"—unendurable—"wretch," Mather asserted, suggesting that he had seen Nanny's behavior for himself. "But God called you to patience, and meekness, and goodness, and all possible trials to overcome evil with good—not to knock her o' th' head!"

To this, Hanno could only respond with anguished contrition. "Truly, Sir," he told Mather, "I have a great deal to say of that, but I have done with it. I shall say no more. The Sixth Commandment is, *Thou shalt not kill.* And I have"—here, Hanno wrung his hands for emphasis—"broken this Commandment of God."

Satisfied with Hanno's response, Mather continued, leading Hanno toward the confession of his sin. "How did you proceed in it?" Mather asked. "How long was you purposing and projecting of it?"

"Never till she told me," declared Hanno, "that she had as liev talk with the Devil, as talk with any of God's ministers." Hanno surely hoped this was what Mather wanted to hear; he seems manifestly disingenuous and might have seemed so to Mather as well—though perhaps Nanny had in fact mocked his religious commitments. "This was but a little before I did the fact." As for the crime itself, Hanno explained simply,

"At last the Devil putting it into my heart, in the night, I took my ax, and with the head of it, I knocked her down, and that she might not recover, I gave her the second blow. After this, I put her to bed, and hacked her throat with the razor. So I left her, and went and called the neighbors, and told them, I was afraid of my wife's making away with herself. But God has now brought me out."

" 'Tis time for you," Mather stated, "not only to be sensible of this horrid crime, and the cry of blood in the ears of Heaven against you, but also to come into some sense of all your other sins." Hanno was now to cast a harsh light on his sinful life.

"You have broken all the Commandments of God," Mather proclaimed, suggesting that Hanno had not only killed, but also had failed to keep the Sabbath, worshipped false gods, and stolen, among other transgressions. "You must now examine yourself by what your catechism"—doubtless that of *The Negro Christianized*—"tells you is forbidden and required in the Commandments. And judge and loath yourself, in view of what you have done, so many thousands of times, denying the God that is above, and harkening to the Devil more than to God, and exposing yourself to all the Evil that pursueth sinners. Yea, procuring of *plagues* upon all about you," Mather remarked, with pointed reference to the pox.

"The first thing you have now to look after is that your Sin may be all pardoned, and that God may be Reconciled to you," he continued. "Look, you," he explained, at once confronting Hanno with the terrors of God's wrath and suggesting where he might turn for mercy. "Sin must be punished. You have sinned, and the punishment of your sin is unavoidable. The law of God has assigned a punishment for it, which there is no avoiding of. The punishment has those miseries in it, which cannot without horror be thought upon. You must either undergo this punishment yourself, and the smoke of your torment under it ascending for ever and ever, or else you must find One to undergo the punishment for you, One to be such a *sacrifice* for you, as God shall be well-pleased withal, the infinite justice of God satisfied withal. Can you tell me where to find such a One?"

Hanno did not now seem to know quite what Mather wanted to hear.

"I fly to the mercy of God," he said.

"But I tell you," insisted Mather, "the infinite justice of God must be satisfied, or else, He that made you will not have mercy on you. Are you willing *yourself* to suffer the punishment of your Sin?"

"I am willing to dy."

"What?" exclaimed Mather. "The second death! Willing to be banished from God, united with Devils, tortured with all the rage of a guilty conscience, thrown down into a devouring fire and everlasting burnings! *Can thy heart endure, when I shall deal with thee, saith the Lord?*"

Now, Hanno finally seemed to understand.

"I fly to the Lord JESUS CHRIST," he told Mather.

"Ay, now you say something," exclaimed the minister approvingly. "This is the only flight for a perishing soul. Fall down before the blessed God, and humbly tell Him, that you beg to have your sins all pardoned, because a glorious Christ has been punished for the sins of all His people."

Mather persisted, explaining the details of Hanno's theological predicament. When he was through, he asked, "Do you understand what I say to you?"

"Yes, Sir," replied the ex-slave. "I have a great deal of knowledge. Nobody of my color, in old England or new, has so much."

"I wish you were less puffed up with it," Mather retorted. "But the more you know, the more your sins are aggravated. The sins of your more ignorant countrymen have not such aggravation as yours."

And so Mather and Hanno continued their dialogue, Mather asserting, Hanno replying, Mather correcting, until finally Mather asked the dispirited Hanno to detail some of his particular crimes against God, as a way to exalt His power and glory. "But what may be the more special sins," he asked, "which you may apprehend, have provoked the Holy One, to leave you unto what are now to come?"

"I can't say," replied Hanno. "For all my sins."

"Which of all your sins gives *most of trouble* to you?" Mather pressed.

"All my sins," said Hanno, exhausted, broken.

Mather decided to close the interview, begrudgingly. "I wish you had glorified God, by being more *particular* in confessing what might be for His glory," he said with disapproval. "But, is there any more that I may do for you?"

"No, Sir," replied Hanno, in words he may have meant as much with irony as with remorse. "I can desire no more."

And with that, their interview ended, Mather departed, and Joseph Hanno was left to contemplate his impending death. He also was left to imagine what Mather might declare the next day, when the two were to meet one last time, in the Old North Church.

. . .

On Thursday, May 25, 1721, Joseph Hanno was brought into the Old North in chains.

It was common in Massachusetts for ministers to give a sermon upon the execution of a criminal, a gallows talk that would transform the act of punishment into a morality play. Mather had a very specific intent in this particular sermon: to resolve the conflict that Hanno's crime brought into sharp relief—that is, to advocate a world of both black Christianity and black slavery, of spiritual equality and secular racial hierarchy. His title was ominous: *Tremenda: Or, the Dreadful Sound with Which the Wicked Are to be Thunderstruck.*

They packed the church, a "great assembly," both black and white, waiting to hear his words. The minister approached the lectern, and then read the scriptural passage that would form the basis of his sermon: "A dreadful sound is in his ears." Taken from the Book of Job, the passage refers to the anxious apprehension of everlasting torment, the "dreadful sound" that haunts those who do evil. The congregation would have immediately recognized the verse as an indictment of the moral laxity of Boston. "The wicked man travaileth with pain all his days . . . ," the verse announces. "And he dwelleth in desolate cities, and in houses which no man inhabiteth, which are ready to become heaps." By this time, at least eight Bostonians had died of smallpox.[30]

Mather began his lecture with the Puritan doctrine that recognition and acknowledgment of sin might lead one toward grace. If the "dreadful sound be now repeated in our ears," he stated, it is with the "design" that "we may be *saved with fear* and be persuaded into the methods of our salvation, *Knowing the terror of the Lord.*" What followed was Mather's effort to put that design into practice, and to lead his flock toward repentance.

Through it all, Hanno stood before Mather's congregation, between the minister and his flock, but not as an outsider, beyond communal sympathy; he was in fellowship and an example to others. The lowest of criminals, Hanno represented what might become of any Christian who failed to heed Mather's admonitions. Mather continually exhorted the congregation to identify with Hanno and to see themselves as his spiritual equals. The sinner—white as much as black—was a "slave unto Satan," bound by "chains of darkness." White sinners and black sinners were together before God. Mather further asked his flock to identify with Hanno not just as a sinner, but also as one about to die. Just as Hanno was to be hanged, so Mather's congregation was facing impending death from smallpox. For both, there was but little time to confront their sins. There are "*Temporal woes* threatened unto the Wicked," proclaimed Mather. For biblical support, he cited Deuteronomy 28:59, "The Lord will Make thy Plagues wonderful." "The Messenger of Death must needs make a dreadful sound in the ears of a man," he asserted, "who perceives himself ready to be seized, and has no view of any but endless torments after the seizure made upon him."[31]

The power of the scene—Mather preaching the end of days, Hanno standing in chains before the congregation, who were made to feel the chains of sin upon their own souls. "*Wo, wo, wo* to the wicked lovers of Sin," Mather declared, midway through his sermon. "Some little rumbling of the woeful sound shall be now heard among you." The congregation was moaning.

"There is a remarkable one," Mather announced, turning toward Hanno, who was crying, "in the condition of that Son of Death, who appears in chains this day among us, and who is within these two or three hours to flee down to the Pit. There may be no staying of him.

"A dreadful sound there is in the ejaculations of this poor creature, upon the view of what he has done, and of what he is now to suffer for it. His weeping & howling for the miseries that come upon him, do make this dreadful sound in our ears. Wickedness! . . . What will it end in! Oh! Let *all Israel hear and fear,* and let none do any more so wickedly!

"It adds doleful murmurs to the dreadful sound," he continued, "that this wretched Ethiopian has been so distinguished from the most of his complexion; and been admitted unto such very distinguishing privileges.

"He was favored with a religious education," he explained angrily, "which enabled him to read the oracles of God, and learn the principles of Christianity. And then had an emancipation into a liberty, which he has been too unthankful for. He made a profession of religion, and was baptized, and stood a candidate for communion in the Church.

"Now, for one who so knew the will of our Glorious Master, to do as he has done, for one under such obligations, to be a pattern of all goodness unto other Ethiopians, to prove of so doubly and so deeply black a character," cried Mather, "Oh! How many and how severe stripes in the Infernal Prison must such a one be worthy of! Ungrateful wretch!"—Mather turned toward Hanno—"What art thou worthy of!"

What Hanno said is not recorded. Perhaps he simply continued to weep.

Mather next addressed the harmony of marriage. "But is the black thing that you have in irons here before you, the only one that may be charged with *murdering his wife* among us?" Mather asked his audience accusingly. "No." Mather believed Hanno's crime was just the most dramatic instance of a general breakdown of male responsibility to family. Men were expected benevolently to exercise their authority over their wives. Instead, they were killing them spiritually and here even physically. Hanno's crime was but that of the community writ large.

"Let all base and bitter and forward *husbands* consider it," Mather thundered against domestic abuse. "Husbands that follow courses which grieve, and even kill their wives; husbands who like the beast we read of speak like dragons and whose words are drawn swords upon their wives; husbands whose vile carriage leaves to their wives no comfort of their lives; it may be they starve them; however they break their hearts for them; the poor wives die before their time, and if their broken hearts might have the cause of their death legible upon them, there would be found some such words as these: *A cruel husband has hastened it!*"

His next lesson was for the human chattel of his flock. "The Ethiopian and other slaves among us" (referring, possibly, to Indian slaves), Mather admonished, "may hear a dreadful sound in the fate of their unhappy brother here before them, and they are to take warning from it. There is a fondness for freedom in many of you, who live comfortably in a very easy servitude, wherein you are not so well-advised as you should be. If you were free many of you would not live near so well as you do. Be your servitude never so hard, yet patience will be your duty under it, while God shall order it for you."

Mather's plea was that to obey Christ, blacks had to obey their worldly masters. Their fate on Earth was not their own, but God's. "Study to please your superiors, because you shall please Him in doing it," he proclaimed. "Then tho' you are poor slaves, yet you will be children of God and *brethren* to the best of men, and your slavery will very quickly, very quickly, expire in a Glory wherein you shall walk with your savior in white and have a part in the royal priesthood."

"Become servants of Christ and you are made free-men immediately," he intoned.

"Now, I lay the charges of God upon you," he ordered, speaking to his own hopes, "that the more you know, the more you be careful to *do* according to what you *know:* and afford not the least shadow of any occasion, for that false complaint, that the worst servants are those that have had most instruction bestowed upon them.

"No," said Mather, "but be the more humble, the more dutiful, the more diligent for what you have arrived unto. Pride goes before destruction. See the pride of your conceited and vainglorious and ostentatious brother here, has gone before!"

After Mather's sermon, prayers were said, and the congregation filed outside.

He later noted that his lecture had left a "great impression." We might picture a subdued crowd, each member of the congregation lost in thought, considering the sins of their own life, as Joseph Hanno was led out of the church and toward the gallows.[32]

Executions were public spectacles in Massachusetts, grim and solemn events that could draw vast crowds. Hanno's must have drawn a throng at least as large as that which heard Mather's sermon, and it is reasonable to imagine the Common aswarm with waiting people. In addition to Hanno's death, spectators also would have enjoyed taunting a married white woman as she was "Whipt several times between the Gallows and the Townhouse" and then forced to sit with a rope around her neck. Her crime: having "been delivered with a Negro Child."[33]

The crowd parted for the condemned man, who was led through the streets by the Suffolk County sheriff. If his was typical of other hangings of the time, Hanno would have had a final, earnest conversation with Mather before climbing the scaffold. He then would have spoken a few words to the crowd, warning them to avoid the sins of his life. After the executioner had slipped a black hood over Hanno's head and tied the rope around his neck, the floor beneath his feet would have dropped open. The crowd would have gasped, or murmured, or remained still and quiet. And then they would have gone home.

That was all. Death itself is a simple matter.

Four days later, a notice appeared in the *Boston News-Letter*. "Boston," read the announcement. "On Thursday last the 25th Current was Executed here One Joseph Hono, Negro, for Murdering his Wife; he had been in the Country about 44 years, and about 14 Years free for himself, and by his Masters brought up in the Christian Faith; and he hoped that all Mankind would take warning by him to keep themselves from committing such Sin & Wickedness as he was guilty of, particularly, Sabbath-breaking and willful Murder, the one being the Ringleader to the other, for which last he was justly Condemned, which had he not been guilty of the first he might probably have never committed the second."[34] Just below the notice appeared another short item, indicating that eight persons had been reported sick with smallpox. Soon, nearly half the town would be infected. Over eight hundred would perish.

Customary methods to reduce the devastation were to no avail. When quarantine proved ineffective, authorities turned to sanitation. The day Mather interviewed Hanno in prison, the selectmen ordered a group of twenty-six free blacks and mulattoes to work for six days clearing away dirt and garbage to stop the spread of the disease. The work crew included Peter Quaquo, Dick Dudley, Exeter Foxcroft, Mingo Walker, Sebastian Levensworth, Charles Menino, Ned Hubbard, and others.[35] But that remedy, too, was ineffectual.

Just as the Puritans held that recognition of sin could lead toward redemption, however, so too from the ravages of plague could come a hopeful sign, and the messenger again was Cotton Mather. Though he believed smallpox was the result of wickedness, the breaking of God's law, Mather thought it his duty to prevent its spread whenever possible. He thus not only developed elaborate theological arguments to explain how physical illness was the manifestation of sin, but also explored new medical treatments to alleviate the suffering of victims. During the 1721 epidemic, he began to advocate a procedure he had recently learned from his servant Onesimus, the black man his congregation had purchased for the minister under the "mighty smile of heaven."[36] When Mather asked Onesimus if he had ever had the pox, the slave explained that he had, and that he hadn't, and that he would never have it again. The slave then revealed to the divine a procedure that was a staple of African folk medicine—inoculation.

After reading similar claims recently published in European journals, Mather decided to press for its use in New England. The day after Hanno's execution, Mather wrote hopefully in his diary: "The Practice of conveying and suffering the *Small-pox* by *Innoculation*, has never been used in *America*, nor indeed in our Nation. But how many Lives might be saved by it, if it were practiced? I will procure a Consult of our Physicians, and lay the matter before them."[37] Doing so cost him dearly, at least at first. Citizens thought he had gone mad, that inoculation could only spread the disease and lay to waste the town. (For his part, Mather believed his critics to have been overtaken by the Devil.) One went so far as to throw a bomb into his home, though by chance it failed to explode. In time, though, the value of inoculation was understood. It was but one of many instances in which the culture and folk knowledge of Africans, preserved during the Middle Passage, would help the whites who had enslaved them: ironic, or perhaps only befitting the spirit of Christian redemption.

2

This Villainous Conspiracy

▲

From the Boston of Joseph Hanno and Cotton Mather, let us travel south, to New York City, and twenty years hence, to 1741. We are in lower Manhattan, in a scrubby ravine beneath a plateau. On today's map, we would be in the civic center, on Broadway, between Chambers and Duane streets, and men and women of every color would be hurrying past in the name of commerce. But now it is remote and quiet. On the plateau above stands the English Commons, once the Dutch Vlackte, with a poorhouse, a prison, and military barracks. New Yorkers graze livestock there, and the English imperium displays its power. Down the northern slope from the Commons just beyond us, are two bodies of water—the Collect Pond, cut in two, from which fresh water streams in two directions, toward the Hudson and East rivers. To our left is Pot-bakers Hill. To our right, a mill wheel grinds saltpeter into a white nitrous powder.

And here, in a silent field dotted with stones and small mounds of earth, is the Negro Burial Ground, the final resting place of the largest African diaspora in the Northeast, and nearly the largest urban diaspora in North America—second only to Charleston's. All around us, slaves and free blacks lie beneath soil that later will be evened out with fill dirt to make a level ground for nineteenth-century construction. Men and women, adults and children, their bones worn from hard labor, buried in coffins and shrouds, facing west. Many are buried with trinkets. Some lie with coins over their eyes. Some with coins in their hands. Or a seashell by their head. One wears a British mariner's uniform, its buttons bearing the anchor-and-cable insignia (once, surely, they gleamed). Another cradles a small child. Their skeletons eventually will number as many as 20,000. And among them are those executed for having taken part in the New York Conspiracy—the "Great Negro Plot"—one of the most important slave revolts, or white panics, in American history.[1]

The story of the New York Conspiracy comprises theft, arson, and racial suspicion; it is the story of an ethnically diverse town with a restive slave population; of interracial camaraderie and friendship; of a young indentured servant with an explosive secret; and of a town caught in the grip of fear. And it is a story that illustrates a very different civic jurisprudential commitment from the one that obtained in the trial of Joseph Hanno: a vision of caste jurisprudence, ritually reinforced through the spectacle of public punishment.

They hung there together, the corpses of two men—one black, the other white—bound in chains, swinging from a tree near the water's edge. The black man was named Caesar, though he also was known as John Gwin, and he had been the slave of the baker John Vaarck. The white man in the red coat was a shoemaker and tavern owner named John Hughson. In life, the two had spent countless hours in Hughson's alehouse by the Hudson, talking, drinking, eating, celebrating—and plotting. Now in death, they were to have one last, extraordinary moment of fellowship.

Caesar had been sentenced to die for stealing silver coins, candlesticks, and linens from Robert Hogg's store off Jew's Alley on March 1, 1741. That same evening, Prince, a fellow slave known to Caesar, had stolen about five pounds of goods from Abraham Meyers Cohen. The two thieves stored their loot with Caesar's white lover, Peggy Kerry, a twenty-two-year-old prostitute known around town as the "Newfoundland Irish Beauty." Peggy lived in Hughson's tavern, and recently had borne Caesar's child (the morning after the robberies, Caesar opened his bag and gave Peggy a child's whistle, a ring, and a locket with four diamonds).

But Caesar and Prince were suspected of being involved in something far more dangerous. They were tried together on May 1, and sentenced to be hanged not only for the robbery, but also for involvement in a larger plot. On May 11, they were executed. According to Daniel

Horsmanden, one of the presiding judges, Caesar had "died very stubbornly," and kept silent, providing authorities with nothing other than the pleasure of watching him die.[2] Once his neck was broken, Caesar's deep-black body was lifted high near the powder house, and hung in chains for all the public to view, a practice known as gibbeting.

Caesar's white friend was in deep trouble, too. He would be executed on June 12 and, like Caesar, he was to be gibbeted. But unlike Caesar, when Hughson was brought from the jail, he predicted that "some remarkable sign" would prove his innocence. As he rode toward the gallows in a cart, he carried his six-foot frame rod-straight, ceaselessly scanning the horizon, and held his chained hands as high as he could, a finger pointing upward (Hughson's wife, who also was executed that day, already stood near the gallows "like a lifeless trunk, with the rope about her neck"). Normally a pale man, Hughson had two bright red spots on his cheeks, each "about the bigness of a shilling." But the execution went as planned, and the Hughsons were launched into eternity without incident.[3]

After the execution, authorities gibbeted Hughson's body alongside Caesar's, and one month later, both corpses still hanging in public view, they were joined by another recently executed slave named York. There they were, swaying together, "blind and blackening" in the heat, as one nineteenth-century writer, quoting Byron, later described the scene, "in full view" of the tranquil bay of the Collect, "a ghastly spectacle to the fishermen as they plied their vocation near by."[4]

Then, a strange transformation took place, one that "drew numbers of all ranks, who had curiosity, to the gibbets, for several days running, in order to be convinced by their own eyes." The two bodies had appeared to change color. The white man had become black, and the black man, white. Caesar's face had been bleached by the sun and wind, and his body had turned pale. As for Hughson, it was said that his face, hands, neck, and feet had turned "a deep shining black," that the hair of his beard and neck was "curling like the wool of a negro's beard and head," and that his face seemed to have assumed "the symmetry of a Negro beauty," with his "nose broad and flat, the nostrils open and extended, the mouth wide, lips full and thick."

New Yorkers gawked at the "wondrous phenomenons," and many "were ready to resolve them into miracles."

The bodies then began to bloat. "The sun at this time had great power," wrote Judge Horsmanden, and in the heat, "Hughson's body dripped and distilled very much, as it needs must, from the great fermentation and abundance of matter within him." Eventually, Hughson's corpse, "unable long to contain its load, burst and discharged pail fulls of blood and corruption" (the stench was so great that, thenceforth, the fishermen "shunned the locality"). "If his corpse becoming monstrous in size, and his complexion . . . as black as the devil, can be deemed remarkable signs or tokens of his innocence," Judge Horsmanden could not resist musing, "then some may imagine it has happened according to his expectation."[5]

How did this grim spectacle come to pass?

In the early seventeenth century, New York was ruled by the Dutch and known as New Amsterdam, but from its earliest origins as a European colony, it was home to a diverse group of people and nations: Germans and French, Scandinavians and English, Sephardic Jews and various Indian tribes—and African slaves.

To what do we attribute the presence of slaves? The answer lies in the reason the Dutch chose to settle in North America at all. For the most part, they did not come to the New World to escape religious persecution. Holland was a tolerant society, a welcoming home for an odd assortment of religious dissenters (including, for a time, the Pilgrims, who found refuge there before embarking to Massachusetts). Nor did they come to fight their way up from endemic poverty. The Golden Age initiated by the revolt of the Protestant Dutch against Spain in the 1560s had lifted Holland into a period of unprecedented material wealth and cultural achievement (Spain asserted a claim over the Netherlands through Philip II, son of the Hapsburg emperor Charles V). The Dutch also lacked the belief among great powers, increasingly common, that extending their social and religious ideals across the globe would be a worthy national endeavor. Mainly, the Dutch came to the New World to increase their riches. They came to trade in lumber, furs, and agricultural commodities. Theirs were the dreams of merchants and bankers. And those dreams became especially seductive after 1609, when Holland and Spain entered a twelve-year truce: with the cessation of naval warfare, the New World was clear for trade and profit.

But there was a problem. New Netherland was just one small part of the vast commercial empire of the Dutch West India Company, which was founded in 1621 and enjoyed a monopoly on trade in West Africa and America. The reach of the West India Company was enormous, and finding men and women to develop a backwater like Manhattan was difficult. Opportunities were greater elsewhere in the world, especially

Asia, Brazil, and the West Indies, to say nothing of Holland itself. And those Europeans who did settle between the Delaware and Connecticut rivers often left their New World plows and fields when they found they could turn a greater profit by trading pelts.

To keep the colony afloat, the Dutch opened their settlement to all who might come and so drew a polyglot immigrant population ready to serve the need for labor, many living in varying degrees of indenture. Beginning in 1625, the Dutch also began to purchase blacks on the transatlantic slave market, and they took them as booty from Spanish ships, captured on the high seas after the end of the twelve-year truce. Traffic in slaves increased particularly in the wake of Dutch independence in 1648, when the West India Company refashioned itself now that war with Spain was finally at an end. The first ship with blacks intended for local purchase, the *Witte Paert*, or *White Horse*, sailed into New Amsterdam's port in 1655, with 300 Guinea slaves in the hold.

Life for these slaves was unlike what it would be later under the British. Much of New Amsterdam could not have been built without slaves, who helped with the first roads, fortifications, and houses; nevertheless, slaves were not central to New Amsterdam's economy or society. Rather than viewing African slavery as part of a cosmic order in which whites reigned and blacks toiled, the Dutch viewed bondage purely as an economic proposition, and the work regime they created was, in the words of one historian, "as mild as the realities of chattel slavery probably allowed."[6] Trained as artisans, a good number of slaves had sought-after skills, and they had bargaining power over when and how much they would work. Slaves could own and dispose of property, and they were allowed to bear arms in times of emergency (a notable contrast to Jews, who were barred from the militia). It also was not uncommon for the Dutch to set their slaves free, and some Africans gained an independence known as "half-freedom," a sort of feudal arrangement by which they were allowed to establish their own houses and farms in exchange for a yearly financial tribute to their former masters. Blacks could join the Dutch Reformed Church. And both freemen and slaves had real standing before the courts. They could sue and be sued, could testify against blacks and whites alike, and were given legal protection from undue cruelty. Naturally, the life of the half-free and the slave was still grim, a captivity filled with pain and sweat, an ocean away from home. Nevertheless, blacks had at least some cause to lay claim to being "accepted" members of the Dutch colonial community.[7]

.   .   .

After the English took over in 1664, the nature of slavery began to change. In New Amsterdam, slavery existed to advance the needs of the colony, to help build a commercial trading center. Under the British, however, the colony existed in good measure to advance slavery, particularly the interests of the Royal African Company (RAC). The RAC was a major slave-trading association whose principal owner was James, Duke of York. James was the second son of Charles I, and had been made Lord High Admiral upon his brother's assumption of the throne in 1660 (James later converted to Roman Catholicism and was deposed in the Glorious Revolution of 1688). The Duke took a special interest in colonial ventures, and after he sent 2,000 troops at his own expense to assert control over New Amsterdam, the town was renamed in his honor. Naturally, the Crown made certain that the Duke's lands were governed with the financial opportunities of the RAC and its shareholders firmly in mind, and it instituted a number of commercial policies that transformed the slave trade into a primary feature of New York commercial life.

Under British rule, the number of slaves passing through the colony on their way to foreign markets began to increase steadily, as did the population residing there. The numbers are striking. In 1664, the counties of New York contained a total of about 600 slaves. By 1746, they held 9,100, almost 15 percent of the total population of about 61,000. Manhattan saw a similar rise. In 1698, there were about 700 blacks in the town. In 1723, there were about 1,300. By 1737, there were 1,700. And by 1746, there were almost 2,500—nearly 25 percent of the island's population—and over half of the town's households owned a black slave.[8]

All this greatly pleased the RAC, as well as the variety of independent slave traders plying the market after the RAC lost its official state monopoly. It also was a great satisfaction to most colonists. Slavery provided cheap labor, the hands that made the colony work. But even more important, the slave trade was lucrative for the community as a whole. The tall ships that docked in southern Manhattan and sold their human cargo in the slave markets at the foot of Wall Street, near the East River, made many New Yorkers rich—merchants and lawyers, scriveners and entrepreneurs of every sort. And those who did not benefit directly from the trade benefited from the resources of those who did. New Yorkers were divided by ethnic suspicions and resentments, especially against the Dutch. But they all could agree that slavery was good business.

In the course of this deep economic transformation, New York changed from a society with slaves into a slaveholding society, and it developed all the attitudes and beliefs of a community dependent on black bondage for its existence. Of course, the Dutch had not been without what we today would call prejudice. But after the English took over New Netherland, and especially beginning in the early eighteenth century, city residents began to take a new view of the bondsmen in their midst. Slavery was no longer an elastic system, from which a black man or woman might exit after years of service. Instead, it came to be seen as the natural state of human affairs, in which whites dominated blacks, who were fit for no other civic status but that of chattel. This change was reflected in a tightening of the law, especially after the town enacted its slave code in 1702. Over time, blacks were denied the ability to testify as witnesses against whites; were made subject to special tribunals and punishments (including floggings from a common whipper for the town); were forbidden from meeting together in groups greater than three; were prohibited from conducting burials at night—the list of restrictions is extensive.

Not all whites were proponents of racial supremacy. A good many poor Europeans befriended blacks, both free and slave, and fraternized with them in local taverns that catered to black clientele, selling them rum in penny drams. Some continued to share food and conversation with blacks, balking at restrictive racial laws, which in any case had always been difficult to enforce. Poor whites and blacks danced together to the strains of a fiddle; they threw dice together; they dreamed of ways to improve their lot; they shared their resentments of superiors; they plotted; and, like Caesar and Peggy, they loved.

But outside the ranks of misfits and outcasts, whites increasingly saw blacks as not only inferior, but as a mass of dangerous, brute energy. As the number of slaves grew, whites believed they had more to fear, and fear is often the mother of disdain. And those fears were not unjustified. Over the course of the early eighteenth century, black theft became a growing problem as slaves robbed white homes, those of strangers and those of their masters, to pay for alcohol and even finely tailored clothing. Whites were alarmed by the wave of attacks on private property—and then there were other, more frightening, crimes.

Above all, whites feared organized rebellion, and that fear came to pass in 1712. On April 6, about twenty-five blacks assembled near midnight, retrieving a cache of pistols, knives, hatches, axes, and other weapons they had laid in the orchard of a local cooper. Most were "Cormantines" and "Pawpaws," African groups renowned for their courage and dignity, and most had been brought directly from Africa to the New World, with no "seasoning" in the West Indies. The rebels had bound themselves to an oath of secrecy, sucking blood from one another's hands, and they had rubbed on their clothes a potion made by a free black named Peter the Doctor, who said it would make them invincible. From the orchard, the slaves proceeded to the house of Peter Vantilborough, a baker in the east ward. There, at about two in the morning, they set fire to his outhouse, and waited.

Fire was a deadly threat in colonial times, and when someone sounded the cry for help, the communal response was immediate. As the townsfolk ran to the rescue, the slaves struck without mercy. Eight whites were killed instantly. The rebels thrust daggers into their backs, chopped at their necks with axes, and shot them in the chest at close range. Governor Hunter asked that the largest gun in Fort Orange be fired to sound the alarm. Then he called out troops to counter the assault. As the rebels withdrew, into the woods of northern Manhattan, six killed themselves rather than be caught. One killed his wife before taking his own life. The town was in a panic, and troops as far as Connecticut and Massachusetts were put on high alert.

The captured fugitives stood trial before a Court of Quarter Sessions of the Peace in City Hall in mid-April and early May. The trials were expeditious to a fault, and the attorney general, May Bickley, seemed alert to public lust for retribution, vigorously prosecuting even those whose guilt seems on the record we have today to be manifestly suspect. Twenty-five slaves were sentenced to death. Most were hanged, but others were not so fortunate, the judges having invented, according to the rebuke of Governor Hunter, "the most exemplary punishments that could be possibly thought of." Three were burned alive at the stake. One was "to be hung up in chains alive and so to continue without any sustenance until he be dead." Another was to be burned over a slow fire "in Torment for Eight or ten hours & Continue burning in the said fire until he be dead and Consumed to Ashes." Another was "broke alive upon a wheel" in front of City Hall, after which a Dutch sailor slowly smashed each of his bones with a crowbar.[9]

The brutality of the punishments may have seemed a prudent deterrent to future rebellion, but it brought stern criticism. Governor Hunter was appalled at the behavior of the attorney general, describing Bickley as a "busy waspish man"—a man who shortly was removed from office. The King's counselors themselves criticized the proceedings as summary justice. Even in faraway England, it was clear that the law had been abused as an instrument of terror. But that, indeed, was the point. The law worked to tutor the emotions, striking fear into blacks, while providing a catharsis for whites of all ethnic, religious, and national groups, binding them together into common identity and cause.

Soon after the insurrection, in December, New York passed a series of edicts further restricting blacks. No person was to trade with any slave without the master's consent. No slave could be out after dark without a lantern. A white person could be fined 5 pounds each night for entertaining a slave in his tavern or home. Masters were obliged to pay 200 pounds bond and 20 pounds a year to any slaves they freed, a regulation that made manumission prohibitively expensive. A slave found guilty of murder, rape, arson, or mayhem could be put to death at the discretion of the justices "in such manner as they shall think fit."[10]

The rebellion had been put down years ago, but its memory lingered, to be revived by the events leading to Caesar's and Hughson's arrests, bringing them together on the gibbet at water's edge.

Those events began, prosaically enough, with simple burglary—but it was no ordinary time. New York had just suffered the longest, most brutal winter in memory. For months, residents were pummeled by snow and ice, and with the rivers frozen around them, their food supplies grew short. More immediately, England was at war with Spain, and hostilities would soon engulf all of Europe. Many New Yorkers had enlisted in the fight, depleting the town of men. Residents feared a military invasion, and tensions were high. They also feared that instability might inspire another slave rebellion. One had recently occurred near the Stono River, in South Carolina, twenty miles from Charleston: on September 9, 1739, when news of war broke, twenty blacks incited by Spanish promises to grant freedom to fugitive slaves began a revolt that swelled to perhaps a hundred men and left about two dozen whites dead. The rebels were apprehended marching toward Florida crying "Liberty" to the beat of drums.

The burglaries occurred in Robert Hogg's and Abraham Meyers Cohen's shops. The next day, Hogg's wife, Rebecca, encountered young Christopher Wilson, an English sailor from the hospital ship *Flamborough*. Rebecca knew that several of Wilson's friends were regulars at the "idle houses in the Jews-Alley," and she thought that he might have heard tell of who had robbed the store. She even had reason to suspect Wilson himself. Days before, she had noticed his eyes alight upon the pile of coins in a register drawer she had carelessly opened in his sight. When she described some of the stolen things —including snuffboxes, silver medals, and a "remarkable eight square piece"—Wilson allowed as how he had been earlier that day to Hughson's alehouse, where a man named John Gwin had pulled from his pocket a worsted cap filled with silver coins, including the square piece of eight she described.[11]

Robert Hogg and James Mills, the deputy sheriff, went immediately to Hughson's tavern in search of John Gwin. But as Caesar stood in the room by the chimney, Hughson calmly told the men that no one by that name had been to the tavern. Hogg and Mills were puzzled, and when they later returned to question Wilson further, he explained that John Gwin was in fact the name of the black man also known as Caesar (whether Wilson intended to deceive during his first interview, we do not know). At three o'clock, Caesar was apprehended and brought into custody. The next day, suspecting he had had a hand in the robberies, authorities made a thorough search of Hughson's premises, but found no evidence. Hughson and his wife were questioned and then dismissed.

The investigation stalled until Tuesday, March 3, when Hughson's indentured servant Mary Burton went to buy a pound of candles from Ann Kannady, the wife of one of the constables who had searched Hughson's alehouse. Did Mary know anything about the robberies, asked Kannady? Mary demurred. Mrs. Kannady admonished her to confess anything she knew, "lest she herself should be brought into trouble." She then tried the carrot, a bit of "motherly good advice": if Mary "knew anything" about the robbery, Mrs. Kannady promised she "would get her freed from her master." Mary took the bait: she said that she "could not tell her then," but would tomorrow—and she indicated that Constable Kannady hadn't been quite assiduous enough in his search of Hughson's home, for he had "trod upon" the stolen goods.[12]

The next day, authorities searched Hughson's tavern once again, but again they turned up nothing. When questioned, Mary claimed she knew something of the robberies but feared "she would be murdered or poisoned by the Hughsons and the Negroes" if she told. For her protection, authorities lodged Mary with the deputy sheriff in City Hall, after which she explained that Hughson's wife, Sarah, had hidden the goods, first in the garret and then under the stairs, and in the end had given them to her mother. Questioned once again, Hughson admitted to knowing where some of the goods were hidden, and he soon surrendered them to Alderman Bancker. The Hughsons were arrested and then released pending trial. As for Caesar, he remained in jail.

It all might have ended there, but more dramatic and dangerous events were to intervene.

A plumber named White was probably the first to spot the flames. It was the day after St. Patrick's Feast, March 18, when many New Yorkers were recovering from a night of revelry. White had been asked to solder a leak in the gutter between the governor's house and the chapel at Fort George. With a strong wind blowing from the southeast, flames suddenly lapped from the governor's cedar roof. The chapel bell was rung in alarm, and men rushed to the scene, soon bringing hand-pump fire engines. Fed by the old wood and wainscoting inside, the fire engulfed the fort, the chapel, the secretary's office, the barracks, and the armory, and then threatened to spread to the nearby residences on lower Broadway.

Panic erupted when thoughts turned to the grenades and gunpowder inside the fort; it was feared that the entire town might burn. Those who lived nearby began to remove valuables from their homes. Cornelius Van Horne, a captain in the militia companies, called up seventy armed men to patrol the streets. Miraculously, it began to rain, and with much work and courage on the part of town residents, New York was saved. But for the fort, it was too late. It burned to ashes in about two hours and would continue to smolder through the night.

Some blamed the fires on the plumber's coal-laden firepot, suggesting that hot ash or sparks had ignited the roof. Others were not so sure: they observed that the fire seemed to come from inside the building, and that it had broken out in several places at once. In any case, the next day, the Common Council ordered one hundred new leather fire buckets, painted with the words "City of N. York."

Suspicions about the fire at the fort were renewed soon after, when another fire broke out, in the home of Captain Warren, on March 25. The captain lived on the southwest edge of town, near the "long bridge," the ferry service to Brooklyn operated by slaves. The fire engines caught this blaze in time, and a faulty chimney seemed to be responsible—or was it? On April 1, fire broke out once more, this time destroying Winant Van Zandt's old storehouse on the east end near the river. New Yorkers rushed to the scene, handing out the burning planks of wood stored within, and madly dousing the flames with buckets of water. The storehouse was destroyed, but the adjoining buildings were spared. Some said a man smoking a pipe had accidentally set fire to some hay inside. But then others noted that the fire was discovered on the northeast end of the roof, before the hay had even caught fire.

On April 4, there were two more blazes. The first was in the cow stable of Mr. Vergerau, who owned a slave named Quick, in the Fly along the East River (the area was named after the original Dutch Smith's Vly, or Smith's Valley). The second fire, which was observed toward dusk, in the house of Ben Thomas, seemed to have begun in a kitchen loft, between some straw and a bed where a black man slept.

On April 5, when live coals were discovered early in the morning under a haystack near the stables of Joseph Murray, New Yorkers began to suspect arson, though at the time, they imagined the culprits' motive to be only "making a prey of their neighbor's goods, under the pretence of assistance in removing them for security from the danger of flames." Many residents recently "had complained of great losses of their goods, and furniture, which had been removed from their houses upon these occasions."[13] Was it the slaves in their midst? There seemed to be a line of coals leading from Murray's fence to a house beside his stables where a black man lived.

Around church time on Sunday, Abigail Earle saw three slaves walking uptown. One spoke to the others "with a vaporing sort of an air," declaiming the frightening words "*Fire, Fire, Scorch, Scorch*, A LITTLE, *damn it*, BY-AND-BY" and then threw up his hands, made a circular motion over his head, and laughed. Abigail quickly reported the incident to her neighbor, Lydia George, who saw the men returning an hour later. She knew one of them, a slave named Quack. Lydia repeated her account of the incident to an alderman.[14]

The next day, April 6, while the city magistrates were meeting to discuss recent events, the alarm sounded at ten o'clock: there was a fire in Serjeant Burns's home, near the fort. It turned out to be a smolder, smoke without fire, but the cause was unclear. Around noon, another alarm sounded—Agnes Hilton's house, near Ben Thomas's, not far from the slave market on Wall Street. This one was clearly set on purpose, with coals cradled in hemp found by the wall plate adjoining Hilton's shingle roof. Was it one of the "Spanish negroes" whom Hilton had purchased not long before from among a group of blacks taken as spoils of war and condemned to slavery?

Some of the Spanish blacks were taken into custody and were being questioned—when yet another fire broke out, at around four o'clock, at

Colonel Adolph Philipse's storehouse. Flames raced up the shingle roofs of the old timber buildings, but just before the fire was extinguished, another alarm drew residents away—all but a few, including one man on the roof, who, seeing a black man jump out a storehouse window and over several garden fences, began to shout, "A Negro! A Negro!"—and then, more ominously, "The Negros [are] rising!" The black man, Cuff, Philipse's slave, was apprehended and carried off to jail on the shoulders of the crowd.[15]

Residents took it upon themselves to haul a number of other blacks into jail for questioning by the magistrates. The governor ordered a military night watch, and other authorities offered rewards and pardons for anyone who could help capture the arsonists: 100 pounds for whites; manumission and 20 pounds for slaves (plus 25 pounds to the slave's master); and 45 pounds for free blacks, mulattoes, or Indians. Town residents began to evacuate their homes. As the supreme court began a special, extended session to investigate the causes of the fires, some New Yorkers came to suspect that their slaves were conspiring to revolt.

This possibility certainly occurred to Judge Daniel Horsmanden, one of the three officials who would preside over the grand jury investigation and eventual trials. A blue-blooded royalist, trained at the Inns of Court in London, Horsmanden was a stern and suspicious jurist who believed blacks to be truculent and dishonest by nature, and who urged his fellow citizens to rid themselves of slavery, not out of any moral distaste for the institution, but rather for fear it would end in bloody rebellion. For Horsmanden, law was the bulwark protecting white society from the threat of black violence. In the polyglot community of white New York, the law's highest consideration was not the word of God, as it was at least in name in Mather's Massachusetts, but rather the interests of property owners. And so it was mainly a law for whites, a law that embodied white interests and defined blacks as outsiders.

As Horsmanden and his fellow judges administered this law, they did so, perhaps surprisingly, with real concern for what we today would call "due process." New York authorities wished to avoid the criticism they had endured in 1712, and hoped to leave no room to doubt the legitimacy of their legal and civic order. While the odds were certainly against the defendants, the trials of 1741 were not summary judgments. As the proceedings moved forward, the suspects were brought before a grand jury and arraigned upon indictment, and allowed to enter a plea before being tried by a petit jury. They were allowed preemptory challenges to jury selection, as well as the opportunity to call witnesses in their defense and to defend themselves before the bar.

The proceedings began on Tuesday, April 21, 1741, in City Hall, before Justices Frederick Philipse and Daniel Horsmanden. Justice Philipse charged the grand jury, a group of seventeen merchants: Robert Watts, Jeremiah Latouche, Joseph Read, Anthony Rutgers, John M'Evers, John Cruger, Jr., John Merritt, Adoniah Schuler, Isaac De Peyster, Abraham Keteltass, David Provoost, Rene Hett, Henry Beckman, Jr., David Van Horne, George Spencer, Thomas Duncan, and Winant Van Zandt.

The next day, the jury called the indentured servant Mary Burton to testify about the goods stolen from the Hoggs, but she refused to be sworn. The jurors pleaded with her, appealing to altruism and self-interest, but to no avail. In frustration, they then asked Alderman Bancker to send her to jail, which made her think better of her obstinacy. She finally agreed to be sworn and to tell what she knew about the stolen goods, but nothing more. She would not speak, she insisted, about the fires. With that, naturally, the jury's ears pricked up, and after haranguing Mary with threats of damnation in the afterlife if she remained silent, "representing to her the heinousness of the crime which she would be guilty of," she agreed to be deposed. Even then, however, her words were hesitant, and they "came from her, as if still under some terrible apprehensions or restraints."[16]

In hindsight, Mary's apprehension is hardly surprising. What she had to say was explosive: a number of blacks, especially Prince, Caesar, and Cuff, used to meet regularly at Hughson's, and they often spoke of burning down the fort, and then the entire town; next they would murder the white inhabitants, all with the help of Hughson and his wife, who seemed to be stockpiling arms for the purpose. "A great many people [have] too much," Cuff used to say, "and others too little; [my master] [has] a great deal of money, but in a short time, he should have less, and [I] should have more!"[17] After the destruction, Caesar was to be made governor, and Hughson, king. As many as thirty blacks had met in the tavern at one time, pledging loyalty to the three ringleaders. If Mary ever said a word, they threatened, she would be killed by poison.

The jurors were stunned; a plot to steal goods by setting fires was bad enough, but here were the events of 1712 replayed on an even more horrific scale, and now with the assistance of white people.

For the next months, the conspiracy was revealed, partly through Mary's testimony; partly through an informant, Arthur Price, who was in prison for theft and seemed "very adroit at pumping out the secrets of the conspirators" (who included Peggy Kerry, Hughson's daughter Sarah, and Cuff); and partly through the confessions of slaves themselves, scores of whom were jailed, threatened, or otherwise coerced.[18] The plot seemed to comprise two main parts. The first was an interracial operation for the theft and sale of goods from local homes and merchants. This part centered in Hughson's tavern and the home of a gentleman named John Romme (who fled during the investigation of the Hogg burglary, to be captured later in New Jersey; owing to his high connections to town authorities, he and his wife were eventually allowed to leave the province). The second part seemed to involve two paramilitary slave groups, the "Long-Bridge Boys" and the "Smith's-Fly Boys," in a far more dastardly scheme.

That plot may be recovered from fragments of confessions and the testimony of defectors. Fortune, the slave of John Wilkins, for example, told the grand jury on the morning of May 22 that ten days before Fort George was burned, Quack asked Fortune to accompany him down into the swamp near the powder house to retrieve some article, what it was Quack did not say. Quack then asked Fortune to come to the Fort, where Quack's wife lived, and where Quack would give him some punch. They went—"though the examinant says, that he did not go very willingly"—and stayed in the kitchen until dark. Fortune, fearing the watch, said that he had best be going. But of that, Quack said, there was no danger. Quack then asked Fortune to drink a dram, but he refused, and then they left together.

Two days before the fire, Fortune related, he saw Quack again. "In a few days," he told Fortune, "there would be great alterations in the fort." The transcript continues:

> to which the examinant [Fortune] asked him what alterations? to which Quack answered, that the fort would be burnt: the examinant on that asked him who would do it? Quack replied, you may ask Niblet's Negro, and he will tell you. That he did ask Niblet's Negro who was to burn the fort? to which he answered, Quack, himself, and Cuffee they would do it. That next day after the fire, the examinant met Sandy (Niblet's) who said to him, we have done the business; and the same day he met Quack who

likewise said to him, the business is done; that when Quack told him that the business was done, he asked him what business? to which Quack answered, the fort is burnt; do you not remember that I told you, there would be a great alteration in the fort?[19]

Caesar was first to face punishment, hanged on May 11 and then gibbeted. Other victims followed, conviction upon conviction, as authorities began to sweep the streets of blacks, overcrowding the jails: burned alive in a valley "between Windmill Hill and Pot-Baker's Hill," near the Negro Burial Ground, hanged, or deported to points throughout the Atlantic. Some of those arrested or punished were white, whose motives probably had been some combination of money and resentment of their superiors: John and Sarah Hughson, the first, were hanged, as was Peggy Kerry, and fourteen others were expelled from the province. But most were black. Their names are worth recalling. Burned alive: Albany, Ben, Caesar, Cuff, Curacoa Dick, Cuffee, Cook (also known as Acco and Maph), Francis, Harry the Doctor, Quack, Quash, Robin, and Will. Hanged: Caesar, two slaves named Cato, two named Fortune, two named Prince, Toby, Frank, Galloway, Harry, Othello, Quack, Toney, Tom, Venture, Juan, and York. Among seventy-two deported to the West Indies, Madeira, Hispaniola, Cape François, St. Thomas, Suriname, Portugal, Newfoundland, and elsewhere: Antonio, Bastian (also known as Tom Peal), Bridgewater, Braveboy, Cambridge, Dundee, Deptford, Emanuel, Jasper, Jupiter, Pablo, Pompey, Quamino, Tickle, and Titus.[20]

Punishment addresses itself explicitly to two groups: criminals and potential criminals. As directed toward the first, punishment represents the "just desert" of a crime, and acknowledges a person's individual freedom of action by imposing retributive consequences for misdeeds. Threat of further pain also may deter offenders from undertaking a similar crime in the future: punishments can concentrate the mind on the error of past behavior and so induce criminals to reform their ways. As directed toward the second, punishment is a deterrent. The punishment of one may deter others from perpetrating the same offense.

But punishment also alters those who punish. Public punishments bring a community together, creating civic solidarity through the collective expression of moral values. Indeed, punishment can inform as well as express a community's beliefs. The spectacle of public punishment conditions the emotions, suggesting to a community what they ought to think by inciting what they feel. It is an active, ritual process that changes those who perform it.

The case of Quack and Cuffee is instructive. Found guilty of arson, they were sentenced by Judge Horsmanden, before a courtroom packed with spectators, to be consumed by flames.

"Quack and Cuffee," Judge Horsmanden announced, as much to the courtroom and to posterity as to the condemned, "you both now stand convicted of one of the most horrid and detestable pieces of villainy, that ever Satan instilled into the heart of human creatures" (where Mather's Satan was a palpable force in the affairs of the world, Horsmanden's was a good deal more abstract). "Ye that were for destroying us without mercy, ye abject wretches, the outcasts of the nations of the earth, are treated here with tenderness and humanity. But you have grown wanton with excess of liberty, and your idleness has proved your ruin, having given you the opportunities of forming this villainous and detestable conspiracy, a scheme compounded of the blackest and foulest vices, treachery, blood-thirstiness, and ingratitude.

"Be not deceived," he continued, "God Almighty will proportion punishments to men's offenses. Ye that have shown no mercy here, and have been for destroying all about ye in one general massacre and ruin, what hopes can ye have of mercy in the other world?!

"And here, too, ye must have justice"—with emphasis—"for the justice of human laws has at length overtaken ye. We ought to be very thankful, and esteem it a most merciful and wondrous act of Providence, that your treacheries and villainies have been discovered, that your plot and contrivances, your hidden works of darkness have been brought to light, and stopped in their career, that in the same net which you hid so secretly for others your own feet will now be taken, that the same mischief which you have contrived for others, and have in part executed, is at length fallen upon your own heads!

"You and each of you shall be carried to the place of execution, where you and each of you shall be chained to a stake, and burnt to death. And the Lord have mercy on your poor, wretched souls."[21]

On the appointed afternoon, Quack and Cuffee were carried in chains to a pyre of dry sticks near the Hudson. There, they broke down and confessed their guilt, weeping, offering to give a full account of the conspiracy. The notes of their outcries make a grim report, and in the most essential respects—that there had been a plot centered around Hughson's tavern and the blacks who met there—probably an accurate one. According to Quack:

Hughson was the first contriver of the whole plot, and promoter of it; which was to burn the houses of the town; Cuffee said, to kill the people . . . that Hughson brought in first Caesar, then Prince, then Cuffee . . . that he Quack did fire the fort, that it was by a lighted stick taken out of the servants hall . . . that Hughson desired the negroes to bring in his house, what they could get from the fire, and Hughson was to bring down country people in his boat to further the business, and would bring in other negroes . . . that forty or fifty to his knowledge were concerned, but their names he could not recollect (the mob pressing and interrupting) . . . that Mary Burton had spoke the truth, and could name many more . . . Fortune, and Sandy, had done the same.[22]

After they told their stories, the sheriff began to lead the two back to jail, eager to question them at length. But the howling crowd barred his way, and the sheriff saw that trying to pass would be dangerous.

He helped tie Quack and Cuffee to the stake, and he lit the fire.

Mary Burton would offer still more extraordinary revelations before it was all over. In the feast of punishment and death, in the heat of the ongoing investigations, she claimed that a teacher of Latin who was in fact secretly a Catholic priest had been involved in the plot. There was indeed some evidence that John Ury held rather peculiar, dissident religious views; that he had performed a christening in town, as well as a number of suspicious rites at Hughson's tavern; and that he had perhaps told some blacks and whites that he could absolve them of their sins. It is possible he was a Nonjuror, one of the highly principled Anglicans who refused to swear allegiance to William and Mary after James II (James, Duke of York) was deposed. Whatever his actual religion or role in the fires, Ury would be convicted on August 29 on rather slim evidence; more than any demonstrable guilt, his evasiveness before the court seems to have done him in. Thereafter, with many of the town blacks sailing for distant parts, and others executed or discharged (thirty-four blacks were ultimately released), the major trials of the New York Conspiracy came to a close.

The true nature of the conspiracy—black, Catholic, or otherwise—will probably never be known. The truth most likely perished with the slaves who were burned alive, hanged, or banished to Madeira or the West Indies. Indeed, most of the original records of the conspiracy trials were themselves damaged or destroyed in 1911 in a fire in the New York State Capitol. Today, scholars are more attentive to the lives the blacks themselves led in New York than to their guilt or innocence. And those were lives led increasingly on the margin, the lives of the civic outcasts of a slaveholding society. In British North America, this civic exile was felt by other groups as well—especially Native Americans, who faced expulsion, and Catholics, who faced significant social and political discrimination—but within a world of pervasive hierarchy, blacks came to stand at the very bottom. The increasingly restrictive lives they led would become the norm in a society of caste.

3

Air Too Pure

▲

Did he run? Did he *run*? Did his first steps come with a sudden explosion of boot heels on cobblestone, the sound of a man in rapid motion, joyous and fearful, as this slave—now this free man—sailed through the squalid streets of London, shoving his way through the crowd with a muscular frame? Were carts of goods overturned in his wake, giving merchants cause to shout after him?

Or was it all different? Instead, did this thirty-year-old African man, not large and muscular but small and elegant, savor the first moments of freedom by strolling quietly, at his leisure? As he walked about town in the October air, did he notice with pride how many people gazed enviously at the colorful silk in his well-tailored coat? Did he tarry at St. Giles Church, chatting gamely with some of his friends among the black poor who congregated near its entrance (St. Giles: patron saint of beggars)? Did he pause to look once more at the sites he had admired so often since arriving two years earlier, in 1769, and doing his master's bidding in this expanding seat of colonial power? Did he stop and look at Westminster Hall or the slowly wending Thames and take a deep, contented breath? Or did he simply stride with haste to the home of one of his white collaborators, where a knock on the door was answered by an old woman with a look of grim determination, to whom he announced in excellent English, "I have come"?

As with so many events in Afro-American history, just what happened when James Somerset ran away from his master will probably remain forever obscure. Much of whatever record existed has been lost to fire, theft, and neglect, and perhaps purposeful destruction by those with an interest in burying the facts. But while we do not know the details of Somerset's escape into the London underground, we do know a good deal about the proceedings he set in motion, the case of *Somerset v. Stewart*, or *Somerset's Case*, one of the most important legal actions in the history of the antislavery movement. We also know a good deal about a document the case produced, the judicial opinion of Chief Justice Lord Mansfield, a cautious meditation on Somerset's plight that inspired the abolitionist struggle.

This is the story of a dispute between a North American slave, originally from Africa; his master, a merchant named Charles Steuart; and an impassioned man named Granville Sharp, who helped Somerset before the law. It is a tale that leads to a series of dramatic arguments before the Court of King's Bench in London. And it is the story of a case that advanced a jurisprudential vision that was gaining increasing currency in the late eighteenth century: that blacks were persons before the law like any others, deserving of the official protections due all men within the King's realm, and that chattel slavery was contrary to the law of nature. This was the vision embodied in Somerset's flight from bondage, and so it is that we begin with Somerset's life not as a free man, but as a slave.[1]

The boy looked at the sea, and at the ship on the water. This much we can infer about the child born in Africa who would become James Somerset. We do not know his original name, nor do we know where on the continent he was raised. The historical pattern of the transatlantic trade suggests he may have come from Senegambia, near present-day Nigeria and Sierra Leone; the Bight of Biafra, where the coast draws eastward around Calabar; or the region of Angola, near the present-day Congo. He was probably a Bantu speaker, of somewhat small stature, from a self-sufficient village of what we today would call peasants, a society of male-centered households. At some point in his young life, the boy was taken by slave traders, possibly in a raid of one black village making war against another, and conveyed to the coast in 1749 by canoe or coffle (a caravan, from the Arabic *qāfila*), to be sold to Europeans.

What he thought at that moment and what would later become of him may not have been so different from the enslavement of the great Olaudah Equiano. Captured in Africa as a boy about 1756—and, like Somerset, taken first to America and later to England—Equiano would grow to become a free man, a sailor, and a renowned opponent of slavery. In 1789, he published *The Interesting Narrative of the Life of Olaudah Equiano, or Gustavus Vassa, the African.* The sea and the ship that first "saluted my eyes," wrote Equiano in his autobiography, "filled me with astonishment which was soon converted into terror when I was carried on board." We can imagine for the young Somerset an experience like that of Equiano, who describes how he was "immediately handled and tossed up to see if I were sound by some of the crew." Fascination, confusion, dread—it must have been a common experience for African boys. Somerset would have been sold for some blue Indian cloth, or perhaps some liquor, or bars of iron.[2]

The Middle Passage, the trip across what many slaves called the "Great Water": the exact numbers are disputed, but about 600,000 endured the months-long journey to the present-day United States (about 6 percent of the total 10 or 11 million slaves moved in the transatlantic trade to the Americas).[3] About 10 percent died en route, most from disease. Like many of the men and women subjected to this modern horror, Somerset may have feared that the white-skinned crew intended to eat him, a fear many non-Western societies had of the West, as much as vice versa. Equally, he may have been treated with great indulgence by the crew and allowed to move freely about the ship. He may have walked beneath the rigging and the flapping canvas as these strange men, with their long, stringy hair, moved their immense craft across the ocean as if by magic. He may have gazed in amazement as the other blacks, perhaps two-or-three hundred of them, were fed horse beans, rice, or yams in small bowls or in groups of ten clustered around tubs. He may have heard black men and women speak a Babel of languages, desperately trying to communicate with one another. He surely would have smelled the pestilence of the hold, in which his fellow captives sweated, and cried, and vomited, and suffered uncontrollable diarrhea. He would have seen other blacks try to outrun their captors, break through the ship netting, and throw themselves overboard to drown. And he would have heard the crew shout with joy on first sight of the land where men would peer into Somerset's mouth and probe the muscles of his body, and where he then would be sold at auction. This was the island of Jamaica.

And he would have heard another ship's crew raise a joyful shout weeks later as the wind blew them within sight of the next landfall. Here was the place he would reside for most of his next twenty years; the place where Olaudah Equiano would be taken as well; a watery land with one of the most melodious and tragic names in American geography. How did it sound when he first made the word with his own lips? He had arrived: Virginia.

When Somerset landed in the Old Dominion, the colony was at the end of a slave bonanza, one of the largest periods of slave importation in its history. Roughly 41,000 Africans had landed on its shores between 1720 and 1749, making it one of the great centers of North American bondage. When Somerset was a young man, roughly 40 percent of those around him were black forced laborers. The numbers are astonishing to contemplate. In 1756, seven years after Somerset's arrival, Virginia was home to about 173,000 whites—and 120,000 blacks. Some of these men and women worked as field hands, harvesting and curing tobacco, while others guided rafts through regional waterways or sailed on ships across the Chesapeake. Some worked as house servants, cooking, spinning yarn, while others served as skilled artisans and had trades as blacksmiths or carpenters. Some were the foremen and drivers of other slaves, while others specialized in bricklaying.[4]

And Somerset? Young black men were highly prized for their longevity and versatility. His master, Charles Steuart, could have put him to work in any number of ways. But evidence suggests he was trained early on to be Steuart's personal manservant, a special, trusted underling, the immediate extension of his master's will. Steuart must have taken some pride in having purchased such a slave. After all, he was just twenty-four years old himself and about to launch a career as an independent merchant. Buying Somerset would have been a public statement of his having moved up in the world, a sign of his success. And he must have thought Somerset an especially fine specimen, as Steuart would have surely had his pick of the offers: he himself was a slave trader.

If a single word can be said to define an individual's values and character, in Charles Steuart's case that word was "loyalty," his governing principle in relation to his king, nation, family, and race. He was born in Kirkwall, Scotland, on the green and rugged isle of Orkney, in 1725. His father was sheriff clerk of the remote northerly land, a position once described as "more honorable than lucrative," and both parents traced their roots to the minor aristocracy of the region. He was the second son in a family that included his elder brother James, a successful lawyer, and his beloved sister Cecilia, who married a minister. With his brother's financial support (their father died when Steuart was only six), he attended grammar school in Kirkwall and, beginning in 1737, the University of Edinburgh, where he studied mathematics under a disciple of Isaac Newton. There, he acquired skills in bookkeeping and "a very good hand of write."[5]

Nobody would ever have called Charles Steuart a rebel. For many, to be Scottish in the early eighteenth century was to live between two worlds. The Scots for years had been part of a despised minority in Britain, a conquered people and a backward race. This tension was heightened by the challenge to the Hanoverian succession posed by the Scot highlanders, who supported the noble Stuarts, Prince James Edward and "Bonnie Prince Charlie," in their aspirations to the Crown. Charles's brother, James, for instance, risked a death penalty by holding radical meetings in his home on St. James Square in Edinburgh in the 1740s and 1750s (among his guests was Robert Burns, the future national poet of Scotland). Charles, however, took a different path, at least as records suggest. Rather than advocating Scottish autonomy and the cause of the Stuarts, he seems to have looked forward to the increasing incorporation of Scotland into the British Empire initiated in 1707 by the Act of Union. Over the course of his life, he seems to have sworn loyalty to the Hanoverian kings and to the cause of their empire.

Steuart's first choice of career brought him to one of its vital centers. In 1741, at the age of sixteen, he set sail for Virginia. His first job was as an apprentice in a store on the Rappahannock River owned by Robert Boyd, a prominent tobacco trader from Glasgow (merchants from that city did a brisk business in Chesapeake Bay). While Steuart left Boyd's employ three years later to work in Boston, in the countinghouse of his uncle, he would soon return to Virginia to join a trading firm owned by Robert McKenzie. His reputation steadily rising, Steuart then became partner in a mercantile establishment with William Aitchison and James Parker, and by the early 1750s had struck out on his own, founding a soon-to-be prosperous independent house in the commercial and shipbuilding center of Norfolk. His letters suggest that he did a significant trade in wine, rum, tobacco, molasses, corn, and shingles, among other products, and it would have been typical of a trader in his region also to have exported such items as pork, flour, butter, candles, tallow, bacon, lumber, masts, and hemp. One of his clients was George Washington.

Like many mercantilists, Steuart also traded slaves, large numbers of them, and was deeply committed to a worldview in which white men ruled by birthright and blacks toiled for their betters. "We received your esteemed favor of [the] sixth with forty-eight slaves as per invoice," wrote Steuart to a client in 1751, two years after he had purchased Somerset. "One of the women came ashore very sick & is since dead; four of the rest complained a little & two of them had the same symptoms with which the woman was taken. . . . We made an immediate sale of them at £26 Sterling a head." "We hope this will encourage a further correspondence of this kind," he continued, noting that "Negroes from fourteen to ten years are most saleable." Steuart wrote another client on the same day to "take the liberty to make you a tender of our further services." "We will venture to say," he boasted, "that the account we have now tendered is the greatest sale that has been made in this country, since the war, when they sold £30 Sterling the choice. Indeed we had the misfortune to lose one though all imaginable care was taken of her, but when she came ashore we did not expect she would live; however upon the whole a handsome profit will arise."[6]

Two of Steuart's letters bear similarly graphic testimony to the depth of his involvement in the cruelty of human traffic, an officious cold-bloodedness Somerset must have witnessed more than once in service. "Since writing the annexed," wrote an annoyed Steuart to a client, "we have received a letter from the gentleman to whom we sold your two Negroes, a paragraph of which follows." "'The two old men Jack & [Pedro],'" he quoted, "'are not worth the half of what you charged any one of them at, as you could not be acquainted with their distempers & worthlessness, had they been well. . . . Their gutts [intestines] hang out at their fundaments [anus] longer than the quill we now write with, & one of them has hardly the use of one arm.'" While Steuart insisted that the two slaves be resold at a low price to cover expenses, he explained to the same client one month later that "your Negroes remain yet unsold, nor will they allow themselves to be sold by pretending to be worse than they are & declaring to all that come to see them, that their parents & others of their generation died of the same disorder." "We are apprehensive," cautioned Steuart, "that, instead of a profit, the sale of them will be attended with a loss, which, if so, shall be as small as possible."[7]

And so Somerset came to know the slave trade with a particular, perhaps even clerical intimacy. He also saw Steuart's wrath when his own slaves tried to escape, and had good cause to know his master was not one to suffer transgressions lightly. On December 24, 1751, two years after Somerset's arrival, Steuart announced in the *Virginia Gazette* that he was seeking "a young mulatto fellow, named *Joe,* alias *Josiah Sally.*" "He is a sailor," Steuart explained, "and had on when he went away, a blue fear-nothing jacket, trousers, an old hat and wig, yarn stockings, and shoes." Steuart promised, perhaps with some ominousness, that "whoever will apprehend and bring him to me, or secure him so that I may have him again, shall have a pistol reward, besides what the law allows." Somerset likely also saw the end of a slave named Jack, who in 1752 "sued his present master for his freedom," and later "got drunk" and ran about town "with a drawn cutlass & frightened the people." There is little room to imagine how this rascal may have been dealt with.[8]

In this world, the boy was becoming a man.

Steuart kept a number of his own slaves—there was "old George," for instance, and Lawson and Nanney, and Quashabo and Annake, with their African names, and of course Annake's children—but Somerset was his clear favorite. And that preference would have only increased after Steuart began a new career in the colonial customs, by which time Somerset had likely grown indispensable. Entering the customs administration was a common route of assimilation for Scots in the British Empire. Steuart, however, entered the service in a rather unusual manner, and at a particularly high level. In October 1762, a group of Spanish sailors in Havana had been set aboard the *Amity's Addition* as part of their surrender in the Seven Years War (the European counterpart to the French and Indian Wars; Spain was allied with France), and were on their way to Cádiz when the vessel began taking on water. The captain found harbor near Norfolk, probably on the Elizabeth River, allowing his crew, his officers, and a "lady of distinction" to disembark while he tried to repair the craft. Then events took an ugly turn. A drunken mob attacked the sailors on November 21, killing at least two and seriously wounding several others, including the captain. Steuart jumped into the fray, protecting the Spaniards with great skill and diplomatic sensitivity. In doing so, he received the abiding gratitude of the Spanish officers and helped prevent what might have become an international incident.

Word of Steuart's gallantry reached George Grenville, First Lord of the Treasury and Prime Minister, who wished to reward him handsomely. In 1765, Grenville appointed Steuart the receiver general of the Eastern Middle District of his Majesty's customs, with authority over a region extending from Quebec to Virginia. Steuart recognized what was to be a turning point in his life and commissioned a fine portraitist to depict him in the clothes he wore when presented to George III. Steuart appears in a proper powdered white wig and a dashing mauve coat with gold buttons. He would remain loyal to the last, eventually elevated to paymaster general of the American Board of Customs, where he would help enforce the despised tariffs that fanned the flames of the American Revolution.

As Steuart traveled up and down the North American coast, enforcing the colonial customs laws, Somerset was by his side. Quebec, Salem, Boston, New York, Philadelphia, Williamsburg. And everywhere, Steuart's associates came to know and admire Somerset's abilities (precisely what services he performed, though, is unclear). From Boston, Nathaniel Coffin, of the celebrated Quaker family, compliments "able Somerset Steuart" in more than one letter, and sends Steuart's slave the greetings of his whole family, as well as "terms of the highest friendship" from "Sapho & Tombo."[9] Steuart seems to have concurred in Coffin's high estimation. His account books indicate that he gave Somerset a variety of expensive gifts unlike anything offered his other slaves, including a pair of stockings at a cost of 14 shillings, a full pound in cash, and, conspicuously, half a yard of expensive silk ribbon, or alamode, at a cost of 1 pound and 16 shillings. His Somerset: brought to Virginia as a boy, speaking English perhaps as well as many white men, serving his master with the greatest of solicitude. Somerset: a good slave, and properly grateful—and always at hand.

Somerset was at hand, too, in October 1769, when Steuart boarded the *Earl of Halifax* for London. At the time, Steuart did not know he would end up remaining there his entire life. The trip was taken out of family loyalty; Steuart planned to help rear his three nephews, the sons of his dear sister Cecilia, whose husband had recently died. One of Steuart's acts of generosity would be to help establish one of the nephews as a slave trader in Barbados. In about a week's sail, he arrived in the heart of London, in the district of Cheapside, home of the architect Christopher Wren's renowned St. Mary-le-Bow Church, with its beautiful white steeple and sonorous bells. Steuart quickly set up quarters in the city and assumed the role of paterfamilias.

As for Somerset, he fell in with the growing number of blacks brought from the colonies by masters returning home. Estimates of the number of blacks in England around this time vary, but there may have been as many as 15,000. Equiano had lived in the city, and in 1773 the poet Phyllis Wheatley visited there from Boston. During his work about town, Somerset would have met many of these "English" blacks. Most would have been slaves, some in positions of relative prestige, much like his own. Portraits of the era are dotted with well-dressed African footmen. But there were free blacks and runaway slaves as well, part of a growing black underground. Some gathered by St. Giles Church and were known as "St. Giles' blackbirds."

English whites could have hardly ignored the growing number of black slaves in their midst. In the Middle Ages, peasants had lived in villeinage, a form of semislavery that tied them to a lord and his land. But slavery itself had not existed in England for hundreds of years. And blacks, of course, were a conspicuous minority. Moreover, it was an open question whether one could legally hold a slave in England at all. Slavery in the colonies was based on municipal ordinances, but these were not recognized in England itself, where Parliament had refused to grant slavery the sanction of law—but had also declined to declare it unlawful. Could one actually be a slave in Britain? Or would a master's property interest fall outside the protection of law? And what if a slave were to be baptized? Would that alter his or her condition? A long line of contrary legal opinions left the issues unresolved. As increasing numbers of bondsmen arrived in England, however, and grim advertisements for slaves appeared throughout London newspapers, the issue pressed itself forward with urgency. In a nation especially proud of its tradition of law and liberty, whites were forced to face a fundamental civic question: whether slavery should be tolerated on Albion's shore. And few grappled more seriously with that issue than an extraordinary man named Granville Sharp.

Born in Durham in 1735, Sharp was the son of an archdeacon and the grandson of the archbishop of York.[10] As a young man, he decided against the ministry and instead was apprenticed to a linen dealer in London. Afterward, he tried to enter business on his own, but without much success. He was a man of strong enthusiasms, who, owing to this temperament, probably could not have settled into a conventional life. He was especially taken by religious questions. In his early years, he had worked closely with a Quaker, a Catholic, and a Jew, honing his skills at theological debate, especially after his friendly opponents challenged him to learn Greek and Hebrew so that he could dispute them in the original (a challenge Sharp met handily). He drifted, eventually finding a minor post in the Ordinance Department of the British government.

The position was not overly strenuous, and it allowed him time to pursue his passions. He perfected his languages, learned music, and conducted rigorous inquiry into biblical and religious issues. He is still remembered today for the "Granville Sharp rule," a tenet of Bible translation.

Sharp was drawn into the antislavery cause almost by accident. One afternoon in 1765, after visiting his brother William's medical practice in Mincing Lane, he saw among the indigent patients awaiting treatment a young black man lying on a bench, beaten and bloody. His name was Jonathan Strong, and his master, David Lisle, a hotheaded lawyer from Barbados, had pistol-whipped him nearly to the point of blindness before casting him into the street. Deeply moved, Sharp and his brother took Strong to the local hospital for extended treatment, after which Sharp helped Strong obtain a position as a messenger for a local surgeon and pharmacist. The matter might have ended there, but two years later, Lisle spotted Strong on the street and, seeking to gain the profit from his newly restored property, had him detained with the aim of shipping him to a buyer in Jamaica. Strong wrote to Sharp, begging assistance, and Sharp prevailed upon the lord mayor to win Strong's release. Sharp further issued a stern warning to Lisle and his agents that he would bring charges of assault against them if they interfered with Strong again. Strong himself would die a short time later, at the age of twenty-five.[11]

To protect himself against counterattack in the courts, Sharp threw himself into legal studies, taking up the law with the same intensity with which he had earlier studied languages and the Bible. In the process, he learned of a disheartening story. In 1729, a group of lawyers gathered together for an after-dinner discussion at Lincoln's Inn, one of the Inns of Court (the unincorporated educational and professional associations that have the power to call lawyers to the bar in England). Among them were two of the greatest legal minds of the day, Attorney General (and later Lord Chancellor) Philip Yorke and Solicitor General Charles Talbot. Over glasses of wine, a delegation representing West Indian slave interests asked the eminences if they might clarify some matters of importance to them. The lawyers obliged, writing a statement of the law that later would be described as the "Yorke-Talbot opinion," in which they asserted "that a slave by coming from the West Indies to Great Britain, doth not become free, and that his master's property or right in him is not thereby determined or varied . . . that baptism doth not bestow freedom on him . . . [and] that his master may legally compel him to return again to the Plantations."[12] Yorke and Talbot's stature led many—including William Blackstone, author of the eponymous *Commentaries on the Laws of England*, who once had suggested the very opposite—to accept their view as an apt summary of the state of English law. And while not in fact legally binding, the Yorke-Talbot opinion became a major obstacle for slavery's opponents.

Though he claimed to have never before read any work of law— "except," he wrote later, "the Bible"—Sharp was certain he could counter the arguments of Yorke and Talbot. Poring over his books late at night, he produced a classic document of the antislavery cause, *A Representation of the Injustices and Dangerous Tendencies of Tolerating Slavery in England*. In it, he contradicted the principle advanced by an English justice in 1706 that "the laws of England take no notice of a Negro," and instead posited that a natural law of human rights lay at the heart of the English nation. Drawn in part from Christian ideals, this law of nature superseded English rights of private property and classed slavery as a fundamental, intolerable evil. "True justice," Sharp wrote, "makes no respecter of persons"—that is, true justice is universal—"and can never deny to any one that blessing to which all mankind have an undoubted right, their *natural liberty*." In this respect, Sharp agreed with Chief Justice Holt, who in an earlier, much disputed opinion, had argued that "as soon as a Negro comes into England, he becomes free." It was a proposition brought dramatically to life when James Somerset came to knock on Strong's door one afternoon in November 1771.[13]

Why Somerset chose to run away at the moment he did is not certain, but he probably had been planning his move for some time. In August of that year, he had been baptized in the Church of St. Andrew, Holborn, perhaps out of genuine religious feeling, or perhaps hoping, as did some slaves in England, that baptism would lead to manumission. As to his "godparents" (possibly both literal and symbolic, as there are three), we know only their names: Thomas Walkin, Elizabeth Cade, and John Marlow. When the man now properly known as "James Somerset" was on the run, he doubtless sought refuge in the home of one of them. In any event, Steuart was shocked not only that his personal attendant should dare leave him, but also that he "insulted his person," as records indicate Somerset did.

Like that of Jonathan Strong, Somerset's freedom was short-lived. Less than two months after his escape, in late November, he was seized by Steuart's agents and placed aboard the *Ann and Mary*, which was bound for the West Indies under the command of Captain John

Knowles. As with Jonathan Strong, however, fate smiled on Somerset before his ship set sail: his godmother, hearing of his plight, quickly obtained a writ of habeas corpus, demanding his release. Often called the foundation of English liberties, the writ is a legal order requiring that a person detaining another bring the prisoner into court to explain the legality of the detention. Taken from the *Ann and Mary*, Somerset was brought before Lord Mansfield, who released him, pending a hearing to determine his fate. It was then that Somerset approached Granville Sharp, now among the most famous of antislavery activists, and asked for his help. "I gave him the best advice that I could," Sharp wrote in his diary that day.[14] An understated overture to what would be a mighty struggle—Sharp's final confrontation with the English law of slavery— that would compel the attention of both slaveholders and their opponents across the British Empire.

How to avoid rendering this decision? That was the main concern of Chief Justice Lord Mansfield. The issues in *Somerset's Case* were great, even revolutionary. The lives of thousands of slaves—and the property interests of thousands of owners—potentially hung in the balance. A Scot like Steuart, Lord Mansfield had risen through the ranks of the bar to the highest judicial post in Britain, and not by being reckless. He was an innovator in the field of commercial law, but in politically charged cases like this one, his legal opinions were models of caution; it pleased him when he could decide a case on technical grounds. But he was also devoted to law's rule, and in their previous encounters over slavery, Sharp had already made some compelling points that called the lawfulness of English slavery into question. In the Somerset case, Mansfield not surprisingly proposed a settlement: he urged the widow who had brought the habeas corpus action to purchase Somerset herself, and then set him free. But to no avail: both antislavery activists and the West Indian slave interests who took control of the case from Steuart demanded a definitive ruling, one that would resolve the issues raised by Yorke and Talbot. They adamantly refused Lord Mansfield's Solomonic solution.

Somerset had skilled and ample counsel: John Glynn, a fiery advocate of freedom; Francis Hargrave, a deeply learned man, who offered his services to Somerset and Sharp without charge; James Mansfield, a solid lawyer and former member of Parliament (no relation to the Chief Justice); a Mr. Alleyne, who had only recently been called to the bar; and William "Bull" Davy, a jocular former druggist, tenacious and fearless in argument. On the side of Steuart and the West Indian interests were the lawyers William Wallace and John Dunning, the latter politically influential, a powerful orator, and something of a mercenary gun, having argued on Sharp's behalf in an earlier case. In technical language, the legal issue before the court was known as "comity," the extent to which one jurisdiction was obliged to acknowledge and enforce the laws of another. It was a familiar principle, that of mutual respect between sovereign authorities, but it was not unlimited. And underlying this technical question was an even more fundamental principle, one of citizenship. While not argued with explicit reference to the term, it was precisely on this pivot that the case would turn, by determining the extent that a law recognizing fundamental distinctions in legal capacity based on color would be allowed to operate in the civic culture of England.

Spectators began to gather early on February 7 and filled Westminster Hall. James Somerset was there, with a crowd of his black supporters. Charles Steuart attended that day as well, though he chose to be absent for the rest of the proceedings. What he may have said to Somerset was not recorded. For his part, Granville Sharp avoided the courtroom altogether, lest his mere presence unnecessarily inflame his opponents and prejudice the judges.

The arguments were technical and heard in sessions over the course of many weeks, but even a small sample is enough to suggest the rhetorical force of Somerset's counsel, who argued for a vision of English law informed by the natural law of human freedom (in fitting with the defense of a status quo, Steuart's counsel offered more legalistic arguments and appeals to the sanctity of slaveholders' property interests).

Davy spoke first, announcing that he intended to prove "that no man at this day *is*, or *can be*, a slave in England."

"With regard to laws of Virginia, do they bind here?" Davy asked. "Have the laws of Virginia any more influence, power, or authority in this country, than the laws of Japan? . . . [A]ll the people who come into this country"—including blacks—"immediately become subject to the laws of this country, are governed by the laws, regulated entirely in their whole conduct by the laws, and are entitled to the protection of the laws of this country, and become the King's subjects."

Turning to Somerset, Davy continued. "Either this man remains, upon his arrival in England, in the condition he was abroad, in Virginia," declared Davy, "or not. If he does so remain, the master's power remains as before"—Somerset would stay a slave and could legitimately be seized for sale in the West Indies. "If the laws, having attached upon him abroad, are *at all* to affect him here, *it brings them all.* Either *all* the laws of Virginia are to attach upon him here, or *none.*" But an earlier case had indicated, Davy declared—in words to which his fellow counsel would return throughout their arguments—"that England was too pure an air for slaves to breathe in." "That was in the eleventh [year of the reign] of Queen Elizabeth," Davy reminded the court. "I hope, my Lord, the air does not blow worse since then." The pure air of England, the life force that fed all men alike, a symbol of the equality of men under law.[15]

After further arguments, Lord Mansfield asked that the case be postponed until May 9, in the next judicial term, hoping again that the parties might settle and relieve him of the obligation to make a decision; again, he hoped in vain. The arguments continued on that first day of the new term, and again on May 14, when Hargrave approached the bar. If Steuart's right to seize Somerset were recognized in England, he proclaimed, "domestic slavery, with its horrid train of evils, may be lawfully imported into this country, at the discretion of every individual foreign and native. It will come not only from our own colonies, and those of other European nations," he warned, "but from Poland, Russia, Spain, and Turkey, and from the coast of Barbary, from western and eastern coasts of Africa, from every part of the world, where it still continues to torment and dishonor the human species."[16]

Mr. Alleyne was not to be outdone in ringing oratory. He closed his argument for Somerset as follows. "Ought we not, on our part, to guard and preserve that liberty by which we are distinguished by all the earth!" he cried. "The horrid cruelties, scarce credible in recital, perpetuated in America, might, by allowance of slaves amongst us, be introduced here. . . . Could your Lordship, could any liberal and ingenuous temper, endure, in the fields bordering on this city, to see a wretch bound for some trivial offence to a tree, torn and agonizing beneath the scourge?" Turning to Somerset, he proclaimed, "This man is *here:* he owes submission to the laws of England, and he claims the protection of those laws; and as he ceases to be a citizen of Virginia, and stands in no such relation *now* to Mr. Stewart, so he is certainly not bound to him; and therefore he stands, like any other man in this kingdom, entitled to his freedom."

"[W]hen . . . the judgment of this Court is given," Alleyne concluded, "Stewart, as well as the rest of the slaveholders, will know, that when they introduce a slave into this country, *as a slave,* this air is too free for him to breathe in."[17]

Davy's arguments ended in a similar vein. "The air of England," he told Lord Mansfield, "has been gradually purifying ever since the reign of Elizabeth. . . . This air is too pure for a slave to breathe in. I trust, I shall not quit the Court without certain conviction of the truth of that assertion."[18]

Opposing counsel made their arguments, too: that Somerset was Steuart's slave, that Steuart's property interests should be respected in London as much as in Virginia, that English law did not condone slavery but neither did it condemn it, that the law should allow Steuart to seize Somerset just as it would allow a master to compel his apprentice to work, that the Yorke-Talbot opinion was correct from the start. There were practical considerations, too. "Let me take notice," Dunning announced, "neither the air of England is too pure for a slave to breathe in, nor have the laws of England rejected servitude. . . . It would be a great surprise, and some inconvenience, if a foreigner bringing over a servant, as soon as he got hither, must take care of his carriage, his horse, and himself in whatever method he might have the luck to invent. He must find his way to London on foot. He tells his servant, Do this; the servant replies, Before I do it, I think fit to inform you, Sir, the first step on this happy land set all men on a perfect level; you are just as much obliged to obey my commands. Thus, neither superior or inferior, both go without their dinner."[19] Each counsel was in high form.

After a few weeks, the court retired to consider its verdict. Lord Mansfield urged a settlement one last time—and lessened doubt as to which side would be better served by seeking accommodation, warning Steuart and the West Indian interests that, if forced to decide, he would do so, "*fiat justitia, ruat caelum*": let justice be done, though the heavens may fall.

Monday, June 22, 1772. The justices of the King's Bench filed into Westminster Hall. "On the part of Somerset, the case which we gave notice should be decided this day," intoned Lord Mansfield, "the Court now proceeds to give its opinion." The Chief Justice summarized the case pro forma, and reviewed Captain Knowles's explanation of why he detained Somerset aboard his ship: "That James Somerset is a Negro of Africa, and long before the return of the King's writ was brought to be sold, and was sold to Charles Steuart, then in Jamaica, and has not been manumitted since; that Mr. Steuart, having occasion to transact business, came over hither, with an intention to return; and brought Somerset to attend and abide with him, and to carry him back as soon as the business should be transacted. That such intention has been, and still continues; and that the Negro did remain till the time of his departure in the service of his master Mr. Stewart, and quitted it without his consent; and thereupon . . . the said Charles Stewart did commit the slave on board the *Ann and Mary*, to safe custody, to be kept till he should set sail, and then to be taken with him to Jamaica, and there sold as a slave."

Somerset's enslavement, his youth, his escape, and his peril—over twenty years: in this way, the law ruthlessly whittles a man's most important experience down to a bare essence.

"We pay all due attention to the opinion of Sir Philip Yorke and Mr. Talbot, in the year 1729," continued Lord Mansfield, "by which they pledged themselves to the British planters for the legal consequences of bringing Negro slaves into this kingdom." And, he noted, "we feel the force of the inconveniences and consequences that will follow the decision of this question."

Judges generally are appropriately cautious, loath to make sweeping pronouncements where a case may be decided on narrow grounds. And the question before them at that moment, claimed Lord Mansfield, was much smaller than that raised by Yorke and Talbot. That question was simply whether Captain Knowles's explanation for detaining Somerset was valid, whether the reply to the habeas corpus writ was sufficient.

"The cause returned is, the slave absented himself and departed from the master's service, and refused to return and serve him during his stay in *England;* whereupon, by his master's orders, he was put on board the ship by force, and there detained in secure custody, to be carried out of the kingdom and sold," Lord Mansfield stated. "So high an act of dominion," he reasoned, "must derive its authority, if any such it has"— if any such it has—"from the law of the kingdom *where* executed"—that is, from the law of England. "A foreigner cannot be imprisoned *here* on the authority of any law existing in his own country."

Lord Mansfield continued, theorizing as to where slavery could find its legal justification. "The state of slavery is of such a nature," he explained, that "it must take its rise from *positive* law; the origin of it can in no country or age be traced back to any other sources." A state of slavery, that is, had to be explicitly granted by human law. It derived no power from the law of nature. "Tracing the subject to natural principles," stated Lord Mansfield, "the claim of slavery can never be supported."

"The power claimed by this return," Lord Mansfield declared, "was never in use here, or acknowledged by the law. No master ever was allowed here to take a slave by force to be sold abroad because he deserted from his service, or for any other reason whatever. We cannot say, the cause set forth by this return is allowed or approved of by the laws of this kingdom."

"And therefore," he concluded, "the man"—Somerset—"must be discharged."[20]

In the courtroom, there was jubilation. Somerset's black supporters bowed to Lord Mansfield, then to the bar, "with symptoms of the most extravagant joy." They then shook each other by the hand, and according to one newspaper, "congratulated themselves upon the recovery of the rights of human nature, and their happy lot that permitted them to breathe the free air of England." A few days later, nearly two hundred of them gathered in a tavern near Westminster Hall, "to celebrate the triumph which their brother Somerset had obtained over Steuart his master. Lord Mansfield's health was echoed round the room, and the evening was concluded with a ball."[21]

Immediately after the decision, Somerset raced to tell his benefactor the news. Granville Sharp's diary entry was a simple one: "June 22d.— This day, James Somerset came to tell me that judgment was to-day given in his favor. . . . Thus ended G. Sharp's long contest with Lord Mansfield, on the 22d of June, 1772."[22]

With Somerset set free, it is understandable that many observers took Lord Mansfield to have affirmed the very principles he sought to side-step. The Chief Justice had not "ended slavery in England," as many seem to have thought—and as antislavery activists would try to suggest. Instead, he had issued a very limited ruling that Steuart had no right to forcibly take his slave from England to the colonies on the basis of the reasoning supplied in Steuart's reply to the writ of habeas corpus.

But the most carefully delimited judicial pronouncements have a way of assuming lives beyond the intent of their authors: just as it is for judges to be judicious, so, too, it is natural for the people to infer what larger principles they will from their opinions. This is the nature of legal conversation, a push-and-pull between the law and moral aspiration. Thus it was with *Somerset's Case*. Lord Mansfield's decision became a symbol for the antislavery movement, as activists and sympathetic judges seized upon the high rhetoric of its litigants and their appeal to natural law. And as we will see in the next chapter, both the case itself and the ideals it was said, rightly or wrongly, to have advanced would become sources of hope for American abolitionists, who fused its liberal principles—as Sharp himself attempted—with those of Christianity.

As for Somerset, he seems to have made good use of his freedom, as at least one story suggests. In March 1772, John Riddell, a charming gentleman and wit making the social circuit, wrote to his friend Charles Steuart, whom he hoped to meet in Bath. "I flattered myself that I should have had the pleasure of seeing you here amongst the crowd this winter," Riddell declared. "But I hope you only put it off, to invite yourself in the more pleasing spring, which now begins to appear in all its usual splendor—the beauties of the country at this season of the year, is a sufficient inducement for a gentleman of much less taste than Mr. Steuart to fly to paradise while he can embrace it. I won't say any thing of the number of female Beauties that are here," Riddell continued, "and are daily coming, lest you should be too precipitate in your departure from the Metropolis." Then gently mocking a misrepresentation of Steuart's name and title in recent newspapers, Riddell teased, "I am doubtful that the plague Capt. Steward has had with that black man of consequence Somerset Esqr. has been the means of preventing your coming to Bath."

On July 10, Riddell wrote again, though this time his tone was distressed. He had traveled to "Bristolle Wells," having first concluded a large transaction for some real estate. Despite having arrived "well" at his destination, it was eighteen days after the *Somerset* ruling, and an unforeseen problem presented itself to Riddell in the person of his slave Dublin. "I was to have set off tomorrow for Weymouth," Riddell wrote, even in his affliction maintaining his accustomed linguistic playfulness with status and titles:

> But I am disappointed by Mr. Dublin, who has run away. He told the servants that he had received a letter from his Uncle Somerset acquainting him that Lord Mansfield had given them their freedoms, and he was determined to leave me so soon as I returned from London—which he did without even speaking to me. I don't find that he is gone off with anything of mine. Only carried off all his own clothes which I don't know whether he had any right so to do. I believe I shall not give myself any trouble to look after the ungrateful villain. But his leaving me just at this time, rather proves inconvenient. If you can advise me how to act you will oblige.[23]

Somerset's letter to his "nephew" Dublin—whether there was in fact a blood tie we cannot know, but the likelier symbolic one seems to have sufficed—provides a glimpse into the black community of eighteenth-century Britain, hinting at its tenacious solidarity. It also suggests the process by which blacks spread word of the Mansfield decision among themselves, and how they voted, with their feet, on their understanding of its liberal jurisprudential significance. With the Riddell document, Somerset once again disappears from the historical record, except for one tantalizing clue. In October 1773, Steuart sought to identify a black man in the region who had robbed a coachman. Though "the coachman . . . never heard him give any account of himself," it seems that Steuart suspected the man to be someone he knew.[24]

PART TWO

White Republic,

1776–1849

National Identity on Trial

Memory is a powerful force in human society, but the repression of memory is even stronger, especially when the past is upsetting or morally difficult to confront. In the early decades of the nineteenth century, America held two political values we now see as contradictory but which—we tend to forget—then coexisted comfortably side by side. The first is egalitarianism, and the second is white racial supremacy. On one hand, the "Age of Jackson" celebrated and pursued principles of individual liberty and equality to a degree almost unprecedented in world history. From immigration to property ownership, the nation's laws made record strides toward allowing common people a social and economic stake in their communities. It was a time of mass politics, when up to 80 percent of the electorate voted, and vast numbers of previously excluded, often poor, men gained a real place in American civic life. At the same time, it was an era of caste, a time of self-aggrandizing, virulent racism practiced on a national scale. Many Americans after the founding decades of the republic espoused a fervent belief in the cause of Anglo-Saxon racial dominance, and in both spirit and practice, the United States was a nation of and for white Americans, a nation of black slavery and Indian removal and genocide.

The trials in this chapter all resulted from efforts to expose the contradiction within this comfortable ideological marriage, to reveal it as a conflict of civic values—a struggle whose legal terms were now set by the federal Constitution. The cases concern three critical issues for black citizenship in the antebellum period: the civic status of northern free blacks, whose numbers were rapidly increasing; the transatlantic slave trade, which continued despite a national ban on slave importation in 1808; and fugitive slaves escaping the South, a matter closely tied to the explosive question of slavery in the western territories. The first trial centers on a young schoolteacher named Prudence Crandall, who in 1833 established an academy for free black girls in Connecticut, provoking the violent ire of town residents and the state government. Her case became an abolitionist cause célèbre. The second follows a rebellion in 1839 aboard the slave ship *Amistad.* The ship was plying an illegal trade from Africa to Cuba when its captives broke free and, under the leadership of Sengbe Pieh, tried to steer their way back home. Before they could, the ship was seized in Long Island Sound and towed to shore. The third case concerns a devout Christian stationmaster of the Underground Railroad named John Van Sandt. In 1842, Van Sandt tried to smuggle a slave family from Kentucky through Ohio in his wagon but was caught in a dramatic early-morning chase. The resulting legal action against Van Sandt would allow one of the great antislavery lawyers of the day to test the constitutionality of the Fugitive Slave Law of 1793 before the U.S. Supreme Court.

To understand the significance of these cases for the history of black trials, let us return to the era just before they took place, to the Revolutionary and Early National periods. In 1790, shortly after the ratification of the Constitution, there were about 757,000 blacks in the United States, over 90 percent of whom were held in bondage. The vast majority of the total, a full 99 percent, lived in the South, almost 40 percent of them in Virginia. They mainly worked in agriculture. There was reason to believe that, as agricultural output leveled off, the slave trade would gradually become unprofitable and slavery itself might eventually wither away. But in 1793, a Yankee inventor named Eli Whitney perfected a type of cotton gin that helped reverse both trends. Whitney's gin made it possible to harvest vastly greater quantities of cotton than was possible by traditional methods, enabling farmers to meet soaring demand and encouraging cotton cultivation throughout the South, especially in Georgia and South Carolina. Increased cotton production, in turn, created a vastly increased demand for slaves. From 1771 to 1790, before Whitney's gin, about 55,000 slaves were imported to the United States.

In the following decade, that number rose to 79,000. And from 1801 to 1810, it was 114,000. Between these imports and the high birth rate of existing slaves, the black population grew in the twenty years after Whitney's advance to about 1.4 million, constituting nearly 20 percent of the national population as a whole.

Why increasing numbers of whites began to question the legitimacy of an institution that had the sanction of history, theology, and self-interest is one of the mysteries of modern Anglo-American history.[1] Even at the start of this transformation, however, a good number believed the existence of black bondage was inconsistent with American values. After all, in the 1770s and 1780s, colonists both north and south had fought a war in which thousands died for the cause of liberty. The Revolution generated countless tracts celebrating the struggle for human freedom.[2] Thomas Jefferson advanced such Enlightenment ideals in the Declaration of Independence, loftily announcing that "all men are created equal," possessed of equal claims to the rights to "life, liberty and the pursuit of happiness." In the wake of the Revolution, northern states in particular put these ideals into practice by banning slavery in their constitutions and by passing statutes aimed at gradual emancipation. One black trial of the era, the case of Quock Walker of 1783, involved a successful suit for freedom brought, in part, under the new Massachusetts Declaration of Rights.[3]

But while some ideals of the Revolution condemned slavery, others fortified the institution. The liberalism of many Revolutionaries cut in other directions. One basis of colonial liberalism, in particular, was the inviolability of private property, a foundation of individual liberty that included, some argued at the time, the sanctity of property in slaves. To abolish black bondage, in this view, would have undermined one of the nation's founding principles. Similarly, the same Enlightenment ideals that fed the rhetoric of Jefferson's Declaration also supported the development of early racist science, whose findings human law was said to ignore at its peril. Indeed, Jefferson himself was among the influential theorists of race who believed in the natural inferiority of blacks. Jefferson was not alone in arguing that blacks naturally emitted a repugnant odor or that black women in Africa had sexual intercourse with orangutans, but his influence helped establish modes of thought that would lead directly to the more virulent and systematized racism of the nineteenth century.

If the ideals of the American Revolution seemed to point in two directions for blacks, the Constitution of the new nation was Janus-faced as well. The precise role of slavery in the making of the document is a subject of historical debate, but it is clear that members of the Constitutional Convention walked a precarious line between the demands of southern slaveholders and those of northerners who objected to slavery or feared southern political dominance. Just how a balance was struck is a story of high intrigue and sometimes low-down negotiation, but the resulting moral compromise was certainly that. The Constitution created a national government of limited powers that left the legality of human bondage to be decided by the states; it apportioned the relatively less populated South's congressional representation through the "three-fifths clause," which granted states House seats based on the number of free persons plus three-fifths the number of slaves within their boundaries; it forestalled any federal ban on the transatlantic slave trade for twenty years; and it required that fugitive slaves be "delivered up on Claim" of their owners. Opponents of slavery also gained important concessions in the Constitution and in the First Congress; the most important of these were the consensus that Congress possessed the authority to abolish international slave imports after 1808 and the Northwest Ordinance of 1787, which prohibited slavery in the Northwest Territory.[4]

The new nation taking shape in the 1830s wove both strands of the American civic inheritance, liberty and racism, into a simple idea: that Americans were entitled to liberty not because of abstract ideals of universal human freedom, but rather by virtue of being white. Few in the political mainstream doubted that blacks were an inherently inferior race; and, as the number of blacks in the United States grew to 2.3 million by 1830, the question of slavery was kept off the national stage, thanks especially to southern Jacksonian Democrats. In time, however, certain pressing national issues—the status of free blacks, the international slave trade, fugitive slaves, slavery in the territories—brought the issue of slavery and race to the fore. Abolitionists also began to make themselves heard, countering visions of caste with legal and civic ideals of their own—ideals drawn, most potently, from the egalitarian spirit of antebellum Christianity. Before the Revolution, a handful of religious men, especially Quakers, had condemned bondage as a violation of Christian principles. But the evangelical revivalism of the antebellum years not only was profoundly democratic and antitraditionalist, but also was able to yoke its leveling commitments and spiritual energy to the republican principles of the Revolution. In the process, a battle took place at once for the spirit of Christianity and for the young nation.[5]

4

I Should Not Turn Her Out

▲

In central Connecticut, in the town of Canterbury, at the junction of two country roads, stands a stately white colonial house. Shaded by a cluster of tall trees, the house looks out over a wide green lawn and is encircled by a white fence with thin, elegant rails. The easy rhythm of its rectangular windows, the Palladian glass above the front door, its simple form and exact proportions all suggest a dream of an ordered world, a dream of reason. It is a beautiful spot. It also is a memorial, a fractured one, to some of the best and worst impulses in American civic history, a testament to hope and to violence. Built in the early 1800s, the house was purchased in 1831 by a pious young schoolteacher named Prudence Crandall, who came to Canterbury to instruct the daughters of the local elite. Before two years had passed, Crandall would stun the town by declaring her plan to convert the house into an academy for "young ladies and little misses of color." The reaction was swift and, in the end, brutal. After a protracted legal battle, Crandall's home was sacked by a mob who came by night to prevent its owner from promoting the evils of racial amalgamation and turning Canterbury into the "Liberia of the North." Fearing for her safety and that of her students, Crandall closed the school, soon to leave her white house, and Connecticut, forever.[1]

"My whole life," Prudence Crandall would declare in her final years, "has been one of opposition. I never could find anyone near me to agree with me."[2] She was born in 1803, the eldest daughter of Pardon and Esther Crandall, farmers. Her mother had been indulged as a child and had acquired a taste for extravagance, but her father was famously stubborn and soon brought Esther under his strict and simple rule. Pardon's ancestors were Anabaptists, though soon after marriage he and Esther joined the Society of Friends, many of whose members heeded not preachers or sermons, but rather the guidance of their Inner Light.

Prudence was not to follow in her parents' Quaker path, but she herself was subject to religious enthusiasm—she followed the spirit of her time and became a Baptist, acknowledging her acceptance of Christ's redemption with full immersion in the Quinebaug River. This was a time of evangelical revival, and on an immense scale. In camp meetings across the country, crowds gathered to hear several plain-speaking sermons each day; cast hopeful glances toward the "anxious bench," where those considering conversion could ponder the fate of their souls; sang hymns ordered precisely to lead them toward salvation; and listened to inspiring testimonials of the saved. Crandall herself attended such meetings, where the evangelical vision was brought to life with a visceral force, and she heeded their call.

The antebellum revival encouraged social activism, with a distinctive theological accent. For antebellum evangelicals, Christ's death on the cross was the ransom paid by God to redeem His children from their enslavement to sin, a bondage incurred by their failure to live by His law. It was a transaction in which humanity literally was purchased from sin through a form of legal substitution: Christ's death for ours. Accordingly, Christ's atonement on the cross enabled all people, not just the elect, to find salvation, provided they placed their faith in Christ and followed God's commands, inspired by the perfect sacrifice. This was an active process of individual spiritual aspiration. Antebellum revival emphasized the power of individuals to turn actively away from sin by establishing a personal relationship with Christ—a vision that encouraged Christians to work toward righteousness on Earth, as true desire for salvation was said to manifest itself in moral and social commitment. Christians were to remake American society and government according to the principles of their faith, just as that faith itself transformed a symbol of Roman administration—the cross, instrument of an ultimate corruption and cosmic injustice—into a sign of infinite justice and love. Temperance, feminism, education and prison reform, utopian socialism, and abolitionism were all forged in the smithy of this growing religious feeling.

Prudence brought this activist Christian ideal to her career as a teacher. After attending the Brown Seminary, she returned to Connecticut to work in a boarding school in Plainfield before proposing to found a new women's school in her hometown. The proposal was welcome among the well-heeled of Canterbury, who yearned for a finishing school nearer than Hartford or New Haven to which they could send their daughters. On the school's board were a physician, a lawyer, a merchant, a justice of the peace, and the minister and secretary of the local Congregational Church. There was also a politically ambitious lawyer named Andrew Judson, who lived directly across the street from Crandall's future home. Judson was the Canterbury town clerk, a state's attorney, a former state senator, director of the county bank, and an active member of the Democratic Party—an important man in the area. He had high hopes that the new institution would attract the daughters of wealthy families from across Connecticut, bringing prestige and influence to the town.

Crandall must have seemed the perfect candidate for her job. A bright local girl made good, a well-educated, pious convert, she seems to have been a model of primness and propriety. In a painting of her, she has a broad face, pulled-back hair, and the self-satisfied expression of a schoolmarm. With help from Canterbury residents, one of whom provided a mortgage on favorable terms, Crandall established herself in the former home of Luther Paine in October 1831, a house so lovely it must have promised a lifetime of possibility and satisfaction. About twenty students shortly enrolled in the Canterbury Female Boarding School and were adeptly taught a range of subjects from mathematics to music. Their instructor was a great success with the board and other townsfolk. Hearing of this general approval, Prudence was cautioned by her brother Reuben, a respectable doctor in Peekskill, New York: "I sincerely hope that you will use discretion in all your undertakings."[3] Reuben knew too well that his sister's name did not bespeak her foremost quality.

In the fall of 1832, a black twenty-year-old named Sarah Harris asked Crandall a simple question whose answer would reverberate across Connecticut: could *she* enroll in the Canterbury school? Sarah had already attended the local district school, where black children sat together alongside white ones, and now she wished to acquire "a little more learning" so that she herself might become a schoolteacher. Crandall knew Sarah's future sister-in-law, Mariah Davis, who worked in the school and sometimes listened to classes when her chores were done. Sarah and Mariah belonged to one of about twelve free black families in the area.

Despite its obvious difficulties, the prospect of enrolling a black student must have appealed to Crandall's heart from the first. After all, she had been raised by Quakers, the first religious group in history to prohibit slaveholding among its members. Recently, she had also been reading William Lloyd Garrison's fiery abolitionist newspaper the *Liberator*, furnished by Mariah, whose father was its local agent. In his inaugural issue, in early 1831, Garrison resoundingly proclaimed, "I am in earnest—I will not equivocate—I will not excuse—I will not retreat a single inch—and I WILL BE HEARD," words that must have resonated with Crandall's own temperament. After some initial hesitation, Crandall welcomed Sarah, with the promise of standing by her new pupil should parents complain.

And complain they did, which came as little surprise. Although Connecticut had adopted a gradual emancipation policy in 1784, and had only about two dozen slaves resident by 1830, color prejudice loomed large. The 8,000 free blacks in the state felt it constantly, accused not only of inciting restlessness and rebellion among southern slaves (a threat to national political stability, particularly worrisome after Nat Turner's bloody revolt in 1831), but also of being predisposed to poverty, crime, and lawlessness. Moreover, as in the South, most people in the North, Democrats and Whigs alike, believed at bottom that the United States was a white man's country. And this was true even among those opposed to slavery. Members of the American Colonization Society, for instance, many of them foes of the institution, hoped to encourage free blacks to emigrate "back" to Africa, even those born in Virginia or Rhode Island, and they helped establish the colony of Liberia for the purpose. The society was popular in Connecticut and had the support of many prominent citizens.

In a world dedicated to white supremacy, advancing the welfare of free blacks could promote public wrath—especially if such activities hinted at a vision of racial equality. After the Third National Convention of Free Blacks in Philadelphia in 1831, for instance, the abolitionists William Lloyd Garrison, the Reverend Simeon Jocelyn, and Arthur Tappan, a wealthy businessman who funded a range of reform causes, tried to establish in New Haven a school for free black men so that students might "obtain a useful *mechanical* or *agricultural* profession." New Haven seemed appropriate, given the reputation of the town for enlightened thought. But the effort failed miserably. Town authorities were little prepared to countenance blacks attending what had provocatively been called an industrial "college." Among other criticisms, the would-be founders were told that blacks would create a threat to the peace of mind of "the institutions for the education of [white] females . . . already existing in this City."[4] For most whites, black education meant black equality, which could lead only to the most frightening specter of all, interracial marriage and racial amalgamation.

When Crandall decided to admit Sarah, then, the matter of black education was already an open wound—not that Crandall particularly cared. When the wife of a local Episcopal minister visited to protest, Crandall's response was pure ice. The minister's wife demanded that Harris be dismissed. If Crandall did not send her away, her school "could not be sustained." *"It might sink, then,"* Crandall replied, *"for I should not turn her out!"* She was not one to waste higher rhetoric on the benighted.[5]

Amid the growing controversy over Sarah's admission, Crandall decided to undertake an even more radical scheme. On January 13, 1833, she wrote to William Lloyd Garrison. "I wish to know your opinion," she wrote, "respecting changing white scholars for colored ones. I have been for some months past determined if possible during the remaining part of my life to benefit the people of color." Crandall was proposing not simply to admit another Sarah Harris, but to dismiss all her white students and reopen her school as a black academy. She wondered whether Garrison might assist her in obtaining twenty to twenty-five eligible and willing "young ladies of color." And she set out for Boston to discuss the matter with him personally.[6]

Nobody in Canterbury knew her plans, it seems not even her family. Crandall had said she was taking the trip to purchase "infant school apparatus" (teaching material for small children). She even asked a storekeeper, Richard Fenner, and her own Baptist pastor, to provide letters of introduction she might use in Boston. And so, with secret designs, Prudence Crandall traveled north.

William Lloyd Garrison was the son of a drunken sailing instructor who had abandoned his family. A devout Baptist like Crandall, Garrison was an up-from-your-bootstraps self-starter who rose from nothing to become a successful printer, editor, and polemicist. Though his work as a reformer began with advocating colonization and gradual emancipation, by 1831 his views had radicalized. He now believed slavery was an abomination in the eyes of God that had to be repudiated immediately, and without compensation to slaveholders. By temperament and conviction, he was an absolutist, known for his defiant, scathing style. Shortly after meeting Crandall in 1833, he would found the American Antislavery Society, the most important abolitionist group in the United States (he already had helped create the New England Antislavery Society in 1831). Eventually, he would call for disbanding the Union, echoing Isaiah 28 to argue that the Constitution's tolerance of bondage made it a "covenant with death and a compact with hell." He also would embrace a form of Christian anarchism and support a range of radical social causes, including temperance, pacifism, anticlericalism, and women's rights, allegiances that helped alienate him from many of his original allies.

Crandall met him in Boston's Marlborough Hotel and found the young editor eager to offer his assistance. She traveled next to Providence, where she visited Elizabeth Hammond, a black woman with two young daughters, who were her first potential students. Hammond in turn introduced Crandall to the abolitionist brothers George and Henry Benson, which broadened her passage in antislavery circles. She then continued on to New York for further missionary work. The wealthy businessman Arthur Tappan rallied to her side. So did the abolitionist Reverend Simeon Jocelyn, white minister to a black congregation. Crandall's sponsors now included white and black abolitionists from New York, Philadelphia, Boston, Providence, and Connecticut. No longer just another reader of the *Liberator*, she had been graduated to activist.

On February 24, 1833, Crandall stood before her students and announced her plan. The next morning, four prominent townsmen came to her home to advise her in the strongest terms to reconsider. Ever unbending, Crandall showed the gentlemen the door. On March 1, they returned, this time as the town's official delegation, but Crandall remained unmoved. Their warning to Crandall articulated the prevalent anxiety: "[I]f she received her expected scholars, the blacks of the town . . . would begin to look up and claim an equality with the whites; and if they were all placed upon an equal footing *property and life* would no longer be safe." Ever plainspoken and pointed, Crandall shot back, "Moses had a black wife!" (Zipporah, as they all surely knew, was a descendant of Ham).[7]

Local leaders called an emergency town meeting for that Saturday night. Crandall asked one of her supporters, Samuel May, a local Unitarian minister, to represent her there. May agreed, attending the meeting along with Arnold Buffum, president of the New England Antislavery Society, as well as the antislavery Benson brothers from Rhode Island. Hundreds filled the Congregational Church, where Andrew Judson of the Canterbury school board read a statement warning that if Crandall proceeded with her plans a flood of blacks from "foreign jurisdictions" would descend upon the village. Citing the town of New Haven, he urged that they follow suit. "Shall it be said," he cried, that "*we* cannot, that we dare not resist?" Judson announced that he would invoke an old pauper law to impose a fine on Crandall for the presence of each black student in the town (in time, students would be threatened with fines as well). He would defeat the school by bleeding its resources—words that were met with wild applause.

When May and Buffum asked to speak, Judson began to rant, and others shouted and waved their fists. The meeting ended, everyone was ordered outside, and the church doors were locked. Learning of what had transpired, Crandall was only more resolved. For his part, Garrison printed the names of the school's enemies in the *Liberator* in boldface letters beneath the headline "heathenism outdone." Proposing a "Liberia" his adversaries could call their own, Garrison proclaimed fiercely: "to colonize these shameless enemies of their species in some desert country would be a relief and blessing to society."

On April 21, the first young woman from out of state arrived at Crandall's academy, Ann Eliza Hammond from Providence. The next evening, Sheriff Roger Coit delivered an official warning that Ann Eliza was to leave the town or be fined $1.67 per week. Failing to pay, the young woman would be publicly whipped. The sheriff returned later to order Crandall and Ann Eliza, along with Crandall's sister Almira, who was assisting with the school, to appear on May 2 before a justice of the peace. The six students now matriculated must have been afraid, but they betrayed no want of courage. When one was issued a warning like Ann Eliza's, she declared her willingness to be whipped for the school's sake. More pupils began to arrive, and the success under adversity seemed to hearten Crandall. To Reverend Jocelyn, she wrote, "In the midst of this affliction, I am as happy as at any moment of my life."[8]

Meanwhile, in Hartford, the state legislature responded to the pleas of Canterbury residents by drafting what later became known as the Black Law. "We are under no obligation, moral or political," declared the committee that drafted the bill, "to incur the incalculable evils, of bringing into *our own State* colored emigrants from abroad." The foolishness of Crandall's school was obvious: "The records of criminal courts, prisons and asylums for the poor," the committee concluded, "admonish us of the dangers to which we are exposed, and evince the necessity, in the present crisis, of effectual legislative interposition." The "Act for the Admission and Settlement of Inhabitants of Towns," the Black Law, required that "no person shall set up or establish in this State any school, academy, or literary institution, for the instruction or education of colored persons who are not inhabitants of this State" without first obtaining the written consent "of a majority of the civil authority" and selectmen of the town in which the school was to be located.[9]

An act to prevent the education of blacks. The law was a response, specifically, to the situation of Canterbury, a legislative effort to close a single school, but more generally the statute promulgated and reinforced a particular vision of race and citizenship. Article IV, Section 2, of the U.S. Constitution guarantees all citizens temporarily residing in a state the rights and privileges enjoyed by the state's permanent residents. "The citizens of each State," the article reads, "shall be entitled to all privileges and immunities of citizens in the several States." By restricting the free movement of blacks across state lines, the act implied that blacks, even if free, were not citizens of the American nation, insofar as it denied them the same constitutional privileges and immunities accorded whites. The law asserted blacks' constitutional incapacity, enacting a principle of civic exclusion in the deepest jurisprudential sense.

At least some state residents, including some prominent ones, were apparently against it, though the proposal seems to have encountered little organized opposition. Proponents, however, were well organized indeed. For instance, the local chapter of the Colonization Society, a critical lobby, voiced its strong support. Among those testifying in favor of the law was an expert in phrenology, who argued that the "facial angle" of blacks was "almost to the level of the Brute." According to the expert, it was "reasonable to suppose that the acknowledged meanness of the Negro's intellect," their "want of capability to receive a complicated education, renders it improper and impolite that [they] should be allowed the privileges of CITIZENSHIP in an enlightened country."[10]

The measure became law on May 24, 1833. Teachers in violation were to be levied a $100 fine for the first offense, a substantial penalty, the equivalent of about $2,000 today.[11] A second offense would carry a $200 fine, with the penalty doubled for each successive violation. Illicit students could be compelled in court to testify against their teacher and physically removed from the state. The people of Canterbury were well pleased. The town cannon was fired thirteen times, the bells peeled in the Congregational Church, men shot guns in the air and lit bonfires.

Difficult as things now were for Crandall and her thirteen students, worse was still to come. As Crandall and her charges walked across town in two neat columns, boys would follow them down the street, taunting them and blowing horns and jangling cowbells. One morning, manure was found spread on the front steps of the school. And then there was the official harassment of the town government: on June 27, Crandall was arrested under the Black Law and charged to appear in the next court session, in August. Bail was set at $150.

If the authorities imagined they had routed Crandall when they signed her arrest warrant, however, they were about to discover the depth of her obstinacy. Claiming penury, Crandall refused to post bail. It was a calculated move. Abolitionists had a potential sensation if Crandall went to jail, even for a short time. An otherwise respectable white female, a New England schoolteacher, forced into a cold cell: it was unthinkable. The publicity opportunities would be legion. Crandall and her supporters, especially her Unitarian ally Reverend May, had already contacted her friends and family, urging them not to produce funds for her release in the event of her arrest.

When Crandall claimed indigence, Judson sent a messenger to Reverend May soliciting the bail money. The minister told the astonished messenger that he refused to pay. "But are you not her friend?" the messenger blurted. May replied that, indeed, he was too good of one. Good as his word: When Crandall was taken to jail, May was waiting there for her. As she stepped down from her carriage, he whispered, "If you now hesitate, if you dread the gloomy place so much as to wish to be saved from it, I will give bonds for you even now." In his pocket was $150. "Oh no," replied Crandall, "I am only afraid they will not put me in jail."[12]

She occupied a cell reserved for debtors, though abolitionists did nothing to quash rumors the cell had been vacated of a wife murderer lately put to death. In truth, it was not an especially trying ordeal. The walls of the cell had been freshly whitewashed, and Reverend May and George Benson brought clean bedding. Anna Benson, George's sister, was allowed to spend the night to keep the prisoner company. The next afternoon, Benson produced the necessary bonds, and Crandall was released, returning to teach her ever-growing student body (they would soon number nineteen).

Abolitionists braced for the trial, hiring three prominent Connecticut lawyers. Chief among them was the eloquent William Wolcott Ellsworth, son of Oliver Ellsworth, former Chief Justice of the United States Supreme Court. Ellsworth was a professor of law at Trinity College, a Connecticut representative to the U.S. Congress, and, later, the governor of the state.

The trial of Prudence Crandall began in the Windham County Court on August 22, 1833. Despite the summer heat, spectators had come from miles around the rolling New England farmland and the courthouse was packed. Crandall had little cause for optimism, seeing among the three presiding judges Chief Judge Joseph K. Eaton, who had argued on the floor of the legislature for the Black Law.

The prosecution charged two counts. First, in the legal parlance of the day, "that the said Prudence Crandall, on the 24th day of June last, with force and arms, in a certain school which before that time had been and then was set up in said Canterbury, for the instruction of teaching colored persons, to wit, Theodosia De Grasse, Ann Peterson, Amelia Elizabeth Wilds, Ann Eliza Hammond and others whose names are unknown, who at the time so taught and instructed were not inhabitants of any town in this state." In other words, that Crandall had taught black girls in her school who were not from Connecticut. The second count charged "that the defendant . . . did willfully and knowingly harbor and board, and aid and assist in harboring and boarding certain colored persons . . . who when so harbored and boarded were not inhabitants of any town in this State," without the consent of the civil authority.[13] Crandall's plea: not guilty.

During this period of American history, drawing on a common-law inheritance, juries often decided cases not only "on the facts"—that is, determining whether or not the accused had, in fact, violated a particular statute—but also "on the law." They were asked to decide whether the law allegedly broken was itself legitimate or constitutional, an office from which juries now are in theory excluded (though some scholars recently have irresponsibly argued that juries should assert their supposed power of "nullification"). Crandall's defense therefore pursued a twofold strategy: to prevent the admission of evidence that implicated her in the teaching of black children, shielding her students as well from legal penalties; and second, and more important, to show that the Black Law itself violated basic state and national civic principles.

Only overweening prosecutorial confidence can account for the state's repeatedly addressing Crandall as "Prudy." State counsel began by calling a selectman of Canterbury, Asahel Bacon, who testified that he and Captain Sanger, another selectman, had visited Crandall soon after she opened her school. Crandall had received him "very politely," introducing him to some of the students, four of whom, she had said, were from New York. The prosecution then called Deputy Sheriff George Cady, who testified that when he had gone to Crandall's school to summon witnesses for the prosecution, Crandall had told him that "she did not see that there was any need of witnesses at all, for she should confess that she had broken the law."[14]

When the prosecution next called Ann Peterson, one of the students from New York, William Ellsworth rose to object. Peterson, he stated, was not obligated to answer any question that could incriminate her, despite the Black Law's requirement to do so. Ellsworth denied altogether "the competency of the Legislature to compel a witness to testify, or to answer a question that might implicate him." It was "contrary to fundamental principles" and of the state Constitution and the Bill of Rights to compel a witness to testify in such a criminal case. Judson stood and read at length from a legal treatise on evidence to prove Ellsworth wrong, and Ellsworth, in reply, read from various judicial opinions. The judges found in Judson's favor, but just as Peterson was about to testify, Ellsworth jumped in again. He had, he said, advised the witness "not to answer interrogatories in regard to her knowledge of the School," and "he felt it his duty now to repeat this advice."[15]

Anna Peterson heeded her lawyer. When, asked by the prosecution, did she come to Canterbury? She took the fifth, as we would say today, politely refusing to answer on grounds that she might incriminate herself. "Has Miss Crandall kept a school for Colored Misses not inhabitants of the State?" Again, no reply. "Will you say whether the defendant has or has not instructed any person of color other than yourself, since the 10th of June last?" All questions met with Peterson's solemn demurral. The same occurred when the prosecution called Catharine Ann Weldon and Ann Eliza Hammond. Prudence's Baptist pastor, the Reverend Levi Kneeland, was likewise unhelpful. But after he was taken to prison by the sheriff, he thought better of his silence. He told the court only that he had been to the school, had eaten and prayed there, and had spoken to the students on religious topics, providing just enough testimony to keep himself from confinement but not enough to advance the prosecution's case, which fared little better with the other witnesses they called.

But the threat of imprisonment finally proved to be the limit of silence. The next day, another student, Eliza Glasko, took the stand and, though a resident of Connecticut, refused to testify on grounds that she, too, might incriminate herself and be subject to penalty. The court clerk was asked to make out an order for her arrest. Moments before she was to be removed, however, Ellsworth rose again. Rather than have the girl committed to prison, he announced, he would advise her to speak. What Eliza had to say was straightforward and, naturally, a blow to Crandall's defense: She was a student in Crandall's school, as were the other girls in the court, one hailing from Providence, the others from New York. Crandall was the teacher, and instructed them in standard subjects of reading, writing, grammar, and geography. School usually was opened and closed with a prayer. The Bible was read and explained each day, and students were required to commit scriptural passages to memory. Realizing Crandall's defense had now, to a degree, been botched, George Benson's sister Mary also testified, explaining that she had visited Crandall's school and seen Ann Eliza Hammond there. She also admitted to recognizing a number of the students in the courtroom, some of whom were from New York and Rhode Island, and to having heard Crandall instruct the students in geography and arithmetic. In the eyes of the prosecution, the case was made.

In their arguments to the jury (we have no record of Ellsworth calling witnesses), Judson and Ellsworth expressed, in ways more or less subtle and direct, two of the fundamentally different visions of law that animated debates about black civic belonging in America. We can read their speeches as rhetorical performances specific to the case at hand, but their contemporaries would have also understood them as salvos in the intensifying battle between abolitionists and their opponents. For Ellsworth especially, it was rhetoric meant for the court but also for those who might later read his words with the fervor of an evangelical convert hearing a sermon.

Judson, first to speak, began by laying out the facts of the case and reading from the Black Law. The statute, he argued, "did not prevent any black from attending the district schools in the state, or any higher schools." The only purpose of the law, he argued, was to prevent blacks from other states from coming into towns without written permission from the town authorities. The issue at hand, he averred, involved placing schools and their students under the proper control of the local government. "This was all," Judson claimed, "and this was perfectly lawful."

It also was in keeping with the traditions of Connecticut. The legislature, he pointed out, had exercised authority over schools for more than a hundred years. In Judson's view, towns "had a right to say who should be allowed to become inhabitants by residence in their limits and this law gave them no more power than was necessary for the exercise of that right." The law did not reflect, as alleged, "disgrace on the state." On the contrary, "there are now more than 15,000 schools in the state, supported by our fund of $1,800,000, to which blacks may go without the payment of a cent." And of that, he was proud. "Where could a parallel be found in the Universe?"[16]

As for the constitutionality of the law, Judson believed this issue hinged on the definition of citizenship. The law, Judson asserted, was like many others directed at regulating a class. Physicians, lawyers, tanners, barkeepers, and manufacturers—all were subject to state regulation as a matter of public policy. In Connecticut, as in other states, so were blacks. Indeed, other states had enacted far more extreme measures: Georgia and North Carolina, for instance, authorized imprisonment of blacks entering the state, "even if they came in the capacity of cooks and stewards of vessels." If these laws did not violate constitutional principles, surely the Connecticut law did not. As for the federal Constitution's guarantee that the citizens of each state would enjoy the "privileges and immunities" of citizens of other states, Judson argued, the term "citizen" had a "technical signification—a legal meaning" that "did not include colored persons." Indeed, he noted, the Connecticut constitution itself excluded blacks from citizenship by denying them the opportunity to be electors.

Judson closed with an appeal to public safety. If the law were overturned, he warned, "the southern states might emancipate their slaves and send them all to Connecticut instead of Liberia. The influx of that species of population might be so great as to be overwhelming." Judson was no advocate of slavery. He desired "not to oppress any class of population," and "heartily wished that every slave might be emancipated that very day." But, he intoned, "if it could not be done without destruction to our constitutions, and desolating our land, he could not desire it." He concluded by emphasizing that the evidence against Crandall was "abundant and conclusive."

Central to Ellsworth's summation in Crandall's defense was his view that there was no tension between black civic belonging and the health of the nation as a whole—indeed, that blacks were already incorporated into the spiritual body of the United States. If his earlier tactic in cross-examination was patient silence, his method now was virtuosic rhetoric. We have his eloquent remarks in full written form, word for word. He began by immediately admitting that Crandall had broken the law. "True it is," Ellsworth stated, "my client had kept this school, but whether this is a *crime* is for you to determine." "You may find," he continued, "that she has violated an act of the Legislature of this state; but if you also find that she is protected by a higher power, it will be your duty to acquit. . . . Each one of you must be satisfied, both upon the law and the fact, beyond every *reasonable doubt*, that a *crime* has been committed. I flatter myself, that I shall be able to lead you to the conclusion that the law in question is a violation of the constitution of the United States. The constitution of the United States, where it controls, is the highest power in our land: beyond this no Legislature can go; and if you find that this law conflicts with that, you will by your verdict, say so."[17]

In the fashion of all good lawyers, Ellsworth next formulated the question before the court in the manner best suited to his client's interests. The issue at hand, he stated, was the rights of free blacks as *citizens* of the United States: "[C]an the Legislature of Connecticut prohibit the citizens of other states in this Union, from residing here, to pursue those avocations, which are open and lawful to our own citizens; or more exactly, can our Legislature prohibit a citizen of New York or Rhode Island from residing here, to pursue the acquisition of knowledge open to all citizens of this state?" And this question, Ellsworth proclaimed, "reaches deep and wide," indeed "deeper and wider than is perhaps imagined." "It is not a question of *color*, as might seem to be, at first thought," he said, but of state powers to contravene the protections of all citizens are granted by the federal Constitution. If a state were able to exclude "a colored citizen of another state," he reasoned, it could then also exclude "a *white* citizen." This conclusion was inevitable "unless their political rights are different." A state could exclude blacks from the privileges of citizenship only if there were "some admitted distinction, some qualification of right, growing out of color"; otherwise it was "quite certain" that "a prohibition today, extending to a colored man, may tomorrow be extended to others. If today we may expel from Canterbury, people of color, tomorrow we may expel from New Haven, every youth who was not born in the state."

Ellsworth's case rested upon a liberal vision of black citizenship—the civic universalism Granville Sharp had advanced in *Somerset's Case*. "The criterion of citizenship in the view of my friend from Canterbury," he argued, "is complexion; in mine, it is *birth* and *naturalization*." A series of rhetorical questions elaborated the claim: "Is it so that a person born on our soil is not a citizen of our soil? In the days which tried men's souls, did not men of color stand side by side with our fathers and shed their blood for this country, which was THEIR country? The country to which they owed indefeasible allegiance? Are not their names inscribed on the pension rolls of the government? And are they not now receiving the honorable testimonies of the services they rendered? Can they not be guilty of treason? Where does the gentleman get the doctrine, that the rights of man depend on his complexion, and above all, where does he learn to make a distinction, among *free born citizens*, on such ground?" The answers to these questions, by Ellsworth's shrewd implication, were simply a matter of common sense.

They also were guided by the central document of the War for Independence. "I am so much of a republican," Ellsworth declared, "that I love to refer, now and then, to that immortal instrument which our republican fathers put forth, as the ground work of all true government"—the Declaration of Independence. "There, gentlemen, we read, 'we hold these truths to be self-evident, that all men are created *equal*, that they are endowed by their creator with certain *unalienable* rights.'" Similar language could be found in state constitutions. Ellsworth advocated reading "these great land marks of free government, as they *are*," and he declared he would "not give my consent to have them interpolated as is done to day." "The gentleman," he said, perhaps pointing to Judson, "would [have us] read 'people of color excepted.'"

Ellsworth then addressed each of Judson's claims in turn. In reply to Judson's argument that blacks' ineligibility to vote proved they were not citizens, Ellsworth scoffed. "[W]hat then becomes of all white females and minors under age? Are they denationalized because the constitution does not allow them to vote? Is the wife of my friend an alien? And what is the condition of all those white males, who were born here, but have not the necessary qualifications of electors, such as property, paying taxes? Right or qualification to vote is no criterion of citizenship, either by birth or naturalization." As for the educational alternative the states furnished to all blacks, Ellsworth dismissed it as worthless: In the public schools, he said, blacks were "but hewers of wood and drawers of water; literally in many instances the objects of taunt, contempt and ridicule." And Judson's other assertions about black education, those were hypocritical obfuscations. "Let the gentleman tell me where, *where* in this state the doors are not barred against pupils of color. The Black Law declares it is *dangerous* to have them in this state, and why then talk of the liberality extended to them in the exceptions of certain schools?" The Black Law, he told the jury, "means nothing else, it was designed for nothing else, but to drive this school from Canterbury: its professions are one thing and its objects another." If blacks are to be educated, Ellsworth stated, "it is necessary that they should have schools of their own; public sentiment, at present, demands it; they cannot enter our schools without being made the cause of excitement—unless therefore their minds are to be sealed up in darkness, they must be permitted, according to their circumstances to form schools of their own."

Ellsworth's legal claims seem compelling enough today, long after they have been assimilated into our understanding of national identity, and fifty years after *Brown v. Board of Education* focused the nation's concern on the quality of black education. But the underlying logic was far from widely accepted at the time. Thus to persuade the jury to exonerate Crandall, Ellsworth needed to make his case not only on legal, but also on emotional terms. He needed to convince them that the Black Law was not only unconstitutional, but also unfair and un-Christian. He needed to appeal to white sympathy. "The people of this country," Ellsworth proclaimed, "forced the ancestors of these pupils from Africa; they have since kept their descendants in bonds, and darkness, and now talk of right and prejudice founded on slavery and the degradation of the Negro, as a justification for our continued wrong, and the deprivations, this day, attempted to be maintained on principle and morality." Such hypocrisy, Ellsworth suggested, inverted the real relation between whites and blacks. "Gentlemen, need I tell you, we owe a debt to the colored population of this country, which we can never pay—no, *never,* NEVER, unless we can call back oceans of tears, and all the groans and agonies of the middle passage, and the thousands and millions of human beings, whom we have sent and are now sending, ignorant, debased and undone, to eternity."

This debt ought at the very least to be acknowledged, he continued, and it required the absolute repudiation of the Black Law and the vision of civic exclusion it expressed and embodied. Ellsworth painted a vivid picture for his audience: "Let this law perish. Be *you* the executioners. Its object is to extinguish the light of knowledge; to fasten chains of ignorance upon those whom the God of all has made equal with ourselves; whose future destiny is as high; whose hopes are as dear as ours. For Heaven's sake, let us not, by legislative enactments and the solemn forms of judicial sanction, add to the prejudice which already exists against the descendants of the Negro. Let us not verify the declaration of Montesquieu, 'that we must not allow negroes to be *men* lest we ourselves should be suspected of not being *Christians.*'" The law, he said, "is a most wanton and uncalled for attack upon our black population—it opens wounds not easily healed, it exasperates to madness many who live among us; it strengthens the unreasonable prejudice already pervading the community against blacks, and in short, it rivets the chains of bondage and makes our own state an ally in the unholy cause of slavery itself." "Slavery," he warned, "is a volcano, whose fires cannot be quenched, and whose ravages cannot be controlled. We already feel its convulsions— and if we sit idly gazing upon its flames, as they rise higher and higher, our happy republic, will be buried in ruin, beneath its overwhelming energies."

His final words were a simple declaration of faith. "I trust," he said, "you will see your way clear before you convict my client of a crime, for teaching children of color, what is daily taught to your children— for endeavoring to elevate and enlighten an unfortunate portion of our race"—that is, a portion of the *American* race. "Are you, gentlemen," Ellsworth intoned, "prepared to say, *that teaching the word of God is a crime?* . . . My appeal is to the PEOPLE, who you are, and WITH THE PEOPLE I LEAVE MY CAUSE."

After the remaining arguments, the court charged the jury, advising jurors that, in its opinion, "the law is constitutional and obligatory on the people of this state"—but affirming that "the law of the case . . . also belongs to you to decide."[18] Deliberation lasted several hours. When the jury returned, they must have surprised many, not least Crandall and her allies: they could not reach a verdict. The court ordered them to deliberate again, but once more they returned divided. A third attempt produced the same result. Seven jurors favored conviction, the foreman revealed, and five acquittal—and they were irreconcilable. The case would have to be heard a second time, in the superior court, on the second Tuesday of December.

In her second trial, Crandall again faced a presiding judge firmly against her case. Chief Justice David Daggett, one of the early proprietors of the institution that would become the Yale Law School, was formerly mayor of New Haven (where he had stood in staunch opposition to the black industrial college), a vice president of the Hartford Colonization Society, and a public proponent of the Black Law. And this time Judson was in far better form, the records left to us showing his nimble responses to

Ellsworth's arguments and his eloquent plea on behalf of racial discrimination and black civic exclusion. Judson began his case by insisting, first, that Connecticut had "done more for the *education* of the blacks, than has been done in any other portion of the civilized world," and that his purpose was simply to "oppose the importation of blacks from other countries, for any purpose" into the state. He also noted that he was a firm opponent of slavery. Nevertheless, he said, the facts of the case were clear, as was the constitutionality of the Black Law.

Judson focused his arguments on the long-standing status of education as a matter of local concern, asserting that localities and states had never relinquished their control to a higher jurisdiction. But even more, he met Ellsworth's objections to the Black Law head-on, arguing baldly that free blacks were simply not citizens and therefore not entitled to the privileges and immunities guaranteed by Article IV. "We are told on this trial," he argued, "that persons of color are *American citizens*, within the meaning of this section of the Constitution, and therefore a law of Connecticut, which requires that schools set up for *colored persons*, not inhabitants of this State, without the consent of the board named in that act, is a violation of this Constitution. I am willing to meet this argument at the threshold, and, without evasion, answer it in such a manner as shall be satisfactory to the court and jury.

"*Colored persons*," announced Judson, "*are not citizens*, within the meaning of that term, as technically used in the Constitution." For support, he unleashed a wide range of arguments, appealing to the original intent of the founders, as evidenced by their own racial views; various acts of the federal Congress concerning race and citizenship; state constitutions that excluded blacks from civic life; and the history of legislative and judicial decision-making about blacks in America. Did blacks fight in the Revolutionary War? asked Judson, responding to Ellsworth's earlier arguments. Yes, but so did Hessians and Frenchmen, and they were not now citizens. Does the Declaration of Independence contain ringing proclamations about liberty? Yes, he said, "but go back with me, and see whether that declaration will not disprove the position. *When* was that declaration made—by *whom* was it signed—and against *whom* did it speak? It does say that '*all men are created equal.*' But who does not know, that on the 4th of July, 1776, every Colony or State tolerated slavery—they had laws to hold their slaves in bondage." Judson had done his homework, grounding his argument in a wealth of references to American history and law.

"The white men were oppressed and taxed by the king," he proclaimed, echoing common wisdom of the time. "They assembled in Convention, and at the peril of their lives declared this *white nation* free and independent. It was a nation of *white men,* who formed and have administered our government, and every American should indulge that *pride* and *honor,* which is falsely called prejudice, and teach it to his children. Nothing else will preserve the *American name,* or the *American character.*" Judson turned to the jury. "Who of you," he asked, "would like to see the glory of this nation stripped away, and given to another race of men? Give up this distinction, and you part with all which makes the name of an American our pride and boast." He, too, could argue that his opponents had resorted to evasive rhetoric. "The *professed* object" of Crandall's school, he said, "is to *educate* the blacks, but the *real* object is, to make the people yield their assent by degrees, to this universal amalgamation of the two races, and have the African race placed on the footing of perfect equality with the Americans." He concluded: "This is not the case of the town of Canterbury alone, against Prudence Crandall." To Judson's way of thinking, Crandall was "the mere nominal defendant, put forward by others, whose machinations would disturb the tranquility of this whole nation." "[I]t is *the case* of the State of Connecticut," he insisted, and as a result, "every town, however remote, and every citizen, however unconcerned, has involved in it, a deep interest. Let the law be pronounced unconstitutional, by this high tribunal, and a corresponding school for males will be immediately established in some other town. . . . In a very few years the evil will spread over the State."[19] Judson was playing for the highest of stakes, asserting and clarifying a vision of caste jurisprudence that would haunt the country long into the future.

Chief Justice Daggett was equally strong in his charge to the jury. He instructed them to rule based on the facts presented, which were scarcely in controversy. And though he admitted that it was "an undeniable proposition, that the jury are judges of both law and fact, in all cases of this nature"—and therefore empowered to rule on the constitutionality of the law—he allowed it "equally true, that the Court is to state *its* opinion to the jury, upon all questions of law" (judges could exercise such influence, surely a salutary one from the standpoint of the development of the rule of law).[20] In the strongest terms, Daggett declared that the defense was in error, that the Black Law was constitutional, because free blacks were not, in fact, American citizens. "To my mind," the Chief Justice intoned, "it would be a perversion of terms, and the well known rule of construction, to say, that slaves, free blacks, or Indians, were citizens, within the meaning of that term, as used in the Constitution. God forbid that I should add to the degradation of this race of men, but I am bound by my duty to say, they are not citizens."

This jury was able to concur and made short work of the matter: they found Crandall guilty. Her lawyers quickly filed a motion in arrest of judgment to prevent her sentencing. Their charge was technical: first, that the superior court had no legitimate jurisdiction over the crime; and second, that the formal charge itself had not been prepared correctly. Crandall returned to Canterbury, to await the next phase of her ordeal. She found the well of her stately house had been contaminated with manure and a stone thrown through her window. There were numerous other affronts: a local doctor refused to treat a sick student; a black and white cat was left on her fence post with its throat cut; and, in late January, a would-be arsonist tried to set the house ablaze (Crandall and her students were able to douse the fire before it could do much damage). At the same time, she was the toast of abolitionist society, showered with well-wishes from around the United States and across the Atlantic.

Ironically, in the end, Crandall had nothing to fear from the law of her state. Her final trial took place in the Supreme Court of Errors in Brooklyn, Connecticut, beginning on July 26, 1834. Chief Justice Daggett presided again, sitting with judges Samuel Church, Clark Bissell, and Thomas Williams. The others had no wish to overrule explicitly the eminent chief justice but hoped to undermine his decision without confrontation. And so they availed themselves of a familiar judicial maneuver, dismissing the case on technical grounds. Announcing the decision in Hartford, Judge Williams stated that there had been a defect in the warrant for Crandall's arrest. While it had charged Crandall with violating the law, he argued, it had not explicitly stated that her school had no license to operate, identifying a central feature of the statute which, he asserted, was aimed against *unlicensed* schools. The dismissal left all parties dissatisfied: Judson because Crandall was free without penalty, abolitionists because it deprived them of legal grounds for appeal to federal court, where they could have advocated for an explicit proclamation of principles against the law. It was a fittingly inconclusive end to the case that had taken up the indeterminate status of black civic belonging at this moment in history.

But Crandall was subject to one other law, and it was this one that ultimately determined her fate: the law of the mob. On September 9, her school was surrounded by angry men, yelling and beating on the house with lead pipes and wood timbers. They tore out two windows and smashed many more panes of glass. Some broke into the house, overturning furniture, wreaking destruction. One girl was so upset that she was said to have coughed up a pint of blood. Reverend May came as soon as he could and advised against repairing the house. It would only be destroyed again, he said. With her students terrified, Crandall's back was finally broken. Going into seclusion, she put up the house for sale. She was so disconsolate that May had to inform her students that the school was closing—she couldn't face them. "My heart glowed with indignation," May said later. "I felt ashamed of Canterbury, ashamed of Connecticut, ashamed of my country, ashamed of my color."[21]

On August 12, 1834, Crandall was married to a minister who had courted her since the trial had begun. After her school was destroyed, she moved to New York with her new husband, who bled her dry of her money and, it seemed, of joy. After he died, she moved to Kansas, gaining a name for her advocacy of feminism and spiritualism. She kept several framed photographs of William Lloyd Garrison hung throughout her home. She lived her final years in isolation, in conversation, it was said, with spirits of the dead—the other world from which the subjects of the next black trial, prisoners in an unlawful transatlantic trade, sought desperately to escape, sparking another confrontation of American liberalism, Christianity, and caste.

5

All We Want Is Make Us Free

▲

The handle is just a square block of steel. The blade is two feet long, and broadens outward to a width of three inches at the tip. Along its curving edge, the metal is scratched and nicked from weeks of cutting obstinate stalks in the sugarcane fields of Cuba. Splinters of green bark still cling to the blunt edge. The ocean swells as the schooner slowly plies its way through the Atlantic from Havana to Puerto Príncipe (now Camagüey). As a black hand carefully lifts the knife from the broken carton where it was hidden, the steel makes a soft scraping sound as it drags, clanking over the cache of other knives stacked in the box. The other knives make the same sound of scrape and clank as they are removed one by one. The blades are heavy, and the knives swing pendulously as they point toward the floor.

The hold is dark and foul, but there is air on the deck above, where the sky is moonless, the dawn yet to break. Bare black feet walk quietly on deck. Two shipmen, one white, the other mulatto, are sleeping on mattresses. In an instant, the blades fly and enter the bodies of the men with a succession of soft thuds. Another knife falls, and another, and many more, especially on the mulatto, bringing forth swells of blood. The mulatto dies without a sound, the white man is strangled after a horrifying struggle, and soon shouts of "Murder!" pierce the darkness.

The law at times is swift and terrible—at times, its instrument is a cane knife—and so, at times, in acts like this the law has been redeemed.[1]

His name was Sengbe Pieh, and he was born a Mende, in Sierra Leone. We know almost nothing of his early life, except that his father was a "big man" in the village. Of Sengbe's childhood, his occupation, or his wife and children, the facts are lost. Sengbe generally kept silent about such matters, probably out of caution. What we know, for certain, dates from 1839, when Sengbe was in his early twenties, and found himself in Lomboko, at the mouth of the Gallinas River, imprisoned in a vast facility holding the most valuable merchandise on the African continent, black slaves. There are conflicting stories about how he got there, ready for shipment across the Atlantic to harvest cotton or sugar under threat of the lash. By his own account, Sengbe was hunting one day in the forest when he was seized by a group of black men. Later, during his extensive travels through the American legal system, some whites would accuse him of having been a slave trader himself, and claim that he had been seized as payment for a debt he owed to another trader in human flesh. Neither story can be verified.

Sengbe was loaded aboard the slaving brig *Tecora*, bound for Cuba. During the first decades of the nineteenth century, European nations gradually outlawed the transatlantic slave trade through a variety of legal instruments. Spain had promised to end the traffic in 1817 through a treaty with Britain, reaffirming the commitment in 1835, two years after England abolished slavery in her West Indian colonies. The *Tecora* was a criminal vessel, and its captain was courting a possible death sentence for the high profits of the black market. The journey to Havana took about two months, and for hundreds of captives, mostly women and children, the conditions were extreme. Chained together at their wrists and legs day and night, they lived in a hold not higher than four feet. They lacked for water and were whipped for not eating enough of the rice the sailors slopped at them. About one-third died along the way, their bodies tossed overboard. Finally, the ship neared Havana, but the captain chose to wait until nightfall to unload his cargo. The slaves would be falsely identified in import papers as having been shipped to the island before the 1817 ban—as being, in the language of the day, *ladinos* rather than *bozales*, or native Africans—allowing their future owners to buy and sell them without fear of reprisal. But for now, the *Tecora* had to be wary of British ships cruising the area to uphold the trade interdiction by force.

Sengbe and his fellow captives next were locked in oblong, roofless corrals, and in these barracoons they would await their day of sale. In late June, after being poked and prodded with a thoroughness for which the slave trader was renowned, in every part of their bodies, fifty-three were purchased by José Ruiz and Pedro Montes, aged twenty-four and fifty-eight, respectively. Ruiz bought forty-nine adult men, and Montes four children: three girls and a boy. In the dark of night, with false papers, they were loaded onto the slave ship *Amistad*, to be transported to Puerto Príncipe, a two-day journey to the other side of Cuba. The Africans found no relent from their suffering. They were bound hand, foot, and neck. Antonio, the captain's black cabin boy and slave, taunted them ceaselessly. And then there was Celestino, the mulatto cook; he painted a grisly portrait of what awaited them: through hand gestures, he described how their throats would be cut and their bodies chopped to pieces, to be eaten as dried meat. According to Grabeau, the second leader of the bloody revolt to come, Celestino's jest "made their hearts burn."

Sengbe found a slightly loose nail lodged in the ship's wall. Slowly prying it out, he used it to open the lock on his chains and release his fellow captives. Once free, the Africans found a cache of cane knives in the hold and carefully padded to the deck above. The captain and Celestino lay sleeping on mattresses dragged into the open air. Celestino was first to die, hacked to death for describing their dishonor. The captain put up a struggle, killing and wounding some of the rebels with his dagger, desperately calling to members of his crew to "throw some bread at them"—but Sengbe flattened him with his knife, and the others set about strangling him. The crew jumped overboard and disappeared, probably drowned. Montes ran to the hold and hid beneath an old sail, but was soon discovered, as were Ruiz and Antonio. The Africans demanded that Ruiz and Montes sail the ship back to Sierra Leone. They did so by daylight, sailing the ship east toward Africa, but at night, they headed northwest, seeking to hug the American coast. The possibility of being spotted by a British or American vessel seemed their only hope.

The *Amistad* was hard to miss. Rumors soon spread through the Northeast of a mysterious ship, a "long, low black schooner," manned by a group of Africans with cane knives. Were they pirates? Smugglers? A number of ships met the *Amistad* as it zigzagged north, but the Africans always hid Ruiz and Montes from sight while they tried their hand at trade (one ship from Kingston sold them a jug of water for the astronomical price of one doubloon). With supplies perilously low, some of the Africans desperately quaffed the various medicines on board and ransacked the vessel for hidden stores. The deck was strewn with a "disorderly profusion" of "raisins, vermicelli, bread, rice, silk, and cotton goods," and the hold was filled with "silks, crapes, calicoes, cotton, and fancy goods of various descriptions," "all mixed up in a strange and fantastic medley."[2] Eventually, the *Amistad* came to an unknown coastline, and the Africans sent a small boat to investigate Culloden Point, at the tip of Long Island. As Sengbe and the scouting party traded with a group of white men they met on shore, they were spotted by Lieutenant Commander Thomas Gedney of the U.S.S. *Washington*. Peering through his looking glass, the seaman thought the *Amistad* seemed suspicious. He boarded it and took control of the vessel at gunpoint.

Ruiz and Montes fell to their knees and gave thanks to the Holy Virgin. The *Amistad* was guided to New London, Connecticut, where the Africans were held in the town jail.

Little did the *Amistad* rebels know as they were led ashore that their revolt and arrival raised an issue at the center of American national identity: were blacks presumptively persons or property? Would federal law be guided by the principles of caste or the dictates of liberal jurisprudence? On one view, slavery was the prerogative of the states—in accordance with the federal Constitution—and white supremacy was a fundamental principle protected by national law. This position was especially held in the South but was not without its many northern advocates as well, owing to the depth of racial solidarity and a commitment to national unity. Against it were opposed a range of antislavery groups that found in the Constitution the very letter of the Declaration of Independence, which plainly affirmed that "all men are created equal." From this view, the core principle of the American nation was that of universal individual liberty, the natural rights vision that underlay the arguments in *Somerset's Case*. The law of human bondage, that is, was unalterably and unambiguously opposed to the law of America.

Those in the latter, less popular camp, it should be said, were driven by a range of motives and expressed their opposition to slavery in various ways. The American Colonization Society, for instance, which figured in the trial of Prudence Crandall, hoped that American blacks would form independent colonies in Africa, creating a home for free blacks currently living in the United States. Such advocates typically were guided less by a commitment to human equality than a suspicion that freedmen might incite rebellion among domestic slaves in the South and doubts that blacks and whites could ever live together peaceably in America. As for the ranks of abolitionists, they were typically motivated by Christian egalitarianism and a profound commitment to bringing American society, politics, and law into line with the spirit of their faith. Men like William Lloyd Garrison thus believed that slavery should be repudiated immediately as immoral, even at the risk of national disunity. They were widely seen as a dangerous, mad lot, though their ideals have been in large measure vindicated by time.

The advocates and opponents of slavery viewed the *Amistad* rebels in diametrical legal terms. To slaveholders, the Africans were assassins, their crime proof of the necessity of racial discipline. Such criminals should be returned to Spain or Cuba for trial, where they would either be put to death or returned to bondage after a memorable flogging. For abolitionists, on the other hand, Ruiz and Montes were forces of lawlessness; Sengbe was the guardian of law. With courage and dignity he had overturned the white supremacist vision that deemed blacks incapable of the self-possession at the heart of a society of legality. And if some might have blanched at the un-Christian taking of life, others would have acknowledged the occasional historical necessity of the Christian warrior. Even more, the Africans were exercising their natural right to resist sale into bondage, no less than the colonists had in 1776 resisted their own enslavement by Great Britain—republicanism and Christianity mingling in the evangelical mind.

Soon after the captives arrived in Connecticut, antislavery networks formed an "*Amistad* committee" to advocate on their behalf in court and with the Van Buren administration. Sengbe and his compatriots were free, they argued, and should be allowed to return to Africa—preferably after having been converted to Christianity, so that they could serve as missionaries. Other interests, however, had other plans: Ruiz and Montes demanded that the blacks be returned to them; the nation of Spain demanded that the rebels be extradited for trial; and Captain Gedney of the *Washington* demanded the value of the slaves as a reward under the law of the sea for salvaging the ship from certain loss.

The committee fighting for the Africans' freedom included the Reverend Joshua Leavitt, an abolitionist editor, and Lewis Tappan, a prosperous merchant from New York (the younger brother of Arthur Tappan, one of the early supporters of Prudence Crandall). The group hired a number of prominent antislavery attorneys, notably abolitionist Roger S. Baldwin. They also enlisted an important statesman to their cause: the former Senator, Secretary of State, President, and current Congressman John Quincy Adams. Known as "Old Man Eloquent"—he was the author of a standard text on rhetoric and oratory—he had tire-lessly opposed the "gag rule" preventing discussion of antislavery peti-tions on the floor of the U.S. House of Representatives. The *Amistad* captives moved him to enter the fray to advance the principles for which his ancestors, most notably his father, the second President of the United States, had fought the Revolution.

Sengbe and his fellows were soon moved to the jail in New Haven, on the town green, where local residents, a steady stream of gawkers, could view them for a small fee, to help pay for their defense. In the afternoons, the Africans also could be seen exercising on the lawn, per-forming somersaults and other physical feats for petty cash (money many soon learned to spend in a local grog shop, much to the dismay of abolitionist supporters). A professor at the Yale Divinity School fur-nished them with attentive religious instruction (some eventually con-verted to Christianity), and Josiah Gibbs, a Yale professor of linguistics, helped the committee find Mende interpreters, one an African sailor aboard a British brig of war docked in New York. What Sengbe and the others thought throughout the ordeal is difficult to say. What is certain is that they longed to return home, little knowing they would have to wait for two years as the courts determined their fate.

One of the judges who would make that determination was none other than Andrew Judson, who, in 1833, had fought against Prudence Cran-dall's school. That effort had proved a good career move. Judson rose through the ranks of the Democratic Party to be awarded a judgeship shortly after the Crandall affair. In the interim, his views on race and civic life had not changed; America, he still believed, was a white man's country. As the case came before Judge Judson in federal district court, sitting in admiralty, first in Hartford and then in New Haven, it gener-ated a welter of legal claims and counterclaims, from Captain Gedney's demands for salvage payment, to Ruiz and Montes's demand for their slaves, to a suit by the Africans against Ruiz and Montes. But running through all the technical arguments lay the central question: were the Africans persons or property, free men or slaves? If free, the question was, what to do with them? Should the federal government return them to Africa? Should they be allowed to stay in the United States if they so chose? Should their abolitionist friends be entrusted to send them home? If slaves, the question became, who would own them? Captain Gedney? Ruiz and Montes? The Spanish government?

With observers following the testimony closely, the Court heard a procession of witnesses, including Dr. Richard Madden, a British investigator of the illegal Atlantic trade who had been posted to Cuba. Madden described how slaves were kidnapped from Africa to the Spanish colony in contravention of international treaty. He also detailed the routine forging of papers falsely establishing captives as *ladinos*—to the island born or else imported before the international ban—and asserted that in his judgment, the *Amistad* captives were *bozales*, slaves captured recently from Africa. It was a forceful account from a man who had seen the wickedness of Cuban slavery firsthand. "I have already said, and I repeat the words," he would recount in his memoirs, "so terrible were these atrocities, so murderous the system of slavery, so transcendent the evils I witnessed, over all I have ever heard or seen of the rigor of slavery elsewhere, that at first I could hardly believe the evidence of my senses."[3] The Yale linguist Josiah Gibbs testified as well, planning to show why the *Amistad* captives were surely *bozales*. Before he could launch into his explanation, however, Judge Judson shocked the courtroom by announcing that he "was fully convinced that the men were recently from Africa" and that "it was idle to deny it"—a crucial statement in a case that might turn on whether the blacks had been legally imported into Cuba.[4]

After Professor Gibbs spoke, Sengbe rose to testify, dressed in a blanket, and assisted by one of the interpreters. The courtroom was mesmerized as he described his capture while working on a road in his homeland, and his subsequent sale in Lomboko. To illustrate how his limbs had been bound in chains, he sat on the floor of the courtroom. And he showed how, in Havana, Ruiz had probed his body—"[h]e described by actions (which spoke louder than words)," one report noted delicately.[5] Aboard the *Amistad*, he testified, captives were allowed one plantain, two potatoes, and half a cup of water per day. Soon, his fellow captives rose to confirm his story.

It was a story Judge Judson believed. On Monday morning, January 13, he rendered his decision before a jammed courtroom. Captain Gedney, Judson announced, was entitled to salvage payment for the value of the *Amistad* itself and its nonhuman cargo, all of which was to be returned to the Spanish government. As for the Africans, the judge announced that they had been "born free" and "ever since have been and still of right are free and not slaves." According to Judson, the Africans had been "kidnapped" against "their own rights and the laws of Spain," and in Cuba had been sold "unlawfully"—the identification papers indicating otherwise had been a fraud. The men aboard the *Amistad*, Judson ruled, rebelled from a "desire of winning their liberty and of returning to their families and kindred." "Here then is the point," he announced, "the point upon which this great controversy *must* turn!" Because the *Amistad* captives had been illegally imported into Cuba, they had to be freed, and not be returned to Spain, where they would surely stand trial for murder that, in the context of such a kidnapping, was justified. Based on a congressional act of 1819, the captives would be placed under the care of the president of the United States, who was to return them to Africa.

For abolitionists, Judson's decision was not an unalloyed victory. They distrusted Martin van Buren, in whose hands the judge had placed the fate of the captives (his administration had lobbied throughout for the interests of Spain). Moreover, while Judson's decision stated that the *Amistad* captives were free men, in principle it upheld the lawfulness of slavery itself. According to the decision, had the blacks been imported legally into Cuba before the ban, Judge Judson would have proclaimed them to be slaves and returned them to Spain. Indeed, Antonio, the cabin boy, legitimately enslaved, was by the decision to be returned, still a slave, to Cuba. Yet the partial nature of their victory did not prevent them from capitalizing on the case, such as they could, in the media. They hailed Judson for upholding "great principles of justice." When informed of the decision, the Africans threw themselves prostrate on the floor, proclaiming "Thank you, thank you!" having learned a little English in the course of their ordeal. Sengbe seems to have learned more than a little. When Roger Baldwin, who had argued the captives' case in court, visited them in jail the next day, Sengbe is said to have dropped the book in his hands (likely the Bible), stood up, almost jumped over the table before them, and, taking Baldwin's hand, said with full depth of emotion, "We thank you, we bless you, this is all we can do for you."

His gratitude, however, was premature; naturally, the case would be appealed.

As the *Amistad* captives awaited their fate on the New Haven Green, sympathetic reporters recounted their lives in anthropological detail. "Ornaments are much esteemed," explained one writer, and "the natives adorn themselves with strings of beads, shells, and the like." The writer admitted that "many submit to the painful process of tattooing," noting that "the breasts and arms of some of the captives display in every part the incision of the knife"—but, he was told, the purpose of tattooing was "'to make them proud,' i.e. to make them beautiful."

Many of the captives had removed one or two of their teeth. One had even filed his front teeth into sharp points, which projected from his mouth, earning him the nickname of Cannibal. Asking why he had done so, the writer was told "to make the ladies love him." ("It is proper to add," the writer noted, "that the captives without distinction appear filled with horror at the idea of feasting upon human flesh.")

Their social organization was more troubling, at least to democratic sensibilities. To one observer, their government "appears to be despotic," and was based on patrilineal descent. "Attempting once to explain to Cingue the nature of our government," the observer explained, "when in answer to his inquiries I informed him that our 'great man' was not great man for life, but was elected once in four years, he seemed not a little astonished; surprise however soon gave way to boisterous laughter at my expense, in which nearly all his companions joined. The ideas of a democracy, and rotation in office, seemed to him new, strange, and ridiculous." The Africans' marital practices, especially polygamy, aroused in turn some amusement among Americans. "The remark was made by them to one of their friends," according to one account, "that in case he returned with them, he should have ten wives, expressing thus the honorable station he would probably hold." Such was the patriarchy among the Mende that "seldom does [a man's wife] eat at the same time. To use the language of one of the captives 'man come, eat, eat—go; then woman come, eat, eat—go.'"

Funerary practices aroused special interest. "Soon after a person dies," wrote one observer, "the body is wrapped in a mat, an article somewhat like cloth, made from the fibrous bark of a certain tree that grows in their country; in this, without any coffin, the body is carried out at evening, within two or three days after the decease, and deposited in a place set apart for this purpose with the head always lying to the west. The funeral is attended with weeping and mourning, so loud that the stillness attending exercises of this kind among us seems to them surprising, and to be accounted for only on the ground of insensibility." But here, too, there were opportunities for the captives to learn. When one of the "Amistads" died, for instance, a clergyman came to minister: "Prayer was offered in the room, and remarks made, the substance of which was, 'Ka-pe-ri is dead. His body is still, and will be laid in the ground. The soul of Ka-pe-ri is alive. It will never die. Our souls will never die. They will live after our bodies are dead and cold. The Bible tells us how our souls may go to the good place. You must learn to read the Bible. Pray to God, become good, and then when your bodies die, God will take your souls to the good place, and make you happy forever.'" The Africans were said to listen "with serious attention," and "appeared interested and solemn."

The interior life of the captives, in fact, seemed cause for the deepest concern among their sympathizers, who provided them daily religious instruction. In the morning, the captives were to assemble for prayers, conducted through their interpreter. In his absence, a boilerplate prayer had been transcribed aforehand into Mende: "O ga-wa-wa, o great God, bi-a-bi yan-din-go, thou art good, bi-a-bi ha-ni gbe-le ba-te-ni, thou hast made all things." Some of the Africans seem to have approached their tutors with great seriousness, but their apparent interest cannot have been wholly pious. Asked whether he understood that God would punish him for violating his legal oath to tell the truth, one of the captives asked, in reply, "[W]hat will be done to the people of the United States if they send us back to Havana?"[6]

The abolitionists had by no means a monopoly on white aspiration for Christian justice. Some Christian-minded whites sat on the Supreme Court—toward which the *Amistad* case slowly made its way. Five of the nine justices were southerners: John Catron of Tennessee, John McKinley of Alabama, James M. Wayne of Georgia, Philip P. Barbour of Virginia, and Chief Justice Roger Brooke Taney of Maryland. One northerner, Henry Baldwin of Pennsylvania, was a supporter of southern property rights in slaves. But the court also included Joseph Story of Massachusetts, to whom the writing of the *Amistad* opinion ultimately fell. Justice Story, a scholarly lawyer, was also a committed nationalist. Born in the Commonwealth in 1779, he was graduated from Harvard in 1798, soon to begin a life in politics and at the bar. After his appointment to the Supreme Court in 1811, he would assume the first endowed professorship of law in the United States, becoming Dane Professor at Harvard in 1829.

Story was both a strict adherent of the law and a committed Christian who believed in the social usefulness of his faith. In his eyes, Christian principles were inseparable from American law, animating the very spirit of the nation. For instance, upon assuming the Dane Chair at Harvard, he declared that "[t]here never has been a period in which the common law did not recognize Christianity as lying at its foundations." And the law of nature, he argued, is the basis of all other human laws, encompassing "those rules, which human reason deduces from the various relations of man, to form his character, and regulate his conduct, and thereby insure his permanent happiness."[7] But even that law is no mere product of human reason; contra Thomas Jefferson, he argued, natural law follows from revealed truth: "With us . . . who form a part of the Christian community of nations, the law of nature has a higher sanction, as it stands supported and illustrated by revelation." Its congruence with the Word of God was no accident: "Christianity, while with many minds it acquires authority from its coincidences with the law of nature, as deduced from reason, has added strength and dignity to the latter by its positive declarations. . . . It unfolds our duties with far more clearness and perfection than had been known before its promulgation."[8]

Story tried where possible to incorporate these views into actual judicial decisions, especially those concerning slavery. In 1822, for instance, in the circuit court case of La Jeune Eugénie, he was called upon to determine the fate of an abandoned slave ship that, flying the French flag, was captured in Africa and taken to Boston by the American navy. Story used the decision to characterize the slave trade as "abhorrent to the great principles of Christian morality, mercy, and humanity," while acknowledging that slavery was sanctioned by local laws. "It would be unbecoming in me," he wrote, "here to assert that the state of slavery cannot have a legitimate existence, or that it stands condemned by the unequivocal testimony of the law of nations." But his ethical and judicial views of the institution were unambiguous, even to the point of bombast: "[I]t necessarily carries with it a breach of all the moral duties, of all the maxims of justice, mercy and humanity, and of the admitted rights, which independent Christian nations now hold sacred in their intercourse with each other. . . . It is repugnant to the great principles of Christian duty, the dictates of natural religion, the obligations of good faith and morality, and the eternal maxims of social justice. When any trade can be truly said to have these ingredients, it is impossible, that it can be consistent with any system of law, that purports to rest on the authority of reason or revelation."[9]

In the tug-of-war between divine and human law, however, between Christian and caste jurisprudence, the latter generally triumphed in federal courts. Addressing Story's opinion in La Jeune Eugénie, for instance, the great Chief Justice John Marshall, in an 1825 case concerning the Antelope—captured off the coast of Florida carrying 281 African captives—allowed that the slave trade was "contrary to the law of nature," but he firmly asserted that it had the sanction of "long usage and general acquiescence."[10] In the ultimate compromise, more than 120 of the Africans on the *Antelope* were sent to Liberia by the American Colonization Society, and more than 30 were sold into slavery in the United States, with the remaining men and women having died in captivity. The Court might take cognizance of the ethics of antislavery Christians, but the law of the land supported slavery and could be stretched only so far. The *Amistad* committee had taken careful note of Chief Justice Marshall's view.

The case of the *Amistad* came before the Supreme Court on February 22, 1840. At the time, the Court did not occupy its present marble temple across from the Capitol, but rather convened in a small, damp room beneath the Senate, into which light streamed from three small windows behind the justices. It was an ironically confining space in which to consider the fate of the African captives. With the justices looking on solemnly, Attorney General Henry Gilpin argued on behalf of the United States that the wishes of Spain should be honored and the captives returned. According to Gilpin, there were two matters at issue: first, whether there was "due and sufficient proof" concerning "the property" on board the ship (was it clear that the Africans were slaves?), and second, whether the United States had "a right to interpose in the manner they have done, to obtain its restoration to the Spanish owners." According to Gilpin, the case in this respect was straightforward. The certificate held by the captain indicating the Africans were *ladinos* should be taken as prima facie evidence that the blacks were property under Spanish law and so should be returned to Spain.

Next to speak was Roger Baldwin, the New Haven abolitionist lawyer, later one of the great senators in the history of Connecticut. He argued that the case of the *Amistad* was unique: "It presents, for the first time, the question whether that government, which was established for the promotion of JUSTICE, which was founded on the great principles of the Revolution, as proclaimed in the Declaration of Independence, can, consistently with the genius of our institutions, become a party to proceedings for the enslavement of human beings cast upon our shores, and found in the condition of free men." The implications of casting the Africans back into slavery, warned Baldwin, were monumental. "The American people," he cautioned, "have never imposed it as a duty on the Government of the United States to become *actors* in an attempt to reduce to slavery men found in a state of freedom, by giving extraterritorial force to a foreign slave law. Such a duty would not only be repugnant to the feelings of a large portion of the citizens of the United

States, but it would be wholly inconsistent with the fundamental principles of our Government, and the purposes for which it was established, as well as its policy prohibiting the slave trade and giving freedom to its victims."[11]

Who were these men, whose fates now depended on the decision of the Court? They "were not pirates," asserted Baldwin; instead, they were rebels on behalf of the principle of liberty. "Cinque, the master-spirit who guided them," he stated, "had a single object in view . . . the deliverance of himself and his companions in suffering, from unlawful bondage." "They were on board the *Amistad* by constraint," Baldwin continued. Their object "was to free themselves from the fetters that bound them, in order that they might return to their kindred and their home." There was only one way his opponents could prove the Africans should be returned to Spain. "They must show that some law existed [in Cuba] by which 'recently imported Africans' can be lawfully held in slavery." And here he assaulted the caste tradition. "Such a law is not to be presumed," Baldwin stated—that is, the Africans were not to be supposed to be slaves simply because they were black—"but the contrary." The Africans "having been born free" had "a right to be everywhere regarded as free, until some law obligatory on them is produced authorizing their enslavement." They could be slaves only "by reason of some positive law of Spain"—except that "no such law is exhibited. On the contrary, it is proved by the deposition of Dr. Madden, one of the British commissioners resident at Havana, that since the year 1820 there has been no such law in force there either in statute or common law."[12]

"The only evidence exhibited to prove them slaves are the *papers of the Amistad*," Baldwin said derisively, "giving to José Ruiz permission to transport 39 *ladinos* belonging to him from Havana to Puerto Príncipe, and a like permit to Pedro Montes to transport three *ladinos*. For one of the four Africans, claimed by Montes (the boy Kale) there is no permit at all." And the fraudulence of the certificates that could be produced, Baldwin said, was clear. "These permits or passports are in the printed custom-house forms," he noted, "which are evidently prepared for the purpose of giving a particular description of the individuals for whom they are intended. But in both, the column left for that purpose, remains a blank." The only part of the form that was completed, he said, was that indicating that the blacks were to be "called by certain Spanish names"— to which, he said, "*these* Africans do not answer, and by which they have never been known." "The permits were for *ladinos*—a term exclusively applied to Africans long resident in the island—acclimated, and familiar with the language of the country," said Baldwin. "But the Africans of the *Amistad* are *bozales*, and not *ladinos*," and as such could not be forcibly returned to Spain as property, but must rather be acknowledged as men who had justly if violently resisted their kidnappers.[13] In Baldwin's argument, the facts of the case and the letter of the law called out for the simple application of the universal legal principles of the Declaration of Independence.

On February 24, John Quincy Adams, a living symbol of the traditions of American liberty, addressed the Court. His address was long even by the standards of the time, two full days—as opposed to the thirty minutes allotted to each side today—and also, in the words of Justice Story, "extraordinary" for "its power, for its bitter sarcasm."[14] Adams saw the case of the *Amistad* as a struggle between law and lawlessness—the lawful struggle of the Africans to rebel, and the lawlessness of those who would enslave them—and this struggle had also put the demands of "justice" at odds with those of white racial "sympathy." Adams was especially troubled by the efforts of the Van Buren administration to return the Africans to Spain by an act of executive fiat, or "gubernativamente." "Is there any such law at Constantinople?" asked Adams. "Does the Celestial Empire allow a proceeding like this?" "That charge I make against the present Executive administration," he stated, "is that in all their proceedings relating to these unfortunate men, instead of that *Justice*," they have "substituted *Sympathy!* . . . Sympathy with the white, antipathy to the black. . . . The sympathy of the Executive government, and as it were of the nation, in favor of the slave-traders, and against these poor, unfortunate, helpless, tongueless, defenseless Africans, was the cause and foundation and motive of all these proceedings, and has brought this case up for trial before your honors."[15]

At bottom, Adams held that the case of the captives should be adjudicated according to the liberal jurisprudential principles of the Revolution, the true law of the nation. "One of the Judges who presided in some of the preceding trials," said Adams, referring to Judge Judson, "is said to have called this an anomalous case." It was indeed anomalous, he continued, insofar as he knew of "no law, statute or constitution, no code, no treaty, applicable to the proceedings of the Executive or the Judiciary, except that law"—the former President now pointed to one of the copies of the Declaration of Independence hanging from the pillars of the courtroom—"that law, two copies of which are ever before the eyes of your Honors." He announced with all the authority of a descendant of one of the foremost signatories of the sacred document, "I know of no other law that reaches the case of my clients, but the law of Nature and of Nature's God *on which our fathers placed our own national existence*. . . . That law, in its application to my clients, I trust will be the law on which the case will be decided by this Court." Adams was asking the Court to do more than decide the case of the *Amistad* Africans. He was asking it to reaffirm the fundamental jurisprudential principles that he believed animated American national identity—to establish, in the face of the caste legal principles of southern slave interests, the fundamental character of the nation (a view of American civic identity on which other minorities would draw to advance their cause of inclusion in the twentieth century).[16]

Against that fundamental law Adams bitterly contrasted the lawlessness of slavery itself. His arguments were vividly derisive of his opponents, whom he painted as criminals. Addressing a call by the Spanish government for "public vengeance" to answer the murder of the *Amistad* captain, Adams let loose a torrent. "'The public vengeance!'" he cried. "What public vengeance? The vengeance of African slave-traders, despoiled of their prey and thirsting for blood! The vengeance of the barracoons! This 'public vengeance' is not satisfied. Surely, this is very lamentable." The Spanish minister, he announced incredulously, "demands that the President should keep these *persons* all—all—adult males and children of both sexes included—in close custody, and convey them to Cuba to be tried for their lives." Were the captives "with flesh, and blood, and nerves, and sinews, to be tortured, and with lives to be forfeited and consumed by fire, to appease the public *vengeance* of the lawless slave-traders in Cuba? . . . Is it possible to speak of this demand in language of decency and moderation?" he asked. "Has the expunging process of black lines passed upon these two Declarations of Independence in their gilded frames? Has the 4th of July, '76, become a day of ignominy and reproach?"[17]

As for the case of the Attorney General, Adams showed nothing but disdain, accusing Gilpin of, in effect, begging the question of the certificate—"he assumes, throughout the whole argument, that these negroes were slaves." "There is the basis of his opinion," continued Adams scornfully, "that the comity of nations requires, that such a paper, signed by the Governor General of Cuba, is conclusive to all the world as a title to property. If the life and liberty of men depends on any question arising out of these papers, neither the courts of this country nor of any other can examine the subject, or go behind this paper." But the paper was merely a lawless ruse. "In point of fact," he argued, "the voyage of the

Amistad, for which these papers were given, was but the continuation of the voyage of the slave trader, and marked with the horrible features of the middle passage. That is the fact in the case, but this government and the courts of this country cannot notice that fact, because they must not go behind the document. The Executive may send the men to Cuba, to be sold as slaves, to be put to death, to be burnt at the stake, but they must not go behind this document, to inquire into any facts of the case. That is the essence of the whole argument of the late Attorney-General."[18]

And Adams was no less disdainful of the executive branch itself, indeed more so. "Was ever such a scene of Liliputian [*sic*] trickery enacted by the rulers of a great, magnanimous, and Christian nation," he asked, referring to the Van Buren administration. "Contrast it with that act of self-emancipation by which the savage, heathen barbarians Cinque and Grabeau liberated themselves and their fellow suffering countrymen from Spanish slave-traders, and which the Secretary of State, by communion of sympathy with Ruiz and Montes, denominates *lawless violence.*" To understand the Africans, and their place within the order of natural law, he counseled, required one to see beyond their color, to think of them not as black but white, indeed not as Africans, but as ancient Greeks. "Cinque and Grabeau are uncouth and barbarous names," he said wryly. "Call them Harmodius and Aristogiton"—two Athenian tyrannicides—"and go back for moral principle three thousand years to the fierce and glorious democracy of Athens. They too resorted to *lawless violence,* and slew the tyrant to redeem the freedom of their country. For this heroic action they paid the forfeit of their lives . . . and in gratitude to their self-devoted deliverers [the Athenians] decreed, that thenceforth no slave should ever bear either of their names." "Cinque and Grabeau are not slaves," said Adams. "Let them bear in future history the names of Harmodius and Aristogiton."[19]

When determining the fate of men like these, said Adams, the Court should be guided by its most basic law—which, in truth, made the decision clear. "The moment you come to the Declaration of Independence," he asserted, "that every man has a right to life and liberty, an inalienable right, this case is decided. I ask nothing more in behalf of these unfortunate men, than this Declaration." No other law mattered—and most decidedly not the precedent of the *Antelope,* in which Chief Justice Marshall had rebuked Justice Story's claim that the law of natural right underlies the law of nations.[20]

Adams closed his analysis with a plea for simple justice. "I said, when I began this plea, that my final reliance for success in this case was on this

Court as a court of JUSTICE," he said as the Court observed the end of his rhetorical marathon. It was to be the final appearance of the elderly statesman before the Court, as the justices well knew. An opportunity no good lawyer would waste, it ended with a peroration of fond remembrance of his own extraordinary career in government, and of humble hope for the mercy of a still greater justice. "In taking, then, my final leave of this Bar, and of this Honorable Court," closed John Quincy Adams, "I can only ejaculate a fervent petition to Heaven, that every member of it may go to his final account with as little of earthly frailty to answer for as those illustrious dead, and that you may, every one, after the close of a long and virtuous career in this world, be received at the portals of the next with the approving sentence—'Well done, good and faithful servant; enter thou into the joy of thy Lord.'"²¹

One week later, on March 9, Justice Story announced the decision of the Court: it upheld the district court's order that the Africans should be set free—but not, as Judge Judson announced, remanded to the care of the Van Buren administration, but simply free to go as they wished or could.

The decision was made on the notably narrow basis of the Cuban import certificate's having been found fraudulent. The Court stressed that had the blacks been in fact *ladinos*, or the certificate not so clearly counterfeit, there would have been no choice but to return the Africans to bondage. Notably, too, the Court declined to address slavery's inherent contradiction of liberal and Christian values as posited by Baldwin and Adams. "If these negroes were, at the time, lawfully held as slaves under the laws of Spain," Justice Story explained, "and recognized by those laws as property capable of being lawfully bought and sold, we see no reason why they may not justly be deemed within the intent of the treaty, to be included under the denomination of merchandise, and, as such, ought to be restored to the claimants." But the certificate itself was merely tissue. "It is plain beyond controversy, if we examine the evidence," he asserted, "that these negroes never were the lawful slaves of Ruiz and Montes, or of any other Spanish subjects. They are natives of Africa, and were kidnapped there, and were unlawfully transported to Cuba, in violation of the laws and treaties of Spain, and the most solemn edicts and declarations of that government." *Under such circumstances*, said the Justice, following at once positive law and the dictates of his Christian conscience, "eternal principles of justice and international law" guided the decision—and the *Amistad* captives were free to go.²²

Like all high court rulings, that of the *Amistad* is interesting as much for what it omits as for what it includes. On one hand, Story had sanctioned the right of slaves to rebel against unlawful captivity with an appeal to "the eternal principles of justice." At the same time, the decision hinged on local laws, and on the fraudulence of paperwork, thus in principle upholding slavery as an institution when sanctioned by duly enacted law. Indeed, like Judge Judson, the Supreme Court chose to send Antonio, the cabin boy, back into bondage in Cuba (though as often happens in Afro-American history, human impulses outran the law, literally—in late March, Antonio would escape to Montreal, with the help of Lewis Tappan). As for the *Amistad* Africans, they were sent to wait in Farmington, Connecticut, while funds were raised for their return home. They waited for a long time, almost nine months, long enough for more of them to die, one apparently a suicide. Their yearning was incalculable. "All we want," wrote one of the captives to Adams, "is make us free."[23]

On November 27, 1841, the thirty-five surviving Africans, along with one of their interpreters and five white missionaries and teachers, left New York on board the *Gentleman* to found a Christian mission in Sierra Leone. They reached their destination in January 1842, almost three years after they boarded the *Tecora*. Thereafter, their fate becomes a historical mystery. Some would later say that Sengbe returned home to find his town in ruins, his country in civil war; others, that he returned and became a slave trader himself. But no matter what happened to them in fact, their memory, the image of men who had struck for liberty against unjust laws, remained a powerful symbol among abolitionists—their lives, the active embodiment of a universalist vision of law, an embodiment that others strove to achieve, as we will see, in rather different, if no less dramatic ways.

6

Christian Witness

▲

As they walked silently in the dark, their first sight of the Ohio River must have looked like deliverance. A thousand miles of waterway for flatboats and paddleboats, flowing all the way from Pittsburgh and emptying into the Mississippi at Cairo, Illinois. The French called it La Belle Rivière, the beautiful river. That night, Saturday, May 23, 1842, the nine slaves had escaped from their master, Wharton Jones, a farmer in Boone County, at the northern tip of Kentucky. Letta was about twenty-five years old, and her husband, Henry, was about forty-five. Accompanying them were their children: Henry, age eight; George, age four; and Jane, age two. Four friends and confidants were with them as well: Andrew, age thirty; Jerry, age twenty-three; Mary, age sixteen; and Jackson, age thirteen. Together, they crossed the Ohio, approaching Cincinnati, and a man known only as Mr. Alley directed them to Lane Seminary, a hotbed of the antislavery movement. There, they climbed inside a wagon and waited until three o'clock the next morning, when the owner, a tall, middle-aged white man, climbed onto the back of the wagon and closed it fore and aft. While a hard rain washed the morning sky, John Van Sandt told Andrew to take the reins and drive the horses down the road.

What happened next, as they sped north toward Sharon and Lebanon, was to be a turning point in all of their lives, and in the life of the nation. For the runaways, it would end with eight of the nine back in Kentucky in bondage. For Van Sandt, a stationmaster of the Underground Railroad, it would initiate a closely watched court battle with Wharton Jones. A claim for money by one white man against another, *Jones v. Van Zandt* would ultimately prove a case of national civic importance. The battle would go on for years, into the early 1850s, outliving both litigants, and it would cost Van Sandt dearly, leaving him to die, poor and sick, but without regret.[1]

When Henry, Letta, and their family and friends climbed into John Van Sandt's wagon, Hamilton County, Ohio, was among the breadbaskets of the nation. On the border of Kentucky and Indiana, in the southwestern corner of the state, Hamilton was covered by gently rolling hills with alluvial valleys, fertile land for droves of settlers who had been arriving from the East since the early nineteenth century. The second county to be carved from the Northwest Territory of 1787, Hamilton had grown tremendously in fifty years. By 1840, it boasted over 80,000 residents, 77 per square mile, not including Cincinnati, which alone was home to over 46,000 people. Van Sandt and his family lived on a small farm, in Sycamore township, in a region known as Oak Hill. There, John and Nancy had built a hilltop home they called Mt. Pierpont, after the Reverend John Pierpont, an abolitionist minister, poet, and social reformer from Massachusetts. Van Sandt seems to have had a certain personal reserve, which moved a contemporary to describe him as "one who could not be estimated justly upon casual acquaintance." He was "tall and lean, but of a wiry, muscular frame," and his face, "though cast in an angular mold, had a peculiarly frank, open and mild expression." There was, however, "just enough firmness about his compressed lips and beaming from his calm, steady eye to give assurance of a deep inward consciousness of right and unswerving purpose."[2]

Van Sandt was born in Fleming County, Kentucky, to Elisha Van Sandt and Margaret Crawford, on September 23, 1791, when the American Revolution was still a fresh memory (his ancestors had emigrated to Pennsylvania from Holland in the late seventeenth century). We know little about his family or early life, but that little is intriguing. Van Sandt was rich. He owned a "large plantation" and possessed what one amateur biographer called "everything that men longed for."[3] A devout

Methodist, he accepted the evangelical doctrines of Wesleyanism. Most noteworthy of all, the young John Van Sandt owned slaves. We do not know how many, nor what life was like for his bondsmen, but in general, slavery in Kentucky differed substantially from slavery in the Deep South. In a state where, in some regions, more than 40 percent of the population was black, slaves tended to receive better treatment than those in Georgia, Alabama, or Mississippi, especially in the northern counties—a difference undoubtedly resulting, in part, from the distracting presence of free Ohio just across the border.

But Van Sandt's career as a slaveholder was not to last. He seems to have spent a good deal of time meditating on moral principles and, in the spirit of the day, his ideals were drawn not only from the Bible but also from the Declaration of Independence and other documents sacred to the Revolutionary generation—then even more than now the immediate paragons of idealistic self-sacrifice. Van Sandt gradually became convinced that slaveholding was a sin, and he resolved to free his own bondsmen. How the realization came to him, we do not know, but in one account his change of heart came after God spoke to him in a dream.[4] Van Sandt sold his farm and moved north, to Ohio, not far from property owned by his father-in-law, and rented a home with his second wife and children. He soon purchased a plot of land in Hamilton County, near the town of Sharon, using the bricks from a demolished Presbyterian church to build his new hilltop home. A sketch from the 1890s shows a two-story house, open and inviting, seven lattice windows in its façade, a scattering of trees, all enclosed by a wooden fence. The walls of the kitchen were said to be painted a bright yellow. Settling down to farm at Mt. Pierpont, Van Sandt also became one of the first trustees of the Methodist Episcopal Church.[5]

Following his Christian convictions, his vision of Christian law, Van Sandt turned Mt. Pierpont into a station on the Underground Railroad, a stop point just before the one at the Spread Eagle stagecoach inn, and harbored fugitive slaves on their way north, to Canada. There is probably more myth than reality in our collective memory of the Railroad. The number of slaves who escaped from the South is relatively small (the very highest estimate is 50,000), and the popular image of a vast, tightly organized network of stationmasters is likely illusory, originating after the Civil War, when it became fashionable in the North to claim a heroic abolitionist past. Still, the work of northern free blacks and of white activists like Van Sandt played an important part in the struggle against slavery, and the danger Van Sandt courted was serious. Southern

Ohio was southern indeed, and a substantial part of the population supported slavery and its racial vision. Deadly race riots struck Cincinnati in 1829 and 1841, sending many blacks fleeing as far as Canada, and on various occasions, rioters targeted the office of the abolitionist newspaper the *Philanthropist*. In the antebellum North, abolitionists, to put it mildly, were no heroes.

We do not know the extent of Van Sandt and Mt. Pierpont's role in the Underground Railroad. Van Sandt was a notable enough figure, at least, to have been immortalized by Harriet Beecher Stowe, the daughter of the director of Lane Seminary. "Honest old John Van Trompe," as Stowe called him in *Uncle Tom's Cabin*, "was once quite a considerable land-holder and slave-owner in the State of Kentucky. Having 'nothing of the bear about him but the skin,' and being gifted by nature with a great, honest, just heart, quite equal to his gigantic frame, he had been for some years witnessing with repressed uneasiness the workings of a system equally bad for oppressor and oppressed. At last, one day, John's great heart had swelled altogether too big to wear his bonds any longer." In another passage, apparently based on an actual incident, Stowe describes how Eliza Harris, a young runaway, walked over the precarious ice sheaths of the Ohio, carrying her baby, led by a white senator, to find refuge in Van Sandt's home. "Are you the man that will shelter a poor woman and child from slave-catchers," Stowe's senator asks. "I rather think I am," replies Van Trompe. "If there's anybody comes," he continues, "stretching his tall, muscular form upward . . . why here I'm ready for him: and I've got seven sons, each six foot high, and they'll be ready for 'em."[6]

"On a rainy evening in June 1843," writes William Cornell, another contemporary, "I was returning from Cincinnati by way of Reading turnpike, with a team attached to a hay wagon. When about a mile from the old corporation line, two young colored people, a boy and a girl, asked if they might ride. Upon being answered in the affirmative, they seated themselves on the wagon." His companions were silent, and neither spoke a word. "I suspected they were trying to reach Van Zandt's station," Cornell continued, and after passing Reading, "they were wide awake and alert as if suspecting something, but said nothing to me or to each other. Finally, when we reached the farm of John R. Dick and Mt. Pierpont loomed up in the distance, the lad impulsively exclaimed, 'there it is!' I told them I thought they were looking for that place and would show them the road leading to it. They said nothing, but dismounted and started toward the house on the hill . . . I never heard from my silent companions afterward," he concluded, "but I have no doubt that they met with a hospitable reception at the home of John Van Zandt."[7]

As to the dangers of helping fugitive slaves, Van Sandt, as portrayed by Stowe at least, declared himself ready: "'I'm up to all that sort o' thing,' pointing to two or three goodly rifles over the mantel-piece . . . 'and most people that know me know that 't would n't be healthy to try to get anybody out o' my house when I'm agin it.'" But the cost was not to be underestimated. He was shunned by other residents in Hamilton County, including members of his own parish (the Methodist Episcopal Church was split on the slavery issue, officially dividing into northern and southern factions in 1844). Aiming to curb his efforts, an ecclesiastical court barred Van Sandt from church privileges for "lying" by declaring that he "harbored no slaves" (Van Sandt probably had a semantic rationale: in his mind, property in persons violated the law of God, and thus no person could truly be a slave).[8] Moreover, as we will see, to help slaves escape north was a federal criminal offense under the Fugitive Slave Law of 1793.

As Van Sandt's wagon sped forward in the rain, jostling back and forth along the road to Lebanon and Springboro, it passed through the town of Sharon, thirteen miles north of Cincinnati, shortly after daybreak. There, it was spotted by two men, one named Hefferman, the other Hannibal Hargrave. Recognizing the wagon as Van Sandt's, and noticing that the notorious abolitionist was not at the reins, they became suspicious. Hoping for a reward, the two gave pursuit. Approaching the wagon near the property of Asa Bates, they signaled for it to stop, possibly with a rifle shot in the air. Riding up next to the wagon, Hargrave demanded that Andrew come to a halt, while Hefferman brought his horse around to the front. Andrew checked the team, but then Van Sandt's voice was heard from inside, beneath the canvas—drive on, he ordered, and run them over. Andrew cracked the whip, and Hefferman was knocked off his mount to the ground. The wagon sped forward for two hundred desperate yards, until Hefferman, back in the saddle, drew alongside, seized the reins from Andrew, and steered the wagon into a corner of a fence.

Andrew jumped off the wagon and ran. Van Sandt emerged from inside and took the reins, trying to drive the wagon forward, but Hefferman held the horses fast. The young Jackson, age thirteen, also made his escape. And then came a cacophony of shouts and queries. Hargrave looked inside the wagon and, seeing the black men, women, and children, asked Van Sandt if he knew they were slaves. He did, Van Sandt replied—but they had been born free. Other men now approached the wagon. Bates looked inside and turned to the old man. "Van Sandt, is that you?" he asked. "Have you a load of runaways?" To this taunt, Van Sandt replied resolutely, "They are, by nature, as free as you or I."[9]

Henry, Letta, Jerry, Mary, young Henry, George, and Jane were loaded into a wagon and taken to Covington, Kentucky, to be held in custody before their return to Wharton Jones some days later.[10] "If you had let me alone," Van Sandt later cried ruefully, "the Negroes would have been free, but now they are in bondage."[11] Van Sandt was thrown in jail, too, and Hargrave and Hefferman approached Jones and demanded the reward that was due to them under Kentucky law. Though the two were indicted in Warren County, Ohio, for kidnapping the slaves and forcing them back to Kentucky, the action was doomed to fail. Defended by Ohio Governor Thomas Corwin and a former member of Congress, Hargrave and Hefferman were quickly acquitted. As for the two slaves who managed to escape the melee at Sharon: Andrew was never to be seen again, but the thirteen-year-old Jackson would travel back to Kentucky, back to Wharton Jones, and return himself to bondage. We do not know why.

Wharton Jones had suffered a considerable loss. Not only had he paid Hargrave and Hefferman a mandatory reward of $450, as required by a Kentucky statute, as well as $150 for their expenses, he also had lost the services of Andrew, which he valued at $600. He intended to make Van Sandt pay, at the very least to make him forfeit the $500 due him under the terms of the Fugitive Slave Act (the present-day equivalent of $10,000).[12] The 1793 act grew out of a problem the framers faced in 1787, endemic to all slaveholding societies: those in bondage do on occasion try to flee to territory where they would be free. We do not know precisely how many slaves may have escaped in the period of the Constitutional Convention. They were never so numerous as they would be in Brazil, for instance, where there developed significant colonies of escaped slaves, or "Maroons." But if the number of advertised rewards for recapture is any indication, the number was significant.

The specific problem of 1787 was that two legal worlds, one slaveholding and one free, existed side by side within a single would-be nation. If southern states were to join the North in political union, they would require guarantees of their property rights. Unless the peculiar institution were safeguarded by law, the nation itself was sure to unravel. We have already noted some of the Constitution's safeguards of slavery: it implicitly gave slavery the sanction of local law, prevented the abolition of the international slave trade until 1808, and gave southerners extra representation in Congress through the three-fifths clause. It also addressed the problem of slave runaways, in Article IV, Section 2, Clause 3, which states that "no person held to service of labor in one State"—constitutional parlance for "slaves" or indentured servants—"escaping into another shall, in consequences of any law or regulation therein, be discharged from such service"—that is, the slave would not be considered free—"but shall be delivered up on claim of the party to whom such service shall be due."

Four years after the Constitution was ratified, the first Congress elaborated and strengthened the principles behind this guarantee. The impetus came in 1791, after a slave catcher kidnapped a free black man from Pennsylvania and took him to Virginia. Pennsylvania twice demanded the return of the kidnapper, as a fugitive from justice. When Virginia refused, President Washington asked Congress to act, and the House responded, voting 48 to 7 for a comprehensive plan for forcing states to extradite both criminal fugitives and fugitive slaves to the state from which they had escaped. By the terms of the law, "An Act respecting fugitives from justice, and persons escaping from the service of their masters," a fleeing slave could be pursued to another state by the owner or the owner's agent, who could seize the property, and upon furnishing proof of ownership to either a federal judge or local magistrate, secure permission to remove the slave to the owner's home state. Proof of ownership could take the form of direct testimony before the judge or an affidavit made in the owner's home state. The act further provided that anyone "who shall knowingly and willingly obstruct or hinder" a master or his agent from seizing his slave, "or shall harbor or conceal such person after notice that he or she was a fugitive from labor," would be forced to pay the owner $500 if the owner chose to sue him in court.

The Fugitive Slave Law bound together two social and geographic worlds, two contradictory understandings of American law and black legal capacity. But more than simply protecting southerners' rights in their property (slaves), the act tainted northerners with complicity in the hated institution, and in effect extended the southern legal vision to the whole nation. While the act did not require northerners to take part in slave recapture—that coercion would be left to the draconian Fugitive Slave Act of 1850—it still turned the North into an extension of the slave owners' will. It also placed northern free blacks in danger of unjust seizure and kidnapping. In this respect, the Fugitive Slave Law could be seen as overcoming, with the decisive tool of positive law, the legal principles announced in *Somerset's Case*. In 1772, American slaves who escaped in England could not be seized and returned to the colonies. In 1793, under the Fugitive Slave Law, the ideals promulgated by Somerset's attorneys were rendered meaningless by a compact that underlay the federation of the new country.

In the antebellum years, northern states resisted the full odious implications of the Fugitive Slave Law by enacting a series of statutes known as "personal liberty laws," which gave blacks greater due process protections after their capture, generally by holding slave catchers to a higher standard of proof of ownership than federal law required. These were struck down in the landmark case of *Prigg v. Pennsylvania* (1842), a cause célèbre of its day, with its own particularly dispiriting story of hope, betrayal, and death. A black woman named Margaret had long believed herself to be free (her parents having been allowed virtual liberty by their owner, Mr. Ashmore), though she had never received a formal grant of manumission. In 1832, Margaret moved from Maryland to Pennsylvania with her husband, a free black man named Jerry Morgan. Five years later, Margaret and her children, at least one of whom had been born in Pennsylvania, were seized by an attorney, Edward Prigg, on behalf of Ashmore's niece and heir, who claimed them as her property. Prigg took Margaret before Justice of the Peace Thomas Henderson, and though Henderson had issued the original warrant for Margaret's seizure, he now "refused to take further cognizance" of the case, perhaps because Prigg could not produce the documentation necessary for slave recapture under Pennsylvania's personal liberty law. Taking the law into his own hands, Prigg took Margaret back to Maryland by force.

Pennsylvania demanded that Prigg be extradited for trial, and under an agreement between the two states, the case was directed immediately to the Supreme Court. There, under the leadership of Justice Joseph Story, of the *Amistad* case, the Court ruled with near unanimity (only Justice McLean dissented) that state personal liberty laws interfered with the Fugitive Slave Law, and thus were unconstitutional. The efforts of northern legislatures to resist the extension of southern property interests, of the southern vision of race and law, were thus overruled by the federal government. The brutal relations between slave and slave-holder would be nationalized. The opinion also held that slave catchers like Prigg could forcibly take their slaves back south without consulting a magistrate at all, so long as they did so without breaching the peace. What effect this ruling would have on the nation, time would tell. For Margaret and her children, the effects were immediate: they were to return to slavery. As for Jerry Morgan, after Edward Prigg kidnapped his family, he visited the governor of Pennsylvania to plead for assistance. On the way back from Harrisburg, he took a boat south down the Susquehanna and, during the trip, one of the boat hands lost his jacket, which held his papers. Suspected of being a runaway, he was seized and bound aboard the ship. Upon reaching Columbia, he tried to escape, leaping from the boat for a nearby wall. But he fell backward into the lock, was drawn under the boat, and drowned.[13]

Wharton Jones brought two civil actions against Van Sandt in federal court. The first was for $1,200, to recover the costs of Andrew, whom he valued at $600, and the $600 he had paid to Hefferman and Hargrave. The other suit was for the $500 owed to him under the provisions of the Fugitive Slave Law. When Van Sandt received his first court summons on June 21, 1842, facing a potential liability of $1,700, not including court costs, he badly needed legal counsel. Fortunately, while Ohio had many supporters of slavery, it was also home to steadfast opponents whose ranks included several very able lawyers—the antislavery bar.

Perhaps the most prominent member of this now hallowed (then reviled) fraternity was a big, burly, often sanctimonious character named Salmon Portland Chase. In 1842, Chase was an ambitious young attorney and recent convert to the Liberty Party. Over the course of twenty-four years, he would be elected senator from Ohio (1849–55 and 1860–61) and governor (1856–60), serve as Abraham Lincoln's Secretary of the Treasury and—the capstone of his career—as Chief Justice of the United States (1864–73).

Chase was born in New Hampshire in 1808. His father was a farmer and small businessman who died bankrupt in 1817, leaving Salmon the poor relation in a family that included Dudley Chase, twice elected to the Senate from Vermont, a disparity the boy felt acutely. In the early 1820s, his mother was forced to send Chase to live with his uncle Philander, the Episcopal bishop of Ohio. Forceful, imposing, and accustomed to having his own way, Bishop Chase demanded a regime of hard physical and mental labor from the boy, firmly believing that a strict rule of godly work improved one's character. Under his uncle's thumb, young Salmon would labor in the fields, as well as study Latin and Greek, principles of Christian theology, and mathematics. Like Cotton Mather, Chase would also apply himself to overcome a speech impediment (a lisp in his case, supposedly induced by the rigors of his uncle's sponsorship), and he was later known for his exemplary elocution. A pious, evangelical Protestant, Chase had exceptional worldly ambition and, forgoing a career in the ministry and a life of farming, he scraped together what money he could to enroll at Dartmouth College.

During a brief stint as a teacher in Washington, D.C., he found favor with the father of one of his pupils, Attorney General William Wirt, one of the great political power brokers of the day. Wirt opened a door to elite Washington, whose society Chase craved, and set him on a career in the law. After passing the legal licensing examination, Chase returned to Ohio in 1830 to practice in Cincinnati. Much of his work, like that of most lawyers in our own time, was commercial, and he prospered, throwing himself into his career, especially after the deaths of his first two wives. But increasingly, as his wealth and security grew, he directed his efforts where he imagined they would do the most social good, and he was drawn particularly to those involved in opposing, or fleeing, southern slavery.

Chase did not come to Cincinnati as an abolitionist rebel. His initial political tendencies were conservative. In matters of race, he was a colonizationist, supporting the settlement of American blacks in Africa. His sister Abigail, however, had married a local physician, who introduced Chase to Ohio abolitionist circles. On July 30, 1836, a mob dumped the printing press of the antislavery newspaper the *Philanthropist* into the Ohio River before sacking the black neighborhood of Little Africa. Chase was outraged. Hearing that the editor, James G. Birney, was holed up in the Franklin House Hotel, he rushed to help, physically blocking the entrance with his imposing frame until the mob dispersed. It was his great initiation. Thereafter, he became increasingly involved in the antislavery cause. He ultimately came to a new view of divine law—that "man could have no property in man." He also came to believe in what he called "freedom national," according to which the United States, under the Declaration of Independence, was the manifestation of divine principles of right, and could have no part in bondage—a conflation of liberal republicanism and religion characteristic of the mid-nineteenth century. The Fugitive Slave Law was a direct affront to this vision of national civic life and to Chase's developing understanding of constitutional law, which drew freely on Christian morals.

Chase brought his enormous energy and ambition to his cause of freedom national, winning friends and enemies alike (after one of his more eloquent pleas defending a runaway slave, an older attorney in the courtroom was heard to say, "There goes a young man who has ruined himself today").[14] He soon would become known as the attorney general of fugitive slaves, an insult he bore with pride. The defense of John Van Sandt would prove one of his most celebrated cases, helping him to launch his national political career and to achieve the professional success he so desired.

The first trial was held in Lebanon, before John McLean, the justice who had dissented in the case of *Prigg v. Pennsylvania* (before 1869, Supreme Court justices were required to regularly "ride circuit," acting as judges in the various circuit courts of the United States). A devout Methodist himself, Justice McLean was no stranger to the contradictions represented by slavery; all his judicial life he had felt their tension, caught between his private, Christian antislavery principles and his judicial oath to the Constitution, which required him to uphold the basic compromises of the Union. In sitting circuit in Ohio, Justice McLean was returning to the land of his youth. Born in New Jersey in 1785, he moved with his family to Warren County in 1797. He began his law practice in apprenticeship to the clerk of the Hamilton County Court of Common Pleas, and he later sat on the Ohio Supreme Court. A man of principle, he also is known as one of the most politically ambitious justices in the history of the Ohio Supreme Court bench.

All the witnesses were examined with respect to the issue of whether Van Sandt had actual notice that the blacks were runaways and whether he had in fact "harbored" and "concealed" them (under the evidentiary procedure of the time, Van Sandt could not testify and explain his own motives). The first witness, recorded only as "Jones," perhaps Wharton's son John, attested to the background facts: that Jones owned nine slaves, Andrew, Henry, Jerry, Letta, Jackson, Mary, young Henry, George, and Jane, and that he resided in Boone County. Most of the slaves had been born on Jones's estate; others had been purchased. On that Saturday evening, he said, he had seen the blacks at Jones's house at about nine o'clock; the next day, he saw seven of them in the Covington jail, ten miles north. While Jackson returned in a few days, Andrew had remained absent "and has not been reclaimed." He confirmed that Hefferman and Hargrave had been paid a reward of $450, plus $150 in expenses, and that Andrew, aged about thirty, could be sold in Kentucky for $600.

Hefferman took the stand, explaining how, shortly after dawn, on the road to Cincinnati, he had seen a black man driving a wagon quickly through Sharon, covered, fore and aft. He knew the wagon was Van Sandt's, he said, and "his suspicion was excited." He recounted how he and Hargrave pursued and overtook it near Asa Bates's property, six miles north. He also described the attempted flight and recapture, two hundred yards up the road.

Hargrave in turn corroborated Hefferman's account of the chase. He knew Van Sandt, he explained, certainly well enough to know that it had been his voice inside ordering Andrew ("the colored boy") to run him over. Seeing him inside with the blacks, he said, he had asked Van Sandt whether he knew they were slaves. Van Sandt had replied that he knew they were slaves, but that they had been born free, and said that he was traveling with them to Springboro, a village in Warren County.

A local man, Isaac Hume, followed, explaining how he had seen the wagon moving fast early Sunday morning, two men pursuing it on horseback. When the wagon had been overtaken, he, too, looked inside and saw Van Sandt with the black fugitives. He confirmed Van Sandt's statement: that the slaves were by nature as free as anyone. "Witness," state the court documents, "took the Negroes to Covington in a wagon. Some time after this, he saw the defendant, who said to him, 'If you had let me alone, the negroes would have been free, but now they are in bondage.' And the defendant said it was a Christian act to take slaves and set them at liberty."

Asa Bates told much the same story. "The witness," the court papers document, "heard the defendant say that, having been at market in the city of Cincinnati, he returned to Lane Seminary, a distance of two or three miles, to spend the night with Mr. Moore. That he left his wagon standing in the road, and when he came to it, about three o'clock the next morning, he found the Negroes standing near it; that he did not know how they came there, or where they wished to go." According to Bates, Van Sandt said that he had not conversed with the blacks at all—he simply geared his horses, hitched them to the wagon, and the blacks got inside. But later, said Bates, Van Sandt had said that he had received the blacks from "Mr. Alley."

A Mr. McDonald spoke next, recounting Van Sandt's own explanation of how he came to be driving on the road toward Sharon with nine fugitive slaves. He testified that Van Sandt had told him he had received the blacks in Walnut Hills, by Lane Seminary, and that, at three o'clock on Sunday morning, he found them standing near his wagon, in the road. Van Sandt claimed to have risen early so that he might "have the cool of the morning." The blacks got inside the wagon, Van Sandt told him, and then he had started for home.[15]

To counter this testimony, the defense, which included the attorney Thomas Morris as well as Chase, made three basic arguments. First, they defended "the fundamental principles of human rights and the paramount claims of justice, equity, and humanity"—that is, they argued on the grounds of conscience. As Chase had in earlier cases, they also asserted the inapplicability of the 1793 law, objecting not only in general constitutional terms, but also in specific regard to Van Sandt's case. The plaintiff, Chase argued, had not established that Van Sandt had unlawfully harbored or concealed the slaves, because it had not proved his having had notice that the blacks were escaped slaves from Kentucky. Such notice, he added, had to be firm and clear, in accordance with the statute. His argument seems not to have been preserved, but we know it ran about three hours, moving the editor of the *Philanthropist* to exult, "Whether viewed as a legal argument or a specimen of forensic eloquence, it has seldom been equaled."

Chase closed, by the editor's account, "with one of the finest efforts of oratory we ever heard. The blind Samson of Longfellow was brought upon the stage; and when we say that so far from impairing this noble allusion, as used by the poet, he really added to its munificence and power, we say but the truth. Not a foot-fall was heard, not a movement made. Every form was a breathing statue—every eye was fixed upon the blind Samson, standing between the massive pillars, while the jeering multitude scoffed at his rights, mocked his apparent helplessness, sported themselves with his bonds, till, bowing himself in the greatness of his strength, in a moment, in the twinkling of an eye, the temple was in ruins and the multitude buried beneath them."[16] Henry Wadsworth Longfellow's poem "The Warning" had just been published in 1842 in his *Poems on Slavery*:

> *Beware! The Israelite of old, who tore*
> *The lion in his path,—when, poor and blind,*
> *He saw the blessed light of heaven no more,*

Shorn of his noble strength and forced to grind
  In prison, and at last led forth to be
  A pander to Philistine revelry,—

Upon the pillars of the temple laid
His desperate hands, and in its overthrow
  Destroyed himself, and with him those who made
A Cruel mockery of his sightless woe;
  The poor, blind Slave, the scoff and jest of all,
  Expired, and thousands perished in the fall!

There is a poor, blind Samson in this land,
Shorn of his strength and bound in bonds of steel,
  Who may, in some grim revel, raise his hand,
And shake the pillars of this Commonweal,
  Till the vast Temple of our liberties
A shapeless mass of wreck and rubbish lies.

While doubtless feeling some sympathy for Van Sandt, Justice McLean showed little patience with Chase's appeals to "higher law." He charged the jury, straightforwardly, to direct itself to the facts of the case in relation to the written law of the Fugitive Slave Law. "The attention and patience with which you have heard this case, gentlemen of the jury, show that you appreciate its importance, and I doubt not that, in deciding it, you will follow the dictates of an unbiased judgment." The question at issue, he said, was whether Van Sandt harbored and concealed the runaway slaves, having had notice that they were fugitives. "If the evidence should not sustain these counts," continued McLean, "the plaintiff can not recover."

Addressing the issue of notice, his instructions gave voice to the national conundrum. "In Kentucky, and every other state where slavery is sanctioned, every colored person is presumed to be a slave. This presumption arises from the nature of their institution and from the fact that, with few exceptions, all the colored persons within those states are slaves. On the same principles," the justice explained, "every person in Ohio, or any other free state, without regard to color, is presumed to be free. No presumption, therefore, arises, from the color of these fugitives, alone, that the defendant had notice that they were slaves. A notice in writing to the defendant was not necessary, nor any special notice from the plaintiff, his agent or attorney. But if, at the time the defendant was connected with the Negroes, he had a full knowledge of the fact, however acquired, that they were slaves and fugitives from labor, it is enough to charge him with notice.

"What shall constitute a harboring or concealing within the statute?" he asked. "This offence is not committed, in my judgment, by treating the fugitive on the ordinary principles of humanity. You may converse with him, relieve his hunger and thirst, without violating the law." To harbor and conceal required more, an unambiguous action. "But any overt act which shall be so marked in its character," continued Justice McLean, "to not only show an intention to elude the vigilance of the master, but is calculated to attain such an object, is harboring of the fugitive in violation of the statute.

"In the course of this discussion," cautioned the justice, "much has been said of the laws of nature, of conscience, and the rights of conscience. This monitor, under great excitement, may mislead, and always does mislead, when it urges any one to violate the law. Paul acted in all good conscience," he said, "when he consented to the death of the first martyr; and also, when he bore letters to Damascus, authorizing him to bring bound to Jerusalem all who called upon the name of Jesus." Such appeals, he made clear, had no bearing on the jury's duty to the law. "I have read to you the constitution and the act of Congress," he admonished. "These bear the impress of the nation. The principles which they lay down and enforce have been sanctioned in the most solemn form known in our government. We are bound to sustain them. They form the only guides in the administration of justice in this case." The jury was also warned against judgment based on personal sympathies, with or against Van Sandt. "I charge you, gentlemen," said Justice McLean, "to guard yourselves against any improper influence. You are to know the parties only as litigants. With their former associations and views, disconnected with this controversy, you have nothing to do. It is your duty to follow the law, to act impartially and justly," he concluded, "and such, I doubt not, will be the result of your deliberations."[17]

Indeed, there was little room for doubt. The jury decided in favor of Jones. Chase quickly filed a countermotion and demanded a new trial, alleging a variety of procedural errors—especially that the Court erred when it instructed the jury as to what acts would prove Van Sandt had harbored the runaways intentionally and that he had actual notice of their fugitive status. Moreover, he reiterated the claim that the Fugitive Slave Law was contrary to the Constitution, as well as to the Northwest Ordinance of 1787, which had established the region of Ohio as free.

Justice McLean did not take kindly to Chase's loftier assertions. "I was not prepared to hear, in a court of justice," he explained on hearing the motion, "the broad ground assumed, as was assumed in this case before the jury, that a man, in the exercise of what he conceives to be a conscientious duty, may violate the laws of the land. That no human laws can justly restrain the acts of men, who are impelled by a sense of duty to God and their fellow creatures. We are not here to deal with abstractions," he declared sternly. "We can not theorize upon the principles of our government, or of slavery. The law is our only guide. If convictions, honest convictions they may be, of what is right or wrong, are to be substituted as a rule of action in disregard of the law, we shall soon be without law and without protection."

"The pretext for violating the rights of those who may become obnoxious to censure," cautioned the justice, "can easily be assumed and maintained. And the same plea of the rights of conscience, and the high motive of duty, will be asserted, however absurd, everywhere, in justification of wrongs. What one man, or association of men, may assume as the basis of action, may be assumed by all others. And in this way society may be resolved into its original elements, and then the governing principle must be force. . . . Every approximation to this state is at war with the social compact. If the law be wrong in principle, or oppressive in its exactions, it should be changed in a constitutional mode. If the organization of our government be essentially wrong, in any of its great principles, change it. Change it in the mode provided. But the law, until changed or abrogated, should be respected and obeyed. Any departure from this inflicts a deep wound on society, and is extremely demoralizing in its effects. No good man, in the exercise of his sober judgment, can either feel or act in violation of this rule."[18]

In the end, however, Justice McLean did grant Chase's request for a new trial in Jones's action for the value of Andrew and the reward he had paid to Hefferman and Hargrave. He had been unmoved by counsel's broader arguments, but he allowed that there had been some technical faults in how the case had been originally brought. He also postponed exacting the judgment of $500 against Van Sandt under the Fugitive Slave Law until the Supreme Court, through a special judicial request, determined a series of specific questions about how the act should be applied, particularly regarding questions of notice. And so, with Justice

McLean's mixed blessing, in 1847 the case was certified for hearing before the Supreme Court.

To what degree did a person have to be aware—have notice—that he or she was harboring runaways to be liable under the Fugitive Slave Law of 1793? Did picking them up in a wagon and taking them down the road constitute harboring? Simple questions, on the face of it. At a higher level, however, they had implications for the extension of the southern legal vision into the North, the nationalization of slavery, and the exclusion of blacks from the law. For if no substantial notice were required for a man to be liable under the act, whites in the North were effectively obligated to presume that any black might be a runaway slave; this was in effect to be forced to accept the southern vision of race and law on northern free soil. On the ostensibly dry technical question of notice hung the question of whether the racial principles of southern law would become the civic basis of the nation as a whole.

When the case reached the Supreme Court, none of the lawyers appeared personally; they instead presented their arguments entirely in written form. Chase's brief—"upwards of one hundred pages . . . in length," according to a chagrined court reporter—spoke eloquently of the "law of Creation" and the Declaration of Independence to argue that the Fugitive Slave Law was contrary to the animating legal principles of the Union, and that the federal government could have no hand in slavery itself.[19] On the particulars, it asserted that Van Sandt had insufficiently clear notice that the blacks were runaways, and that merely to have driven them in his wagon did not constitute harboring or concealing them.

Chase portrayed Van Sandt as a kind, rather hapless geriatric drawn into a situation for which he could not be held accountable. "I beg leave to submit to your consideration an argument in behalf of an old man, who is charged, under the act of congress, of February 12, 1793, with having concealed and harbored a fugitive slave," Chase began. "The defendant, John Vanzandt, is an old man, of limited education and slender means, but distinguished by unquestioned integrity and benevolence of heart," he continued. "He is a farmer, occupying a small property in the neighborhood of Cincinnati, and maintaining himself and family by the sale of its products in the markets of the city. On Saturday, the 23rd day of [May], 1842, after attending the market as usual, he went out of the city to Walnut Hills, where he passed the night with a friend.

"The next morning," wrote Chase, "when he rose very early to go home, he found in the road a company of Negroes, consisting of a middle aged man, his wife, their children, the wife's mother, and two or three other persons—nine in all" (here, Chase was either mistaken about the runaways or purposefully altered the facts to suit his needs). "These persons, it appears," he continued, "had escaped from slavery in Kentucky, and had been conducted, some twelve miles or more, from where they crossed the Ohio, to Walnut Hills. Vanzandt saw them for the first time in the road where he found them. He had nothing to do with their escape. But, upon their solicitation, or that of the person who had conducted them to Walnut Hills, he undertook to convey them in his wagon to Lebanon or Springboro, thirty or thirty-five miles north-ward from Cincinnati. There was no evidence that he had any positive knowledge that they were fugitives from slavery, or any information whatever on the subject, except what he derived from the statements of the Negroes themselves. He *believed*, doubtless, that they were fugitive slaves," Chase admitted, "but he had no notice whatever—unless such intelligence as this be notice—that the Negroes had been held to service or labor in Kentucky under the laws thereof, and had escaped from that state into Ohio."[20]

Chase also argued for the application of higher law, his confidence founded, in part, on the transformation of English law that he avowed had been established by *Somerset's Case*. "If what I urge has not the sanction of reason and truth," Chase stated, "let it be condemned: if it has, I trust it will prevail—I am sure it will ultimately prevail—whatever opinion and authority may stand in the way. Opinion and authority may stand for law, but do not always represent the law. . . . For many years, opinion and authority sanctioned the doctrine that slaves might be held in England; but, after thorough investigation, this doctrine was over-thrown, and that maxim, so fraught with important results, established, that slavery is strictly local, and cannot be extended beyond the territo-rial limits of the state allowing it."[21]

Chase had as co-counsel future Secretary of State William Henry Seward. "We appeal to the Court to restore that revered instrument [the Constitution], its simplicity, its truthfulness, its harmony with the Dec-laration of Independence—its studied denial of a Right of Property in Man, and its jealous regard for the Security of the People," Seward declared. "We humbly supplicate, that Slavery, with its odious form and revolting features, and its dreadful pretensions for the Present and for the Future, may not receive in this great Tribunal, now, sanction and countenance, denied to it by a Convention of the American States more than half a century ago. Let the spirit which prevailed in that august assembly, only find utterance here, and the time will come somewhat more speedily, when throughout this great empire, erected on the foundation of the Rights of Man, no Court of Justice will be required to enforce INVOLUNTARILY obligations of LABOR, and uphold the indefensible LAW OF PHYSICAL FORCE."[22]

The Court rejected all the appellant claims, in a vote of 9 to 0. Justice Levi Woodbury, who wrote the opinion, firmly brushed aside Chase's objections, both the technical and the lofty. Van Sandt's actions indicated sufficient notice, and he had certainly harbored and concealed. Moreover, the 1793 act was perfectly constitutional, following reasonably from the basic compromise in the Constitution itself regarding slavery. So long as those constitutional compromises were in force, wrote Woodbury, the Court could not find otherwise.

"Before concluding," he wrote in the penultimate paragraph of his opinion, "it may be expected by the defendant that some notice should be taken of the argument, urging on us a disregard of the constitution and the act of Congress in respect to this subject, on account of the supposed inexpediency and invalidity of all laws recognizing slavery or any right of property in man. But that is a political question, settled by each State for itself; and the federal power over it is limited and regulated by the people of the States in the constitution itself, as one of its sacred compromises, and which we possess no authority as a judicial body to modify or overrule. Whatever may be the theoretical opinions of any as to the expediency of some of those compromises, or of the right of property in persons which they recognize, this court has no alternative, while they exist, but to stand by the constitution and laws with fidelity to their duties and their oaths. Their path is a strait and narrow one, to go where that constitution and the laws lead, and not to break both, by traveling without or beyond them."[23] In the matter of fugitive slaves, the nation would be defined by a law and jurisprudence that served the needs of a slaveholding society. Chase's Christian vision of a national liberal freedom, as we will see, would be forged only through blood.

Even after the decision of the Supreme Court, the case of *Jones v. Van Zandt* continued, taking on an inexorable life of its own and outliving both of its litigants, moving beyond their control—irrepressible, like the national cataclysm to come.

The strain of the case seems to have been too much for Van Sandt, and as it continued, his health deteriorated. In April 1847, Chase wrote to Seward: "I saw poor Vanzandt a day or two ago. He came into town in his wagon, & sent up his son to ask me to come down to him, as he was unable to get up stairs to my office. He was very weak. Pulmonary disease had made sad work with his hardy frame. The probability is strong that before the mandate of the Supreme court [to pay the fine] can be carried into a judgment of the Circuit Court the old man will have gone to another bar, where aid to the worn & suffering will not be imputed as a crime. I said to him that I could hardly suppose that, in view of his approaching end, he could feel any regret for having aided the fugitives, whose appeals to his compassion had brought him into his present troubles. The old man's eye lighted up, as he answered, 'No; if a single word could restore the man who escaped and save me from all sacrifice, I would not utter it.' And such I believe is the universal spirit of those who have aided the oppressed in regaining their freedom."[24]

Van Sandt died destitute on May 25, his estate split and sold to pay the judgment against him. His gravestone, which stood near Mt. Pierpont, was repeatedly vandalized, and eventually it was moved by some of his friends to what is now the Wesleyan Cemetery in Cincinnati. Its inscription reads: "In him Christianity had a living witness. He saw God as his father, and received every man as his brother, the cause of the poor, the orphan and the oppressed was his cause. He fed clothed sheltered and guarded them. He was eyes to the blind, and feet to the lame. He was a tender father, a devoted husband, and a friend to all. He is what is here described, because he was a Christian Philanthropist who practiced what he believed and he thus lived practicing his faith." Some of his descendants live today in the state of Washington, well aware of their legacy.

As for Wharton Jones, he would die in 1849, two years before the final settlement of his suit.

His nine slaves disappeared from the historical record. The trace of their lives has been lost.

PART THREE

New Americans,

1850–1896

Fulcrum

The evolution of American society, of all human societies, is a narrative that proceeds at different speeds, moving slowly in some eras, in others undergoing a rapid transformation. Time is routine, passing steadily in regular degrees, minute by minute, day by day; history is spasmodic. The trials in this chapter all took place during a period of swift change, a pivotal era in American civic life marked by the implacable approach of the Civil War, its unimaginable bloodletting, and the painful, long-lingering aftermath. Over the course of twenty years, hundreds of thousands of Americans would lose their lives; the nation would emancipate its vast slave population; and the federal government would undertake an ambitious plan to assist those who had been held in bondage—only to retreat from that effort, ushering in the era of Jim Crow. The black trials that took place during this volatile time were motivated by a series of persistent jurisprudential questions, whose answers we are only beginning to understand today. Would it be possible to destroy the caste system of the South, a traditional legal order based on principles of racial hierarchy and humiliation? Could that order be replaced by an emerging national liberal vision? Could that new vision itself be sustained? How would the nation reckon the moral significance of the war, the civic meaning of mass death, in its struggle over the basis of civic belonging in America?

The nation that would go to war in the 1860s looked very different from the political union that Sengbe Pieh left behind as he sailed toward Africa. The United States had grown substantially in size. The great migration over the Oregon Trail; the settlement of the Utah and New Mexico territories; the annexation of Texas; the discovery of gold near Sacramento; the Treaty of Guadalupe Hidalgo; the Gadsden Purchase— all the forces of Manifest Destiny had pushed the nation progressively outward. At the same time, the number of blacks and slaves had grown as well. In 1850, there were about 3.6 million blacks in the United States, constituting 15.7 percent of the total population. About 3.2 million of these were slaves. By 1860, there were about 4.4 million blacks in America, about 3.9 million of whom were slaves, an increase of 700,000 people classed as southern property, with a corresponding growth in the southern material interest in black bondage. Most white southerners were not slave owners. Only about 384,000 southern families possessed slaves, and 50 percent of those held fewer than five. But nearly all whites below the Mason-Dixon line were intricately connected to slavery as an institution, bound to its fate, and bitterly opposed to agitations against it. Slave owners especially resented northerners who worked to limit their ability to take their bondsmen into nonslaveholding territories, declaiming that such limits placed unjust restrictions on private property, one of the essential institutions government was designed to protect.

The growing tension over slavery expressed itself in terms of the quintessentially American antagonism between state and federal law. For the northern minority who opposed slavery outright, as for the many northerners who opposed its expansion or demanded that slaves not be recognized as seizable property on northern soil, the national government implicitly became the seat of American civic identity. More practically, it was a potential safeguard against the encroachment of the slave power northward and westward and, after the war, a tool for imposing liberal legal order over the nation as a whole. For southerners, by contrast, the national government posed a threat to state sovereignty, endangering the very communities—with their distinct legal systems— that had entered into the constitutional union in 1787. (For this reason, southerners fought so hard to control it, giving rise to northern fears of a Slave Power conspiracy.) When war finally came, the price in blood was paid not only to bring insurrectionary states back into the Union, but also to forge a new national identity, inaugurating a distinctly national jurisprudence that held the promise of ending Afro-American legal exile—and that would serve as a beacon for other groups seeking greater civic inclusion in a nation remade.

The first trial I examine from this momentous period in history is that of John Brown, the militant Christian visionary of violence and redemption, who attacked the federal arsenal at Harpers Ferry in 1859. Through his trial, imprisonment, and execution, Brown became a martyr of the abolitionist cause and drove America further on the road to war—a conflict that would result in an amended federal Constitution that placed liberal ideals more firmly at the heart of American civic life. I next turn to the years 1871–72, when the federal government undertook a major effort to prosecute and destroy the Ku Klux Klan in up-country South Carolina. The Klan had formed in the wake of the Confederate surrender to oppose Republican political power and reassert the caste principles of southern white supremacy, and it had terrorized blacks and liberal whites throughout the South in acts of intimate hate. Finally, I consider the linked legal dramas of *The Civil Rights Cases* and *Plessy v. Ferguson,* in which blacks fought against racial segregation in commercial public space—here, theaters and trains—and whose outcomes helped bring an end to liberal Reconstruction. With *Plessy,* we are brought to the precipice of the twentieth century, which would witness a revolution in American civic life that, in its reaction against *Plessy* and black trials like it, would create the civic world in which we live today.

The Law of Blood

▲

Beneath the feet of an old man, the scaffold door opens, and he falls through space. Between the first flash of his descent and the instant his body hangs finally limp from the rope around his neck, he makes a sequence of rapid gestures, each of which we can bestow with the name of a moment in the old man's life. His body sinks. *Blow, trumpet!* His mask flutters. *Black boy, black boy.* His neck strains. *My hand, my oath.* His neck snaps. *These men, their force.* His arms fly upward. *The law, its blood.* His body quivers. The body hangs.

More than a thousand soldiers look on in silence, while a single uniformed man raises his voice to proclaim, "So perish all such enemies of Virginia! All such enemies of the Union! All such foes of the human race!"

John Brown, killer, Christian, failure, prophet, was dead.

Dead and yet, for some, now immortal. "On the day of his translation," wrote the New England rebel Henry David Thoreau, imagining a deathless progress toward spiritual exaltation, "I heard, to be sure, that he was *hung,* but I did not know what that meant. . . . Of all the men who were said to be my contemporaries, it seemed to me that John Brown was the only one who *had not died.*"[1] A man most alive in death: that strange elevation would best define the paradox of Brown's historical role.

This is the story of John Brown, who was born in Connecticut, fought against slavery in Kansas, and was executed in Virginia after leading an unsuccessful attack on the federal arsenal at Harpers Ferry. His hanging was one of the most important deaths of a single man in Afro-American legal history, and his trial was the fulcrum for a transformation more fundamental than any other in American civic life.[2]

Born in 1800 in West Torrington, Connecticut, John Brown was taught to honor his parents and to fear God. His mother was the daughter of a Congregationalist minister, and his father, a farmer and tanner, was a stern disciplinarian who never stinted with the lash (according to W. E. B. Du Bois, relying on an earlier Brown biographer, the elder Brown could not speak without stammering "except in prayer").[3] In the Brown household, Calvinist piety went hand in glove with abolitionist fervor, but another powerful force also promoted his egalitarian moral convictions: the grief and bitterness of John's childhood. For after his family moved to Ohio's Western Reserve, in 1805, the boy's life began to be touched by a spirit of loss that would permanently ground his sympathetic identification with the oppressed.

At first, there were many small dispossessions, though they were large for a child on the frontier. An Indian boy gave John a yellow marble, "the first he had ever seen," a gift he treasured, until "*he lost it beyond recovery*" and it "*took years to heal the wound*" (the words are Brown's, writing of himself in the third person, in an 1857 letter to a young boy). John captured a live squirrel, accidentally severing its tail in the hunt. He nurtured the animal back to health, taming it as his friend, and soon "almost idolized his pet." But in time, "Bob Tail" disappeared, too, like the yellow marble, sending John into "a year or two" of mourning. Again, John lost: his father gave the boy a ewe lamb, a special prize indeed, but the lamb sickened and died, initiating "another protracted *mourning season.*"

Finally, when John was eight years old, came the dispossession of which the others were merely harbingers: he was left "a Motherless boy." That loss, wrote Brown, "was complete & permanent." Though the elder Brown remarried "a sensible, intelligent, & on many accounts a very estimable woman," John "*never adopted her in feeling,*" and "continued to pine after his own Mother for years." According to Brown, his mother's death "operated very unfavorably upon him," as it "deprived him of a suitable connecting link between the different sexes, the want of which might under some circumstances have proved his ruin." Precariously, the boy was becoming a man.

It was within this milieu of abandonment that Brown was to have his first taste of American slavery, which he would remember the rest of his life. After a long cattle drive through Michigan in 1812, Brown stayed for a time "with a very gentlemanly landlord, since a United States Marshall." This future lawman owned a slave boy nearly John's own age who was "very active, intelligent, & [of] good feeling; & to whom John was under considerable obligation for numerous little acts of kindness." But while the master treated young John with fond affection and made a "great pet" of him, "the *negro boy* (who was fully if not more than his equal) was badly clothed, poorly fed; *& lodged in cold weather.*" Most shockingly, John saw the boy beaten "with Iron Shovels or any other thing that came first to hand."

According to Brown, seeing that black boy brought him to "reflect on the wretched, hopeless condition, of *Fatherless & Motherless* slave *children:* for such children have neither Fathers or Mothers to protect, & provide for them." Sometimes, Brown wrote, he even would ask, *"is God their Father?"* Under whose protection were those wretched black youths? The identification marked a turning point in the child's sentimental life. It showed him the deep chasm between divine and human law, and it made him, he would later write, a "most *determined Abolitionist:* & led him to declare, or *Swear: Eternal war* with slavery." *Black boy, black boy.* By helping him feel the social death-in-life of others, his own grief had helped him better understand God's word.[4]

In time, Brown would become a father himself and raise nine children (he would marry twice, first in 1820 and, as a widower, again in 1833). According to one biographer, he ruled his family like an Old Testament patriarch, with "a Bible in one hand and a rod in the other," always acting toward his sons and daughters with a stringent religious purpose. He was especially concerned with the doctrine of atonement, the principle that Jesus' sacrifice was a ransom paid for the redemption of man from the slavery of sin. Once, for instance, he forced John Jr. to keep an account book of the lashes that were due him for his frequent misbehavior. When Brown decided the time had come for the debt to be paid, he began to thrash the boy "masterly" with a blue-beech switch—but, then, after laying on about one-third of the boy's accounted due, he abruptly stopped. Taking off his own shirt, Brown got on his knees and ordered the boy to mete out to the father the remainder of the punishment. The boy did so, drawing blood from his father's back. It was, John Jr. would later write, a "practical illustration" of how guilt could be washed away by the blood of an innocent. Brown was likewise theological in his tender moments. When he felt paternal affection, for instance, he would hold one of his children on his knees and sing his favorite hymn, Charles Wesley's "Blow Ye the Trumpet, Blow," whose title refers to the *shofar,* or ram's horn trumpet, to be blown at the time of Christ's return, and whose refrain refers to the time in which ancient Israelite slaves were to be freed:

> *Blow ye the trumpet, blow!*
> *The gladly solemn sound*
> *Let all the nations know,*
> *To earth's remotest bound:*
>
> *The year of jubilee is come!*
> *The year of jubilee is come!*
> *Return, ye ransomed sinners, home.*
> . . . .
> *Extol the Lamb of God,*
> *The all atoning lamb;*
> *Redemption in his blood*
> *Throughout the world proclaim:*
>
> *The year of jubilee is come!*
> *The year of jubilee is come!*
> *Return, ye ransomed sinners, home.*

The meaning of Jesus' death infused Brown's life. It was a story that lived inside of him, as intimately as his own blood.[5]

As a young man, Brown hoped to serve his atoning Lord by entering the ministry, and he prepared for the calling in Plainfield, Massachusetts, and Litchfield, Connecticut. Though his ambitions were thwarted by chronic eye irritation and a shortage of funds, he would never tire of playing the old-line cleric. He heeded the commandments assiduously, keeping the Sabbath so holy he asked his brother-in-law not to call at the home on Sunday. In his self-righteousness, he also had a passion for pointing out the sins of others. If no minister was available to lead services in a church Brown had organized, he himself would read to the congregation from the sermons of Jonathan Edwards. Brown brought something of the preacher into his worldly affairs as well. A man of action, and always certain his cause was just, he threw himself into a range of entrepreneurial ventures—among them tanning, sheep herding, and speculating in real estate and fine wool—with a distinctly Protestant zeal. In financial terms, Brown's fervor tended to work to his disadvantage. A man utterly convinced of the correctness of his beliefs, indeed of their godly virtue, is liable to neglect his own interests, not to mention those of his creditors. Most of Brown's ventures failed, some of them spectacularly, and he was dogged by a multitude of lawsuits. But the very qualities that had sunk Brown in business would ensure his place in American history.

November 7, 1837, Hudson, Ohio: a Christian antislavery editor named Elijah Lovejoy was killed in Alton, Illinois, by a proslavery mob from Missouri. In the wake of the murder, abolitionists throughout the North held meetings and memorials elevating Lovejoy to martyrdom as they pondered the moral and political meaning of his death. Together with his elderly father, Brown attended one of those services, organized by a professor of theology at Western Reserve College, Laurens P. Hickok, at the local Congregational Church. "The crisis has come," Hickok proclaimed. "The question now before the American citizens is no longer alone, 'Can the slaves be made free' but, are we free, or are we slaves under Southern mob law?'" Listening quietly, Brown was deeply moved. As the gathering drew to an end, he stood up, raised his right hand, and declared to all present, "Here, before God, in the presence of these witnesses, from this time, I consecrate my life to the destruction of slavery!" *My hand, my oath.* How the congregation reacted is unclear. But Brown's father, perhaps moved as much by his son's vow of atoning sacrifice as by the meeting itself, rose and stammered, "When John the Baptist was beheaded, the disciples took up his body and laid it in a tomb and went and told Jesus. Let us now go to Jesus and tell him." The elder Brown then offered "a very fervent prayer, weeping," which ended the meeting.[6]

While Brown's life would lead him at times away from a solitary focus on abolition, ultimately he remained true to his pledge. With help from the wealthy philanthropist Gerrit Smith, for instance, he founded a black farming community in upstate New York, in North Elba, where his body lies buried. As a conductor on the Underground Railroad, he helped uncounted numbers of slaves escape north from bondage, into Canada. In Massachusetts, he created a group called the League of the Gileadites, dedicated to forcible resistance of the Fugitive Slave Act of

1850 (the name taken from the Book of Judges, after an army that owed its victory to faith in God). Everywhere, he supported individual blacks in business. He made plans to start a black school and to adopt a black child into his own family. He befriended black militants, staying in their homes, praying with them, and plotting an end to bondage. And he began to dream of a complex design to ferry vast numbers of slaves north in an exodus through the Allegheny Mountains, an extensive underground railroad system that would follow a route he called the "subterranean pass way"—a dream of a people in motion that ultimately led him to Harpers Ferry.

Brown was guided throughout his work by a theory of law similar to that of John Van Sandt, Prudence Crandall, and other antislavery Christians; his vision was also a distinctive blend of his particular views on race, manhood, atonement, and covenant—which furnished him with an unusually potent justification for political violence. It was a vision that would have its day in court, in the wake of his Harpers Ferry raid, and that would linger long after, embodied by Brown's memory, influencing national thought about race into the latter half of the twentieth century.

We might see Brown's jurisprudence in three parts. The first, its theory of legitimacy, was drawn from the Bible, especially the Old Testament. Brown's affinity for the Hebrew scriptures was deep. Just before his death, he would present a local Virginia confectioner who had shown him some kindness with the Bible he had read while in prison. In it, he had marked a range of passages that spoke to his convictions or perhaps simply comforted him as he awaited execution. Of the 300-odd marked verses, about 250 were drawn from the Old Testament, and of those in the New, all but one were from the Gospel According to Matthew, the most Jewish of the gospels in its sensibility. Brown's jailhouse reading focused on a set of related themes: the covenant between Yahweh and Israel, in which the Jewish people are strictly enjoined to observe the Law given through Moses; the sharp distinction, particularly in the latter half of Isaiah, between the righteous and the wicked, between those who follow the Law and those who stray from it; the price God's people would pay for failing to keep his commandments, especially as proclaimed in Jeremiah and the preexilic passages of Proverbs; and the parts of Exodus, Leviticus, and Deuteronomy enjoining the Israelites not to "oppress the stranger," to be kind to the alien in their midst—injunctions reiterated in the egalitarian evangels of Matthew, especially in the Golden Rule.

Brown believed that as a Christian nation the United States was as much obligated to follow God's law as the ancient Israelites had been. Christians were the spiritual descendants of Abraham, and they had become parties to the Lord's new covenant through the universal blood sacrifice of Jesus. Even stricter than the first, the new covenant required that the law be brought into one's heart, not merely obeyed in one's deeds. In such a nation, no state or federal statute could be legitimate if it contradicted divine principles and put man's law and God's in conflict, for final jurisdiction over the righteous could reside only with the Almighty. In this light, Brown found American law fundamentally illegitimate in forcibly denying black inclusion in the circle of civic brotherhood. The "Good Book," he asserted, "says we are all equal." Still, Brown was no Christian anarchist. He acknowledged the importance of secular legal institutions and deeply respected the idea of America as a nation. But he argued that any human law ordering different statuses for blacks and whites was a violation of the will of God that undermined the compact between the United States and its Christian Lord, and that it thus should be disobeyed and immediately abolished (Brown did not fret over the ethical quandaries of civil disobedience). Indeed, he believed that until such laws were overthrown, the American people lived at risk of divine vengeance, of being punished just as the ancient Israelites had been for falling away from the Law.

In an 1854 letter to his friend Frederick Douglass, which he had planned to entitle "Law and Order," Brown complained of "the extreme wickedness of persons who use their influence to bring law and order and good government, and courts of justice into [the] disrespect and contempt of mankind." Such "fiends clothed in human form," he explained, were present throughout society. They had become, for instance, "a majority in our national Legislature," where they passed "unjust and wicked enactments, and call them laws." They also included chief magistrates, who "affix the official signature to such enactments," and those "from the same horde" who "fill the offices of judge, justices, commissioners" and "follow that which is altogether unjust." They even included wicked ministers. "What Gospel do they preach?" Brown asked, referring to men who defiled their priestly office by condoning laws like the Fugitive Slave Law. "The Son of God said—'Therefore all things whatsoever ye would that men should do to you, do ye even so to them; for this is the law and the Prophets.' The conscience of every man that ever heard or read that command says Amen! But what say these so-called Divines? You must obey the enactments of the United States

Congress, even to the violation of conscience, and the trampling under foot of the laws of our final judge." Referring to a South Asian tree whose vapor was thought at the time to be poisonous, Brown continued, "What punishment ever inflicted by man or even threatened of God, can be too severe for those whose influence is a thousand times more malignant than the atmosphere of the deadly Upas—for those who hate the right and the Most High?" In a "Declaration of Liberty" written in advance of his Virginia raid, Brown condemned those who made and executed the laws of slavery and caste as "pirates," "swarms of blood suckers," and "a blot upon the character, the honor, of any nation, which claims to have the least shadow or spark of civilization above the lowest, most inferior cannibal races." "Their laws," he proclaimed, "are no laws."[7]

The second component of Brown's jurisprudence might be called his theory of civic emasculation. No metaphor bespoke the capacity for full civic membership as fully as did that of manhood. To attain manhood in this civic sense was to be frank, independent, dutiful to God and family, dedicated to principles of right, and engaged in active, useful work. For Brown, such manly virtues were the basis of citizenship and the civic order, a view not uncommon at the time—except that Brown's ideal included black men. The majority of Americans had subscribed to the view of slavery's supporters that most blacks lacked the requisite manhood for law and citizenship, but Brown denied the vision of innate black inferiority behind these claims. Instead, foreshadowing arguments to be developed by radicals such as Malcolm X one hundred years later, Brown argued that American society had in effect emasculated blacks not only by the lash, the active enforcement of servility, but also by encouraging them to participate in their own subordination. Brown argued that blacks had habituated themselves to the very sort of conduct that prevented them from overthrowing bondage and preserved the stereotypes of inferiority by which whites justified oppressing them. By bringing the ideals of a slave society into their own hearts, blacks were engaged in civic suicide.

In his celebrated essay "Sambo's Mistakes," written in 1847 or 1848 for the short-lived black newspaper the *Ram's Horn* (a name taken from the trumpet that would be blown at the time of jubilee—the trumpet of Wesley's hymn), Brown presented the advice of a fictive elderly black man who, having "committed a few mistakes in the course of a long life," hoped to confer the benefit of his experience on "others of my colored brethren." "For instance, when I was a boy I learned to read," the article began, but, instead of giving my attention to sacred and profane history, by which I might have become acquainted with the true character of God and man, learned the true course for individuals, societies, and nations to pursue; stored my mind with an endless variety of rational and practical ideas; profited by the experience of millions of others of all ages; fitted myself for the most important stations in life, and fortified my mind with the best and wisest resolutions, and noblest sentiments and motives—I have spent my whole life in devouring silly novels and other miserable trash, such as most newspapers of the day are filled with; thereby unfitting myself for the realities of life, and acquiring a taste for nonsense and low wit, so that I have no relish for sober truth, useful knowledge, or practical wisdom.

Other common black errors, according to Brown, included a penchant for wasting money on luxuries rather than saving and developing capital; a tendency to talk too much; and rather than organizing effectively as a group a propensity to criticize one another and splinter into social and political factions. Above all, Brown condemned the failure of most blacks, free as much as slave, to stand up to personal rebuke and oppression. "I have always expected to secure the favor of the whites," wrote the author of "Sambo's Mistakes," with palpable anger, "by tamely submitting to every species of indignity, contempt, and wrong, instead of nobly resisting their brutal aggressions from principle, and taking my place as a man, and assuming the responsibilities of a man, a citizen, a husband, a father, a brother, a neighbor, a friend,—as God requires of every one (if his neighbor will allow him to do it)." In this, Brown—who, it should be noted, was far more eager to criticize the sinful or simply appeasing behavior of whites—called on blacks as critical allies in their own emancipation.[8]

The third element of Brown's jurisprudence—ultimately its most important—might be called a theory of legal deliverance. For Brown, if blacks could be brought into the circle of national civic belonging, America could fulfill its divine covenant and reclaim its legitimacy under Christian law. Particularly toward the end of his life, Brown believed that redemption would require not simply the abolition of slavery, but its destruction through the specific means of physical force. National legal redemption, that is, demanded directed violence on behalf of the political ideals of Christianity. Why violence? For one, it was in keeping with God's promised retribution against the wicked, a scripturally precedented justice by which slaveholders would know the wrathful God of the Old Testament, in which the Law is vindicated by the smiting of God's enemies. In addition, violence would help blacks to reclaim their manhood, to prove themselves worthy of civic belonging by a show of self-assertion with force of arms. This, in turn, would help change common white perceptions of black inferiority. "Nothing so charms the American people as personal bravery," wrote Brown. "Witness the case of Cinques, of everlasting memory, on board the 'Amistad.' The trial for life of one bold and to some extent successful man, for defending his rights in good earnest, would arouse more sympathy throughout the nation than the accumulated wrongs and sufferings of more than three millions of our submissive colored population."[9]

Finally, violence had a symbolic function of ritual sacrifice. The Law would be redeemed by the shedding of blood, an act of collective atonement for a sinful nation. Blood figures centrally in Christian jurisprudence, a symbolism dating back to the ancient Israelite practice of animal sacrifice by which their covenant with God was fulfilled. Hundreds of pure, unblemished animals were sacrificed each year by the Aaronic priesthood. The attendant theological lessons were not unlike those of other religious systems in which the killing of animals plays a role: that disobedience of God's law results in death (the "wages of sin"); that the purging of sin is a costly, difficult matter; and that only those duly purged can righteously stand before God. "Almost all things are by the law purged with blood," proclaims a verse in Hebrews to which Brown would refer in his final written words, "and without shedding of blood there is no remission."[10] For Brown, just as the ancient Israelites were purified through animal sacrifice, and all men were brought into a new covenant with God through the sacrifice of Jesus, so the American nation would be returned to Christ through the atoning sacrifice of the just. The blood of the righteous would have to be spilled in the Lord's fight, and it was a sacrifice Brown himself was quite willing to make.

His first full taste of combat would come in 1856, when Brown joined his sons in a hardscrabble camp in Kansas to battle southern "border ruffians" who sought to win the future state for slavery. In that engagement, which earned him the moniker "Captain Brown," he became a murderer. It happened one night in May. Lawrence had recently been sacked by proslavery forces—the free-state citizens were virtually helpless to defend themselves—and Charles Sumner had been beaten within an inch of his life by Preston Brooks on the floor of the U.S. Senate. Brown slaked his thirst for retribution by leading a small band, including two of his sons, in a massacre of five men under cover of night. The raid was as brutal as God's law was unflinching. Some of those Brown helped kill were dragged from their cabins in the dark and summarily executed with swords as their wives and children wailed inside. Their throats were slit, their heads bashed in, and their bodies thrown into the brush and water. *The law, its blood.* Brown's act of terror came to be known as the Pottawatomie Massacre, after the nearby creek, and in the eyes of many Americans it revealed him as simply a cold-blooded killer. But in the eyes of others, it transformed the abolitionist into a warrior of God, a man of action who could fight on behalf of Christian ideals against the immense sin of southern slaveholding. It made him a hero of a higher law.

That image would serve Brown well as he later made his way north, seeking funds for what he elusively called his "Rail Road business on a *somewhat extended* scale," the child of his dream of a subterranean pass way.[11] Brown made his tour at a time when like-minded people thought American law more than ever in need of redemption. In 1857, the Supreme Court handed down its opinion in *Scott v. Sanford,* or *Dred Scott,* the most notorious decision in American constitutional history. With that stroke, the law of the land flatly denied blacks national legal and civic capacity, and to many the Court and its law of race and slavery seemed to have reached its low point of illegitimacy. *Dred Scott* provided an important jurisprudential context to Brown's raid on Harpers Ferry, and the meaning of his death cannot be understood without at least briefly considering that momentous case.

While *Scott v. Sanford* involved a complex array of proceedings dating from 1846, the essential facts were straightforward. In the 1830s, a slave named Dred Scott was taken by his master from Missouri, a slave state, to Illinois and on to Fort Snelling, in what is today St. Paul, Minnesota, but which at the time lay within the free territory of Wisconsin. Scott resided in Fort Snelling for some time, and there married a black woman named Harriet Robinson, the slave of Major Lawrence Taliaferro, a local Indian agent and justice of the peace who performed their civil wedding. After later traveling to Louisiana and Texas, Scott returned to Missouri with a new master—and there he brought suit to gain freedom for himself, his wife, and their two children. Scott claimed that Missouri's long-standing legal principle of "once free, always free" applied to him, that, by moving north and residing in a free territory, Scott had become a free man. James Somerset's counsel had made similar arguments before the King's Bench in England. The reasons why Scott and his wife did not bring their suit sooner remain unclear. It is possible their first master had promised Scott his manumission on a certain date, and that he had been biding his time, or that Scott and his wife simply had not been aware of their legal rights (one conjecture has it that Harriet learned of the possibility of a suit through her church, whose minister had worked for Elijah Lovejoy). It also is possible that the Scotts felt no pressing need to be free of their bondage: they seem to have made no attempt to escape during their many miles of travel together across the United States without white supervision.

No matter the catalyst, when Scott brought the case in 1846, it should have been open and shut. Missouri precedent was clear on situations such as his. Unfortunately for Scott, however, a problem with hearsay evidence in the original proceeding forced the judge to declare a mistrial, and by the time the Missouri Supreme Court was asked to make a final disposition of the matter in 1852, the political winds in America had shifted substantially. Southern courts now felt intense pressure to defend the peculiar institution against northern attack, and so the Missouri high court ruled to reverse years of state precedent and deny Scott his freedom. Announcing that "times now are not as they were," the Court repudiated the principle of "once free, always free" with a variety of proslavery assertions fortifying the legal interests of slaveholders. Scott next took his case to the federal courts, where his owners sought to have the Missouri decision upheld mainly on the basis of two arguments. First, they maintained that as a black man, Scott was not even entitled to sue in federal court, as blacks could not be citizens of the United States, leaving his status to be determined entirely by the courts of Missouri. Second, they contended that it was false for Scott to claim that he had resided in the *free* jurisdiction of Wisconsin, because Congress had never truly possessed the constitutional power to prohibit slavery in the territories. The Missouri Compromise of 1820, Scott's owners asserted, was invalid from the start, and Fort Snelling had always been a territory open to the lawful practice of black bondage.

While it seemed at first as though the Supreme Court might exercise judicial self-restraint by asserting that it was for Missouri to determine its own law, and so avoid pronouncing on any of the volatile issues the case raised, the slaveholders on the bench, especially James Wayne of Georgia, demanded a more extreme course. They hoped by judicial action to resolve some of the most fundamental issues in the debate over slavery, matters that had proved insoluble by political and legislative processes. The ringing endorsement of slavery they produced was written by Chief Justice Roger Brooke Taney of Maryland, one of the most respected jurists of his time (and, despite *Dred Scott*, still one of the great justices in the history of the Court). First, Taney rendered the Missouri Compromise invalid by agreeing that Congress had never had the power to abolish slavery in the territories. Scott's movement north, in this respect, was no legal movement at all: he had always remained within jurisdictions where slavery was permissible. Moreover, the Chief Justice asserted that Scott had no right to bring suit in federal court because blacks—and not just slaves, but all blacks—were ineligible to be citizens of the United States. Invoking the racial beliefs of the framers, as Andrew Judson had in the case of Prudence Crandall, Chief Justice Taney asserted, in the most notorious words of his opinion, that blacks in Revolutionary America had "no rights the white man was bound to respect." They had lived outside the circle of national legal life at the time the United States was born, and so by all rights should continue to live in that state of civic exclusion (a holding that, ironically, seemed to render the Court's invalidation of the Missouri Compromise merely nonbinding dicta: if Scott could not bring suit in federal court, the Court would have lacked jurisdiction over the other matters implicated in the case).

The *Dred Scott* decision struck the nation with thunderous force, much as the case of *Brown v. Board of Education* would one hundred years later. While Scott himself eventually was purchased from his master by white friends and set free, Chief Justice Taney's opinion seemed to establish slavery and black subjugation as one of the bedrock principles of national life. Naturally, such a line in the sand elicited both heated fury and ringing praise. "It is not too much to say that this decision revolutionizes the Federal Government," wrote the *New York Daily Times*, "and changes entirely the relation which Slavery has hitherto held towards it. Slavery is no longer local: it is national."[12] Many northerners saw *Dred Scott* as part of a tyrannical plot on the part of the Slave Power. Southerners and their northern allies, conversely, were overjoyed, and they frequently characterized their opponents as treasonous. "Our republican friends," wrote the *New York Journal of Commerce*, "have fairly raised the standard of insurrection, and are giving us the higher law in all its moods and tenses with a vengeance. They declare in every way and shape . . . that the decision in the *Dred Scott* case is not law, that the Judges who decided it don't know what law means, that their decision is absurd and nonsensical, oppressive and tyrannical, that nobody is bound by it, that nobody ought to obey it, and finally, that it shall not be submitted to. . . . The long and the short of it is, that the so called Republican Party is only another name for Revolution and anarchy."[13]

It was in this volatile legal climate that John Brown set upon his northern tour, moving through the antislavery parlors of Ohio, Massachusetts, and New York, traveling throughout the country, dreaming that God's trumpet might soon blow. During much of that expedition, the abolitionist wore a white beard in the manner of a Hebrew prophet, a biblical lawgiver, and he assumed an alias: Shebuel Morgan. In the Bible, Shebuel is the grandson of Moses, and his name means "returned to God." In German, *Morgen* means "tomorrow" or "dawn."

Brown ordered a Connecticut forge master to build him 1,000 iron pikes, which he hoped soon to put into the hands of slaves, weapons of manhood and citizenship. His plan went beyond boldness: attack the federal arsenal at Harpers Ferry, seize its storehouse of arms, and rally the bondsmen from the region to follow him into the mountains, from where he would begin a military campaign that would sweep the South, destroying slavery at the end of the sword. The idea had more than an air of madness about it, but there had been successful slave uprisings elsewhere, in Haiti and Santo Domingo for instance, and Brown was by no means alone in his readiness to pledge himself to a bloody death for black freedom. When the general outlines of the plan were revealed at a secret convention in Chatham, Ontario, in May 1858, twelve whites and thirty-four blacks warranted their assent and together adopted a constitution that Brown had drafted at the home of Frederick Douglass, a provisional constitution for the territory he and his men would seize in their campaign.

The constitution reflected both Brown's religious scruples and his loyalty to the forms and principles of American government, making plain his desire to redeem the nation rather than destroy it. The illegitimacy of the American law of bondage is declared immediately in the preamble. "Whereas, Slavery throughout its entire existence in the United States," it begins,

> is none other than the most barbarous, unprovoked, and unjustifiable war of one portion of its citizens against another portion, the only conditions of which are perpetual imprisonment, and hopeless servitude, or absolute extermination in utter disregard and violation of those eternal and self-evident truths set forth in

our Declaration of Independence: Therefore, We, the citizens of the United States, and the oppressed people, who, by a recent decision of the Supreme Court [*Dred Scott*], are declared to have no rights which the white man is bound to respect, together with all the other people degraded by the laws thereof, do, for the time being, ordain and establish for ourselves the following Provisional Constitution and ordinances, the better to protect our people, property, lives, and liberties, and to govern our actions.

In his movement's Declaration, Brown proclaimed as basic the principle that the "labourer is worthy of his hire"—a reference to Luke 10:7—and asserted "that the Slaves are, & of right ought to be as free & as independent as the unchangeable Law of God requires that All Men Shall be."[14]

The specific articles of the constitution similarly reflected the range of Brown's jurisprudential concerns. Some bore the mark of theocracy: Article 40, for instance, declares that "[p]rofane swearing, filthy conversation, indecent behavior, or indecent exposure of the person, or intoxication or quarreling, shall not be allowed or tolerated, neither unlawful intercourse of the sexes." Another stated that "[s]chools and churches shall be established . . . for the purpose of religious and other instruction, and the first day of the week shall be regarded as a day of rest and appropriated to moral and religious instruction." At the same time, Article 46 stressed the aim not to destroy America, but rather to redeem it according to its own principles. "The foregoing Articles," it asserted, "shall not be construed so as in any way to encourage the overthrow of any State Government or of the General Government of the United States: and look to no dissolution of the Union, but simply to Amendment and Repeal. And our flag shall be the same that our fathers fought under in the Revolution." And then there was Brown's particular inspiration for fostering racial equality: Article 43 announced that "all persons known to be of good character, and of sound mind, and suitable age, who are connected with this organization, whether male or female, shall be encouraged to carry arms openly" (with other radical abolitionists, Brown supported women's rights).

Brown's guerrilla band was a strange assortment, some twenty men in all, most of them far younger than Brown. They were students, free blacks, former soldiers, runaway slaves, cranks, romantic idealists, and some of Brown's own sons. Brown's secretary of state was a poet named Richard Realf, protégé of Lady Byron, who would later write some of the most popular songs of the Civil War. Among his most trusted men was an avid reader of Thomas Paine. Few shared Brown's deep religious passion. Some did not even consider themselves Christians. But all agreed with Brown's main goal, and they agreed with his methods. They were ready to kill to end black slavery. *These men, their force.* They were as ready to die as to kill, and must have expected to do both. Nineteen would join the attack on the arsenal.

There is no need here to examine in detail Brown's movements shortly before or after the Chatham convention in May 1858: his meeting with wealthy supporters on the East Coast; his military training in Kansas and Iowa; his secretive family correspondence; his calling of his sons to join him in this great work; his receipt of the 1,000 iron pikes; or his establishment of a clandestine base of operations in Maryland, not far from his intended target, on an old farm where he and his men trained; or the many extraordinary events and schemes that took place in advance of Brown's invasion. Nor need we examine the details of the invasion itself, other than to remember, as many Americans learn in school, that it was a miserable failure. The day after they took the arsenal, Brown and his men were overrun by a juggernaut under the command of Colonel Robert E. Lee. The record shows that no slaves actively rallied to Brown's side, though it is possible that some knew of his plan and retreated only once they saw its defeat. In any case, the pikes remained in their boxes and Brown waited in vain for the black storm that would overwhelm the South.

Some of his men escaped, but most were killed, including two of his sons, who died in slow agony by their father's side. Brown himself was run through the gut with a sword but, though badly hurt, he survived. He even managed to exhibit a remarkable clarity of mind despite his bleeding wounds. Shortly after his capture, Brown was interviewed for over three hours by a company of politicians and military men, including Virginia Governor Henry Wise and Senator James M. Mason—author of the Fugitive Slave Act—and in the presence of the reporters who would publish his words across the country, he gave what all agreed was a manly performance.

"Mr. Brown, who sent you here?" demanded Clement L. Vallandigham, a Democratic congressman from Ohio.

"No man sent me here," replied Brown. "It was my own prompting and that of my maker, or that of the devil, whichever you please to ascribe it to. I acknowledge no man in human form."

"What was your object in coming?" asked Senator Mason.

"We came to free the slaves, and only that."

"How do you justify your acts?" asked the Senator.

"I think, my friend," said Brown, who was remarkably respectful toward his captors, "you are guilty of a great wrong against God and humanity—I say it without wishing to be offensive—and it would be perfectly right in any one to interfere with you so far as to free those you willfully and wickedly hold in bondage. I do not say this insultingly" ("I understand that," replied the Senator, acknowledging the respect).

"I think I did right," Brown continued, "and that others will do right who interfere with you at any time and all times. I hold that the golden rule, 'Do unto others as you would that others should do unto you,' applies to all who would help others to gain their liberty."

"Did you get up this document that is called a Constitution?" Representative Vallandigham asked.

"I did," said Brown. "They are a constitution and ordinances of my own contriving and getting up."

Holding a copy of the constitution, Senator Mason later asked Brown if he considered his group a "military organization." Brown replied that he did, "in some sense," and then pointedly advised, "I wish you would give that paper close attention." (Brown need not have feared on that score: all his papers would be examined in detail; carelessly left behind at his Maryland hideout, they incriminated not just Brown and his men, but many of their secret northern backers.)

"What wages did you offer?" asked Senator Mason.

"None," said Brown—to which Lieutenant J. E. B. Stuart, present among the onlookers, gave a sarcastic retort: "'The wages of sin is death.'"

"I would not have made such a remark to you," Brown shot back reproachfully, "if you had been a prisoner and wounded in my hands." No doubt he spoke the truth.

An unnamed bystander asked Brown if he considered his actions to be part of "a religious movement."

That was perhaps the simplest question of all. "It is, in my opinion," the old man replied, "the greatest service a man can render to God."[15]

Brown had planned to vindicate the law of his Christian Lord. Now Virginia, asserting its jurisdiction over the crime rather than delivering Brown into the hands of Washington, prepared to vindicate the law of the South. The abolitionist had declared in word and deed that southern law was barbarous. By placing Brown and his men on trial in nearby

Charlestown, Virginia would reassert the strength and legitimacy of its institutions by observing its own legal process, much as New York City had attempted to do in 1741. As Virginia and the nation would soon discover, however, Brown's trial served his own purposes as well as those of the South, translating him from the world of the living into that of legal martyrdom.

On the morning of October 25, 1859, Brown and his companions were led into magistrate's court with a guard of eighty armed men. The court, wrote one observer, was "bristling with bayonets on all sides." Brown was haggard, and his eyes were swollen from his wounds (a medical examiner reported, however, that he was in a good enough condition to stand trial). "I did not ask for any quarter at the time I was taken," he exclaimed. "If you seek my blood, you can have it at any moment, without this mockery of a trial. . . . I am ready for my fate."[16] But a trial he would have, in accordance with procedure. The charges: conspiring with blacks to commit insurrection, murder, and treason to the Commonwealth of Virginia. Technically, the treason count was contentious, as Brown was not a citizen of Virginia. But the prosecutor successfully argued that Virginia, like other states, defined treason in broad terms, and that as a citizen of the United States who sought residence in the state, the abolitionist had duties to the Commonwealth in the same measure as he received its privileges and immunities.

When State's Attorney Charles B. Harding first presented the facts of the case and read the applicable law, he must have known there was little doubt as to the result. He explained to the jury that he would show "that the prisoners' whole object was to rob our citizens of their slaves, and carry them off by violence"—which, he "was happy to say," went "against the wills of the slaves, all of them having escaped, and rushed back to their masters at the first opportunity." Harding also must have been assured of the sympathies of the gallery. One of the first witnesses to be examined was asked to describe the interview that took place after Brown was captured, and he told how the old man had discussed his constitution and the military organization he had formed to bring it to power. When he testified that Brown had stated "there was an intelligent colored man" elected to his provisional House of Representatives, there was a "sensation" in the courtroom.[17]

The trial lasted four days. Brown could scarcely have expected better treatment, but any defense would have been futile. Prosecutors presented the jury with a copy of his constitution, pointing out the most incriminating articles, and there could be little more damning evidence than that great legal document of the Chatham convention. The constitution required an oath of allegiance. It purported to establish a provisional government. It explicitly stated Brown's intention to confiscate the personal property of slaveholders and arm slaves. His organization, prosecutors noted, was "the real thing, [and] no debating society"—a direct attack upon the law and state of Virginia. As for local slaves, testimony seemed to confirm their "faithfulness," imputing that they had no desire at any point to challenge the principles of a caste society. According to John Allstadt, a white man Brown took prisoner, the Harpers Ferry raiders had forcibly liberated seven of his slaves, but while "the negroes were placed in the watch-house with spears in their hands," they "showed no disposition to use them." Later, Allstadt reported happily, he saw one of his slaves "making port-holes by Brown's order" while the others were "doing nothing, and had dropped their spears." Some, he continued, "were asleep nearly all the time"—a comment that elicited laughter.[18]

Brown's defense was sparse. After he forcefully rejected an effort by his counsel to save his life by reason of insanity, there was little to be done. Against the witnesses who testified in detail as to his actions in and around Harpers Ferry and the federal arsenal, all Brown could do was repeatedly indicate that he had treated the prisoners he had taken with care and claimed that he had no intention of starting a violent insurrection—a seeming falsehood, contradicted by his 1,000 iron pikes. Whether Brown was lying, in a most un-Christian manner, or imagined his subterranean pass way scheme succeeding without a vicious uprising, or meant something else entirely, is unclear.

But if the facts clearly proved Brown's guilt under the laws of Virginia, his physical presence in the courtroom elevated him into another jurisdiction altogether. With "three sword stabs in his body and a saber-cut over the heart," and unable to stand on his own, he indeed made a "pitiable sight."[19] For most of his trial, he lay upon a cot on the floor. As if miraculously, his health improved somewhat over the course of the proceeding, but anyone at all inclined could easily see the unrepentant man who claimed to be following God's law as what abolitionists most desired: a manly Christ, suffering before Pilate for his truth. The prosecution might call its witnesses to show how Brown and his men had killed a handful of Virginia citizens and soldiers in their raid, they might place Brown's constitution before the jury to reveal his treason, and they might even demonstrate how, if successful, his raid would have resulted in a massive slave insurrection. But Brown's real defense before the nation following the proceedings in Charlestown lay in the physical presence and spiritual symbolism of his body, the wounded man near death, his frailty accentuated by the formalities of due process, which thus were rendered absurd. His wounds become stigmata, markers of the higher law by which he asked to be judged, and by which he would be counted not among the guilty, but among the righteous. "The cut is on the crown," Herman Melville would write in "The Portent," "[a]nd the stabs shall heal no more."

As the good and lawful men returned, after but three-quarters of an hour, the crowd stood "anxious but perfectly silent," spilling out of the courtroom and stretching beyond the courthouse doors, the mass of them "terrible to look upon." Straining their necks, they all "moved and agitated with but one dreadful expectancy—to let the eyes rest for a moment upon the only calm and unruffled countenance there." Not the "slightest sound" was heard, while Brown stood, impassive, "a man of indomitable will and iron nerve." After the foreman pronounced him guilty, as all expected, Brown turned to adjust his narrow bed, and then "composedly stretched himself on it." The court recessed until the following day, when it would reconvene for the sentencing.[20]

When Brown entered the court on that November 2, the building was "immediately thronged." The Court made a few preliminary remarks, in accordance with strict procedure, before asking Brown whether he had anything to say that might bear upon the judgment. The old man was caught somewhat off guard, unprepared for this final chance to speak, but finally he rose and began speaking in a "clear, distinctive voice."

"I have, may it please the Court, a few words to say. In the first place, I deny everything but what I have all along admitted, of a design on my part to free slaves. . . . I never did intend murder or treason, or the destruction of property, or to excite or incite the slaves to rebellion, or to make insurrection." It was again a seeming falsehood, and Brown would later indicate he had not intended to make such a global denial of his acts, but however intended, the words portrayed him as an innocent soldier fighting for a pure cause—surely he was aware of his impending "translation" and did what he could to facilitate it. "I have another objection," he continued, "and that is that it is unjust that I should suffer such a penalty. Had I interfered in the manner which I admit, and which I admit has been fairly proved" (ever respectful of manly conduct, Brown expressed his admiration for "the truthfulness and candor of the greater portion of the witnesses who have testified in this case")—"had I so interfered in behalf of the rich, the powerful, the intelligent, the so-called great, or in behalf of any of their friends, either father, mother, brother, sister, wife, or children, or any of that class, and suffered and sacrificed what I have in this interference, it would have been all right, and every man in this Court would have deemed it an act worthy of reward rather than punishment.

"This Court acknowledges, too, as I suppose, the validity of the law of God," he said, beginning to probe a fissure of hypocrisy. "I see a book kissed, which I suppose to be the Bible, or at least the New Testament, which teaches me that all things whatsoever I would that men should do to me, I should do even so to them. It teaches me further to remember them that are in bonds as bound with them. I endeavored to act up to that instruction.

"I say," Brown continued, "I am yet too young to understand that God is any respecter of persons." God's law, that is, included all people, and blacks as much as whites were included within the Lord's church. (The reference is to Acts 10 and to James 2:8–9, where it is written, "If ye fulfil the royal law according to the scripture, Thou shalt love thy neighbour as thyself, ye do well: but if ye have respect to persons, ye commit sin, and are convinced of the law as transgressors.") "I believe," Brown thus declared, "that to have interfered as I have done, as I have always freely admitted I have done in behalf of His despised poor, is not wrong, but right. Now, if it is deemed necessary that I should forfeit my life for the furtherance of the ends of justice, and mingle my blood further with the blood of my children and with the blood of millions in this slave country whose rights are disregarded by wicked, cruel, and unjust enactments, I say let it be done."

Let it be done. When Brown was through, the judge sentenced him to die by hanging on December 2, 1859, which sentence he received "with composure." The courtroom, too, was composed. The only "demonstration made," wrote a reporter, was a single man clapping his hands—a man, it was emphasized, "who is not a resident of Jefferson County." The clapping "was promptly suppressed, and much regret is expressed by the citizens at its occurrence."[21]

While awaiting his execution, Brown received a steady stream of visitors, exchanged countless letters with supporters, and addressed the nation with an equanimity that impressed even his enemies. "With John Brown, as with every other man fit to die for a cause," Frederick Douglass would write, looking back in 1881 to Harpers Ferry, "the hour of his physical weakness was the hour of his moral strength—the hour of his defeat was the hour of his triumph—the moment of his capture was the crowning victory of his life. With the Alleghany mountains for his pulpit, the country for his church and the whole civilized world for his audience, he was a thousand times more effective as a preacher than as a warrior."[22]

He was now consciously preparing for his martyrdom, his translation into a symbol of legal principles—a transformation for which allies across the nation were also steadily preparing. "'Commonwealth of Virginia!'" cried the blue-blooded antislavery agitator Wendell Phillips. "There is no such thing. Lawless, brutal force is no basis for a government, in the true sense of that word." Virginia, he proclaimed, was "only a pirate ship." "I mean exactly what I say," cautioned Phillips, "I am weighing my words now. She is a pirate ship, and John Brown sails the sea a Lord High Admiral of the Almighty, with his commission to sink every pirate he meets on God's ocean of the nineteenth century."[23]

On the morning of his death, Brown read the Bible and bade his fellow raiders farewell, urging them to meet their fates like men. He shook their hands and gave each a quarter as a parting token. He was then led outside (though the incident never happened, artists would later depict him with a flowing white beard, bending to kiss a black child in the outstretched arms of its mother), and he gave one of his attendants a slip of paper, on which he had written a final prophecy. "I John Brown," the note read, "am now quite *certain* that the crimes of this *guilty land will* never be purged away; but with Blood. I had *as I now think: vainly flattered myself* that *without very much* bloodshed it might be done."

To purge a crime with blood. According to Hebrews 9:22, "all things are by the law purged with blood." And Jesus' bloody death redeemed mankind from sin for all time. Drawing his meaning from the old covenant as well as the new, Brown offered a two-part blueprint for civic redemption. It suggested, first, the need for God's followers to smite the wicked, to kill southern slaveholders and their allies in the manner of Old Testament justice. But even more vital was the need for a massive communal blood sacrifice, the widespread death of the righteous, in the manner of Jesus, to cleanse America of its wickedness and put it again at one with the Lord.

Brown stepped into the wagon waiting to take him to the gallows and sat upon his coffin. The wagon moved forward, flanked by six companies of infantry and a cavalry troop. The soldiers—the security detachment constituting an unintended honor guard—were under the command of General William B. Taliaferro, a relative of the Indian agent who had owned Harriet Robinson, Dred Scott's wife.

"Captain Brown," said an undertaker who rode with him, noting the condemned's almost cheerful confidence, "you are a game man."

"Yes," Brown answered, "I was so trained up; it was one of the lessons of my mother."

Then Brown remarked, "This is a beautiful country; I never had the pleasure of seeing it before."

On reaching the gallows, Brown said goodbye to his prosecutors, and shook hands and said farewell to his jailer and the presiding sheriff, thanking them for their kindness during his imprisonment. Brown's step toward the rope was firm and quick. A mask was put over his face before the noose was tightened around his neck. The jailer asked him to step forward onto the trapdoor.

"You must lead me," Brown replied, "I cannot see."[24]

Soldiers marched and countermarched for ten minutes, taking up positions as if an enemy were in sight.

He was hanged shortly after eleven o'clock and died about thirty-five minutes later. His body was cut down, and then carried to a train at four o'clock, the whole affair conducted with military precision, according to law.

Less than two years later, the country would be at war, and Union soldiers singing "John Brown's Body" would begin to fulfill the martyr's dream. "He captured Harper's Ferry with his nineteen men so true," they sang (*Blow, trumpet!*):

> *He frightened "Old Virginny"*
> *'Till she trembled through and through.*
> *They hung him for a traitor,*
> *Though themselves a traitor crew.*
> *His soul goes marching on!*

At Manassas, Shiloh, Antietam, and hundreds of other battlefields, Americans both white and black would prepare the way of the amended federal Constitution that would be the war's greatest legal achievement. They would create a new nation, a second republic, with a terrible, swift sword, and all the atoning blood of boys and men.

8

Original Purity

▲

The hooded men rode for law and honor, breaking into homes at night while their victims slept. One evening, they came for Clem Bowden and his wife, Minerva. It was October 19, 1870, in Spartanburg County, South Carolina. A farmer, a carpenter, and a black man, Bowden, sixty-one years old, lived a few miles northwest of Limestone Springs. "I myself worked about," he would explain months later to three visiting congressmen. "I was clearing up a plantation, and starting it."

As the congressmen listened, a stenographer recorded Bowden's story. They had traveled here, to the South Carolina up-country, in July 1871, as part of a committee investigating the activities of a secret paramilitary group called the Ku Klux Klan. Their charge: to "inquire into the condition of affairs in the late insurrectionary States, so far as regards the execution of the laws, and the safety of the lives and property of the citizens of the United States."

"Begin at the beginning," instructed the committee chairman, Senator John Scott of Pennsylvania, "and tell us the occurrence."

"When they first came to me I was in a chair asleep, and had not stripped," Bowden began. "My family had laid down on the bed. The first thing I heard was the report of pistols, and men going around my house, and then they ran against the door, and by this time a portion of them got around on the other side to the other door, and ran against it and burst it open. . . . They came in the house and laid hold of me. . . . They went to the bed and pulled my wife out."

At the same time the men were seizing Clem and Minerva Bowden, another mob was breaking into the home of William Champion, a white man. Champion was a farmer and miller, a trial judge, a Republican— and, like Clem Bowden, one of the township managers of the upcoming gubernatorial election. "Go on and state if, at any time, you have been visited by any men in disguise," asked Senator Scott, "and, if so, what they did and said to you, and all that occurred."

"Yes," Champion replied, "but I hate to tell it."[1]

The stenographer took down the white man's words, and his story became public record, forever binding his life to that of Clem and Minerva Bowden. Their collective story is a horrific portrait of civic violence—but, as we will see, it also was not unusual. It mirrored the experience of thousands of blacks across the South following the surrender at Appomattox as white southerners sought to resist and subvert the liberal civic principles of three new provisions of the federal Constitution: the Reconstruction Amendments.[2]

"Come out here!" the men shouted in the moonlit night, swearing and firing into the air as they broke down Clem Bowden's door. Bursting inside, more than two dozen strong, they ordered one of Bowden's daughters to kindle a light, and searched the home for weapons (they found none). While dogs barked furiously, they dragged Clem and Minerva Bowden outside.

The men marched the Bowdens three-quarters of a mile away, to the home of Daniel Lipscomb, who was sharecropping on the land of his former master, "Major" Lee Linder. The seventy-five-year-old Lipscomb had been a "favorite servant" of the major for twenty years. During the war, he brought Linder "the bulliest crop he ever had on his place" and hauled two loads of coal for him a day. "I never made a step in my tracks to get away the whole time of the war," Lipscomb said proudly. "I attended to my business." So high was his master's regard that Lipscomb had been entrusted to hold and deliver as much as $1,000 of the major's money at a time.

The old man, having been dragged out of his home, too, was standing in front of his door with a rope around his neck. He was guarded by eight men, shortly joined by the mob that had assaulted the Bowdens. Some wore masks, but others showed their faces. One of the more brazen, Columbus Petty, had visited Major Linder's home earlier that evening. Lipscomb knew "Clum" well. He had "raised him up from a child," and recently had been "electioneering for him to court my young mistress, and talked for him." (The young Miss Linder rebuffed the suggestion. "Uncle," she told Lipscomb, using the more respectful diminutive by which whites referred to older black men, "I wouldn't notice him any more than I would a cat.")

While the Bowdens watched, the mob accused Lipscomb of being a Republican, a "rattler," a member of the party of Lincoln and the Union. "I'll not deny my principles," Lipscomb replied, with a courage that today seems almost unimaginable. "I'll make you deny them," said Clum Petty, who then beat Lipscomb so fiercely that his arm would swell to twice its normal size. "[M]y fingers on this arm will never get right in the world," he would tell the Senate committee. "My fingers have no feeling." Stripping off Lipscomb's clothes, the mob took turns whipping him over the head and across his entire body, cutting deep welts into his flesh. One kicked Lipscomb so hard in the gut that, months later, he would still be incontinent. The mob finally kicked Lipscomb back toward his door and then dragged the Bowdens to a field a half-mile away.

The men had blindfolded Clem Bowden with his coat and put an ox halter chain around his neck. At the field, they kicked up his shirt, pulled down his pants, and made him lie on the ground. With strips of brush, and limbs torn from trees, they began beating him so hard he thought he might die (but "through the Merciful Master I did get away," he testified). The mob accused Bowden of trying to form a company of armed black militia in the area, a charge he denied. They accused him of being appointed one of the managers of the upcoming election—"I told them I supposed I was." They warned that if he participated in the election, they would come back and kill him. They asked whether he would cast his vote for the Republican candidate for governor, Robert K. Scott—"I told them if I voted at all, I would." They accused him of declaring that he would "commence on the white people at the cradle, and kill from that up"—"I told them I had never thought of such a thing, and I never had." One of the men cut off part of Bowden's left ear with two or three licks of his knife, cursing all the while.

Another crowd of whites, about fifty men, was approaching. Thinking they had come to rescue the Bowdens, those holding them scattered and formed a battle line, ready to fight. But they soon discovered that the new group was part of the same conspiracy, and had brought with them a new captive, William Champion. Clem Bowden knew "Buster"

Champion well. "I went to mill to him," he would tell the committee, "and he was also teaching a Sunday school. We were sort of engaged in teaching the Sunday school close to my house, and he was going to change it into a two-day school; two days in the week."[3] Champion also knew local blacks through his participation in the Union League, a Republican club, and was known to have read legal books to former slaves, advising them of their property rights. Among the local Democratic elite, of course, he was a man of "rather low repute." Among his other transgressions, real or imagined, he was alleged to have said that whites in the area "might just as well come to social equality with the negro first as last, and invite them to eat at their tables and sleep in their beds; if they did not they would be made to do it by the bayonet."

Champion had been dragged from his home much as the Bowdens had. "You damned radical son of a bitch!" the mob shouted, tearing through his house, guns firing. Rufus Erwin, who happened to be staying with Champion that night, took a shot directly under the collarbone. The mob warned Champion to start praying. "I told them," Champion said, "that I was praying all I could." The men led him to the field where their compatriots had taken Clem and Minerva Bowden. There, the mob blindfolded him, took down his pants, and whipped him "as much as I was able to bear," all the while shouting "you damned old radical son of a bitch!" The beating was so severe that by the time Champion could remove his shirt, it was "stiff with blood," and his back "was black, and so sore that I could scarcely go anywhere for days."

Just as Champion was about to faint, the beating stopped. The men made him kiss Bowden's head. They held open Bowden's buttocks and forced Champion to kiss his anus, making Bowden "tell them when his mouth was at the place." They then forced him to kiss Minerva Bowden's "private parts," and ordered him to "have sexual connection with her" (when Champion told the mob that "they knew, of course, I could not do that," some "begged" him to do so, while others beat him). "How do you like that for nigger equality?" the men shouted. "I told them," Champion said, "it was pretty tough." After the men removed Champion's blindfold, they forced him to whip Clem Bowden. They then forced Clem Bowden, with what little strength he had left, to whip William Champion. In the meantime, the men beat Minerva Bowden "[u]ntil she was helpless," accusing her of boasting that she wanted to kill a Democrat, and admonishing her "that she might have taught [her husband] better than to be a radical."

About three weeks after the beating, Champion received a note marked "Headquarters Ku-Klux Clan, Algood, S.C." "Mr. Buster Champion," the note read, "We have been told that our visit to you was not a sufficient hint. We now notify you to leave the country within thirty days from the reception of this notice, or abide the consequences." Champion remained in the area, but like other Republicans, black and white, he slept in the woods at night, terrified for his life. Daniel Lipscomb went into hiding as well, lying out at night in the hail and rain, losing most of his crop of potatoes, cabbages, and molasses. As for the Bowdens, when they returned home that night, they were so badly hurt that they "could not kindle up a fire to warm ourselves by, if our children had not been there to kindle it for us." They left their home immediately, traveling thirteen miles despite their injuries, and lost most of their crop of corn and cotton. Beginning in February, Clem and Minerva Bowden began to sleep apart. Clem stayed at the edge of town, while Minerva and the children kept their distance, afraid to stay with their husband and father "for fear of being destroyed."[4]

Leather strap, oak switch, or rope lash, the whip has been an eloquent orator in American civic life. The welts it articulates upon a man or woman's body proclaim a host of political ideas to which few others, short of the noose, could give such clear expression. The whip is the tool but also the rhetorical incarnation of a particular vision of race and jurisprudence. The whip says: you are black flesh only, dirt and blood. It says: you are dead already, honor lost. It says: stay, live in exile beneath us. The whip speaks and, in speaking, endeavors to create a world. Even after the whip ceased to be the enforcer of slavery's dominion, it remained an enforcer of the American caste system. There are few more effective ways one human can humiliate another.

In 1870, the whip spoke with terrifying force in South Carolina, as it did throughout the former Confederacy. The triumph of the Union had set in motion an unprecedented challenge to the foundation of southern society: a demand that blacks be called citizens. The challenge came, especially, from the Thirty-ninth Congress, which included such radicals as Charles Sumner and Thaddeus Stevens, who were enraged by the work of southern legislatures that had gained power under President Johnson's conciliatory postwar administration. Believing that the Confederate states would be promptly reincorporated into the Union on easy terms, southern leaders had enacted a host of so-called Black Codes designed to ensure that if blacks could no longer be slaves, at least their social and political inferiority to whites would be preserved. And so not long after Appomattox, new battle lines were being drawn, with a victorious northern army and a Republican congress arrayed against a recalcitrant South, in a fight over the right of blacks to greater or equal place within national civic life.

The range of efforts to extend black citizenship during this era, known as Reconstruction, represents one of the most promising reform movements in American history. The best known of these was the Freedman's Bureau. The Bureau provided freedmen with food, shelter, and medicine; it helped them find family members from whom they had been separated under slavery (after emancipation, blacks took to the roads by the thousands in search of lost loved ones); it established an extensive network of free schools; it helped blacks make legal contracts; it settled disputes; and it sought to quell racial violence. In a far more radical vein, some officials, especially in the government of South Carolina, also made scattered efforts at land redistribution, putting property confiscated from former Confederates into the hands of their one-time servants—an extraordinary idea in a nation committed to the sanctity of private property, yet one not beyond moral reason considering blacks had produced much of the wealth of the antebellum South through their unremunerated labor. (Such efforts to establish black economic self-sufficiency were abandoned too early to have wide or enduring effect.)

Notably, the most lasting efforts to bring former slaves into the circle of American civic life were legal—especially the three so-called Reconstruction Amendments to the U.S. Constitution. The first of these was the moral capstone of the Union victory. Ratified in 1865, the Thirteenth Amendment banned slavery and involuntary servitude throughout the United States, except as a punishment for crime, and so abrogated the basic legal disability underlying black subordination in the South. Lincoln's Emancipation Proclamation of 1863 was the harbinger, but the Proclamation applied only to those areas of the Union still in rebellion. The Thirteenth Amendment was the actual instrument that ended two hundred years of chattel slavery in America and made blacks free under law. It would have pleased John Brown that one of the most important forces behind the amendment had been the action of blacks themselves, who had sought protection with Union forces during the war and, in their drive to fight the Confederacy, helped make emancipation a feature of northern military strategy.

The Fifteenth Amendment, ratified in 1870, was aimed at black enfranchisement. "The right of citizens of the United States to vote," it announced, "shall not be denied or abridged by the United States or by any State on account of race, color, or previous condition of servitude." In theory, the measure provided black men with the most basic privilege of citizenship in a republic: the right to participate in the election of political leaders. It was by no means an act of pure idealism, free of partisan calculation (it was assumed that black voters would constitute an essential base for keeping the Republican Party in power in the South), yet its civic vision could have scarcely been more radical. In 1860, most blacks lived in a world of absolute political disability. The notion that a largely illiterate servant class, presumably vulnerable to bribery and coercion, would be given a say in determining the composition of their state and national political leadership seemed absurd, indeed dangerous. But by 1870, black men who had been slaves only a few years earlier were placing tickets in ballot boxes.

The Fourteenth Amendment, ratified in 1868, was potentially more radical still, and it has been the subject of more litigation than any other part of the Constitution. Its first section reads as follows:

> All persons born or naturalized in the United States, and subject to the jurisdiction thereof, are citizens of the United States and of the State wherein they reside. No State shall make or enforce any law which shall abridge the privileges or immunities of citizens of the United States; nor shall any State deprive any person of life, liberty, or property without due process of law; nor deny to any person within its jurisdiction the equal protection of the laws.

The final section granted Congress the power to enforce these rights "through appropriate legislation." The amendment may seem unassumingly vague, but it enacted a fundamental change, a revolution, in our understanding of civic capacity—for blacks and other minorities alike, for the amendment speaks of "persons" without regard to race—and, ultimately, in the distribution of power between state and national governments. If the Thirteenth Amendment defined what blacks were not (that is, slaves), the Fourteenth spelled out what they were: as persons "born or naturalized in the United States," they were "citizens of the United States and of the State wherein they reside"—*Dred Scott* was dead. The amendment further shielded blacks from attempts by state governments to undercut their civic membership, by declaring that states could not deny blacks the "privileges or immunities" of national citizenship, nor lawfully withhold the "due process of law" and "equal protection of the laws" to which they were entitled.

The precise meaning of the phrases "privileges or immunities," "due process of law," and "equal protection of the laws" would be the subject of intense debate over many decades and in important ways to this day. They certainly guaranteed the right to make contracts, to marry, to hold property, and to have access to the justice system, some of the basic elements of the Civil Rights Act of 1866, for which the Fourteenth Amendment was intended to provide a firm legal foundation. It remained an open question whether they also referred to most of those rights enumerated in the Bill of Rights—for instance, the right to keep and bear arms guaranteed in the Second Amendment (the Bill of Rights applies to the federal government, and the place of the Second Amendment in relation to states remains unclear even today).

In the most simple and dramatic terms, the Reconstruction Amendments may be understood in the following way. The Thirteenth Amendment guaranteed blacks *freedom from bondage:* it ended slavery. The Fourteenth Amendment promised blacks *civil rights:* it made them citizens. And the Fifteenth Amendment promised them the key *political right:* it gave blacks the vote. Moreover, the amendments signaled a fundamental cultural change, or at least the promise of it: the destruction of one vision of civic jurisprudence and its replacement with another, one incorporating blacks directly into the circle of national belonging; a civic culture of caste would be supplanted by one of liberal rights.

These were radical commitments, unthinkable before the war, and they drew contempt and resistance throughout the South, resistance in which the rule of the whip would play a central role. Such was the case in South Carolina, where two organizations in particular symbolized for whites the liberal threat. Those groups were a political association called the Union League and a collection of military units known as the black militia. The Union League was a political club, originating in the North, dedicated to supporting the Union during the war and to facilitating Republican rule during Reconstruction. In its support of black voting, it also was the ideal of the Fifteenth Amendment made flesh. It was composed of both white and black members, and its expressed objective was "to preserve liberty and the Union of the United States of America; to maintain the Constitution thereof and the supremacy of the laws; to sustain the Government and assist in putting down its enemies; to protect, strengthen and defend all loyal men, without regard to sect, condition, or race; to elect honest and reliable Union men to all offices of profit or trust in National, State, and local government; and to secure equal civil and political rights to all men under the Government." At League meetings, an American flag was draped upon an altar, upon which was placed an open Bible and copies of the Declaration of Independence and the Constitution. On initiation, new members stood before the altar to swear their allegiance, surrounded by a circle of old members holding hands. They were then admitted into the circle, "in which all are welcome."[5]

The welcome had more than symbolic effect. Under the terms of southern readmission to the Union, Confederates who had taken an oath to uphold the federal Constitution before the war—that is, all men who had served in positions of political and legal authority—were stripped of their voting rights. And so former slaves, assisted by the Union Leagues, were casting their ballots even as the "best men" of the state were barred from the polls, a stunning inversion of the traditional political order. Republicans thereby won a handy majority in the South Carolina elections of 1868, resulting in a lower house of the state legislature that was mostly black, an upper house roughly half black, and a "carpetbagger" governor, Robert K. Scott, who was a former Assistant Commissioner in the Freedman's Bureau. The new South Carolina legislature passed a variety of measures to assist former slaves in their transition to freedom, and financed the programs with substantial property tax increases, forcing whites to finance black social reform. Whites who failed to pay risked forfeiture of their land, which might then be redistributed to former slaves.

The black militias represented an even greater threat. A South Carolina law of 1869 gave the governor authority to form militia companies to suppress insurrection and counter resistance to law. Most South Carolina whites viewed bearing arms side by side with former slaves as repugnant and dishonorable, and were loath to enforce the decrees of a state government they considered to be illegitimate, and so the militias became Republican and notably black. Between 90,000 and 100,000 blacks joined and 11,000 were furnished with breech-loading weapons. The fear this aroused in whites can scarcely be overestimated. In the racial powder keg that existed before the war, the slightest suggestion of black violence toward whites could incite a panic. Blacks were barred even from owning drums for fear these would be used to communicate secret bloody plots. Only a decade later, blacks were filling the air with drum rolls and brandishing rifles, courtesy of a government indebted to armies that had recently reduced a good deal of the South to scorched earth. Whites now feared a race war of vengeance—and who, imagining oneself in the place of a recently freed slave, would deem such fears were entirely unjustified?

In constitutional terms, if the Union Leagues embodied the promise (and, for southern whites, the dangers) of the Fifteenth Amendment, the black militias symbolized the threat of the Fourteenth. They represented the amendment's incorporation of blacks into the civic world of the Bill of Rights, transforming them into the sort of gun-bearing citizens contemplated by the Second Amendment and long central to republican notions of citizenship. Moreover, in a state with a strong military tradition, uniformed black militias, like those blacks who served in the Union Army, were emblems of white humiliation: blacks parading in the streets, drilling on the town square, refusing to yield the sidewalk to white men—and white women. Even more forcefully than the Union Leagues, the militias brought blacks into the circle of American civic belonging by making them party to the ultimate power of the state: the lawful taking of life. Calling upon blacks potentially to kill and die in defense of the law, the militias placed blacks in a new relation to legality. For this is the movement of the soldier: by offering his body as a sacrifice to the state, he is taken into its fold.

The blue may have vanquished the gray on the field of battle in 1865, and the Reconstruction Amendments may have been ratified shortly thereafter, but the traditional law of the South did not simply vanish in the wake of northern armies and constitutional amendments. It continued to live within the hearts of those who held it dear. While many northerners considered southern civic jurisprudence destroyed, repealed, and transformed, to most white southerners their law was merely in abeyance—temporarily stateless. The great hope of the defeated but unbowed Confederacy was to continue its enforcement by informal means, nurturing its memory among both whites and blacks and, ultimately, to reestablish the civic principles of racial purity and pollution as the foundation of government. The instrument of their vision was an extralegal conspiracy called the Ku Klux Klan.

Though all related, there have been three distinct flourishings of the Klan in American history, one of the 1950s and 1960s, another of the 1920s, and the original one of the 1870s. (As it exists in the early twenty-first century, the Klan is so isolated, disorganized, and small as to

scarcely merit mention with its predecessors.) Our contemporary sense
of the Klan is based largely on the organization of the 1950s and 1960s,
which arose in opposition to Communism and the Civil Rights Movement. That Klan was largely southern and urban, and drew its membership from poor, ill-educated whites. Its members were dedicated to and,
in principle, prepared to engage in racial violence, though in practice it
was much less potent than in lore, and it never numbered more than
17,000. By contrast, the Klan of the 1920s, known for its Protestant fun-
damentalism and its loathing of blacks, Jews, Catholics, immigrants, and
organized labor, while drawing its membership largely from urban
whites of the lower middle class, also boasted leaders from the highest
ranks of society, and its active membership extended well north of the
Mason-Dixon line. At its height, this Klan counted three *million* members, and achieved political power in states as far flung as Indiana, Oklahoma, and Oregon. Significantly, the Klan at this time did not engage in
extensive physical violence; its primary activities were directed at symbolic politics, for instance marching in parades (the lynchings of the
1920s were by and large not directly attributable to the Klan, but rather
to informal bands of white citizens acting in concert).

The original Klan, the Klan of Reconstruction, was substantially
different from both of these later manifestations in both numbers and
activity. Founded in 1866 in Pulaski, Tennessee, the Klan drew its name
from the Greek word *kyklos*, meaning "circle" or "band," which was
transliterated into "Ku Klux," with "Klan" added, one supposes, for
alliterative effect. The Klan quickly transformed from a kind of local
social club for ex-Confederates into a secret paramilitary organization
throughout the South; while its leaders came from the upper crust of
white society, its rank and file spanned the social spectrum, and its sympathizers included most whites of the former Confederacy. Loose and
relatively decentralized, the Klan was divided into "covens," or county
chapters, all committed to black subjugation and intimidation.

Included among the Klan's arcane bylaws was a chivalrous oath
sworn by every Klansman during an initiation ceremony. Before "the
immaculate Judge of Heaven and earth," the initiate pledged himself of
his own free will to the following "sacredly binding obligation": "1. We
are on the side of justice, humanity, and constitutional liberty as
bequeathed to us in its original purity by our forefathers. 2. We oppose
and reject the principles of the radical party. 3. We pledge mutual aid to
each other in sickness, distress, and pecuniary embarrassment. 4. Female
friends, widows, and their households shall ever be special objects of our

regard and protection. Any member divulging, or causing to be divulged, any of the foregoing obligation, shall meet the fearful penalty and traitor's doom, which is death! death! death!" As a statement of the legal and civic ideals of the Klan, the oath entwined opposition to the Reconstruction Amendments, which had sullied the Constitution "in its original purity"; hatred of the Republican Party that had caused those impure amendments to be ratified; and a courtly reverence of the southern white womanhood that stood at the heart of traditional caste society. These principles translated into a specific set of practical objectives: to prevent blacks from voting and so undermine the Republican Party; to disarm blacks and so diffuse any real or symbolic threat they posed to whites; and to subordinate blacks socially through the instrument of humiliation.[6]

In 1870, the Klan rode throughout up-country South Carolina, where the balance of political power between Republicans and Democrats was delicate enough to be tipped by physical intimidation. Typically, raiders came by night on horseback in solid-colored gowns, hoods, or "false faces," some with horns strapped to their heads to suggest demons from the underworld. In addition to searching for weapons and violently interrogating black men, including savage beatings and threats of murder, at times Klan raisers would beat and sexually molest black women. In the furtherance of their disguise, they would speak in foreign accents or in outlandish tones (sometimes to no avail: many of the blacks they whipped knew them very well, and could identify them by some distinct feature such as the shape of their fingers—such was the intimacy of the violence). As for the black victims, many of their voices have been preserved, in the transcripts of the Joint Select Committee to Inquire into the Condition of Affairs in the Late Insurrectionary States, which form some of the most extensive records of black life during Reconstruction—and which constitute a lasting cultural legacy of the federal effort to destroy the Invisible Empire.

It is worth pausing to hear some of those voices, if only to understand how routine was the ghastly brutality that befell Clem and Minerva Bowden.

Samuel Bonner, twenty-nine, a sharecropper, was visited by seven or eight men at his home "about corn-planting time," in early April 1870. "It was between midnight and day," testified Bonner, who along with his mother and sister, was in bed. "When I woke up they had come to the door and knocked it down, and were standing hallooing. The first I heard was, 'Come out, come out, God damned you, come out.' It amazed and scared me, and I got up. I stood there a few minutes, and after a time I came out among them. They said, 'Shoot him, shoot him, shoot him.'" Bonner asked the men what quarrel they had with him. "They said God damn me," he reported, "I had done nothing, but they 'low'd to whip me to let me know I had a master." Firing their guns near Bonner's head, scaring him "within an inch of my life," the men asked whether he had voted for Robert K. Scott. When Bonner replied affirmatively, they shouted, "Yes, I can smell you now, you are a damned radical." Bonner said he supposed he was a radical, and that "I thought it was right." The men then whipped Bonner's mother and sister, shouting "damn her, she is a nigger; just whip it on her, damn her." Then they dragged him to a field about fifty yards away, where there were thirty others waiting on horseback, in gowns and horns, to beat him senseless.[7]

Here is Harriet Hernandes. She was visited one night by a gang of Klansmen looking for her husband, Charley. "They took me out of bed," Hernandes testified. "They would not let me get out, but they took me up in their arms and toted me out—me and my daughter Lucy. He [one of the unidentified assailants] struck me on the forehead with a pistol, and here is the scar above my eye now. Says he, 'Damn you, fall!' I fell. Says he, 'Damn you, get up!' I got up. Says he, 'Damn you, get over this fence!' and he kicked me over when I went to get over; and then he went on to a brush pile, and they laid us right down there, both together. They laid us down twenty yards apart, I reckon. They had dragged and beat us along. They struck me right on top of my head, and I thought they had killed me; and I said, 'Lord o' mercy, don't, don't kill my child!' He gave me a lick on the head, and it liked to have killed me; I saw stars. He threw my arm over my head so I could not do anything with it for three weeks, and there are great knots on my wrist now."[8]

Caleb Jenkins reported. "They came in on me, and the gentlemen hit at the door and called my name, 'Caleb, open the door.' I got up and said, 'I will open the door.' As I got up he fired three balls, and shot three times in the house, and told me to raise a light. I hastened and raised a light. He asked me did I know him. I looked at him and said, 'I thought I knew your voice, but I can't say I know you.' He says, 'You don't know me, I am from Manassas.'"[9]

The Klansmen who called on Dick Wilson, a member of the Union League, claimed to have risen from the dead. They ordered Wilson to drop his pants and stretch out on the ground, before whipping him with white oak and, perhaps, iron ramrods. "One went that side, and two on this side," he testified. "Well, they commenced whipping me; I commenced begging them so powerful. 'Don't beg, God damn you. If you beg I'll kill you.' . . . They just ruined me; they cut me all to pieces; they did do it, and I wouldn't mind it so much if they had scattered the licks, but they whipped all in one place. That is what they done. They stopped on me then for a while. 'Will you vote the democratic ticket next time?' 'Yes, I will vote any way you want me to vote. I don't care how you want me to vote, master, I will vote.' . . . I was whipped badly. I had on me a pair of pants too large, and next day I had to tie a string on them so they would meet." Wilson knew some of the men who had beaten him. Of Mr. Lowrey, for instance, he testified, "He has a white hand, but has a finger that stands crooked." It was a keen observation considering his duress. "I went a purpose to see who they was," he said, "whether they were spirits, or whether they were human; but when I came to find out, they was men like me."[10]

Such stories are innumerable: Tom Roundtree, murdered by a mob of fifty or sixty, shot, his throat cut; Anderson Brown, shot and killed; Alexander Leech, shot, his body thrown into Bullock's Creek to be found two weeks later; Mathew Boyce, shot in the head; Lot Campbell, shot in broad daylight; Creecy Adams, whipped almost to death; John Moss, a white man, whipped; Charley Barron's wife, beaten; Sam Simmrell, severely whipped, his house burned; his wife, whipped and "ravished"; Jordan Tate, beaten severely; his son, whipped and beaten; Martha, a girl living at the Tates', whipped; Abraham Webb's daughter, "whipped and made to dance"; Abner Hambright, a white man, whipped and partly hanged; Peter Watson, whipped; Sylvester Barron, a boy, whipped with clubs and pistols; Addison Woods, beaten with a gun; Reverend Elias Hill, a crippled black man unable to walk, sit, or crawl, who could turn himself over in bed only with his "prize-stick," and yet a literate leader of his community, dragged and beaten in the cold, his house ransacked; June Moore, cursed and abused; Polly Weaver, a white woman, whipped; Reverend Elias Hill's mother, whipped; Pink Johnson, pursued and persecuted; Lucinda Hill, his wife, whipped; Julia Barron, whipped; Preacher Foster and his wife, beaten; William Wright, whipped, his house burned; Wilson Thompson, whipped; Edward Patterson, whipped; John Wright, whipped; Robin Black, whipped—and these events only a handful among many more, largely within a few months and in a single county.

Major Lewis Merrill had led a renowned cavalry unit, "Merrill's Horse," which had fought Confederate guerrillas in Missouri. Now as commander of the 7th Cavalry, he began in early 1871 to investigate allegations of the "Ku-Klux" conspiracy in the South Carolina up-country. A paragon of integrity, when asked about his political affiliations, he replied sternly, "I am an officer in the Army, bred up in a school which taught me that officers of the army were not proper persons to mix in politics." Upon arriving in South Carolina from Kansas, this man of hard facts later recalled, "I fully believed that the stories in circulation were enormous exaggerations." At the very most, he expected "a few occasional cases [of violence] that might be regarded rather as vigilance committee matters than anything else." And during his first days in York County, the major's initial suspicions were confirmed, especially in conversations with the "principal people" of the area.[11]

But with Major Merrill's further methodical inquiry, he discovered that the hold of the Ku Klux Klan on the South Carolina up-country was more absolute and violent than he or his superiors in Washington could ever have imagined. "I am now of the opinion," he told congressional investigators in July 1871, after five months in the Palmetto State, "that I never conceived of such a state of social disorganization being possible in any civilized community as exists in this county now." And after witnessing how civil authorities conspired with the Klan, he reported to the Secretary of War in early January 1872: "The facts as now found are astounding, and it is impossible to make even the most temperate statement of them without risk of being suspected of exaggeration. . . . [T]he conspiracy may be stated to have practically included the whole white community within the ages when active participation in public affairs was possible." He was particularly aggrieved at those "principal people" whom he had originally trusted. "The social leaders," wrote Major Merrill, "have a most uncompromising hostility to the citizenship of the negro, and have never yet recognized his right to fair and just treatment, or to the equal protection of the law, and their hostility extends to all who maintain his rights and politically fraternize with him. These men have ruled Northwest South Carolina with a rod of iron."[12]

Defying what the major called "[t]he theory of all ordinary regulations of civilized society," in which "every hand will be against criminals," the situation demanded drastic action. With every white hand raised in support of the conspiracy, the major argued, "it is certainly evident that . . . no ordinary methods are equal to the suppression or punishment of [Ku Klux] crime." The extensive, coordinated violence of the Klan threatened not only South Carolina blacks and Republicans, but the foundation of government itself. To this extraordinary situation, President Ulysses S. Grant, who succeeded President Johnson, responded decisively, lobbying Congress to strengthen the ability of federal authorities to safeguard black rights. The so-called Ku Klux Klan Act would be one in a series of three "Enforcement Acts" empowering federal officials to enforce the guarantees of the Fourteenth and Fifteenth Amendments against not only state governments, to which the amendments explicitly referred, but also private parties—to which they did not. The first, passed in May 1870, sought to protect the black right to vote, in part by making it a crime for individuals to conspire to ride public highways to deprive a citizen of "any right or privilege granted or secured to him by [the] constitution or laws of the United States." The Ku Klux Klan Act, passed in April 1871, was designed to destroy the Klan itself. It not only outlawed a range of conspiracies to deny civil rights, but also increased federal authority directly to quash Klan activities, most controversially by authorizing the President to suspend the writ of habeas corpus. The Enforcement Acts became the first comprehensive national criminal law, enabling Klansmen to be prosecuted en masse in federal court under the direction of the national Department of Justice.

With the authority of the Ku Klux Klan Act behind him, President Grant declared nine counties in up-country South Carolina to be in active rebellion: Newberry, Laurens, Fairfield, Chester, Lancaster, Chesterfield, Union, York, and Spartanburg. The suspension of the writ of habeas corpus there allowed federal authorities to take bold action—with the assistance of the 7th Cavalry and Major Merrill's network of black spies, they swooped down upon the Klansmen with a wide net. "The troops were so disposed," the major wrote,

> that a large number of arrests were effected simultaneously over [York] county. The effect of this, coupled with the fact that it was instantly apparent to the Ku-Klux that no blow was struck in the dark, and no arrests made at random or on mere suspicion, was surprising. The rank and file were bewildered and demoralized. Looking about for their chiefs and counselors, and finding that, to get orders or advice, they must go to them in jail or follow their flight, they recognized the fact that the game was up, that the organization was broken, and all over the country they betook themselves to flight or came in and surrendered. . . . Conspirators against the well-being of society, of every grade of criminality, have come in and surrendered by the score. . . . In some instances whole Klans, headed by their chief, came in and surrendered together.[13]

Prosecuting all of those taken into custody would have been impossible and, indeed, by legal principles of culpability, undesirable. But in York County, 169 Klansmen were charged with a violation of the law and given the choice of confessing their guilt or standing trial in Charleston.

The judges who would oversee those trials would be Hugh Lenox Bond of Maryland and George Seabrook Bryan of South Carolina, men with almost opposite views of the legal questions at issue. Appointed to the federal bench by President Grant, Bond was committed to enforcing black rights in the South, and saw himself as part of a federal team working to destroy the Klan—"even," he said, "if it costs me my life." Yet his commitment to this effort was checked by his doubts about the constitutionality of the Ku Klux Klan Act, its application to individuals, and his respect for states' rights. Federalism, on the other hand, was at the very center of Judge Bryan's legal ideals. A Democrat and former slave owner, he had argued against secession before the war, and on that basis President Johnson appointed him to the bench, allowing him to reopen federal civil courts in his state. Judge Bond, the presiding judge, was under no illusions about the chance of obtaining his colleague's sympathy. "I am with a peck of trouble with old Bryan," he wrote. "The democrats have got hold of him—visit him in crowds & persuade him to be a stick between our legs at every step. . . . [T]hey have stuffed him full of the idea that the Democrats will make him Gov[ernor] if he differ[s] with me."[14]

The prosecution was geared for a fight. Guided from afar by Attorney General Amos T. Akerman in Washington, first head of the Department of Justice (which had been created in 1870), the trial team was led on the ground by Daniel T. Corbin and Daniel H. Chamberlain. The United States Attorney for South Carolina from 1867 to 1876, Corbin was a prominent Republican whose résumé included undergraduate study at Dartmouth, law practice in Vermont, a stint in the Union Army and the Freedman's Bureau, and, after the war, election to the South Carolina State Senate. The trial record shows him to be an able and tenacious litigant. His colleague, Daniel Chamberlain, a scholarly abolitionist from Massachusetts who attended Harvard and Yale, had served as an officer in the Civil War in command of a black troop (though he saw no fighting) before entering South Carolina politics at war's end. And behind them both stood Major Merrill.

As it needed to be, the defense team was no less eminent—indeed, it was more so. It included Reverdy Johnson, former U.S. Senator from Maryland, and Henry Stanbery of Ohio, each of whom had served a term as Attorney General of the United States. Their fees were paid in part by a subscription campaign led by Wade Hampton, a Confederate war hero and future reactionary governor of South Carolina. Johnson, a Union man who welcomed the end of slavery, nevertheless harbored strong sympathies for the white South. An expert in constitutional law, and perhaps the most expensive lawyer of his day, he had argued on behalf of southern interests in *Dred Scott*. He was especially concerned with protecting state power and resisting the extension of national authority over individual civil rights, and after many years would succeed in having the Enforcement Acts declared unconstitutional. Johnson's well-bred charm during the Klan trials masked a desire for obstruction and nullification. His cocounsel, however, dispensed entirely with charm. A tireless Democratic critic of Reconstruction, Henry Stanbery had defended President Johnson during his impeachment trial, and he looked forward to the restoration of the "best men" of the South to political power.

The prosecution and the defense had their eyes on the same prize: both sought to extend the meaning of the Ku Klux Klan trials beyond their implications for the individual defendants and to address themselves to the constitutional issues underlying the Enforcement Acts. And so Corbin and Chamberlain's goal was not simply to convict the steady stream of poor whites and "best men" who stood accused, a relatively straightforward matter under the conspiracy provisions of the Act. Instead, they wanted to secure the incorporation of blacks into the national civic community by asserting a broad, nationalist interpretation of the power of the Reconstruction Amendments. The defense, for its part, was not hoping merely to keep its clients out of prison. It aspired instead to persuade the judges that the Enforcement Acts, or at least their most important provisions, were null and void as beyond the scope of federal power.

In this larger legal effort, both prosecution and defense would be disappointed. Defense objections forced the prosecution to drop the central constitutional claims from its indictments, rendering it impossible for either party to satisfy its grandest doctrinal ambitions through appeal to the Supreme Court. But victories were to be had in other ways, especially for federal authorities, political and institutional benefits to blacks in the immediate term alongside a host of cultural triumphs.

The proceedings against the Klan began on November 28, 1871, with crowds of spectators, reporters, and black witnesses thronging the courtroom. As prospective jurors in Enforcement Act proceedings were required to swear an oath that they had never taken part in Klan activities, most of those empaneled were not white—fifteen of the twenty-one grand jurymen and over two-thirds of the petit jurors were black. For former Confederates, it was a world, or at least the law, turned upside down.

The first case that came to trial concerned the murder of Jim Williams, also known as James Rainey, a Republican captain of a company of black militia in York County who, during the war, had served under General Sherman. Among blacks as among some whites, Williams was known to be a respectful, peaceable, law-abiding community leader who insisted on his rights, but nothing more. Other whites, however, considered him a "pretty independent negro," a term of foreboding derision, a "bad boy" with a violent streak. They believed Williams had probably incited several acts of arson that had destroyed a handful of white gin houses and barns in the area. Some even claimed to have heard Williams vow to kill whites "from the cradle to the grave."[15]

These are the basic facts of his death. On March 6, 1871, a group of between forty and sixty whites met on horseback in the Briar Patch, an old muster field in York County. They included Chambers Brown; Sylvanus, William, James, and Hugh Shearer; Robert Riggins; Hugh Kell; Henry Warlock; Napoleon Miller; Alonzo Brown; William Johnson; James Neal; Addison and Miles Carroll; Harvey Gunning; Robert and John Caldwell; Rufus McLean; Bascom Kennedy; Holbrook Good; Richard Bigham; Eli Ross Stewart; Samuel Ferguson; Joe Martin—and the first man who would be tried for the crime, Robert Hayes Mitchell. Their leader was Dr. James Rufus Bratton, one of the local "best men"; his immediate Klan superior was Major James Avery, another of the "best men," who ordered the raid and murder to come. Bratton was a descendant of Revolutionary War heroes, the first cousin of the great Confederate General John Bratton, and himself a distinguished surgeon during the war. For all their public service, the Brattons' dedication to preserving the Old South partook of none of the paternalism or noblesse oblige that at times had characterized race relations under slavery. From General Bratton, you "expected nothin', got nothin'."[16]

According to the prosecution, that night Dr. Bratton and his gang tore through the county, dragging scores of blacks from their homes, whipping them, and seizing their guns. They warned their victims that if they cast another vote it would be their last. During the rampage, about twelve men separated from the main group of Klansmen and followed Dr. Bratton to the home of Jim Williams. They then broke inside, dragged him from his screaming wife, and hanged him in the nearby woods. After the murder, they rode to the yard of John S. Bratton, Dr. Bratton's kinsman, where they ate cheese and crackers and drank two bottles of whiskey.

Like many Klan leaders in the South Carolina up-country, Dr. Bratton had fled after President Grant declared the area to be in active rebellion; he was now hiding in Canada, newly confederated in 1867. An attempt by U.S. agents to seize and bring him to justice had outraged the Canadian authorities, who successfully petitioned for his return; the memory of Union threats to invade its British northern neighbor during the war remained. But the rank-and-file Klansmen who had joined Bratton's raid, many of them poor, uneducated whites, had remained in York. Among them was the first defendant in the Ku Klux Klan trials, Robert Hayes Mitchell.

Robert Mitchell had not taken direct part in the killing of Jim Williams—he had stayed behind when Bratton and the others rode to Williams's home. Accordingly, he was charged not with murder but with two counts under one of the Enforcement Acts: participating in a general conspiracy to prevent citizens from voting in future elections on account of their race, and participating in a conspiracy to injure Jim Williams for having previously exercised his right to vote. The task of the prosecution was, therefore, to show that the Ku Klux Klan was formed, among other purposes, as a conspiracy to prevent blacks from voting; to show that on March 6, a group of Klansmen terrorized York County and, during their raid, killed Jim Williams; and, finally, to show that Robert Hayes Mitchell participated in that night's organized terror. As for the defense, it took the path of obfuscation. Its strategy was to argue that the Ku Klux Klan was formed not to prevent blacks from voting, but to defend whites against black assaults; moreover, it hoped to confuse the jury by asserting that Mitchell had taken no part in the actual murder of Jim Williams—an irrelevant issue legally but a ruse that might lead to an acquittal.

The prosecution opened its case with a nod to the black jurors' new legal and civic capacity and an assertion that it laid at the heart of the trial. "May it please the court and gentlemen of the jury," Corbin began, the novelty of the honorific doubtless not lost on the twelve to whom it referred. "The case now to be presented to you is one of an unusual importance. . . . The defendant, who is now called before you, is charged with having entered into a conspiracy, and it will be our purpose, gentlemen of the jury, to prove to you that he has entered into the conspiracy, for the purpose of preventing and restraining divers male citizens of the United States, of African descent, and qualified to vote, from exercising the right of voting.

"We shall endeavor to show an organization," he continued, "perfect in all its details, armed and disguised; that this organization was bound together by a terrible oath, the penalty for breaking of which was declared to be that of a traitor—death! death! death! We shall show that this organization had a constitution and bylaws; that it pervaded the whole country, or a large portion of it . . . that great numbers of colored citizens, who were entitled by law to vote in [this] county, were visited by the party and whipped, and many of them murdered. . . . In this case we shall show to you that this organization deliberately planned and executed the murder of [Jim] Williams."[17]

Corbin's first witness was Lieutenant Godfrey of the 11th Cavalry, who was stationed in Yorkville. The prosecutor handed him a piece of paper.

"Will you look at that paper and say whether you recognize it?" Corbin asked.

"I do recognize it."

"State where and how you obtained it."

"I was ordered on the night of the twentieth of October, Friday, by Colonel Merrill, commandant of the post at Yorkville, to proceed to the home of Samuel G. Brown, to obtain there the constitution and bylaws of the Ku-Klux Klan." The copy was found in Brown's desk, with the assistance of his daughter; it had been given to Brown by Albertus Hope, a white neighbor. In the desk, Godfrey had also found a list of members of the local Klan.[18]

The best men who remained for Corbin to call as witnesses, unsurprisingly, were less forthcoming about the document that Lieutenant Godfrey had found and, indeed, about the existence of the Klan. Ultimately, though, they broke under his examination. Asked to identify the same document as the one he was alleged to have given Brown, Albertus Hope haplessly tried to deny the chain of evidence: "I cannot say positively that it is; the paper has been used; I was not familiar with the handwriting of the document; if this be the paper, it has been used since it passed out of my hands."

"What do you mean by that?" asked Corbin, incredulously. "That it is dirty?"

"Yes, sir; it has been some time since it passed out of my hands, and I cannot be positively certain that it is the paper."

"Where did you get that paper that you gave to Mr. Brown?" Corbin asked.

"I think, as near as my memory serves me, that it was given me by Major Avery."

And so it went.

"Have you ever been a member of that Klan?" Corbin asked.

"I have not been a sworn member," Hope replied.

"Have you been inside the order and recognized as a member?"

"I never have, as I consider it."

"Did you ever attend meetings of this order?"

"Yes, sir; I did attend one, a statement of which I have given."

"Was it a meeting of the Ku-Klux Klan?" Corbin asked.

"I did not consider it so."

"Were you or not elected chief that night?"

"I was elected to govern that party; and allow me to state—"

"That is all I desire."

"The condition of the up-country demanded something at that time," Hope blurted. "They had been burning and making threats in the country, and it certainly did demand that something should be done. Word was left to my house to go to that meeting. I came very near not going; but when I did go I asked the object of the meeting, and it was said that, inasmuch as there had been so much burning and threats made round our country, it was necessary we should come to some understanding; that we should know where to get assistance if we needed it."

"Well, you organized a Klan?"

"Yes, sir; if you consider that an organization."

"And they elected you chief of that crowd, did they not?"

"They elected me leading officer of that party."[19]

As the outcome seemed more certain, other whites testified more readily, turning state's evidence in exchange for leniency. Kirkland L. Gunn, who had lived in York County since birth, admitted joining the Ku Klux Klan in January 1871 and to taking its oath.

Corbin asked him to describe this oath.

"The obligation, sir, that I took," Gunn explained, "was that I should not divulge any part of the secrets of the Klan that I had joined, and it was for the purpose of putting down radical rule and negro suffrage." During his initiation, Gunn said, he knelt, and was read the constitution and bylaws of the organization.

Corbin handed Gunn the paper retrieved from Brown's desk. Gunn examined it and replied: "Sir, that is in substance the same that I heard read. This obligation is the same, sir, and I think the constitution is the same in substance."

"Mr. Gunn," Corbin continued, "you have stated the general purposes of the order, now will you please state to the jury how those purposes were to be carried into effect?"

"Well, sir, that is known, I think," Gunn replied. "But the way that I was told that they were going to carry this into effect was by killing off the white radicals, and by whipping and intimidating the negroes, so as to keep them from voting for any men who held radical offices."

"Now tell us what some of the signs and passwords of the order were," Corbin asked. The secrets of the order poured forth.

"This was the first sign," Gunn explained, passing his hand forward over his right ear. "It was to be answered the same way by the left hand. This is the next sign," he continued, inserting the four fingers of his right hand into his pantaloons pocket, his thumb remaining outside.

"What was the reply to it?"

"It was to be returned that way," Gunn demonstrated, giving the same sign with his left hand. "Then," he continued, "when you were sitting about, you could give the sign by turning your right heel into the hollow of your foot, to be returned with the left the same way. . . . The password was, if you met any one in the night you should spell the word, I-s-a-y, and not pronounce it; if it was a member of the order whom you met you would spell, N-o-t-h-i-n-g, and not pronounce it."

Their signal whistle, Gunn explained, was a shrill, gurgling noise.

Gunn even described attending a meeting in Georgia, indicating the extent of the Klan network. Asked to describe the agenda, Gunn replied, "The meeting that I was at was to raise money for the purpose of sending to South Carolina, they told me."

"For what purpose," Corbin continued.

"For paying lawyers' fees," Gunn replied, eliciting laughter in the courtroom, and sotto voce comments from the defense.

"I hope they raised it," said Reverdy Johnson under his breath.

"That is encouraging," added Henry Stanbery.

"I should think," noted Corbin to his opponents, "that would be comforting information to you."[20]

The most dramatic testimony came from those blacks whom Corbin and Chamberlain called to describe what happened the night Williams was murdered. Gadsden Steel, for instance, told of how the disguised, armed band that beat him that night had demanded to know which blacks in the area had guns, and that he replied that many had owned guns at one time but had voluntarily surrendered them recently to the governor. Asked whether Jim Williams had guns, Steel allowed he had heard as much, but was uncertain. "Don't tarry here too long with this damned nigger," one of the Klansmen then said, "we have to get back to hell before daybreak." Perhaps the Klansmen were trying to play on black folk beliefs, though in the process they conjured only their own misassessment of black credulity. "You go home and go to bed," another ordered, "and if you are not there when we come along we will kill you the next time we call on you; we are going on to kill Williams, and are going to kill all these damn niggers that votes the radical ticket; run, God damn you, run."

Jim Williams's widow entered her memories into the trial record as well. Her husband had dashed under the house before the Klansmen came that night, Rosy Williams testified. Once they burst through the door, though, he came inside, helpless and humiliated, and gave up two guns. The men asked "for the others, and cussed, and told him to come out." After persuading the raiders there were no guns in the house, "they went out, and after they had went out there I heard [Jim] make a fuss like he was strangling.

"Then I went to the door and pulled the door open, and allowed to go down and beg them not to hurt him. They told me not to go out there. Well, I didn't go out. Then they told me to shut the door and take my children and go to bed. I shut the door but didn't go to bed. I looked out of the crack after them until they got under the shadows of the trees.

"The next morning I went and looked for him, but I didn't find him. I was scared, too. Then I went for my people, to get some one to go help me look for him; and I met an old man who told me they had found him, and said he was dead."[21]

A black man named Andy Timons, a member of Captain Williams's company, helped complete the story.

"Do you know [Jim] Williams?" Corbin asked.

"Yes, sir; I knew him before he died; had been knowing him for some fifteen or twenty years."

"What occurred that night that he was hung," Corbin continued.

"That night, sir—I think it were something after 2 o'clock—there were three disguised men came to my house—came up cussing and swearing a great deal."

"Tell what they said."

"They said 'Here we come. We are the Ku-Klux. Here we come, right from hell'; and two rode up on one side of my house, and one to the other. . . . They commenced with their guns and beat at the doors, and hollering 'God damn you, open, open the doors.' I told them I would, and jumped out of bed; and before I got to the door they bursted the latch off, and two came in; and one got me by the arms and says, 'We want your guns.' I told them I didn't have any guns; there was one there, but not mine. It was turned over by some of the company.

"They got the gun, and asked for the accouterments belonging to the gun, and I got them for them; and after they got these things they asked for a pistol. I told them I didn't have any pistols at that time, and then they asked if I knew where Captain Williams lived. I told them I did. 'How far?' they asked. I told them about two miles, I think. Says he, 'We want to see your captain to-night. We don't want any more of you to-night.' Upon this they got on their horses."

With a group of other blacks, Timons then sped to Williams's house. When we got there," he explained, "Mrs. Williams was sitting in the door," and Williams was gone.

The men raced to assemble Williams's militia company and took off after the Klan. At Robert Linday's, "we noticed a great many tracks left the road. . . . [B]efore we got to the house we saw the tracks where they had come out of the field. We pursued on until we came to where the horses were hitched, which I thought was about one hundred yards. We saw Williams hanging on a tree."

It was now between nine and ten in the morning. Jim Williams hung from a pine. A note placed on his breast read: "Jim Williams on his big muster."

John Caldwell was a minor Klansman who had participated in the raid, but like Robert Mitchell remained behind while the murder took place.

"Before I got off my horse," Caldwell explained when Corbin examined him, "I heard someone call for ten men, and that party then went off. I saw them go off; and they were gone probably one hour when they returned." When the group returned, Caldwell asked if they had seen Jim Williams. "Mount your horses," some of the men ordered, taking off over a fence. When Caldwell rode to the front of the pack, led by Dr. Bratton, he asked once again "if he had found the negro." After Dr. Bratton said they had, Caldwell inquired as to his whereabouts. Dr. Bratton replied, "He is in hell, I expect."

"What further was said?"

"I asked him, 'You didn't kill him?' He said, 'We hung him.' I said, 'Dr. Bratton, you ought not to have done that.' He then pulled out his watch, and said, 'We have no time to spare; we have to call on one or two more.' "[22]

Having revealed the purpose of the Klan conspiracy, and how Jim Williams died that night, the prosecution now had only to show that Robert Hayes Mitchell was a member of the Klan. Many would hasten forth from the sinking ship to oblige the prosecution's needs.

In the prosecution's closing arguments on December 16, Daniel Chamberlain reiterated evidence of conspiracy by citing the Klansman's sacred writ: "[T]hat article 51, section 1, requires that every member of this order is to provide himself with a pistol, and Ku-Klux gown, and a signal instrument. Note that, gentlemen of the jury; this conspiracy or this agreement is to be carried out, in the first place, by arming every member with a pistol, and by disguising him in a Ku-Klux gown, and providing him with a signal instrument. Armed, disguised, and with a signal instrument, which shall make it unnecessary to use the human voice, is the first feature of this agreement. Now, what is the next significant agreement? That any person who shall divulge, or cause to be divulged, any of the doings or purposes of this organization, shall suffer death. Is that an innocent agreement, gentlemen?"

And in focusing on the provision barring black membership, Chamberlain inferred the Klan's constitutional commitment not only to black exclusion but to the denial of legal capacity: "[T]his order is seen not only to be a political organization, but it is found now to be aimed against those of a particular color. 'No person of color shall ever be admitted as a member of this order.' Why not? Can we not suppose that persons of color may be on the side of 'justice, humanity, and constitutional law, as bequeathed to us in their purity by our forefathers,' in the language of this oath? Yet no person of color, whatever his principles, whatever his life, shall ever be a member of this order. Here you reach the touch-stone of this conspiracy, and you find it an armed, secret, disguised confederacy."[23]

In his closing argument, Henry Stanbery for the defense could scarcely conceal the contradiction between his private views and federal law. Even his attempts at courtroom civilities betrayed his contempt: "It is gratifying, gentlemen, not only to my learned friend who has just taken his seat, but to all parties, to witness with what close and undivided attention you have listened to the argument which has just been delivered. You know, gentlemen, those of you, at least, who belong to the colored race, that grave doubts have been entertained whether, in consideration of your previous condition, you have arrived at this time at a state of improvement which would justify your receiving the right to sit in judgment upon your fellow-men, where you now sit in that jury-box. So far, gentlemen, you have shown a disposition to give undivided attention to the case. You have at least shown one qualification for a juryman; you have listened but as yet to one side—perhaps to that side to which your sympathies are most drawn. Now, gentlemen, can you hear the other side? Can you give the same undivided attention to the advocate for the defendant as you have given to the advocate who has stood up for the government?" His rhetoric was virtually a taunt, pointedly suggesting that the jurors' very entitlement to their legal rights depended on their taking his side. "[I]f you can go that other step forward, then, gentlemen jurors, I am ready to say that you, at least, are entitled to sit in the jury-box."

According to the defense, the killing of Williams was no conspiracy at all but, rather, an act of self-defense on the part of whites faced with a newly freed black population among whom the governor, Robert Scott, had unthinkingly distributed weapons. "What further, gentlemen?" said Stanbery. "Not merely one company, but at least three companies of black men were armed in the county with the public arms, but not a single company of white men. A black face was a recommendation to [the governor] for a musket; a white face was no recommendation.

"I think, gentlemen, you will for equality," he continued, so completely ill at ease addressing black jurors that his words would seem laughable to our ears were they not so offensive. They betray an utter incredulity that his black listeners might not only have taken seriously their new rights but also understood them—and do so in a tone that blends condescension and threat. "I hope you of the colored race will not expect or desire to rule white men. You don't want to be better off than they are, do you? You don't want to stand above them, do you? You don't want to have arms and let them have none?" His ill-advised threats to the jury extended by implication to all the blacks of South Carolina. "Let me tell you, if you go for anything like that your triumph will be short and your doom inevitable, if you insist upon being armed while he is defenseless. Why, gentlemen, he will put a stop to that. If, instead of living on equality with your white brethren, you seek to rule them, you will commit a terrible mistake, take my word for it, gentlemen. I am not an alarmist. You can only maintain your position here by fairness and justice to your white fellow-citizens."

Trying his best to confuse the issue at hand, according to the defense's strategy of obfuscation, Stanbery concluded, "The right man is not here; you have the proof, but not the offender. When he or they, whoever they may be, shall be arraigned, then will be the time to confound the just with the guilty. I pray you, gentlemen, do not allow your feelings to run away with your judgment, but deal fairly with this man, now before you; measure out justice to him. If he is not found guilty of these offenses, gentlemen, acquit him, and you will do honor to yourselves and give a guarantee to the community that a black man knows how to acquit as well as white men, and hold in even poise the scales of justice. But, gentlemen, if you must always have a victim; if, when the right men do not appear, you can get any man with a white face and punish him, vicariously, I do not want to see one of your race on a jury again."[24]

On the final day of closing arguments, Monday, December 18, Corbin placed the proceedings the jury had heard in the historical context they knew from hard experience.

"Gentlemen," he began, "we have lived over a century in the last ten years. The ballot, which is the symbol of power in this Government, has passed into the hands of those who were lately slaves, to be wielded by them in common with the white citizens of the country. The ballot, which has heretofore been, in the eyes of the colored race, the symbol of oppression, has now become to them the symbol of protection and the symbol of power. Not only the symbol but the power, in fact. The colored race, and I rejoice in it, has been emancipated. Two hundred years of unbroken bondage have been terminated, and the slave who once traveled his lowly round, driven by the lash of a master, now stands forth a freeman, clothed with all the rights of an American citizen. In this case, gentlemen, we have charged, and we have attempted to prove, that these newly acquired rights, this franchise conferred upon the emancipated African, has been conspired against; that a terrible conspiracy has been inaugurated not only in this State, but in adjoining states, to rob our colored citizens of African descent of their newly acquired rights—the rights of American citizens.

"Gentlemen," Corbin asked, referring to the constitution of the Klan, "what does that mean, 'constitutional liberty as bequeathed to us by our forefathers'? Let us dwell for a moment upon it. Our forefathers framed a Constitution which the Supreme Court of the United States has declared, over and over again, recognized slavery, protected slavery. . . . The Supreme Court of the United States has said that this meant that the master might pursue his slave into any State in this Union and return him to bondage. This was the Constitution, this the constitutional liberty in reference to the colored man that was handed down to us by our forefathers. That Constitution, the Supreme Court of the United States said, meant this, that the black man had no rights that the white man was bound to respect.

"This article of the Constitution protecting African slavery was in the Constitution as handed down to us by our forefathers, and that is what is meant in this first section of the Ku-Klux constitution. It meant . . . that we stand by the Constitution in that respect *as it was*, not *as it is now*—not with the thirteenth, fourteenth, and fifteenth amendments in it. It means, we reject the results of the late war. That is what this Ku-Klux oath meant, and the distinguished counsel on the other side cannot remove it by argument. . . . Gentlemen, this organization which has this instrument for an exposition of its principles, is for the purpose of destroying the principles of the radical party, and the Constitution as it now is. . . . It is the foundation-stone, and the bottom of this organization."

Corbin carefully reviewed the testimony of the witnesses. He laid out the plot that had ensnared Jim Williams. He showed, in fact, that by all the evidence blacks in York County had generally acted with an abiding respect for law, peaceably and with no apparent urge for retribution so as to cause legitimate fear in whites. He reiterated the terrible purpose of the Klan conspiracy, and that Robert Hayes Mitchell had been a part of it. And in so doing, he laid the ground for his own final appeal, not to the jury, but to those whites who would hear his words and might spread his warning throughout South Carolina and the South generally.

"We have discovered, gentlemen," Corbin concluded, "a fearful conspiracy against [the Reconstruction Amendments] in an armed, equipped organization, composed, alas, gentlemen, of many soldiers in the late war who promised to lay down their arms, retire to their homes, and behave like good citizens. This organization, composed of many of the soldiers in the late rebellion, is found bearing arms, marching in squadrons at night, and for what? To defeat the very principles achieved in that contest by the Government of the United States.

"I say to them," he proclaimed, "I say to every individual in this armed organization—in the name of God, disband!" And he issued a threat of his own: "Go to your homes; meet no more; because the uplifted arm of this nation, otherwise, will crush you, grind you to powder!"[25]

The jury was charged and returned in less than an hour. Whether the verdict indicated their confusion or their care, it is difficult to say. Their verdict: "guilty of the general conspiracy"—a verdict that, in departing from the form of the indictment and the judge's instructions, furnished grounds for an appeal.

And so Henry Stanbery demanded that the verdict be recorded as rendered.

"No!" said Judge Bond emphatically. He reminded the jurymen they were obliged to find the prisoner guilty or not on each count of the indictment: the first, for conspiring to prevent blacks from voting; the second, for conspiring to injure the black man Jim Williams for having previously voted.[26]

Returning quickly again, the jury rendered the following verdict: "guilty on the second count, not guilty on the first." Mitchell's sentence was lenient but not trivial—eighteen months in prison. He had been fairly cooperative with the court, had not taken part in the murder itself, and was not a leading Klansman. Like other convicted Klan riders, he would spend his term in a penitentiary in Albany, New York.

Robert Hayes Mitchell was but one Klansman. Hundreds more awaited trial, many of whom either pled guilty or were swiftly convicted of their crimes. But the "best men" who led the organization, like Dr. Bratton, managed to evade Major Merrill's grasp entirely. And, in the end, federal authorities simply lacked the resources to deal with a conspiracy of this size and scope. The night riders who served time were few in relation to the enormity of the Invisible Empire. The replacement of Attorney General Amos Akerman in late 1871 by George Williams struck another blow to prosecutorial efforts. Akerman was apparently forced from office owing largely to the powerful railroad industry's disapproval of some of his legal positions, though some doubt remains whether the Klan cases played a role in his ouster. In any event, the Department of Justice's commitment to prosecuting the Klan weakened under Williams's leadership, as the new Attorney General showed little interest in securing an expansive judicial reading of the Reconstruction Amendments.

Over the course of the 1870s, the Supreme Court issued a series of rulings that narrowly interpreted the scope and power of the Fourteenth Amendment, foreclosing, for all intents and purposes, the possibility of further federal action against the Klan. Judged in terms of success in shaping constitutional doctrine and in convicting the leadership of the Ku Klux Klan, the prosecutions were a limited failure.

From other perspectives, however, the prosecutions represented a substantial victory for the cause of black civic inclusion. Corbin and Chamberlain may not have been able to bring to justice the "best men" who defied the jurisprudential implications of the Civil War. But through the mass arrests made possible by President Grant's suspension of habeas corpus—which, according to Major Merrill, also had an enormous "moral effect"—they managed to break the Klan's back. In concluding his report for the Secretary of War, Major Merrill wrote that he thought it "proper" to say "that in York County the Ku-Klux organization, as such, is completely crushed." In South Carolina, as throughout the South, the Klan would soon wither entirely.

That victory over the Klan also achieved an important effect in American cultural life; it became a symbol of a rising liberal rule of law on a national scale. The conviction of Klansmen in open court, by black jurors—unimaginable but a decade earlier—represented a searing dramatization of the nation's commitment, at least in this instance, to protect its new citizens in their rights. And by hearing and recording the voices of the Klan's victims, producing hundreds of pages of testimony, the proceedings not only documented the pervasiveness and magnitude of suffering, but drew blacks into the cognizance of national jurisprudence as never before by transforming the speech of freed slaves into legal record. In American law and civic life, it was the first great proliferation of speech from the formerly voiceless, authorized by a state acting on their behalf. The record remains integral to the national memory of Reconstruction and reveals how much the people of a nation can endure in safeguarding its principles.

Minerva Bowden knew that lesson well, for she embodied it. Her descendants, who live in North Carolina, not far from where Clem and Minerva Bowden were beaten, know little about their ancestor's life and trials. But they do know that Minerva Bowden was to see a granddaughter bear her name—and that Minerva Bowden herself, born around 1850, survived well into the twentieth century. Indeed, family history records that she lived to be one hundred.[27]

In the Nature of Things

▲

The most important historical fact about the arrest of Homer Adolph Plessy was that he desired it. On June 7, 1892, the thirty-year-old shoemaker boarded the East Louisiana Railroad in New Orleans with a first-class ticket to Covington, walked through the door of one of the coaches reserved for whites, and sat down. Plessy could have avoided the history-making confrontation with the police that followed. After all, being an "octoroon," a person with "one-eighth African blood," he could have "passed" for white. And many of his fellow passengers, even had they recognized his racial ancestry, might not have been offended by his presence, nor reported him had he kept silent. But it was not Plessy's intention to pass on this trip, nor to accept the indulgence of sympathetic whites. He was intent on breaking the law, and wanted to be noticed doing so. When the conductor asked about his race, he readily admitted he was "colored," and when asked to sit in one of the Jim Crow coaches set aside for blacks, he did not hesitate to refuse. That refusal prompted a detective named Chris C. Cain to arrest him, force him off the train, and throw him into jail—precisely as he had hoped. Indeed, unlike the events precipitating the black trials we have examined heretofore, the odyssey that Homer Plessy began aboard the East Louisiana Railroad, part of a campaign by blacks to secure a liberal, inclusive understanding of the Reconstruction Amendments and to resist their renewed civic exile, proceeded entirely according to his own plans and expectations.

Plessy's actions were part of an effort to create what in legal parlance is known as a "test case." A test case is a legal dispute, often carefully planned in advance, designed to challenge the constitutionality of a disfavored law. Its aim is to see a law revoked not through the political process, by legislative action, but rather through the courts. Not just any case will do for such a challenge. The difficulty in creating a test case is to develop a "fact pattern" so precise as to force courts to address very specific constitutional issues and to foreclose the option of dismissing the case on some technical ground, as courts typically (and rightly) prefer. A test case also is brought before the bar of public opinion, and in this respect, not just any defendant will do. Their personal story must be compelling, and their life should be a symbolic mirror of the legal issues in their case. The test case is a theatrical piece in which setting and casting count for much.

Plessy's boarding the East Louisiana Railroad was the beginning of just such a drama, a legal performance directed by a group known with prosaic clarity as the Citizens' Committee to Test the Constitutionality of the Separate Car Law. With Plessy's arrest, the group hoped to attack an 1890 Louisiana statute that required all railways traveling within the state to provide separate coaches for whites and blacks, a law purportedly designed "to promote the comfort of passengers." But the group's challenge took aim well beyond Jim Crow on Louisiana trains. It was part of a spontaneous campaign of legal and cultural self-assertion designed to affirm black civic belonging and attack the revival of caste jurisprudence—embodied not in acts of Klan violence, but rather in laws that were said to be guided by reason and the public interest.

To understand the full significance of this collective endeavor, we need to consider Plessy's case in tandem with a decision of 1883 remembered mainly by scholars of constitutional law, *The Civil Rights Cases*. The decision consolidated five individual suits brought by black activists under the federal Civil Rights Act of 1875, and though it finds no place in popular memory, no judicial ruling about black citizenship was more important to its time, and it formed the federal component of the jurisprudential trend on which the more enduring symbolism of *Plessy v. Ferguson* rests. *The Civil Rights Cases* were a dress rehearsal of the legal and cultural drama—a theater of exile—for which *Plessy* would be remembered. And so we begin with two of its constituent trials.[1]

In their facts as much as their outcome, the cases were dramas of their historical moment. In the wake of the Reconstruction Amendments, blacks were eager to test their newfound citizenship, and a critical target of their desire lay at the junction of commerce and public space. Blacks understood very early that full citizenship required freedom to enter the places of commerce that, then as now, defined most of public life outside the institutions of the state—that it involved admission not only to voting booths, but also to restaurants, theaters, and trains. Newspapers of the 1870s thus are peppered with stories of black men and women offering their custom and being put off by proprietors, protesting their treatment, and at times seeking legal remedy. Most such acts of self-assertion have disappeared from the historical record with the crumbling of old newsprint. Those that led to *The Civil Rights Cases*, however, are well preserved in the archives of our federal courts. They give the impression of being caught between worlds, at once looking backward and presaging our own era.

Take the story of William R. Davis, a tall, handsome, twenty-six-year-old. Born a slave in South Carolina, Davis became, after emancipation, the business agent of the *Progressive American*, a weekly black newspaper published in New York. He lived at 109 West 27th Street, today a short walk from Pennsylvania Station. On the morning of November 22, 1879, Davis stood with a female companion at Eighth Avenue and 23rd Street, a few blocks from his home. The couple was planning to attend a performance at the Grand Opera House, a premier New York theater with nearly 1,900 seats, two balcony levels, and six stage boxes. The previous month, the theater had presented an operatic production based on Bernadin de St. Pierre's popular 1787 novel *Paul and Virginia*, a sentimental tale of natural man set in the Caribbean and featuring Mary and Domingo, two faithful black slaves. The piece Davis expected to see had a more modern political theme: a matinée adaptation of Victor Hugo's *Ruy Blas*, a love story among the declining nobility that also was a thinly veiled cry for social reform. The featured actor was to be the great tragedian Edwin Booth, brother of President Lincoln's assassin. We know almost nothing about Davis's friend, not even her name, but we do know that she was a "bright octoroon, almost white," whereas Davis was "of full African blood." And that difference made all the difference in the events that followed.

When the couple presented their tickets to the doorkeeper, Samuel Singleton gazed at them and then informed the two that their tickets would not be honored; he advised them to return their tickets for a refund at the box office. If Singleton gave an explanation, it is not recorded. Davis followed the doorman's instructions, though only to a point. He walked to the box office and returned the tickets, but he refused to accept a refund. Instead, he strode outside into the November air, and calling a boy on the street "asked the lad to go to the box-office and buy two tickets for him." Davis gave the boy "10 cents for his trouble," and the couple then tried their luck again. Rather than entering side by side, however, this time Davis's friend walked a few feet ahead of her escort. Her ticket was accepted. But when Davis presented his, Singleton once more declared that it would not be honored. Davis explained that he had purchased his ticket just a moment before, and insisted that "his companion had already been admitted, and that he must also have admission." He then tried to press his way inside, whereupon Singleton grabbed him, forced him back, and called for a policeman. The officer told Davis that the Grand Opera House did not admit blacks and that he had better move along. Perhaps the Opera House did not admit blacks, Davis replied indignantly, but "the laws of the country did admit them, and he would try to have them enforced." He and his companion then left the theater and attended another show elsewhere, leaving Davis to plan his next move.[2]

It was not the first time Davis had been barred at the door of a theater in New York. In 1875, he had brought suit against the managers of Booth's Theater (built by Edwin Booth). But that action never came to trial. Curiously, Davis's witnesses had failed to appear. This time it would be different. Davis approached a U.S. Attorney for the Southern District of New York and asked that a criminal prosecution be brought against the Opera House. Perhaps hoping to deter Davis, the attorney suggested that he bring another civil suit instead. But Davis pressed his case, and in two grand jury sessions, prosecutor Stewart L. Woodford secured an indictment. It asserted that Samuel Singleton, the doorkeeper, had denied William Davis, "being then and there a citizen of the United States," the "full enjoyment of the accommodations, advantages, facilities and privileges of a theater and place of public amusement" for no reason that was "by law applicable to citizens of every race and color." On January 14, 1880, Singleton appeared in court and admitted that he had indeed stopped Davis from entering the Grand Opera House solely because he was black, but he denied his behavior was unlawful. The civil rights law under which he was indicted, he claimed—the Civil Rights

Act of 1875—was unconstitutional. In late February, a two-judge panel reviewed the doorman's argument, failed to agree, and asked the Supreme Court to resolve the dispute. Was "the act of Congress . . . entitled 'An act to protect all citizens in their civil and legal rights,'" they queried, "constitutional so far as it relates to theaters and places of public amusement in the State of New York?" On March 10, their "certificate of division in opinion" was stamped by the clerk of the Supreme Court—where Davis's legal protest, now known as *U.S. v. Singleton*, would linger almost three years (at the time, the Court had little control over its docket, and its backlog of cases was large).

It was perhaps a long time for Davis to wait, but in California George M. Tyler and Charles Green would have to wait even longer. On the evening of January 4, 1876, Tyler and Green hoped to attend the second night of a show at Maguire's New Theater on Bush Street, between Montgomery and Kearny, in San Francisco. Thomas Maguire was presenting the Tennessee Jubilee Singers, advertised as "the far-famed original" and "most superb colored company in America, composed of the sweetest songsters of the Southern clime, singing in aid of the colored school at Lexington." The company, announced Maguire, one of the leading impresarios of San Francisco theater history, "sing with wonderful pathos and power the quaint, weird, touching songs of the slave cabin and the camp meetin' down in de wilderness." Maguire proclaimed the show "The Hit of the Season!" with "Houses Crowded!" and "The Occident Delighted!" The desire of San Francisco blacks to hear the singers must have been high. Whether or not they knew they were being caught in a web of theatrical ballyhoo, however, is not known. In fact, the Tennessee Jubilee Singers were decidedly not the Fiske Jubilee Singers, from Fiske University, the most renowned black singers in America, a company still in existence today and famous for its performance of black spirituals. Maguire's act was a knockoff. And the historical record shows no trace of a colored school in Lexington, Tennessee, in 1876.[3]

Whoever they really were, the Tennessee Jubilee Singers were a smash hit. Their opening night attracted "an overflowing and fashionable audience" said to include "not only those who sought mere amusement, and found it in the exceeding quaintness and oddity of some of the songs," but also "a large number of our most intelligent and thoughtful people" (the latter's appreciation of the "earnestness and sincerity of the colored singers," a reporter observed, "was no less hearty, though less noisy, than the laughter and applause which followed every song"). As for the singers themselves, they included "little Lulu Henderson in the center, quite hidden when she took her seat behind the parlor organ"; Kitty Byrd, contralto; Jennie Mackey, soprano; Frank Grimes, baritone; Albert Byrd, second tenor; Annie Henderson, soprano; Della Reyno, contralto; John T. Henderson, tenor; and Henry Hunly, basso. Most of the group were light-skinned, "the women nearly white, and none of the men really black." We know little else about the ensemble. One clue to their artistic provenance: when they performed, their director, T. R. Jackson, sat at their left, and announced "each song and the singer as their turns came, indicating the singer with a spasmodic gesture of the right thumb." The gesture was characteristic of the "interlocutor" figure in minstrel shows, the blackface performances popular in the nineteenth century based in large part on comedic portrayals of black servility.

The critic for the *San Francisco Chronicle*, while lauding "these earnest but uncultivated exponents of Methodistical music as sung in the slave cabins before the 'Ark of emancipation' set all the negroes free," was not entirely taken in by Maguire's puffery. "The voices," he wrote, "do not perhaps deserve all that the printed circular says of them. We do not find among them 'the finest basso in the country' nor 'one of the most accomplished alto and soprano singers on the continent'; and 'the great baritone' is distinguished chiefly for his lavish interjections, which never failed to excite laughter in the gallery." Still, while he called the singers' voices, on the whole and "in plain English," merely "good," the critic also enthusiastically declared that in their adaptation of slave songs, the singers were "unrivaled." No matter what critics thought, however, San Franciscans were delighted. On opening night, the applause was so insistent that nearly all of the songs were reprised, swelling the program from twenty to thirty-five numbers. Clearly, it was not an act to miss. And so Tyler and Green purchased tickets. Described as "fond of dramatic performances," Green bought a ticket for the fourth row of the house, for one dollar—not a cheap seat.[4]

When Green and a white friend, James H. Whiting, arrived at the theater at half past seven, the doorkeeper, Michael Ryan, told them, "You can't go in." Why not? Green asked. "We don't admit no negroes into this theater," the doorman explained. As a small crowd began to gather, the two exchanged further words, whereupon Ryan conceded that blacks were barred only from the exclusive "dress circle" of the house and directed Green instead to the upper gallery. "You take that ticket and go upstairs," he ordered, "you can't go in here." Tyler experienced a similar rebuff, as did a number of other blacks that night.

The ensuing outrage was swift. The Jubilee Singers, wrote "A Colored American" to the *Chronicle*, "have but recently emerged from slavery, and it is but natural that their own race should desire to hear them to the best advantage, particularly as many colored residents of this city have heard and joined in singing the same melodies on the plantation, in church and at camp meetings." A boycott, asserted the anonymous writer, would be an effective and appropriate response. "I hope Thomas Maguire," he wrote, "will be made to feel in the most sensitive part of his nature, i.e., his pocket, that our civil rights cannot be ignored with impunity." Blacks were not alone in their disgust. Many whites were outraged as well, including those of the *Chronicle* staff. "Mr. Maguire has done a foolish thing," the paper declared on January 9. If a black man were excluded from Maguire's theater because he "was offensive and uncleanly," "if his breath was rank with garlic," "if his character would justify a fear lest he should disturb the audience," "if he was drunk when he offered himself for admittance," then he was "properly excluded." But "that he was black," the editors argued, "was no reason why he should have been treated with indignity." "As to the prejudice that exists against persons of color," the *Chronicle* later announced, rebutting an article supporting Maguire's policies in the *Colusa Sun*, "we say it is an absurd and unjust one, and ought to be eradicated from the minds of all just and generous persons. . . . We see no just reason why this prejudice against color should not be banished as one of the discarded and unworthy relics of an unenlightened and barbarous past."[5]

Blacks in San Francisco did not confine their anger to the printed page. Green immediately initiated an action under the Civil Rights Act against Maguire, who was arrested by a U.S. marshal and released after posting bail of $3,000. And on January 18, black leaders met in the Young Men's Union Benevolent Hall on Pacific Street near Mason, to support Green and engage in "the public assertion of the rights of colored people." The chairman of the group was the Reverend Peter Anderson, and among the vice presidents was a septuagenarian named Solomon Peneton, who had once worked the wharves of New Bedford, Massachusetts, and had become an associate of Frederick Douglass. At the meeting, Green explained that while federal prosecutors naturally would handle his case free of charge, he also wished to hire his own attorney to assist them. A young man named Nathaniel Francis Butts then announced that he, too, "had contemplated bringing an action" against Maguire, and that he had collected about $4 for the purpose, which he then promptly donated to Green. A committee was formed to draft a resolution "embodying the sentiments of the occasion." It appeared in the *Chronicle* the next day. The resolution read:

> Whereas, we are American citizens, the American flag is our flag; we behold it with pride; it floats over us; we yield it our homage and devotion; we glory in its unsullied purity; it assures to us the plenary rights of free men and free women, and we cannot, and we will not, in the sight of that glorious emblem, degrade it and ourselves by accepting anything less than all the liberty it assures to us . . . [therefore] be it resolved . . . That Thomas Maguire, in this act, has violated the laws of the land, infringed the just rights of American citizens, and insulted the honor and patriotism of the colored people of the city and coast, and of the United States.

As for Green, he did not waste the funds entrusted to him. Joining the federal government's effort would be George Lemuel Woods, former Republican governor of Oregon (1866–70) and, by direct appointment of President Grant, governor of Utah Territory from 1871 to 1875.[6]

Green's case came to trial quickly, and on the first morning, the federal courtroom was "filled with spectators, the majority being colored citizens," waiting to hear Assistant U.S. Attorney A. P. Van Duzer and George Woods battle with Maguire's lawyer, R. H. Lloyd. The question at hand was not one of "law" but rather of "fact": was Green excluded from the theater on the night in question because Maguire had a policy of discriminating against blacks? Green was first to testify. He described his experience at the door that night and produced his orange ticket for the performance: "Opera House. Admit one—Dress Circle. . . . Section C, row 4, seat 160." Michael Ryan then took the stand, evidently well coached. He testified that Maguire had never ordered blacks to be excluded from his theater, and that Ryan had refused to admit Green simply because he did not have a proper ticket valid for the performance that night. Had the ticket been meant for that night's performance, the doorkeeper explained, it would have been an altogether different color (a *Chronicle* headline waggishly described the trial as "Involving the Hue of a Ticket and a Man"). On cross-examination, Ryan held fast. He would have admitted no one with Green's ticket, he claimed, white or black, and "never told Green that he was refused admittance on account of his being a negro." As for why he told Green he could go upstairs with that particular ticket, he could offer no explanation. Another doorkeeper, James Rigley, later corroborated Ryan's testimony. He insisted that he had received no "instructions from Mr. Maguire with reference to admitting colored people to the dress circle," and denied, too, any policy of racial discrimination. "If a man presents a ticket for the wrong evening," he stated flatly, "he is not admitted."

Still, the evidence against Maguire was abundant. James E. Allen, a black man, testified that he had gone to the theater with Green and, having presented his ticket to Ryan, was likewise refused admittance to the dress circle; his ticket, he noted, was a different color from Green's. James Whiting, Green's white friend, who was able to sit in the dress circle that evening, testified that Ryan had told him personally "that negroes were not allowed in the dress circle." Nathaniel Butts, the young man who had donated $4 for Green's counsel, provided even more damning testimony. According to Butts, an agent at Maguire's box office had refused even to sell him a ticket, and had told him that Maguire "had given orders not to let my kind of people in." When Butts protested the policy, he continued, Maguire "came up and said to me, 'It is no use talking, you can't get in, and you had better go about your business.'" R. B. Lewis, a black man, testified similarly that "he was present when Green appeared for admission" and that Ryan had explained that he "was acting under orders." And C. D. Griffin, who like Butts had been unable to purchase a ticket to the performance at all, testified that he heard Ryan say that "Mr. Maguire had given orders that no colored persons should be admitted" (on the other hand, Griffin also testified that the doorkeeper told Green that "his ticket would do for another day," a point that Green flatly denied on reexamination). After the testimony, each side addressed the jury, and the court adjourned so that counsel could "look up authorities" on points of law that the judges would address the following morning at ten o'clock.[7]

The next day, the trial drew to a speedy close and, for San Francisco blacks, a disappointing one. Judge Lorenzo Sawyer seemed bent on finding a way to avoid Maguire's conviction, and ruled that any evidence about *Maguire's* policies provided by testimony about the behavior of his *doorkeeper* should be excluded from consideration. Even Lewis and Griffin's assertions of having heard Ryan announce Maguire's orders to exclude blacks did not meet the judge's standards of admissible evidence. "Suppose for his own spite," the judge explained, "[Ryan] excluded this man, and then declared that he did it by the authority of another, so as to take the crime off his own shoulders, would the law presume that he did it by the authority of that other from the mere declaration of the ticket-taker that he did so? Clearly not." The testimony regarding Ryan, he ordered, "must be stricken out" (in this, he had the authority of hearsay law of the time). As for the evidence given by Nathaniel Butts, the judge explained that it was possible that Maguire had said "Go away from here, you can't get in anyhow" without knowledge of the specific conversation that had just taken place between Butts and the agent, and that Maguire may have refused Butts "for some other reason besides his color." In any case, he continued, even if Maguire had discriminated against Butts on the basis of his race, it would be "no evidence" in Green's action that Maguire had "committed an offense the day previous." Woods struggled to save the prosecution's case. The "ticket-taker, being there as the agent of Maguire," he asserted, "made a *prima facie* case, and one which the defendant ought to explain." But Judge Sawyer rejected his arguments, charged the jurors "that there was no evidence before them that Green was excluded by the authority or direction of Maguire," and he demanded that they acquit the defendant—which they did, without even leaving their seats (the procedure, which seems odd to us today, was consistent with contemporary notions of the judicial role).[8]

Undeterred, San Francisco's black community immediately filed another civil rights action, this time on behalf of George Tyler—and this time against not Maguire, apparently beyond their reach, but rather Michael Ryan, the doorkeeper. That case was brought before Judge Sawyer and Judge Ogden Hoffman on February 12. Ryan's attorney demurred to all the charges against him and moved for dismissal. The Civil Rights Act of 1875, he argued, "so far as it is claimed to apply to the theaters and other places which are conducted by private individuals"—rather than the state—"[is] unconstitutional." Theaters like Maguire's, he asserted, were private venues, and their owners had "a perfect right to manage their affairs in the way they deemed most conducive to their interests." The federal government lacked the power to enact a law "that interfered with private rights and feelings"—an argument whose essentials we encountered in the case of the Ku Klux Klan (and that would be invoked against the federal legislation achieved by the Civil Rights Movement, especially the Civil Rights Act of 1964). Van Duzer and Woods countered that even such seemingly private venues were for all intents public places, within the reach of federal action, and that "the object of [the Civil Rights Act] was to level all distinctions pertaining to race and color, and that colored persons had as much right to demand seats in the theaters and accommodations in the hotels as white people." If the national government could not reach acts of racial discrimination like Ryan's, they averred, then "the bill [and, by implication, the Fourteenth Amendment] was a nullity, and its enactment by congress a farce."[9]

Again, San Francisco blacks were to be disappointed: the judges sustained a motion by the defense to dismiss the case as having "no warrant or authority in law." Undaunted, they filed a "writ of error," petitioning the Supreme Court to uphold the law in which their hopes resided. The documents in *U.S. v. Ryan* were filed in Washington on October 14, 1876—though the Supreme Court would not rule on the matter for seven years.

As for the Tennessee Jubilee Singers, they continued their successful run in Maguire's New Theater. And when it was over, two days before the verdict in the first Maguire trial, they took in the sights. On Saturday the singers, "longing to see San Francisco by gaslight," were guided by a special police escort through Chinatown, "visiting the Chinese theater, the Joss house, the restaurants, and the opium dens." Afterward, they made a special visit to the *Chronicle*, the newspaper happily announced, where they "chatted for some moments in the various rooms of the editorial and reportorial staff." They were then shown the composing room, where they "had an opportunity of witnessing the most rapid typesetting on the coast," and the stereotype department, which made the newspaper plates for printing. They next saw the "big press," and "inspected the folding machines and the other apparatus" that made the paper a state-of-the-art wonder. The singers "expressed themselves as highly pleased and interested," the *Chronicle* announced, "and when they returned to the composing-room they sang, for the benefit of the large party assembled, one of their sweetest camp-meeting hymns, and were loudly applauded." We do not know what city was next on the tour, or what happened to the Jubilee Singers after they left San Francisco. But, perhaps moved by Maguire's exclusion of blacks from the dress circle (the singers maintained to the *Chronicle* that they had never experienced such a thing in all their days of touring), they scheduled at least three more performances elsewhere in town. The evening of their Chinatown tour, they planned to sing in the Central Methodist Episcopal Church on Mission Street, and on Tuesday and Wednesday nights, they would bring their show to the "Bethel and Zion (colored) churches." Whether their director's spasmodic thumb made an appearance during those performances is not recorded.[10]

·   ·   ·

When William Davis strode toward the Grand Opera House and George Tyler presented his ticket at Maguire's New Theater, each did so convinced that justice and right, if not the movement of history, were firmly on their side. They did so, too, expecting the protections of an important new federal statute, the Civil Rights Act of 1875. After the Reconstruction Amendments, the Civil Rights Act was the crowning legal promise of Reconstruction and, in the public mind, both black and white, the achievement especially of one man.

Born in 1811, Charles Sumner was a bookish youth whose early ambition was for a literary career. At Harvard Law School, however, he found his true calling not in Shakespeare but in Blackstone and the literature of law. His mentor was Judge Joseph Story, of the *Amistad* case, whose estimation of his protégé was so high he hoped Sumner would one day succeed him as Dane Professor at Harvard. But the judge was to be disappointed, for after some years in practice and as a circuit court commissioner, followed by extensive travel in Europe, Sumner was drawn to social reform and practical politics. And in that world, the tall, independent-minded Bostonian was every bit as successful as his mentor could have hoped. In 1851, after a bitter fight with old-guard Bostonian Whigs led by Daniel Webster, he was elected to the United States Senate. His intelligence, passion, and ringing oratory soon distinguished him, and he succeeded, by his legal and literary facility, to advocate for a wide range of reforms, becoming a leading exponent of a liberal tradition in Massachusetts that continues to this day.

Though Sumner's social reform agenda was broad, by the 1840s he had begun to focus on the cause of abolition and black civil rights—one of his heroes was Granville Sharp.[11] In 1849, for instance, with the black attorney Robert Morris, he argued in the case of *Roberts v. City of Boston* that the Massachusetts constitution prohibited racial segregation in public schools by guaranteeing blacks what he termed "equality before the law," borrowing the phrase from the egalitarian jurisprudence of the French Revolution. But Sumner and Morris lost the case. The opinion, written by Chief Justice Lemuel Shaw, Herman Melville's father-in-law, endorsed the validity of "equal but separate" public schools under the state constitution—a doctrine that would be cited approvingly in 1896 in *Plessy v. Ferguson*. (Massachusetts abolished racial segregation in schools by statute in 1855.)

Historians of the early twentieth century tended to portray Sumner as something of a zealot, and though that image has been substantially revised, there is a grain of truth in it. Given to self-righteousness, Sumner was so inflexible that his own wife left him in exasperation after but nine months of marriage. Whatever his personal weaknesses, however, it is indisputable that the senator from Massachusetts paid a substantial personal price for his passion respecting slavery and racial egalitarianism. In his 1856 diatribe "The Crime Against Kansas," the senator referred to the speech impediment of an elderly colleague, Senator Andrew Butler of South Carolina, which caused the proslavery Butler to spit while he spoke. Sumner ridiculed the "incoherent phrases" with which the octogenarian "discharged the loose expectorations of his speech, now upon [the political] representative [of Kansas], and then upon her people." He also accused Senator Butler of being a congenital liar, alleging that he "touches nothing which he does not disfigure . . . [he] shows an incapacity of accuracy . . . [he] cannot open [his mouth], but out there flies a blunder."[12] The speech so deeply offended Congressman Preston Brooks, Senator Butler's nephew, that, in a notorious incident, he caned Sumner almost to death on the Senate floor. In "bleeding Kansas," the assault drove John Brown and his men wild with fury. Throughout the South, gentlemen applauded the vindication of Senator Butler's honor, rewarding Brooks with gifts of elaborately decorated canes to replace the one he had broken on Sumner's body. The victim would spend over three years in convalescence, mainly abroad, before returning to politics.

From the very start of the Civil War, Sumner believed that abolition should be a primary political and strategic aim of the North. But he also considered the end of slavery but a first step toward the grander achievement of full black citizenship. In the wake of Appomattox, he argued that the federal government had a duty to protect blacks in their newfound freedom and to help them achieve civil and political equality, and to do so through the force of law. The Civil Rights Act of 1866 and the Fourteenth Amendment were powerful expressions of the egalitarian ideals for which he had long fought (the 1866 law guaranteed blacks the ability to make and enforce contracts, to sue, to give evidence in court, and to hold and convey property). But what was needed most, he argued, was legislation that would realize the amendments' radical aspirations concretely through national enforcement. He specifically advocated for a "supplementary civil rights bill" that would outlaw racial discrimination in a variety of public arenas, including inns, streetcars, theaters, restaurants, schools, churches, cemeteries, and state and federal juries. That bill, not surprisingly, inspired both fear and doubt: fear that Sumner's proposal would impose "social equality" among whites and blacks, forcing whites to mingle with blacks in daily public life, which many whites looked upon as a state of social degradation and pollution. As for the doubts, they were intricately bound up with such fears: many commentators deemed the proposal beyond Congress's constitutional power to enact. Just as Reverdy Johnson and Henry Stanbery argued that the Fifteenth Amendment did not give Congress power to reach private efforts deterring blacks from exercising the franchise, so others believed that the Fourteenth Amendment granted Congress the authority to reach only that racial discrimination which might be practiced by state governments.

Sumner responded to these doubts by asserting a jurisprudential paradigm shift. According to the senator, the Civil War had wrought a fundamental change in American civic life by destroying the jurisprudence of caste, the "oligarchy of the skin" as he called it. The destruction of caste as "the great rule of interpretation" in constitutional analysis, he argued, "far beyond the surrender of Lee, was of infinite value to this Republic." That rule had been replaced by an inclusive vision of the liberal rule of law, in which the universalist principles of the Declaration of Independence were fully incorporated into the Constitution. In place of a constitutional jurisprudence of caste, Sumner asserted, there now existed a "new rule of interpretation . . . according to which, in every clause and every line and every word, [the Constitution] is to be interpreted uniformly and thoroughly for human rights." "Beyond all question, the true rule under the National Constitution," he proclaimed, "especially since its additional Amendments, is, that *anything for Human Rights is constitutional.* Yes, Sir; against the old rule, *Anything for Slavery,* I put the new rule, *Anything for Human Rights.*" This jurisprudential transformation, he believed, was "the crowning victory of the war."[13] And in the senator's view, the Civil Rights Act for which he fought implied nothing more or less than putting that "new rule" of interpretation into legal effect.

So deep was Sumner's belief in the legal change wrought by the Union's victory that his most powerful arguments defending congressional authority to pass his bill were grounded not in the text of the Constitution, but rather in evidence of black injury. On the Senate floor, he read from letters he received from black Americans across the country, "to enable the absent to speak—that colored fellow-citizens, whose own Senators had failed them, might be heard through their written word," and offered their experience as the basis for constitutional theory. "I allow a colored fellow-citizen to be heard in reply to the Senator," Sumner announced in an argument against Lot Morrill of Maine, who doubted congressional power to pass the civil rights bill.

> I read from a letter of E. A. Fulton, of Arkansas: "I have seen and experienced much of the disabilities which rest upon my race and people from the mere accident of color. Grateful to God and the Republicans of this country for our emancipation and the recognition of our citizenship, I am nevertheless deeply impressed with the necessity of further legislation for the perfection of our rights as American citizens." This colored citizen is impressed, as the Senator is not, with the necessity of further legislation for the perfection of his rights as an American citizen. He goes on: "I am also thoroughly persuaded that this needed legislation should come from the National Congress." So he replies to my friend. "Local or State legislation will necessarily be partial and vacillating. Besides, our experience is to the effect that the local State governments are unreliable for the enforcement or execution of laws for this purpose. . . ." Here, Sir, he replies again to my friend. I should like the Senator to notice the sentence: "With a care and anxiety which one vitally interested alone can feel"—as, of course, my friend cannot feel, since he has not that vital interest—"I have examined and weighed this subject." What does he conclude? "I am fully persuaded that nothing short of national legislation, and national authority for this enforcement, will be found sufficient for the maintenance of our God-given rights as men and women, citizens of this great and free country."[14]

It was an extraordinary moment in congressional and constitutional history. There on the Senate floor, Charles Sumner offered the letters of black men as evidence of Congress's authority to enact the Civil Rights Bill. To Sumner, the logic was plain, if not strictly constitutional per se: blacks had sustained an injury against their human rights; the national government was intended to protect human rights; therefore, Congress had the power to pass a law to remedy the injury.

Most members of Congress, of course, were unprepared to follow this logic—to embrace, really, a new civic religion of national human rights—to which the senator often responded that such doubters must not truly comprehend the injury blacks had sustained. But Sumner would not yield, and he continued to press for the law up to his death in 1874, worrying about its fate even as he lay dying. Hearing his restless mutterings about his "bill," his secretary thought he was anxious about some household debt that would linger in his absence. "You do not understand me," Sumner said weakly, with what little energy he had left in his body, "I mean the Civil Rights Bill." At ten that morning, he recognized a visitor, his friend and fellow senator from Massachusetts, George Hoar. "You must take care of the civil-rights bill," Sumner said, drawing on the last of his resources, "my bill, the civil-rights bill, don't let it fail." An hour later, Frederick Douglass called, and Sumner exclaimed "with something of the old ring in his voice, 'Don't let the bill fail!'" Sumner died a few hours after, on March 11. His bill was then passed, by a lame-duck Congress, in part to honor his memory. The law had been stripped of certain provisions dear to Sumner (it did not, for instance, prohibit racial segregation in schools, churches, and cemeteries). Nevertheless, it was a statute upon which Americans like Davis and Tyler could stake their right to pass through the doors of public commerce, and into civic life.[15]

But the law would not stand—and its fall would presage the restrictive reading of the Constitution announced in *Plessy v. Ferguson*. To begin, the Court rejected the assertions of Solicitor General Samuel F. Phillips that the Civil Rights Act was supported by the Fourteenth Amendment and the power it granted Congress to enforce its provisions. That amendment, wrote Justice Joseph Bradley for the Court, was plainly applicable to discriminatory practices only of individual states, not of private individuals. To read it otherwise, he argued, was to imply the manifest absurdity that the amendment concerned not civil but "social" rights. A contrary reading, the Court also found, would establish the national government as a purveyor of a "municipal law" that would regulate "all private rights between man and man in society"—a clear contradiction of the Constitution's federalist principles. The Court also rejected the government's argument that the Thirteenth Amendment gave Congress the power to pass the act by banning slavery and "badges of servitude." Mere racial discrimination, the justice argued, could not possibly be considered slavery or a badge of slavery, since such discrimination had been experienced by free blacks in the South before the war, despite their status as free men. To describe exclusion from a theater as a form of servitude, he asserted, was "running the slavery argument into the ground." Indeed, Justice Bradley's distaste for the Civil Rights Act was such that he offered a stinging rebuke to its supporters and beneficiaries. It was time, he counseled, that the black American ceased to be "the special favorite of the laws," that he stop receiving what today would be called "special treatment" and at last have his "rights as a citizen or a man . . . protected in the ordinary modes by which other men's rights are protected." In the future, the opinion cautioned, when it came to advancing the cause of black citizenship, the hands of the federal government would be tied.

Justice John Harlan would write a ringing dissent, but it did not come easily. The justice spent days in the agony of writer's block, and contemplated giving up, until his wife intervened. Years before, Justice Harlan had come into possession of the inkstand in which Justice Roger Brooke Taney had dipped his pen to write *Dred Scott v. Sanford*. Despite fierce disagreement with that opinion, Harlan had so prized the memento that his good wife, concerned more with her husband's self-interest than his chivalry, hid the prize after he had graciously promised to give it to one of Justice Taney's distant nieces. Harlan's wife knew the power of the talisman; when she retrieved the inkstand from its hiding place and put it on her husband's desk—"I have put some inspiration on your study table," she said—the words seemed to flow almost instantly. He lambasted Justice Bradley for "a subtle and ingenious verbal criticism" that ignored both the "substance and spirit" of the Reconstruction Amendments. He attacked Bradley's view of the Thirteenth Amendment, arguing that the Court owed Congress as much power and latitude to ban "badges of servitude" as it had been granted to enact the Fugitive Slave Law in *Prigg v. Pennsylvania*. And as for the Court's narrow reading of the Fourteenth Amendment, the justice reaffirmed that the amendment had established a new national citizenship, in which affirmative rights could be said to include freedom from just the kind of discrimination banned by the Civil Rights Act, especially when viewed in the light of certain long-standing common law principles. If the Court denied Congress the ability to enforce the ideals of the amendment, argued the justice, blacks would effectively be excluded from the very national citizenship the amendment established.

And so, indeed, they were, arguably until after World War II (ultimately, the spirit of Sumner's law would find expression in the Civil Rights Act of 1964, which was sustained under the broad reading of federal power to regulate commerce that the Court began to develop in the late 1930s). Though the Civil Rights Act had effectively been rendered something of a dead letter years earlier through lack of enforcement, the decision came as a bitter blow to black Americans. When the news reached Atlanta, a theater production was interrupted so the decision could be announced. Whites in the house broke into a "wild scene," the men cheering and shaking hands, the women smiling. In the "colored gallery," however, all was quiet. "Not a note of applause came from those solemn rows of benches," reported the *New York Times*; "their occupants were dumfounded."[16]

While the Court's logic in *The Civil Rights Cases* and other decisions may have retarded the movement toward full black citizenship, blacks naturally sought to resist its effects, in part by developing their own legal counterarguments and the organizations needed to advance them. It is during this time, then, that we witness the growth of systematic black legal thought, a nascent vision of law that would go on trial in *Plessy v. Ferguson*. The guiding metaphor of that jurisprudence, and of the cases that advanced it, would be motion.

The most intriguing example lies in the work of the Brotherhood of Liberty of Baltimore, Maryland, a precursor of the National Association for the Advancement of Colored People. Founded in 1884 by a group of black ministers that included the Reverend Harvey Johnson, pastor of the Union Baptist Church, the Brotherhood was dedicated to advancing black citizenship in various public arenas. Early on, the group led a successful campaign for the admission of blacks to the Maryland Bar. The Brotherhood also came to the defense of four men who had killed their white overseers on Navassa Island, a small land mass near Cuba with rich reserves of guano. The black and American Indian workers on Navassa toiled under conditions resembling slavery (if not worse), and one day, the workers staged a bloody massacre that was quelled only when the United States Navy was called to the rescue. Though the men were convicted, the Brotherhood nevertheless celebrated a great victory, for when the case ultimately came before the Supreme Court, Everett Waring, one of the lawyers for the defense, became the first black lawyer to argue before the high tribunal.

Knowledge of the Brotherhood has survived in part because of its historic connection to the NAACP but, more important, because it left behind a fascinating document. *Justice and Jurisprudence*, published in 1889, is the first great, formal analysis in Afro-American legal thought, running almost six hundred pages of small print. Written at the Brotherhood's request that "their counsel" provide "a philosophic account of the jurisprudence of race-prejudice, and of the history of its lineal descent from the ancestral jurisprudence of slavery," the tome examines whether the Fourteenth Amendment still held promise for the advancement of black civil rights and economic progress. Many had doubts. "In the present condition of affairs," wrote the Brotherhood in its forty-page introduction, "every door of industrial aspiration and advancement is barred against the African citizen."[17]

Justice and Jurisprudence is a manifesto and a profession of hope. The preface, addressed to "citizens of the United States of African descent," asserts an abiding confidence in progress through the rule of law. "There is no power to solve the dark problems of the future except law," the Brotherhood asserts, by which it meant no narrow legalism but law "in its highest essence, the soul of the universe—the will of God—not silent, abstract, sleeping law, but law diffused like the fresh air permeating the hidden places wherein race-prejudice coils its dark and venomous folds." More specifically, the book was "designed to be a treatise on the noble principle of *equality of rights by due process of law*, which these addressers insist is the great seminal doctrine of the Fourteenth Amendment, and constitutes an impregnable foundation for the civil tranquility, present and future, of a strong, proud, loving and united people." Notably, the Brotherhood argued that the growing population of blacks in the United States would render the progress of liberty almost inevitable. "We entered 1888 with seven millions," the group announced, "in 1900 we shall be twelve millions; in 1920, twenty-four millions; in 1940, forty-eight millions; in 1960, ninety-six millions, and in 1980, one hundred and ninety-two millions." The predictions were wildly overstated (in 1980, the black population would number only 26 million). Still, like Charles Sumner's reading of the letters of black Americans on the floor of the Senate, the Brotherhood aimed to find in the power of numbers the authority of jurisprudential axiom.[18]

Most of *Justice and Jurisprudence* was written anonymously by John Henry Keene, a prominent white lawyer. We know little about Keene, except that he was probably the child of English parents, and seems to have had a strong grounding in British republican thought of the nineteenth century. The nature of his practice and how he became associated with the Brotherhood are obscure. We do know that he defended Reverend Johnson in a racial discrimination suit against a steamship and later helped Everett Waring defend the blacks from Navassa. He was an eccentric by reputation (he was said to be fond of loud plaids and frequently wrote acerbic letters to local newspapers complaining of streetcar noise), and his personality infuses his contribution to *Justice and Jurisprudence*. At once literary and lawyerly, filled with both fantasy and analysis, the sprawling work purports to be the story of an unnamed foreigner—a man "untainted by race prejudice"—who holds extended conversations about the legal status of black America with the Chief Justice of the Supreme Court and a witty American journalist. Expressing his astonishment at the strange condition of American law, the foreigner retreats into extended research about civil rights and racial jurisprudence.

The findings he presents do not make easy reading. Each chapter begins with a series of obscure, often recondite quotations from classical antiquity intended to present aphoristically what is elaborated more verbosely in the argument. In some chapters, these quotations fill more than ten pages. But the crux of Keene's argument is straightforward enough. Like Charles Sumner, Keene believed that the expression of transcendent human rights in the Declaration of Independence was no less binding on American legal authorities than the Constitution itself. And as Sumner did too, Keene believed that many regions of the country not only denied blacks their legitimate civil rights, but also held to an outmoded conception of law itself. "The *Jus Civile, Jus Gentium, Jus Commune*, and *Jus Singulare*," he argues, "still prevail among the various State tribes in the primeval forests of America." (One of the derogatory terms for blacks at the time, Keene also notes, in addition to "darky" and "coon," was "a fourteenth amendment.") Against a jurisprudence of "Caste" and "Race-Prejudice," Keene argues that true American law in fact is based on a jurisprudence of Christianity and liberal universalism. "Through Christendom, Jurisprudence proclaims that at the creation of man it was written by his Creator upon the tablets of nature that all men are equal. . . . This *lex aeterna*, declaratory of a principle of natural justice, is embodied in the Fourteenth Amendment, that American Magna Charta."[19]

In written form, Keene's arguments probably did little to persuade those who did not already subscribe to them. But his assertions would be put to the test when Homer Plessy stepped through the door of a first-class train coach in New Orleans. The locale was no accident. The history of the city is one of racial flux, and even at the time, New Orleans had a strong tradition of racial intermarriage, especially among French-speaking Creoles, many of whom held prominent positions in society. Plessy probably viewed himself as Franco-American as much as black. His mother's family name was Debergue; the family owned a plot in the famous cemetery of St. Louis No. 1, where Plessy himself is buried. And as for his celebrated last name, it has come down to us with the accent erroneously on the first syllable: the stress likely should be on the second, the name pronounced *ples-SEE*. Indeed, though court records have him as "Homer Adolph," the name on his birth certificate is Homere Patris (he would change his name to honor his father, Adolphe Plessy, who died when the boy was five). The deletion of the "e" in his given first and adopted middle names probably was a gesture of assimilation into the American mainstream.[20]

The character of Plessy's day-to-day life is obscure. Like his stepfather and many in his mother's clan, he was a shoemaker, a trade with a long tradition of political radicalism. But Plessy hardly required tradition in challenging the 1890 Jim Crow legislation. The ambiguities of his name and his skin were bound to set him afoul of Jim Crow's racial absolutism—and, significant for a test case, to highlight its absurdity. Many others in New Orleans were in the same predicament and felt the injustice of the train law with special force. When the Citizens' Committee to Test the Constitutionality of the Separate Car Law approached him, Plessy agreed to participate in their plan, though there probably were many others who would have been eager for the job. Freedom of movement was a key to economic progress for blacks, and trains were one of the great symbols of modern life and its promise. To be consigned to the "second class" in late-nineteenth-century travel by one's race was a great indignity itself, but to be consigned to a Jim Crow train car was to be palpably disadvantaged in America's foremost symbol of progress. Only months before, another "octoroon," Daniel F. Desdunes, under the Brotherhood's guidance, had vindicated a challenge to an "equal but separate" requirement on *inter*state travel (the Constitution assigns the regulation of interstate commerce to the federal government).

How many "common carrier" suits were actually filed by blacks chafing at their second-class status is unknown: many no doubt were settled before they could come to trial. But in the late nineteenth century, a steady stream had made their way through the judiciary, and some ultimately reached the Supreme Court.[21] Most prominent among these was *Hall v. DeCuir*, in which Josephine DeCuir from Louisiana challenged a steamship company's refusal to admit her to the stateroom cabin on a journey from New Orleans to Hermitage. In the late 1870s, a high point of Reconstruction, a Louisiana statute entitled DeCuir to collect damages from the company for failing to offer integrated facilities. The state supreme court found in DeCuir's favor, but the U.S. Supreme Court reversed its ruling, finding that because the steamship also traveled between Louisiana and Mississippi, the statute imposed an undue burden on commerce between states. Most galling, in his concurrence to the unanimous ruling, Justice Nathan Clifford asserted that racial segregation was desirable because antipathy between whites and blacks was "in the nature of things."[22]

In the wake of common carrier cases like *Hall*, one constitutional question in particular remained unresolved by the courts: Whether a law requiring segregation on *intra*state travel would violate the "equal protection" guarantees of the Fourteenth Amendment. Would the federal charter that was remade after the Civil War of its own force strike down segregation mandated by the state? *The Civil Rights Cases* had determined that the federal government had no power to reach private discrimination through the Civil Rights Act. But were state Jim Crow laws that placed no burden on interstate commerce contrary to principles of national citizenship? This was the question posed by Plessy's steps into the first-class cabin.

In truth, there was never any trial. Although the case is known as *Plessy v. Ferguson*, Robert A. Ferguson was not a representative of the East Louisiana Railroad but rather the judge who presided over the court in which Plessy was to be prosecuted. After Plessy's night in jail, he was brought before the judge, but the state had not begun to present its case when Plessy's lawyers moved for dismissal, arguing that the separate-car law was unconstitutional. As expected, the judge ruled against the pretrial motion, a decision Plessy's lawyers challenged in a higher court (thus causing the action to be known as *Plessy v. Ferguson*). The Louisiana Supreme Court ruled against the defense, and the matter was brought into the federal court system with the hope of finding a more sympathetic audience in Washington. The man who supervised Plessy's defense, Albion Tourgée, was in no rush. A northern carpetbagger and author of one of the great literary treatments of Reconstruction, *A Fool's Errand: By One of the Fools*, Tourgée hoped that Plessy's case would not be decided by the Supreme Court until after some of its older justices had retired, perhaps to be replaced by more sympathetic ones. His co-counsel, Samuel Phillips—former solicitor general, who had mounted the defense of the Civil Rights Act of 1875 in *The Civil Rights Cases*—agreed. But almost four years passed without the appearance of an appropriately likeminded justice; most appointees were ill disposed to any broad or liberal reading of the Reconstruction Amendments. And so the show went on, though not quite as the defense had hoped, with *Plessy v. Ferguson* coming up for hearing at the Court on April 13, 1896, before a group of justices generally hostile to its arguments.

Tourgée believed the Civil War had restructured civic life in America in a fundamental and unalterable way. The Fourteenth Amendment in particular, he argued in his brief to the Court, "creates *a new* citizenship of the United States embracing new rights, privileges and immunities derivable in a *new* manner controlled by *new* authority having a *new* scope and extent, depending on national authority for its existence and looking to national power for its preservation." In contrast, he asserted, the "effect of a law distinguishing between citizens as to race, in the enjoyment of a public franchise, is to legalize caste and restore, in part at least, the inequality of right which was an essential incident of slavery." This was the case, he argued, even if the train coaches offered to whites and blacks in fact were equal. Tourgée supported this proposition with a provocative thought experiment, one reminiscent of Charles Sumner's letter reading on the floor of the Senate. "Suppose a member of this court, nay, suppose every member of it," wrote Tourgée,

> by some mysterious dispensation of providence should wake tomorrow with a black skin and curly hair—the two obvious and controlling indications of a race—and in traveling through that portion of the country where the "Jim Crow Car" abounds, should be ordered into it by the conductor. . . . What humiliation, what rage would then fill the judicial mind! How would the resources of language not be taxed in objurgation! Why would this sentiment prevail in your minds? Simply because you would then feel and know that such assortment of the citizens on the line of race was a discrimination intended to humiliate and degrade the former subject and dependent class—an attempt to perpetuate the caste distinctions on which slavery rested—a state in the words of the Court "tending to reduce the colored people of the country to the condition of a subject race."

Just as Mordecai wanted to " 'down' the Jew" sitting at the King's gate through a " 'police regulation' to prevent his being contaminated," asserted Tourgée, so "this act is intended to 'keep the negro in his place' "—in opposition to the principles of progressive liberty that the Fourteenth Amendment had made binding on the states.[23]

However inspiring, his words fell largely on deaf ears. The opinion of the Court was written by Justice Henry Billings Brown, a northern Republican and an active member of the American Association for the Advancement of Science. Prevailing scientific theories of racial hierarchy probably influenced Brown's argument against Plessy. Not that he seems to have needed outside encouragement—his autobiography begins, "I was born to a New England Puritan stock in which there has been no admixture of alien blood for two hundred and fifty years."[24] In his opinion, Brown dismissed Plessy's claim, arguing that Jim Crow legislation was a reasonable exercise of the state's police power to protect public health, safety, and morals. He added that the "equal protection" guarantees of the Fourteenth Amendment in no way implied that segregation was unconstitutional, because, after all, racial antipathy was "in the nature of things" (it was the second time in the history of the Court the phrase had been used in relation to race—echoing Justice Clifford's concurrence in *Hall v. DeCuir*). Indeed, if blacks felt that Jim Crow "stamps the colored race with a badge of inferiority," he wrote, it was not "because of anything in the law itself," but rather because blacks "[choose] to put that construction upon it." By Justice Brown's reasoning, blacks were simply incapable of sustaining constitutionally cognizable injury from a regulation that we today have come to see as symbolizing the essence of a "taunt by law." To support his claim, Justice Brown also cited the Massachusetts Supreme Court opinion in *Roberts v. City of Boston*, the case Sumner had lost.

For Justice Harlan, Brown's opinion was but a "thin disguise" for the reality of the statute. A southerner by birth and a former slaveholder (though a Unionist and colonel in the northern army during the Civil War), Harlan was by early training no racial egalitarian; he had once opposed the Thirteenth Amendment. Yet he underwent a true political conversion after the war and, whatever his continuing views on social equality and his racial pride, came to believe that blacks were fully entitled to the inclusion in American civic life enunciated in the Reconstruction Amendments. He also recognized that full access to public transportation was an essential component of that equal citizenship. "Personal liberty," he wrote, citing the English jurisprudential touchstone William Blackstone, "'consists in the power of locomotion, of . . . removing one's person to whatsoever places one's own inclination may direct, without imprisonment or restraint'"—and "[i]f a white man and a black man choose to occupy the same public conveyance on a public highway," it thus was "their right to do so." In denying that full liberty of movement, the Court's decision, Justice Harlan predicted, would one day be seen to be as "pernicious a case as *Dred Scott.*" (He also raised another civic specter: under the Court's reasoning, he asked, what was to prevent a law requiring separate coaches for "Protestants and Roman Catholics"?) Countering Justice Brown's view that blacks were freighting an erroneous meaning on the separate-car law, Justice Harlan offered an argument for black legal and civic capacity through a metaphor of color and sight taken from Tourgée's brief, which the author himself had drawn from a novel he had published in 1890. "Justice is pictured blind," Tourgée had written, "and her daughter, the Law, ought at least to be color-blind." Justice Harlan agreed. "The Constitution," he declared, "is color-blind."[25] It was a metaphor whose meaning— that government could make no distinctions between persons based on race—would become an important rhetorical weapon in the Civil Rights Movement, and one to which other minorities would lay claim in the future.

But that was to come much later. In 1896, the Court's reading of the Fourteenth Amendment as it concerned private racial discrimination and state-mandated Jim Crow was all too clear: according to *The Civil Rights Cases*, the federal government had little power over the former, and, according to *Plessy*, the latter was fully consistent with our basic law.

Did the Court's decision have any immediate practical effect on black citizenship or racial segregation? It is an old question among scholars. It was long contended that the *Plessy* case opened the floodgates for Jim Crow, though scholars now see the development of modern segregation more as a slow accumulation than an avalanche resulting from a single Court decision. What is certain is that despite Justice Harlan's assertion of its importance, newspapers mostly ignored the case, in stark contrast to the attention they had paid *Dred Scott*. In the wake of the Supreme Court's retreat from Reconstruction in decisions such as *The Civil Rights Cases*, the outcome in *Plessy* was a foregone conclusion, and extended published responses to it were few. The case became famous only in future historical memory, as a retrospective symbol of American law and national civic life.

Curiously, as symbol it would serve double duty. For racial conservatives, the case reiterated common wisdom about the "nature of things," reinforcing a world of caste in which whites ruled and blacks were ritually unclean, and which looked to American law for the wisdom to enforce this natural "Edenic" order.[26] For racial liberals, however, and those who would take up the cause of black civil rights in the twentieth century, *Plessy* became a banner of progressive political and intellectual mobilization. For them, Justice Harlan's assertion that the Constitution is "color-blind" came to symbolize the civic promise of America, the promise some had seen in the underlying principles of *Somerset's Case*.

Plessy v. Ferguson thus would become a token both of black legal incapacity *and* of hope for the defeat of "separate but equal"—that blacks, in the words of W. E. B. Du Bois, would no longer have "the doors of Opportunity closed roughly in [their] face."[27] This aspiration would nourish the network of groups fighting for black equality that came to be known, collectively, as the Movement, groups whose liberal struggle, in time, would be successful. For his part, Homer Plessy would die in obscurity in 1925 after years of working as a life insurance agent, surely little suspecting the changes he helped put in motion—changes of the twentieth century, to which we now turn—through the memory of the case that bore his name.

PART FOUR

Uplift the Race,

1903–1970

Overcoming Jim Crow

In the decades after the collapse of Reconstruction, from roughly the late 1870s through the early 1900s, white supremacy reestablished itself on virulent new terms. For many blacks, life became in some respects worse than it had been under slavery. New forms of labor contract were created that bound blacks to poverty and debt, without offering even those protections that had come, however inconsistently, with slavery itself, when black bodies were investments that whites had some incentive to protect. Intimidation and violence helped whites monopolize political power, and new laws were passed that effectively quashed black voting and established racial segregation, separate and unequal, as the rule in southern society. With southern "redemption," Jim Crow seeped into every feature of society and culture, defining the Afro-American experience from birth to death. "[T]his much men know," wrote W. E. B. Du Bois in 1903 in *The Souls of Black Folk:* "[D]espite compromise, war, and struggle, the Negro is not free. In the backwoods of the Gulf States, for miles and miles, he may not leave the plantation of his birth; in well-nigh the whole rural South the black farmers are peons, bound by law and custom to an economic slavery, from which the only escape is death or the penitentiary. In the most cultured sections and cities of the South the Negroes are a segregated servile caste, with restricted rights and privileges. Before the courts, both in law and custom, they stand on a different and peculiar basis. Taxation without representation is the rule of their political life. And the result of all this is, and in nature must have been, lawlessness and crime."[1]

The twentieth century would see the fundamental transformation of these conditions and, ultimately, the true destruction of caste as a significant principle in American civic life. That change did not come in fleet steps, and it exacted great sacrifice from those who helped bring it about. Blacks faced lynchings in the South, race riots across the country, and in Washington an oblique support of white supremacy. To reckon the distance the nation would travel in the coming years, one need only reflect on the comment President Woodrow Wilson allegedly made upon viewing D. W. Griffith's film *The Birth of a Nation*, which denigrates Reconstruction, glorifies Ku Klux Klan violence, and employs stereotypes of black Sambos: "It is like writing history with lightning. And my only regret is that it is all so terribly true." The reasons for the astonishing transformation during the ensuing one hundred years are complex. Demographics were an important factor. In 1900, there were 8.8 million blacks in America (about 11.6 percent of the population), most of whom lived in the South; by 1960, Afro-Americans numbered 18.8 million, about 10 percent of the American population. Migration played a critical part as well, with an exodus of blacks fleeing the South to the urban areas of the North and West, hundreds of thousands of them in the 1920s and over 1.5 million in the 1940s. World War I and, especially, World War II were also highly significant, prompting realignments in politics, society, and culture and strengthening the claim of black Americans for equal treatment, having demanded of them equal sacrifice.

But in the end, the transformation of black citizenship—and the liberal vision of American identity that resulted from it—was driven most forcefully by the aspirations of blacks for a better life and their collective move to attain it. Afro-Americans did not act monolithically in this enterprise. Their common mission was undertaken through a range of methods amid fundamentally divergent notions of the ultimate goal. Booker T. Washington saw whites and blacks as "separate as the fingers, yet one as the hand in all things essential to mutual progress"; Marcus Garvey embraced black nationalism and improbable schemes of African colonization in his effort to "uplift the race"; Du Bois advocated pan-Africanism and intellectual protest; Martin Luther King, Jr., was an apostle of populist, Christian nonviolence; A. Philip Randolph of socialism; Malcolm X of black separatism.

The trials in this chapter present some of that ideological range. Each involves a particular vision of black civic progress that had a hand in destroying caste and bringing Afro-Americans closer to the center of American civic life: Communism in the case of the Scottsboro Boys, legal liberalism in *Brown v. Board of Education*, and black revolutionary militancy in the trial of Huey Newton. Together, the cases suggest not only the advance of liberal civic ideals in the twentieth century, but also the role that traditions outside liberalism—and sometimes directly opposed to it—played in furthering its principles, especially the redemptive tradition of activist Christianity. The liberal cultural revolution of the era, the assimilation of blacks into American law and national identity, was linked to movements whose dedication to equality often had rather different jurisprudential roots.

10

Black, White, and Red

▲

The train was traveling west across the Tennessee Valley floor, moving slowly into northern Alabama, burning coal. Forty-two cars rattled and clanked in the morning chill: boxcars, flatcars, tenders, gondolas, tank cars. Some held a ballast of gray chert, the coarse gravel quarried from beds of limestone; others held coal—dirty, black, and combustible; and still others held the warm bodies of men, vagabonds riding the rails between Chattanooga and Memphis, scattered from car to car. On this particular stretch of the Southern Railroad, all of this was routine. But in one of the cars, there was something out of the ordinary: two women, poor millworkers (and sometime prostitutes), aged twenty-one and seventeen. Their names were Victoria Price and Ruby Bates, and both were dressed like men, in overalls and caps. Their presence there that morning would make all the difference in the events that followed.[1]

    March 25, 1931. The Great Depression had left millions of Americans without work. At its height, unemployment reached a staggering 25 percent. Tens of thousands took to the road in search of a job, sleeping in hobo jungles, living hand to mouth (a small part of that multitude was on the train as it moved west across the Tennessee Valley). It was an age of dislocation and dispossession. Southerners had suffered as much as any Americans, of course, perhaps even more. The sharecroppers who farmed cotton on leased land were trapped in a brutal cycle of debt, their desperate lives immortalized in works such as James Agee and Walker Evans's *Let Us Now Praise Famous Men*. And if you were black, as so much of the South was, any economic bust was especially hard felt.

The train moved on, pressing forward with its cargo. In addition to Price and Bates, there were among the hoboes riding that day nine young black men. They were poor southerners, some of them care-worn, and some truly wretched. At sixteen, Ozie Powell had completed only the first grade (he could write his name and nothing else). Clarence Norris, nineteen, was the son of sharecroppers. Willie Roberson, aged seventeen, walked with a cane, his syphilis having gone untreated for a year. Olen Montgomery, also seventeen, was blind in one eye and nearly so in the other. Haywood Patterson, nineteen, had begun riding the rails a full five years before. Eugene Williams was just thirteen. Roy Wright was thirteen, too, and with his nineteen-year-old brother, Andy, was hoping to find government work towing logs on boats. Tall, awkward Charlie Weems, who had been a delivery boy, was the eldest at twenty.

Soon, their names would be spoken throughout America, and even beyond. At the very least, Americans both white and black would recognize the collective name by which the nine young men would be known. They were the Scottsboro Boys. Their struggle to escape execution in Alabama is a complex legal drama, intertwining southern law and custom; it is the story of a fight that transformed the jury box into a symbolic battleground for black citizenship; and it presents one of the great ironies in the history of black trials: that a fight to extend certain liberal legal rights to black Americans should have been achieved through the work of a decidedly antiliberal (and by most measures "un-American") organization: the Communist Party.

So far as scholars can determine, the trouble began with a bit of male bluster, and a desire on the part of some of the white tramps to feel a modicum of superiority to the black ones—the narcissism of small differences that captures the dispossessed. Walking across one of the cars where four of the blacks were stowed away, one of the whites stepped on Haywood Patterson's hand, provoking a notably measured reaction. "The next time you want by," said Patterson in response to the provocation, "just tell me you want by and I let you by." "Nigger," he replied, "I don't ask you when I want by. What you doing on this train anyway?"

"Look," said Patterson, "I just tell you, the next time you want by you just tell me you want by and I let you by." "Nigger bastard" was the response, "this a white man's train. You better get off. All you black bastards better get off!" A short time later, as the train was moving slowly uphill, the whites jumped off and began throwing stones from the side of the tracks. After the train left Stevenson, Alabama, they moved to a nearby car and continued the sport.

Then, the whites made a fatal miscalculation: they leaped into a car where many of the blacks had gathered, ready to fight. Clarence Norris would recall that as the white hoboes leaped into the gondola, it was "like jumping into a goddamn wolf's nest." "We beat the hell out of them," Norris explained, with a hint of pride and merriment even decades later. "They was hollering, 'Please don't kill me, please don't kill me.'" When the boys threatened to throw the whites off the train, they begged to be allowed to stay on board. "But we unloaded them," continued Norris. "Others jumped rather than be knocked off. Now I figure, the biggest of them must have been really messed up because this train was moving right along, maybe at thirty miles per hour or so. If they weren't ready when they hit the side of these tracks, there were going to be some banged-up crackers."[2] (They did take pity, however, on one white man who was in danger of falling under the train; they hoisted him back on board and allowed him to stay.)

Those white bullies may have richly earned their drubbing, but no matter his outcast state, a white man was a white man. And it was never in a black man's best interest to beat up a white man in rural Alabama in the 1930s. The victors soon paid a price for wounding white pride. The whites dusted themselves off; bedraggled, enraged, and probably ashamed, they walked back to the Stevenson railroad depot to find the stationmaster. With one of them bleeding from the head, they breathlessly announced that they had been beaten up by a bunch of "niggers" who were still stowed away on the Southern Railroad. The stationmaster duly wired ahead to Paint Rock. Deputy Sheriff Charlie Latham received a call at the general store from his boss, the sheriff of Jackson County, and in less than half an hour he had deputized almost every man around to form a posse.

The Paint Rock depot began to swarm with dozens of men armed with rifles, shotguns, pistols, and pitchforks. At about two o'clock in the afternoon, the Southern Railroad train came to a stop at the water tower. As the posse boarded the train, someone shouted, "Let's take them niggers off of there and put them to a tree and hang 'em!" They searched the wagons from top to bottom and removed every black man they could find, tying them together with a plow line. Had it not been for the sheriff, it would have been one more southern lynching, another forgotten tragedy. Instead, he arrested the nine young men, handcuffed them aboard a truck, and took them to the jail in the nearby county seat of Scottsboro. At the time, the Scottsboro Boys thought they might be killed for what one deputy called "assault and attempt to murder." They little suspected what further accusations awaited them.

For as they searched the train, the men of Jackson County found a surprise: Victoria Price and Ruby Bates. The two millworkers from Huntsville were descended from generations of the southern white dispossessed. Price had toiled in the mills since she was ten years old. Bates lived with her mother in a shack in the black section of town. Neither could be called a paragon of white womanhood; they issued from that strata of society in which poverty trumped the imperatives of race. As one historian writes, "Price and Bates lived among black people, played with them as children, roamed the streets with them as teenagers, bootlegged liquor and got drunk with them as young adults. They also went out with them, slept with them, fell in and out of love with them, apparently unaware of the widespread wishful thinking that made it possible for many white southerners to call all sex between white women and black men rape." In the eyes of southern society, Price and Bates were as low as whites could be. Two nights before, with two male hoboes, they had found a spot by a lake where there were "honeysuckles and a little ditch" and made love three feet away from each other.

The two women were now in something of a bind. They had been discovered as stowaways aboard a train whose only other passengers were black men. The immediate concern—or, rather, assumption—of at least some members of the posse was that they had been raped. In fact, the two had not even spoken with the young men, but to say so would be to admit to being tramps and thus to invite the scorn that polite white society typically showed white female vagrants. By contrast, many poor white women had gained the concern and consideration of their communities by claiming to have been "bothered" by a black man. From this custom of caste society, all whites seemed to gain. By crying black rape, a poor but upright white woman exchanged the scorn for the sympathy of her betters. By avenging the alleged rape through violence, the community of white men reinforced its chivalric sense of itself (the Klan's notion of the knight also derived from this sense).

Just when Price and Bates decided to cry rape is unclear. Some say that the idea may have first been suggested by the sheriff; others say that the women concocted the story themselves. Whatever the catalyst, however, it seems that Price took the lead as accuser, while Bates—nervous and perhaps already regretting the lie—remained mostly silent, seeming to some whites to be in a state of shock. Price's vivid account, however, would more than suffice. "Pour it to her, pour it to her!" the black boys were alleged to have shouted as Willie Roberson splayed her legs and violated her—and so forth, in a stream of lies simply too shocking to disbelieve. (But lies they were: Roberson, for instance, with advanced syphilis, was incapable of intercourse of any kind.)

As Ozie Powell, Willie Roberson, Olen Montgomery, Clarence Norris, Haywood Patterson, Eugene Williams, Roy and Andy Wright, and Charlie Weems awaited their arraignment in the Scottsboro jail, a crowd gathered outside. Soon, it swelled to a mob of several hundred men demanding summary justice. "Let those niggers out," they shouted. "If you don't we're coming in after them!" Williams and Montgomery began to weep. Sheriff M. L. Wann held back the crowd, barricading himself inside with twenty-one deputies; he telegraphed Governor Bibb Graves, who called out the National Guard. But by the time the Guard arrived, most of the crowd had dispersed, and the young suspects passed the night safe but shaken, doubtless aware that their troubles were only beginning.

One might infer from the actions of the Alabama sheriff and governor who protected the nine prisoners that in the South of the early 1930s the law of the courts was secure from mob rule—and that the more general boundary legal scholars have described between "law" and "custom," between "stateways" and "folkways," was as sure as a jailhouse wall. In fact, this line was only beginning to appear when the Scottsboro Boys were taken into custody. Through most of the South, it hardly existed at all.

To understand the character of southern law at this time, the law of a caste society, it is helpful to consider its similarities to the legal life of primitive cultures, wherein distinctions between law and custom, and especially between secular law and religious law, do not yet exist. The South in the first half of the twentieth century bore the deep influence of evangelical Protestantism; but far more important, its low-church Christianity had also become suffused by a potent cosmology, born of slavery and social neurosis, centered on principles of racial purity and pollution—a system not unlike the Hindu caste society of India or, more virulently, Germany under National Socialism.[3] The most immediate manifestations of this vision of tribal purity and pollution were strict taboos against interracial sex and eating. Sexual contact between white women and black men was viewed by whites with the deepest fear, and breaking bread with blacks as equals was taboo, as in any social system that holds a subordinate class to be ritually unclean. This racial hierarchy was established by law but, more meaningfully, it was kept in place by an intricate network of informal controls in whose shadow the law functioned and with which it was contiguous.

If any single institution could be said to embody the essence of this southern civic order, in its legal and extralegal forms, it was the act of "lynching," the mob killing of blacks by whites, from which the notion of "lynch law" issued. From the late nineteenth through the mid-twentieth century, when the practice effectively ended, many lynchings were acts of vigilante justice in the tradition of the American frontier, where with some regularity people of all races had been killed by representatives of a community lacking an effective state bureaucracy. But a significant number of reported lynchings bore unequivocal signs, though never explicitly articulated, of ritualized group expiation and catharsis, and were indifferent to guilt or innocence. Lynching was a public act of human sacrifice—a primitive impulse whose cultural remnant exists in Christianity itself—in which blacks were bound to the symbolic cross of a living tree and, often, the corpse burned in an act of ritual purification. Such was the communal meaning of the act that some lynchings were announced in advance, with railways offering special excursion fares for those wishing to attend. It was also common for whites to share a meal afterward and even to take fragments of the mutilated bodies home with them as souvenirs.

Between 1882 and 1968, there were about 4,700 reported lynchings, mostly in the South, with the decisive majority—though by no means all—of the victims, about 3,400, being black (white victims were guilty of a variety of transgressions against the legal and civic order). But these statistics reveal only a small part of the story. The extent of ritualized racially motivated killings was probably far higher than is suggested by the numbers, which were reported informally or in the press and gathered by antilynching crusaders such as Ida B. Wells-Barnett. And in any event, the actual number of lynchings suggests but a fraction of the manifold communal effects each act wrought. The threat of lynchings gave force to innumerable smaller acts of white dominance and aggression. In symbolic terms, it might be said that the ritualized violence of lynching was the source of ultimate meaning in southern society and jurisprudence. It was a form of civic exile by terror meant to keep all blacks "in their place," to use the dominant metaphor of Jim Crow, outside the circle of civic security. Thus even those who took no part in and gave no explicit support to violence against blacks, even the vast majority of southerners, depended on lynching to maintain their distinctive social and cultural order. If the defining transgression of southern caste was rape, lynching was its defining act of justice and community.

The symbolism and social objectives of lynching, however, were achieved not merely through the ecstatic ritual of mob violence. Its civic principles could also be enacted, if less dramatically, within southern courts of law, a process that was often described as a "legal lynching," which gave the impulses of lynching the sanctity of law and the cover of due process. Indeed, leading up to the 1930s, as the number of actual lynchings began to decline—in part through the efforts of groups such as the Association of Southern Women for the Prevention of Lynching, organized in the 1930s, and the National Association for the Advancement of Colored People, which for decades campaigned unsuccessfully for federal antilynching legislation—the courts assumed an even greater symbolic role in enforcing the codes of Jim Crow. What could no longer be accomplished "at the hands of parties unknown" could nevertheless be achieved through the jury box; and if the gratification was less immediate, the setting endowed it with state authority. Rather than killing blacks upon the cross of a tree, a white jury or judge could send a black man to a lifetime of backbreaking labor in one of the notorious gulags that dotted the South or—in an age even less squeamish about capital punishment than the United States is today—put him to death with a surge of electricity or by the gallows.

It was with such legal sanctification that the court prepared to exact its justice on the nine young men called the Scottsboro Boys, in the first of many trials.

A detachment of over a hundred soldiers from the 167th Infantry of the Alabama National Guard, arriving at five forty-five in the morning on April 6, accompanied the Scottsboro Boys to their appearance before Judge Alfred E. Hawkins. It was an impressive escort but not in comparison with the crowd of 8,000 to 10,000 that had gathered around the town square by ten o'clock, drawn by newspaper accounts of the "bestial" acts aboard the train. One "kind-faced, elderly woman selling tickets at the railroad station" told a representative of the American Civil Liberties Union that one of the "horrible black brutes" had chewed a breast off one of the girls. As for Judge Hawkins, though he expressed forbearance toward the crowd massing around his court, he was determined that the trials be more than kangaroo proceedings, though perhaps not much more; between his own prejudices, his poor judicial handling of the case, and his apparent desire to see the defendants convicted—as well as the extraordinary popular pressures aimed at discouraging potential defense attorneys—the trials seemed destined to bear out Clarence Norris's fear on first hearing that he and the others had been accused of raping two white women, that he was "as good as dead."

The trouble began with the appointment of counsel. Naturally, the nine "boys" had no lawyer (nor did federal constitutional law yet require that they have one appointed). Judge Hawkins's response to their need only made matters worse. He "appointed all [seven] members of the bar" to the case—but only for the narrow purpose of assisting in the process of indictment. Who would represent the boys at their trial was left unclear, and almost every qualified attorney seemed intent on evading the case and not helping the accused (one lawyer even accepted an offer to assist the prosecution before the trials commenced). Later, in condemning the handling of the accused's rights, the U.S. Supreme Court would refer ironically to the "expansive gesture" of appointing the entire bar to the arraignment. And in fact the confusion caused by Hawkins's order did the defendants no practical good, for the stage between arraignment and trial often is the most decisive part of a criminal proceeding, when defense attorneys prepare by sifting evidence, considering applicable law, and investigating the weakness of the prosecution's argument. The nine young men taken from the cars of the Southern Railroad had not been summarily executed, but their lack of due legal protection would make their first trial little more than a charade, notwithstanding the judge's vain pretensions to the contrary.

In the end, the only member of the local bar willing to defend the Scottsboro Boys was Milo Moody, a known drunk, who at nearly seventy years old was "doddering, extremely unreliable, senile . . . losing whatever ability he once had." He would be assisted by a lawyer who had come from Chattanooga at the behest of some of the defendants' families. Stephen Roddy was primarily a checker of real estate titles, and he did some minor police courtroom work; he knew nothing of Alabama law or procedure. And, out of fear, he drank so much on the morning the trial began that "he could scarcely walk straight." Moody and Roddy had a mere thirty minutes with their clients before the trial. It was unclear even which one of them was in charge, as each seemed to decline the honor: Roddy asserted to Judge Hawkins that "[i]f there is anything I can do to be of help to them, I will be glad to do it; I am interested to that extent," while Moody vowed that he was "willing to go ahead and help Mr. Roddy in anything I can do about it, under the circumstances." To such expressions of lawyerly zeal Judge Hawkins responded simply, "All right."[4]

The prosecution had decided as a matter of strategy to divide the case into four separate trials, thereby making the most out of the defendants' conflicting stories. The oldest, Weems and Norris, would be tried first; they would be followed by Patterson, who would be tried alone; next would come the case against Montgomery, Williams, Roberson, Powell, and Andy Wright; finally, the youngest, Roy Wright, would face judgment by himself. The Court made short work of justice. In four days, the nine were found guilty and, with the exception of Roy Wright, condemned to die—on account of Wright's youth, Circuit Solicitor H. G. Bailey had asked the jury to render a sentence of life imprisonment, but as many jurors had demanded that he, too, be executed, his case resulted in a mistrial. On the last day of the proceedings, Judge Hawkins called the other defendants before him and sentenced them all to die. In Alabama, execution was by electric chair. Years later, Clarence Norris would recall, "I never saw so many happy white folks."[5]

The trials themselves had been spectacles of half-truths and outright deceit—and not simply on the part of Victoria Price and Ruby Bates. In the caste society of the American South, the fact of race had created a culture of public mendacity comparable, for instance, to that of the Soviet Union before the fall of Communism—a culture in which countless lies constituted the fabric of daily life, in order to prop up the central, ultimately unsustainable, collective lie. And so despite the testimony of the two medical doctors who examined Price and Bates that neither woman showed signs of real injury, much less the kind that would result from a gang rape, and though the semen recovered from each was "nonmotile," the dramatic story of the two self-described victims was corroborated by other supposed witnesses, including the accusations and counteraccusations of the defendants themselves. According to Price's brash and self-confident testimony, the story happened this way. Just out of Stevenson, twelve black men jumped into the gondola car, where Price and Bates were sitting with seven whites. The blacks were waving knives and pistols and shouting "All you sons of bitches unload!" Then, Norris turned to her and Bates and demanded, "Are you going to put out?" "No, sir," she claimed to have responded, "I am not." The boys then overpowered the two with their weapons, forced Price's legs apart, held a knife to her throat, and raped her again and again while she "begged them to quit." She pointed specifically to Weems, Norris, Roy and Andy Wright, Patterson, and Montgomery as the ones who had brutalized her. It was a mesmerizing story, particularly in a time before the sexual revolution of the 1960s, lacking the pervasive cultural presence of sexually explicit imagery.

Bates told much the same tale, though she was more hesitant, as she had been from the start. She claimed the black men had jumped into the gondola car, pushed the whites off the train, and then raped them. Other witnesses offered supporting evidence, some even claiming they had seen the rape in progress. Indeed, in one of the sadder features of the Scottsboro case, Clarence Norris admitted to seeing the attack as well. Under cross-examination, he claimed that there had been a rape—but that he wasn't involved. "This Weems I was speaking about here is not my friend," he declared.

> I saw him over in the gondola and I saw the girls in there, but I did not go in there. . . . I seen everyone of them have something to do with those girls after they put the white boys off the train. After they put the white boys off I was sitting up on the box car and I saw every one have something to do with those girls. I was sitting on top of the box car. I saw that negro just on the stand, Weems, rape one of those girls. I saw that myself. . . . I did not go down in the car and I did not have my hands on the girls at all, but I saw that one rape her. They all raped her, every one of them. . . . The other boy sitting yonder had a knife around her throat, that one sitting on the end behind the little boy. . . . That little boy sitting behind yonder—I don't know his name—is the one that had a knife around her neck, making her lie down while the others raped her.

From what we know today, Norris was lying to save his life. Patterson followed suit. During cross-examination, he testified that he had seen five of the Scottsboro Boys rape Price (though a short time later, he would also claim that he had never seen Price and Bates on the train at all). Roy Wright said that he, too, had seen nine blacks have intercourse with Price and Bates "with my own eyes" (his older brother, Andy, would maintain that he had not seen the young women at all). And thus lies compounded lies.

The historical meaning of these first Scottsboro trials rests in this vast web of untruth, whereby the neuroses of caste were formalized, even sanctified, by the ritual procedures of law. Fortunately, their outcome, while historically important, would not be definitive. Two days before the Scottsboro Boys were sentenced, Judge Hawkins received a telegram from New York that condemned the convictions as the outcome of "trumped up charges" and warned that he would be held "personally responsible for the verdict." As it came from no controlling authority, he dismissed the message, but it would prove a harbinger of events to come. The following day, a statement was issued, again in New York, charging that the trials had been a "court-house lynching" of nine "Negro workers" perpetrated by the "parasite landlords and capitalist classes of the South." The telegram had come from the International Labor Defense, which would soon take the lead in defending the Scottsboro Boys and make their names familiar throughout the nation. The statement had been issued by the group of which the ILD was the legal arm: the Communist Party of the United States.[6]

The Communists had taken a strong interest in the Scottsboro defendants from the very start. In the Marxist rhetoric of the day, the plight of the young men was a symbol of the "superexploitation" of the black South, and thus their struggle could be deemed a battle in the worldwide war between workers and the ruling class. In the Scottsboro Boys the Party saw a new cause célèbre à la Sacco and Vanzetti, the murder trial of two Italian-American anarchists in Massachusetts that became a focal point of radical organizing throughout the 1920s. The Communists were also eager to make further inroads among Afro-Americans, who were vastly underrepresented in the Party's ranks. But in this effort, as in the specific purpose of helping the Scottsboro Boys, the Communists were opposed by the foremost black civil rights group of the time, the National Association for the Advancement of Colored People (NAACP).

When the Scottsboro defendants were arrested, the Communists believed they stood at a key moment in their history. They had always been revolutionaries, naturally, advocating the ultimate forcible seizure of the state by the proletariat. But especially from 1929 onward, amid the worldwide economic crisis, the time for that seizure in America and Europe seemed fast approaching, and the Party began to advocate with increasing force the tenet elaborated especially in Lenin's 1918 tract *State and Revolution*: that all reformers are as contemptible as the system they aim to reform. To make tinkering improvements to capitalism, easing its yoke on workers, was only to forestall the development of a true revolutionary consciousness among the masses and delay the inevitable rule of the proletariat within a genuine communist society. These years marked the beginning of what Joseph Stalin and the Comintern Executive Committee announced as the "third period" of the global Communist movement, the time that would see the final battle between the exploited and the exploiters—at least once the reformist social democrats, or "social fascists," were destroyed.

The status of blacks in the United States was not high on the international Communist agenda. In 1929, there were only about 200 black members of the Party in the United States. But during the "third period," perhaps precisely because black issues were peripheral, the Comintern discovered, as it were, the potential of race as fact and symbol. At the Sixth Comintern Congress and the Tenth Plenum of the Executive Committee, the international Party declared that American blacks constituted an oppressed nation within the United States and should be given the right to independent political self-determination. The Communist Party in America was charged with "the establishment of a Negro republic in the Black Belt," through the confiscation of white property and the unification of southern counties with black majorities into a single governmental district. The objective was part of a broader effort to recruit blacks in both the South and the North, and by 1930, black membership in the Party had jumped to 1,300.

A notable symbolic step in the organizing campaign was taken in New York in March 1931, shortly before the Scottsboro Boys were charged with rape; the context was a legal and cultural form that global Communism had contributed much to perfecting: a show trial. Earlier that year, a Finnish immigrant and Party member named August Yokinen, who worked as a janitor at the Finnish Workers Club in Harlem, had failed to come to the aid of several blacks who were attending a dance at the club when they were threatened by some of its members. The hostility of whites was understandable, Yokinen asserted, excusing the behavior, because if "Negroes came into the club," they soon also would want to use the sauna, and "he for one did not want to bathe with

Negroes." The Party decided not only to expel Yokinen from its ranks, but also to advertise its antiracist principles by making an example of him. Assembling a jury of seven blacks and seven whites, all of them representatives of various working-class groups, the Party staged a mock trial to which it invited the Harlem community through a mass-leafleting campaign, and on the chosen day, the thousand-chair hall was filled to capacity, with a thousand more standing outside, awaiting the sacrifice.

Yokinen was "prosecuted" by Clarence Hathaway, editor of the *Daily Worker,* and "defended" by Richard B. Moore, the great Afro-American orator of the Party and onetime member of the African Blood Brotherhood, whose advocacy for a black nation had influenced the ideological course of the Party itself. Hathaway declared that Yokinen should be expelled for his "crime" so that the Party could build a truly interracial movement on behalf of working people and surmount the "suspicions, the doubt, the mistrust, that every Negro worker [will have] of whites so long as incidents such as the Finnish dance are tolerated" and until "every member of our Party fulfills *in action* the Communist promise to the Negro masses." Citing the 1930 resolution of the Comintern, Hathaway declared that it was the duty of white workers to stamp out racism in their ranks, that "white workers, every white worker, must unhesitatingly jump at the throat of any person . . . who persecutes a Negro." Moore argued, in turn, that expulsion was too great a penalty for a Party member who had admitted his guilt, and that the fault lay in part with the earlier failures of the Party to instruct its membership in the evils of racial chauvinism. The better remedy, said Moore, was not to expel Yokinen, but to ensure that the Party's white members fought "side by side with the doubly oppressed Negro masses against the bosses [of the] Jim Crow lynching system, for full equality and self-determination."[7]

After such a performance, Yokinen enthusiastically agreed to the staged verdict, a compromise between the positions of the two speakers. He was to accept expulsion from the Party, willingly submitting to exile from its community—but he could be readmitted if he committed himself to leading the fight for black freedom in New York. The drama had achieved its catharsis, though with an unexpected twist. The day after the event, the immigrant Finn was arrested and scheduled for deportation. And shortly thereafter—three days after the Scottsboro Boys were arrested—the Party declared a "national day of struggle against lynching and deportations" to forge revolutionary unity among the white and black masses.

The Scottsboro case came as a boon to the Communists, a perfect sequel to the Yokinen affair. Through its legal arm, the International Labor Defense, the Party sought to gain control of the case after the first trial—and, by their speed, to deny the NAACP that advantage. The NAACP had moved slowly to represent the defendants, a sluggishness that resulted, in part, from its organizational structure, which was slow in alerting the national board to the potential significance of the case. More significantly, the NAACP was precisely the kind of ameliorative organization that Communists held in contempt. No doubt there were radicals in its ranks, but as a group, they were reformers and gradualists who worked within the system and sought to make alliances with the elite to advance their cause. The ILD jumped to the defense of the nine young men as representatives of the oppressed proletariat, their wretchedness being proof of their worthiness. But the NAACP, fearing the taint of association with the Scottsboro Boys, hesitated, preferring to wait until it could better establish their innocence and the extent to which their constitutional rights had been violated.

By the time the NAACP had committed itself in earnest to the defendants, the ILD already had established strong relations with them and their parents, especially their mothers. The Scottsboro Boys found themselves caught in the middle. The NAACP accused the Communists of self-interest, but the ILD showed its ability and readiness to bring the defendants' cause to the world stage. In January 1932, the NAACP ceded the battle and withdrew from the case. From then on, the ILD had a free hand to guide the defendants and, in truth, to use them, taking some of their mothers on tour throughout the United States and, in one instance, to Europe, to generate sympathy for the Communist cause and raise funds. The Communists had seized a rare opportunity to boost their Afro-American membership and to strengthen the cause of multiracial, revolutionary unity—as well as to attack the "social fascism" of mere reformers.

In March 1932, the Supreme Court of Alabama affirmed seven of the convictions (it reversed that of Eugene Williams because he was a juvenile at the time of his trial), but in May, the ILD successfully petitioned the U.S. Supreme Court to hear the case on appeal. And in November, by a vote of 7 to 2, the Court announced its decision in *Powell v. Alabama*, which would become a landmark case in the history of criminal procedure. Writing for the majority, Justice George Sutherland, one of the great libertarian conservatives on the bench, excoriated Judge Hawkins for his careless appointment of counsel. While the

Fourteenth Amendment certainly granted states the right to conduct their trials within a range of legitimate procedures under the broad principles of due process, this case, the justice found, transcended even that considerable latitude. The decision helped push the United States toward a national standard as to what constituted the "fair" procedures that states were required to provide criminal defendants—and, more immediately, it reversed the convictions of the Scottsboro Boys, setting them on a course toward a new trial (double jeopardy applies only after an acquittal), with a very different judge—and a most surprising witness for the defense.

Haywood Patterson's second trial began in Decatur, Alabama, on March 27, 1933. Presiding over the Morgan County courtroom was Judge James E. Horton, a gracious southerner, tall and lanky in a way that reminded many contemporaries of the young Abraham Lincoln. The son of a former slaveholder and the grandson of a Confederate general, he had been elected a circuit judge in 1922 after six years in the state legislature. That Judge Horton was to supervise the new trial of the Scottsboro Boys, now a national controversy—and, increasingly, a stain on Alabama's reputation—seemed a good omen. He was known for his equanimity, fairness, and serious cast of mind. The ILD, for its part, had hired the colorful New York criminal defense attorney Samuel Leibowitz. Of seventy-eight persons charged with first-degree murder, the Romanian-born attorney had won acquittals for seventy-seven (the seventy-eighth case resulted in a hung jury). Leibowitz, a solid Democrat, was no Communist, but he agreed to represent the Scottsboro Boys, with ILD chief counsel Joseph Brodsky, out of a sense of shock and indignation at their treatment, and he accepted the case pro bono. Over the next four years, his main adversary would be Thomas Knight, Jr., the attorney general of Alabama since 1930, whose father sat on the state supreme court that had upheld the original convictions in a 5-to-1 decision (the elder Knight was not the dissenting justice). Thomas Knight, Jr., was a formidable antagonist, a tough prosecutor who would shout at witnesses, belittle them with sarcasm, call black witnesses by their first names only, and who during the trial would refer to Patterson as "that thing."

    Leibowitz's strategy was plain from the start. As soon as Morgan County Solicitor Wade Wright read the grand jury indictments, Leibowitz declared them "null and void" and moved that they be "quashed." Though Judge Horton denied the motion, it was a historic one—an argument for the Scottsboro Boys based not on the factual question of their guilt or innocence, but rather on the process by which they were put on trial, indeed the very nature of the South's system of justice and vision of law. The indictments were defective, Leibowitz argued, because the grand jury that produced them had excluded Afro-Americans, in violation of the Equal Protection Clause of the Fourteenth Amendment. In *Strauder v. West Virginia*, in 1880, the U.S. Supreme Court had ruled that blacks could not be excluded from state juries solely on the basis of race (the case involved a statute that explicitly limited jury membership to "all white male persons"). But southern states dodged the ruling by constructing jury selection schemes that effectively excluded blacks on other, vaguer grounds. Alabama, for instance, excluded blacks from juries by requiring that men could serve only if they were "generally reputed to be honest and intelligent" and "esteemed in the community for their integrity, good character and sound judgment." Naturally, no black man would ever be found to meet these requirements, and thus white jury commissioners routinely excluded blacks from the central institution of Anglo-American law.

In Jackson County, where the indictments against the Scottsboro Boys were originally returned, about 7,800 men were qualified by age to serve on the grand jury. Over 600 were black, but not one of their names was to be found on the jury rolls. "For twenty-five years past," Leibowitz declared, "the officials of Jackson County have systematically refused and neglected to place the names of Negroes on the jury rolls . . . because they are members of the African race." "The State can't hide behind that law," he continued, "because it is not honestly administered. These Negroes as well as 40,000,000 others in the United States"—an exaggeration: there were about 12 million—"can only look to your Honor to uphold the Constitution of the United States and give it force." The editor of the *Scottsboro Progressive Age* confirmed Leibowitz's assertion that no black man had ever served on a jury in the county, but he argued that this was because they all lacked the reflective sagaciousness for such duty. "I know some good Negroes as far as Negroes go," asserted James Stockston Benson. "But I think that sound judgment part of the statute—I think they can't get around that. . . . I don't think there are any Negroes in our county that I'd care to risk in any case which involved justice and law."[8] Other prominent white officials made the same claim. In reply, Leibowitz called nine blacks from the county to testify; John Sanford, C. S. Finley, Mark Taylor, Trap Mosley, Louis Cole, Ples Larkin, John Stapler, Will Watkins, and L. C. Stapler showed themselves perfectly qualified to serve, as doubtless were others who, like these, had never had the chance. Judge Horton overruled the motion to quash. In his effort to quash the empaneled petit jury, Leibowitz next called blacks from Morgan County, which, being more prosperous than Jackson County, had an even greater number of obviously fit black jurors, men such as dentist Frank J. Stykes, a graduate of Howard University; Reverend W. J. Wilson; Dr. N. E. Cashin; Hulett J. Banks; Reverend L. R. Womack; the preacher W. G. Wilson; the high school principal J. D. Pickett; the pool-hall proprietor Robert Bridgeforth; and the undertaker George H. Reynolds. The testimony of J. E. Moody, head of the Jackson County board of jury commissioners, made clear that to place such men in a jury box was beyond the realm of the white imagination.

The climax of Leibowitz's attack came when he asked for the Morgan County jury roll—and the "towering sheriff," Bud Davis, "who stooped a little under its weight and bulk" brought in a "huge loose-leaf tome bound in red leather."[9] On the stand was Arthur Tidwell, one of the three county jury commissioners. Tidwell sat with the huge roll propped in front of him on a chair. "You and your fellow commissioners," Leibowitz demanded, "are required to place on that roll the names of all citizens who possess the qualifications prescribed by law—all citizens—isn't that true." Tidwell agreed. "Now, isn't it a fact," demanded Leibowitz, "that all the names written in that book are the names of white citizens?" Tidwell replied evasively, "I don't know"—to which Leibowitz responded with a shout, "Do you mean that for an honest answer." Tidwell swung around in his chair, making as if about to stand; color rose in his cheeks. "Do you mean to say that I would swear falsely?" he asked. "I don't mean to say anything," Leibowitz snapped, his voice growing louder. "I'm asking you a question. . . . Can you point to the name of any colored citizens on that page." "I don't know whether they are white, black or yellow," insisted the commissioner. Leibowitz was prepared. "It is my purpose and intention to prove that no Negro's name appears upon that jury roll, and I'll do it if it takes till doomsday." In the end, both of Leibowitz's motions to quash were denied—but Judge Horton nevertheless admitted that blacks clearly did not appear in the rolls. For the record, and for a higher court's review, Leibowitz had made his point.

At trial Victoria Price, hard and acerbic, gave little ground. It took Leibowitz a virtual eternity simply to obtain her admission that the model of the South Railroad he used in his examination was a reasonable replica of the train she was riding that day:

LEIBOWITZ: Just look at this little replica and tell me if this little miniature fairly represents the general appearance of the box car you spoke of.

PRICE: It kinda represents one, but it isn't like the one I was on.

LEIBOWITZ: In what way is it different, can you say?

PRICE: I won't say.

LEIBOWITZ: If you can't say why do you say it was different?

PRICE: Because that is not the train I was on.

LEIBOWITZ: Of course you were not on this miniature train, I asked you if this is a fair representation?

PRICE: Just a little bit.

LEIBOWITZ: Only just a little bit?

PRICE: Yes sir.

LEIBOWITZ: How does it differ?

PRICE: I didn't examine it.

LEIBOWITZ: You don't know whether it is different or not?

PRICE: I won't say.

LEIBOWITZ: You don't know do you?

PRICE: It is kind a little bit.

LEIBOWITZ: Little bigger.

PRICE: Sure it was bigger, lots bigger, that is a toy.

She knew what the prosecution required of her, and she almost never flinched:

LEIBOWITZ: They didn't spare you in any way, didn't try to make it comfortable for you in any way?

PRICE: No sir.

LEIBOWITZ: Just like brutes?

PRICE: Yes sir.

LEIBOWITZ: You lay on your back there for close to an hour on that jagged rock screaming?

PRICE: Yes sir.

LEIBOWITZ: Was your back bleeding when you got to the doctor?

PRICE: I couldn't say.

LEIBOWITZ: When you got to the jail did you find any blood on your back?

PRICE: A little bit.

LEIBOWITZ: Are you sure about that?

PRICE: I ain't sure, that has been two years ago.

In the end, the poor millworker would prove one of the most difficult witnesses Samuel Leibowitz would ever face.

Leibowitz's tough cross-examination and his effort to reveal Price's checkered marital and sexual history, however, ended up backfiring. He seemed to be mounting a merciless attack on southern white womanhood, and this attack only added to the danger he faced as a Jewish lawyer from New York defending a group of black men accused of rape in Alabama. The tactics could only have incited the passions of those who wanted to see the Scottsboro Boys dispatched in accordance with southern tradition. So great was the mob animus toward the defendants that Judge Horton issued a long, pointed statement cautioning those who might consider doing them any harm. "I am here listening to this case trying to sift the truth or not the truth of it," the judge exclaimed, "and I am going to strengthen that guard if necessary, and I am going to let everyone know that . . . you have got to kill them before you get these prisoners. That is understood, and they have told me they would, and they will do it. . . . [S]o far as I am concerned I believe I am as gentle as any man in the world; I don't believe I would harm anyone wrongfully, but when it comes to a question of right and wrong, when it comes to the very civilization, men no matter how quiet they are, or how peaceful they are, there comes a time when they must take a stand."[10]

Nor was Judge Horton the only southerner involved in the proceedings who sought to live up to those ideals: so did one of the physicians who had originally examined Price and Bates. Dr. Marvin Lynch's statement was in fact so explosive that he dared not announce it from the

stand—he asked to speak to the judge alone. As a bailiff stood guard outside the door of the men's room, apparently the nearest private space
available, Dr. Lynch explained that from the very start he had believed
the two young women were lying. Neither had been raped, and they had
fabricated their stories seemingly without a second thought. "My God,
Doctor, is this whole thing a horrible mistake?" Judge Horton asked.
"Judge," the doctor replied, "I looked at both the women and told them
they were lying, that they knew they had not been raped, and they just
laughed at me." And there was another southerner who had been converted to the truth as well—Victoria Price's old friend Ruby Bates.
Whether influenced by the workings of her own conscience or the gifts
and acclaim she would receive through the ILD (a bit of both, surely),
she had had a change of heart. Price's story, she asserted, was a complete
fabrication.

Bates testified as to the source of the semen found by the
medical examiners. Two nights before, she had had intercourse with a man
named Lester Carter, and Victoria Price had had intercourse with a
man named Jack Tiller. The day before, they had spent the evening in a
place called Hobo Swamp with Lester Carter and Orville Gilley, who
were also on the train the following day, Carter playing the harmonica
as Gilley sang songs and recited poetry. "Tell the gentlemen of the jury
what happened . . . when you got in that car and when the train started
out for Stevenson," Leibowitz instructed her.

BATES: After the train start out from Stevenson, there was some
white boys come in the end of the car next to where we
were.

LEIBOWITZ: In the next gondola?

BATES: Yes sir.

LEIBOWITZ: What happened?

BATES: And after a while there was a bunch of negroes come
over and started fighting, they was all fighting and
Lester Carter and this Gilley boy jumped over to help
them out.

LEIBOWITZ: You mean Lester Carter and Gilley left the gondola in
which you were in and went into the next gondola where
the fight was between the white boys and the negroes?

BATES: Yes sir.

LEIBOWITZ: Then what happened?

BATES: The negroes put all the boys off but one, Orville Gilley, and he came back in the car where we were.

LEIBOWITZ: Then what happened, when you, Victoria and Gilley were there. Did the negroes come in that car where you were?

BATES: Not that I know of.

LEIBOWITZ: Did any negro attack you that day?

BATES: Not that I know of.

LEIBOWITZ: Did any negro attack Victoria Price that day?

BATES: Not that I know of.

LEIBOWITZ: Did you see any negro attack Victoria Price that day?

BATES: No sir.

.   .   .   .

LEIBOWITZ: You testified at Scottsboro that six negroes raped you and six negroes raped her, and one had a knife on your throat; what happened to her was exactly the same thing that happened to you. Who coached you to say that?

BATES: [Victoria Price] told it and I told it just like she told it.

LEIBOWITZ: Who told you to tell that story?

BATES: I told it like she told it.

LEIBOWITZ: Who told you to do that, who coached you to do that?

BATES: She did.

LEIBOWITZ: Did she tell you what would happen to you if you didn't follow her story?

BATES: She said we might have to lay out a sentence in jail.

But even this recantation was to have no effect. Whether on account of the deft probing of Attorney General Knight, who could unnerve any witness, or of the closing argument of Solicitor Wright, so inflammatory as to make even the attorney general blush—"Show them," Wright told the jury, "that Alabama justice cannot be bought and sold with Jew money from New York"—the jurors did not disappoint the state. On April 9, 1933, they returned a verdict of guilty, and demanded that Patterson be electrocuted. They deliberated for twelve hours. The guilty verdict, they later reported, was arrived at in just under five minutes. It had taken the rest of the time to reason with one of the jurors who had held out for life imprisonment.

Judge Horton was not so expeditious. On April 18, he ordered that the trials of the other defendants be postponed because of the mob atmosphere in the county and the danger the prosecutions would pose to the community. On June 22, amid nationwide protests organized in large part by the International Labor Defense, Horton called the attorneys in the case to the courtroom in Athens, his hometown. The ostensible purpose of the summons was to hear the defense motions for a new trial; the defense expected these would be denied, thus giving them basis for an appeal. Judge Horton's true purpose, however, was to set aside the decision of the jury, vacate Patterson's conviction, and grant him a new trial.

"Social order is based on law," the judge began to read from a prepared statement, "and its perpetuity on its fair and impartial administration." But the trials over which he had presided, he argued, reviewing the witnesses and the evidence, clearly had not been fair. "History, sacred and profane," he continued,

> and the common experience of mankind teach us that women of the character shown in this case are prone for selfish reasons to make false accusations both of rape and of insult upon the slightest provocation for ulterior purposes. . . . The testimony of the prosecutrix in this case is not only uncorroborated, but it also bears on its face indications of improbability and is contradicted by other evidence, and in addition thereto the evidence greatly preponderates in favor of the defendant. . . . It is therefore ordered and adjudged by the Court . . . that the verdict of the jury in this case and the judgment of the Court sentencing this defendant to death be set aside and that a new trial be and the same is hereby ordered.

It was the end of James Horton's career as a judge in the state of Alabama. Previously unopposed, he would lose his bid for reelection in 1934, never again to hold elected office.[11]

· · ·

Attorney General Knight had the cases removed from Judge Horton's court, and they were next to be tried by Judge William Callahan, the sort of jurist on whom the prosecution could rely. Judge Callahan sought first and foremost to "debunk the Scottsboro case" and take it out of the national spotlight. He forbade photographers from his court. He made it difficult for reporters to cover the trial by denying them access to their reserved seats. He asked Governor Meeks Miller to recall the National Guard, and he encouraged prominent citizens not to attend. Described by one reporter from Birmingham as "a perfect ass," Judge Callahan seemed clearly biased.[12] As Haywood Patterson and Clarence Norris faced their third and second trials, respectively, he granted virtually every challenge by the prosecution and contemptuously denied every request of the defense. In his final instructions to the jury, he glared at Leibowitz, heaping scorn on his arguments while giving Victoria Price's testimony every possible benefit of credence. On charging the jury in Patterson's case, Judge Callahan described the form in which they could render a verdict of guilty, neglecting even to describe the form of the contrary verdict until Leibowitz intervened. The jury disposed of both defendants quickly and, in early December 1933, in Decatur, asked that each of them be executed. On December 5, Judge Callahan duly sentenced them to the electric chair.

But in his zeal to see the Scottsboro case over and done, Callahan made an error that would earn him the rebuke of the U.S. Supreme Court. For even before the trials had begun, Leibowitz once again challenged the Morgan County petit jury panel and the original Jackson County grand jury for having excluded Negroes. Under the 1880 Supreme Court decision of *Neal v. Delaware*, states could be deemed to have violated the Fourteenth Amendment not only through explicitly exclusionary jury-selection statutes, but also by extrastatutory means— for instance, through the systematic efforts of commissioners and administrative officers. The doctrine remained in force even if, by the early twentieth century, it had fallen into disuse. While Judge Callahan would have done nothing to revive it, Leibowitz saw an opportunity for a future appeal, and so offered the same evidence of racial exclusion in the petit jury venire he had presented to Judge Horton. Judge Callahan found it no more persuasive than Horton had and concluded that the commissioners had discharged their duties honorably within the bounds of the law. Motion to quash denied. As for the grand jury, Judge Callahan allowed J. E. Moody to testify once again about the state of jury selection in Jackson County. He must have expected a repeat of the performance the commissioner had given before Judge Horton. Samuel Leibowitz surely did, too. Both were mistaken.

When the "mammoth" leather volume containing the names of the potential jurors of Jackson County was brought into the courtroom, Leibowitz asked Moody to read from the list, and indicate any names of black citizens he might find.[13] Moody began to read. He read aloud for an hour. At one point, he grew so weary that C. A. Wann, court clerk, had to take over. The court emptied. Judge Callahan left the bench to chat with a group of reporters. Then Moody read the name of Hugh Sanford. "He's a Negro," said the commissioner calmly. Judge Callahan raced back to his seat. Leibowitz asked to see the page from which he had read. The book registered potential jurors by voting precinct. When Moody assumed office on March 20, 1931, he had asked his secretary to draw two red lines immediately beneath the names of the jurors gathered over the past nine years—the names below the lines could only have been added to the rolls later. The name Hugh Sanford seemed to be written, in green ink, *on* the lines. Moody continued reading. Mark Taylor also was a Negro—indeed, he was among those blacks whom Leibowitz had called in the earlier trial to testify as to his qualifications to serve as a juror. His name seemed to have been the very last one entered for his precinct before Moody took office, just above the red lines. "How about Cam Rudder?" asked Leibowitz, flipping through the book. "Is he black or white?" "Don't know," replied Moody. "For Your Honor's information," Leibowitz announced, "Rudder is a Negro." The two red lines ran *through* his name. "Now," asked Leibowitz, "can you tell us whether the lines are on top of the name or the name on top of the lines?" "Don't know" was the reply. "Never mind," Leibowitz retorted, "we'll have some one here who can tell us about that."

In the next court session, Leibowitz produced John Vreeland Haring, a handwriting expert, who had raced to Decatur from Birmingham. Under a twenty-power microscope, he examined the ten black names on the Jackson County rolls and pronounced them to be new entries, added after Moody had assumed office. The same clerk who had served from 1926 to 1931 had indeed written them, but he had left so little space above the red lines that, in all cases but one, at least part of the new entries had been written on top of the underscores, crossing over the lines. And in the case of Travis Mosley's name, the hook end of its *y* was written directly over the notation "3/20/31" and so could not have preceded the date. Callahan, Leibowitz, and Knight all took turns gazing through the microscope. After about half an hour, Judge Callahan pronounced the evidence too confusing—some of the red lines had been written over dates as well—and so he ruled it unfounded to "presume that somebody committed a crime . . . [or] that a jury board, being sworn officers of the law, have been unfaithful to their duties and allowed tampering. It would be a reflection on them." He concluded "that there were at the time of the indictment the names of colored men on the jury rolls"—and, with that, denied Leibowitz's motion to quash the indictment.[14] For Leibowitz, ironically, it was a triumph. The evidence of forgery by Jackson County officials might well be less "confusing" to another judge. He had discovered sure grounds for appeal.

Fifteen months later, on February 15, 1935, Leibowitz would address the Court of United States Chief Justice Charles Evans Hughes. Describing the systematic exclusion of blacks from Alabama juries, he argued that the state had violated the Fourteenth Amendment doctrine the Court had laid down decades before in cases such as *Neal v. Delaware*. He described the Jackson County rolls as a fraud perpetrated against not only his clients but against the Court itself. When the stern, severe, and fiercely intelligent Hughes looked at Leibowitz and demanded, "Can you prove this forgery?" a page brought the mammoth, leather-bound volume to the Chief Justice. It was a highly unusual moment in the history of the Court. To decide on questions of law was one matter, the role the Court generally played when reviewing cases on appeal. But to review physical evidence already passed upon by a lower court—to seize that book from a state that would shortly become an icon of the southern commitment to states' rights, and to examine it on behalf of the national rights of Afro-American citizens to sit in the jury box—was a historic, symbolic act in the history of black citizenship.

With a magnifying glass, Chief Justice Hughes considered the tome. He silently passed it to Justice Willis Van Devanter, who gave it to Justice Louis Brandeis, who gave it to Justice Pierce Butler, and to Justice Owen Roberts, whereupon the book was brought to the other end of the table to Justice Harlan Fiske Stone. Each in his turn assumed an air of disgust.

On April 1, the Court issued its decision in *Norris v. Alabama*. "The question is of the application of this established principle [of *Neal v. Delaware*] to the facts disclosed by the record," explained the Chief Justice, warding off potential criticism of the Court's active examination of the Jackson County rolls. "If this requires an examination of evidence, that examination must be made. Otherwise, review by this Court would fail of its purpose in safeguarding constitutional rights." And that examination, he continued, had produced rather unseemly facts. "An expert of long experience testified that these names were superimposed upon the red lines, that is, that they were written after the lines had been drawn," explained Chief Justice Hughes. In the face of this evidence, Judge Callahan had justified his denial of Leibowitz's motion by "express[ing] the view that he would not 'be authorized to presume that somebody had committed a crime' or to presume that the jury board 'had been unfaithful to their duties and allowed the books to be tampered with.'" Instead, the Chief Justice explained, Judge Horton chose to conclude "that the names of the negroes were on the [original] jury roll." In response, the Chief Justice stated tersely, "We think that the evidence did not justify that conclusion." He then proceeded to demolish Judge Callahan's ruling in the very words of the county officials whose integrity the judge was so wary of impugning. "The testimony of the commissioner on this crucial question puts the case in a strong light," declared the Chief Justice. "That testimony leads to the conclusion that these or other negroes were not excluded on account of age, or lack of esteem in the community for integrity and judgment, or because of disease or want of any other qualification. The commissioner's answer to specific inquiry upon this point was that negroes were 'never discussed.'"[15]

The next day, Samuel Leibowitz, "thrilled beyond words," announced that he would be returning immediately to Alabama to ask that the case against the nine Scottsboro Boys be dismissed. "Mr. Leibowitz," the *New York Times* reported, "said he will make the trip by airplane." "The victory just won for the 'Scottsboro boys' in the Supreme Court of the United States," he declared, "is the culmination of the hopes and ambitions of 15,000,000 Negro souls in America. More than two years ago when I took up the case on behalf of these innocent Negro boys I knew then that our only salvation lay in the highest court of the land, and I then laid the groundwork for an appeal in the event of a conviction, which was a foregone conclusion." The case, he exclaimed, was a turning point in American civic life and the life of American law. "For the first time in the history of American jurisprudence," announced Leibowitz, "actual proof by way of living witnesses was produced in open court in an attack against bigotry and prejudice which bars the Negro citizen, although qualified, from serving on a jury in any of the State courts in that part of the country." It was, in Leibowitz's view, a triumph of national ideals—and, despite the defense's sponsorship, did not presage the creeping advance of socialism. Indeed, he declared, "[t]he decision of the highest court, just handed down, is a triumph for American justice and is an answer to all those subversive elements who seek to engender hatred against our form of government."[16]

Whether that triumph would now help set the Scottsboro Boys free, however, was another question entirely. For the nine still had many trials ahead.

On January 23, 1936, Haywood Patterson was convicted before Judge Callahan and sentenced to seventy-five years in prison. He escaped in 1948 and settled in Michigan. There, in 1950, he was apprehended by the FBI, but the governor refused to extradite him to Alabama. That same year, Patterson was involved in a barroom brawl and killed a man. He was convicted of manslaughter and died of cancer in the state penitentiary in 1952.

As for Clarence Norris, he was convicted and sentenced to death, but was paroled in 1944. He soon violated the terms of his release by leaving Alabama, and he lived in hiding for decades. Despite several subsequent brushes with the law, he was never caught. He was finally pardoned by Governor George Wallace in 1976. The day he was told of his freedom, Norris called his sister, to whom he hadn't spoken in twenty-three years, and learned that his mother had died the year before.

In 1937, Charles Weems was convicted and sentenced to seventy-five years. That same year, he contracted tuberculosis. In 1938, he was stabbed by a prison guard. He was paroled in 1943.

Andy Wright was sentenced to ninety-nine years. He was paroled with Norris in 1944 but he, too, violated parole. In 1946, he was apprehended and sent to Kilby Prison. He was paroled again in 1950, almost twenty years after the fateful afternoon when he had been bound with plow line and taken to jail in Scottsboro.

The charge of rape against Andy's brother Roy was dropped the same month that Andy was convicted. Roy joined the merchant marine. After returning home from a long voyage at sea, he found his wife at the home of another man and, believing her to have been unfaithful, he shot and killed her. He then returned home and killed himself.

About two years after Samuel Leibowitz won his Supreme Court victory, Ozie Powell pled guilty to assaulting a deputy sheriff while awaiting his trial (during the assault, Powell was shot in the head). He was sentenced to twenty years and paroled in 1946.

All charges were dropped against Eugene Williams, Willie Roberson, and Olen Montgomery. After that they drifted.

Roberson died of an asthma attack in his Brooklyn apartment in the early 1960s.

Williams moved to St. Louis, where his sponsors thought he would enroll in a Baptist seminary.

Montgomery had hoped to become a jazz musician. He bought a saxophone, but nothing ever came of the wish. Like the other Scottsboro Boys, he received some assistance from the ILD, but not for long.

Eventually, the nine young men who had been martyrs for proletarian revolution through much of the 1930s were abandoned by the Communists as the Party moved on to other, pressing matters. In 1935, the Communist International in Moscow decided that the historical moment now called not for opposition to social democrats and other reformers, but rather for collaboration with them in the more urgent struggle against fascism. Groups like the NAACP, with a liberal vision of reform, were no longer derided as the enemy of the black masses, and while the Communist Party remained a decided foe of race discrimination, its program for a black nation in the South was indefinitely postponed.

11

Hearts and Minds

▲

Long after Jim Crow had faded into memory, scholars, lawyers, and journalists would recall the day, May 17, 1954, the U.S. Supreme Court announced its decision in the school segregation cases, and spoke in a language of redemption.[1] They would hail the decision as "a sign of hope" that washed away "shame," "redeemed our national values," and represented "nothing short of a reconsecration of American ideals." Those who witnessed Chief Justice Earl Warren deliver the unanimous opinion of the Court or who waited anxiously by the phone would describe having felt elated, "ecstatic," and "clean." Their emotions were not disproportionate. The decision, better known by the name of one of the four separate legal disputes it consolidated—*Brown v. Board of Education*—was the most important victory for American civil rights in the twentieth century. Most immediately, it declared racial segregation in public schools to be a violation of the Fourteenth Amendment of the Constitution, thereby sounding the death knell for Jim Crow generally. But even more, it began a revolution that would transform American conceptions of civic life, changing the nature of our law and national identity in ways we are still reckoning. In the words of one prominent legal theorist, *Brown* represented "all that the law might be."[2]

The story of *Brown* is one of particular people engaged in specific legal battles over discrete practices of segregation—of individual person-alities and historical particulars. It includes men like Thurgood Marshall, chief legal strategist for the National Association for the Advancement of Colored People; Kenneth Clark, one of the social scientists whose work was cited by the *Brown* Court in its decision and whose "doll stud-ies" became an icon of the case and its reasoning; Earl Warren, whose political skill enabled the Court to make a crucially unanimous ruling; the members of the White Citizens' Council, part of the network of "massive resistance" through which many southerners aimed to defy the Court's order; and the Reverend Martin Luther King, Jr., whose Chris-tian activism helped wrest the civic vision of *Brown* into being. The story of *Brown* is, in addition, a technical story of constitutional law. It is a cen-tral moment in the history of the Supreme Court's interpretation of the Fourteenth Amendment, which guarantees to "all persons" the "equal protection of the laws." It was a counterweight to the Court's notorious 1896 decision in *Plessy v. Ferguson*, swinging with a momentum that had been accumulating through earlier cases that set the stage for *Brown* by considering "intangible" differences between white and black schools.

And while the most visible and dramatic features of the case concern individual actors, *Brown* is also the story of a metaphysical transforma-tion, a change in what scholars have called "the human subject." *Brown* is a tale of the individual personality and the community, of the ways in which the relation between the self and the nation-state was under-stood in American law and culture at mid-century. In the near term, it was an acknowledgment, for the first time, that the Afro-American self had been psychologically damaged by the perverse logic of the law. The acknowledgment would give force to a social and political sea change known by the byword "integration," and usher in the era of modern legal liberalism, with its distinctive vision of law, self, and society. At the same time, *Brown* would crystallize and focus the power of the civic tra-ditions of Christianity and caste. In these ways, its significance would extend beyond its immediate effects on the rights of blacks; the decision would become a touchstone for assessing the civic status of all American minorities.

Brown is one of the great markers of who we are as a people. The case stands at a crossroads in the history of American civic identity that we may still glimpse if we look behind us.

Perhaps before we know it, it will become difficult for Americans to comprehend what our country was like under Jim Crow. Appreciating the experience of the "color line" will be as great a feat of the imagination as reconstructing the worldview of a vassal in medieval Europe. Jim Crow will have become a symbol of a historic abomination, but the precise nature of its evil will have passed beyond direct experience or recollection. The memory of Jim Crow is fading so rapidly, in fact, that today one sometimes hears otherwise sensible people, keen to improve our society, equate the racial inequalities of our own time with those of America before World War II, or during the 1950s and 1960s. At a recent conference at Harvard Law School, for instance, a young scholar berated his older colleagues who had fought in the Civil Rights Movement by pointing to various indicators of contemporary Afro-American social and economic disadvantage; his voice hot with anger, he repeatedly declared "nothing has changed—nothing has changed." It is not an uncommon view, and however preposterous it may be, the moral power it is accorded, with the best of intentions, ensures it some longevity.

We owe the speed with which Jim Crow is passing from the American imagination to the relative peacefulness of its abolition. It would be a terrible mistake to minimize the violence and the great sacrifice involved in fighting segregation: the marches, the jailings, the threats, the murders. But from a comparative, global perspective, the revolution America underwent in abolishing Jim Crow was remarkable for its stability, for its avoidance of mass bloodshed, and, indeed, for not utterly tearing the nation apart. One only has to look to other multiethnic societies that made similar transformations, such as South Africa, to have an inkling of what race relations in the United States might have become. And this relative lack of violence attending the abolition of Jim Crow has, ironically, obscured just how different the world of Jim Crow is from our own—just how *much* has changed. For the American caste system involved not only the social and economic inequality of whites and blacks, and the physical separation of the races (both of which persist today, though as ever-diminishing realities), but also a pervasive vision that divided the world between the quasi-metaphysical polarities of white purity and black pollution. Under Jim Crow, especially in the South, a wall separated blacks from whites not just in the material world but also within the social imagination.

What did that division entail? Jim Crow barred Afro-Americans, by custom and by law, from eating in the same restaurants as whites, lest their presence contaminate the ritual of the meal. The South maintained racially segregated drinking fountains, waiting areas, laundromats, hotels, bars—anywhere the races might come into close contact. Blacks were expected to announce their presence at a white home or office at the back door. Many labor unions were closed to blacks (so much for efforts to unite the proletariat), as were social clubs to those black professionals who could afford membership. In courts of law, jury rolls excluded blacks, and separate Bibles were at times used to swear in blacks and whites. And, especially in rural areas, blacks were barred by various means—law, force, custom, and intricate combinations of the three— from exercising their right to elect political representatives. Let a final example suffice to summarize the rest. When one black civil rights activist of the 1960s attempted to "integrate" a swimming pool by diving in, swimming a lap, and then drying off, the response was to drain the pool entirely and refill it with fresh water.[3]

The group that contributed most to destroying this odious vision of American life was the National Association for the Advancement of Colored People. Founded in 1909 at a New York conference of individuals and groups dedicated to black equality, its expressed goal was "to achieve, through peaceful and lawful means, equal citizenship rights for all American citizens by eliminating segregation and discrimination in housing, employment, voting, schools, the courts, transportation, and recreation." The NAACP was a decidedly liberal group, but the white South viewed it as radical. Though its New York origins stigmatized its members as "outside agitators," its aims were extreme only from the perspective of a caste society thoroughly dedicated to maintaining white supremacy. White racists were not its sole enemies. The group came under the heated criticism of the Communist Party in the 1930s, as we have seen, and in the 1960s and 1970s was derided by black militant groups for being racially inclusive; in fact, its first president, Moorfield Storey, former secretary of Charles Sumner, was a white lawyer from Boston, a shrewd choice that brought the organization influence, while also exemplifying its multiracial civic principles.

During its early years, the NAACP achieved a number of meaningful victories in the political arena and the court of public opinion. In 1915, for instance, it organized a nationwide protest against D. W. Griffith's notorious account of Reconstruction, *The Birth of a Nation*. In 1918, under great pressure from the NAACP, President Woodrow Wilson made a formal public statement condemning lynching. The association advanced its cause through litigation, too, but its success before the bar was piecemeal and uncoordinated (losing control of the Scottsboro case to the Communists was typical of its difficulties). Moreover, though it was the nation's foremost association for black civil rights, it lacked a "grand strategy" for overturning Jim Crow. That began to change in the early 1930s with a grant from a philanthropist. The Garland Fund had been established in 1922 by a Harvard undergraduate, Charles Garland, who rather than enjoy his inherited millions chose out of principle to give the money to liberal and radical groups—"I am placing my life," he explained, "on a Christian basis." Under James Weldon Johnson, director of Garland and former general secretary of the NAACP, the fund pledged $100,000 to the group for "a large-scale, widespread, dramatic campaign to give the Southern Negro his constitutional rights, his political and civil equality, and therewith a self-consciousness and self-respect which would inevitably tend to effect a revolution in the economic life of the country."[4]

Only a fraction of Garland's original pledge found its way to the NAACP (the fund collapsed with the stock market in 1929) but enough seed money had flowed to ensure something would come of it. Among other activities, the NAACP hired a young graduate of Harvard Law School to develop a new comprehensive litigation strategy. Nathan Ross Margold was a Jewish émigré born in Romania who had come to the United States as a child. At Harvard, he became a protégé of Felix Frankfurter—a professor and, later, one of the justices to decide *Brown v. Board of Education*—before serving as an assistant U.S. attorney in New York and beginning a successful career in private practice. Margold has been described as "a brilliant man of the law," and the 1933 document known simply as the Margold Report bore out his reputation. Recommending a concerted attack on segregation in public education as the leading edge of a broader effort to destroy Jim Crow, the report became "the Bible" of the NAACP legal campaign that led to May 1954.[5] In fact, the report was no more radical than the association itself—its approach was legal, its rhetoric technical, and its agenda directed toward influencing a conservative system of courts—but in time it would bear the fruit of a transformation in American civic life that was fundamental indeed.

If anyone can enjoy credit for cultivating that fruit, it was Thurgood Marshall. Born into a middle-class black family in Baltimore in 1908, Marshall was graduated at the top of his class of eleven from Howard University Law School in 1933. There, he had come under the influence of its remarkable dean, Charles Hamilton Houston, who encouraged students to work on behalf of civil rights (he would be celebrated for instructing them that a lawyer was either a "social engineer" or "a parasite on society").[6] After Howard, Marshall joined the NAACP and in

1939 became the director of its new litigation branch, the Legal Defense and Educational Fund. In retrospect, he was clearly ideal for the job. In his private life and his work, he was deeply committed to liberal ideals and a multiracial, integrationist vision. Notably, Marshall also was light-skinned—his father had blond hair and blue eyes—a fact that fed a deep skepticism of black nationalism, whose exponents, such as Marcus Garvey, typically prized dark pigmentation (to the vexation of later black radicals, Marshall would take a Filipina as his second wife). Most important, as a consummate professional, Marshall had an abiding belief in change through law, not force, and proved a superb technical legal strategist, still known as one of the great litigators of the era. Appropriately enough, he would earn the nickname "Mr. Civil Rights."

The Fourteenth Amendment was enacted in the wake of the Civil War to protect the newly freed slaves of the South against oppression by state governments. While the condition of freedmen was its main concern, the amendment has grown over time in scope and consequence. Because it does not mention race, its protections—especially its guarantee of "equal protection of the laws" and "due process of law"—apply to everyone in the United States; indeed, because it speaks of "persons," it applies equally to formal citizens and noncitizens, even illegal aliens. In its broad protection of rights, the amendment would also figure in American economic history; it was invoked in the early twentieth century by the Supreme Court in a way that advanced a vision of laissez-faire capitalism, causing Justice Oliver Wendell Holmes to quip that the conservative majority had used the amendment to enact the social theories of Herbert Spencer as constitutional principle. More fundamentally, as it developed, the amendment became a bridge between two polarities within American political life, the nation and the self. On one hand, the amendment has been a force for nationalization. It has increased the power of national institutions and ideologies relative to those of the states. At the same time, it has been a force of individualization, fostering and protecting the domain of the individual human ego by guaranteeing to all persons a series of rights against state and local government. The Fourteenth Amendment has linked a postbellum rise of national sovereignty with a markedly heightened valuation of the self that is not only fundamental to democratic theories of liberty but, in the latter half of the twentieth century, was in fact the hallmark of our culture. The amendment created a more perfect Union, paradoxically, by strengthening the rights and authority of the individual—a link ever more central to a nation in which individuals make greater claims to have their distinctive traits socially acknowledged and legally protected.

The Fourteenth Amendment as we have it today was constructed through a long process of congressional and judicial interpretation in which the NAACP Legal Defense and Educational Fund's campaign against Jim Crow played a pivotal role. For that campaign was directed against the view of the Fourteenth Amendment that helped sanctify the end of Reconstruction, the view established in 1896 by *Plessy v. Ferguson*, particularly its vision of the Afro-American self and its relation to law. In that case, as we have seen, the U.S. Supreme Court provided a major doctrinal underpinning for Jim Crow by endorsing within Fourteenth Amendment jurisprudence what became known as the "separate but equal" doctrine. The doctrine was significant not only for upholding racial segregation, but also for the manner of its argument: in determining that Afro-Americans, though confined to separate train cars, were not denied the equal protection of the laws, the Court adopted a distinctly psychological cast of reasoning. Specifically, against the claim that racial segregation in public transit harms Afro-Americans in ways that should trigger the protection of the Constitution, Justice Henry Billings Brown asserted that if black Americans felt segregation as a harm, such feeling was all in their minds—that the harm had no tangible reality. Afro-Americans' belief that the "enforced separation of the two races stamps the colored race with a badge of inferiority," he wrote, was not "because of anything in the law itself." It was simply because "the colored race chooses to put that interpretation on it."

By downgrading institutional humiliation to mere touchiness, as it were, on the part of blacks, this argument cleared the way for the increasingly ludicrous practices of the world of Jim Crow, whose affronts to individual dignity could not be called "imagined" by any stretch. The separate drinking fountains, laundromats, hotels, and clubs, the separate Bibles—all this, under the logic of *Plessy*, could be deemed degrading only if Afro-Americans decided to take it that way. With *Plessy*, the Court, in effect, ruled that Afro-Americans were not capable, per se, of sustaining a legally cognizable injury, one that was real, not merely imaginary. There was in principle no way to wrong a black American by any manner of official racial segregation. The legal scholar Charles Black, writing of the *Brown* decision, later asserted that the argument could not withstand the scholar's "sovereign right" to laugh. It was Thurgood Marshall who would force the averted gaze of common sense to take another look at the Court's argument in *Plessy* respecting the status of the black self under Jim Crow.

In this effort, Marshall heeded the Margold Report's advice to focus special attention on segregation in public education, particularly in graduate and professional schools. He began by demanding that the principle of separate but equal be made as good as its word. The NAACP initiated a series of suits to compel states with segregated institutions to implement *Plessy*'s principle of "equality" by allocating equal resources to its white and black schools—a strategy designed to force an end to segregation by putting pressure on southern pocketbooks. These cases, known as equalization suits, began to use the doctrinal logic of Jim Crow against itself. In *Missouri ex rel. Gaines v. Canada* in 1938, for instance, the NAACP achieved an important victory when the Supreme Court ruled that the State of Missouri could not deny Lloyd Gaines admission to its whites-only law school as long as it did not also maintain a separate one for blacks. Nor could Missouri fulfill its obligations under *Plessy* by paying his tuition to a law school outside the state. Missouri was required, the Court held, either actually to provide equal facilities for both whites and blacks or to end its policy of racial exclusion in toto.

Twelve years after *Gaines*, in 1950, the Court elaborated its interpretation of the meaning of "separate but equal" in *Sweatt v. Painter* (and a companion case, *McLaurin v. Oklahoma State Regents*). In *Sweatt*, the Court held that a black applicant refused admission to the University of Texas School of Law had been denied equal protection of the laws—even though, unlike Lloyd Gaines, he had been offered admission to a new law school in Texas created specifically for Afro-Americans. The new black school, not surprisingly, fell far below the white school in its level of resources and quality of education. In the part of its ruling most nettlesome for segregationists, the Court stated that even if the black law school had provided facilities equal to those of its white counterpart—even if the physical premises, the library holdings, and the course instruction had been the same in both institutions—the older white school would necessarily possess "a far greater degree [of] those qualities which are incapable of objective measurement but which make for greatness in a law school." Those qualities included the "reputation of the faculty, experience of the administration, position and influence of the alumni, standing in the community, traditions and prestige." In upholding the claim of the prospective black law student, the Court would consider factors beyond institutional structure and financial

resources to decide whether an educational facility lived up to its obligations under *Plessy*; it would consider symbolic, or "intangible," factors
as well.

This doctrinal acknowledgment of intangibles opened the way for
the NAACP's direct assault on *Plessy*. The invisible, symbolic world the
Court had invoked in *Sweatt* enabled the NAACP not only to attack the
implementation of *"separate but equal,"* but also to show that segregated
facilities, by definition, could never meet the demands of the Fourteenth
Amendment. Under the leadership of Marshall and fellow attorney
Robert Carter, the organization joined four separate lawsuits contesting
segregation in primary and secondary schooling. The Jim Crow schools
at issue, significantly, were not all in the South, but ranged as far north
as Delaware and as far west as Kansas; indeed, the consolidated case
would ultimately take its name from a northern suit, *Brown v. Board of
Education of Topeka*. Unlike the graduate facilities of the earlier NAACP
suits, some of the schools in the cases offered facilities and curricula that
were demonstrably equal to those of their white counterparts or in the
process of being "equalized." In the wake of *Sweatt*, however, the NAACP
could claim that no matter the degree of overt parity, the mere fact that
two schools were divided by race inevitably made the Afro-American
schools inferior to their white counterparts. The law of separate-but-
equal, Marshall would argue, necessarily inflicted an injury on the black
self. The harm it visited upon impressionable children who were black
was intrinsic to its very logic.

Such an attack would require Marshall to contradict the essential
psychological underpinning of the Court's opinion in *Plessy*, to challenge
its view of human personality and its relation to law. "I told the staff,"
recalled Marshall, "that we had to try this case just like any other one in
which you would try to prove damages to your client. If your car ran
over my client, you'd have to pay up, and my function as an attorney
would be to put experts on the stand to testify to how much damage was
done."[7] Here, Marshall made a historic choice. To document such
"intangible" inequality, he depended on more than legal arguments and
turned as well to modern social science, especially sociology and psychology. In an era when such disciplines enjoyed great deference, on the
order of what economics enjoys today among policy-makers, Marshall
called on various academics to testify as expert witnesses and explain
how racially segregated schools traumatized black youngsters and hindered their learning. Such testimony served Marshall both at trial and
on appeal, when the NAACP would attach as an appendix to its brief to

the Supreme Court a "social science statement" on the psychological effects of Jim Crow, a statement still celebrated in academic circles for the social good it brought. Many minds contributed to that statement, but one informed the argument especially: Kenneth B. Clark, the NAACP's chief witness at trial. A psychologist whose "doll study" was to become an emblem of *Brown* itself, Clark was a scholar destined for great renown, and an intellectual whose research flowed naturally from the currents in social science and political thought characteristic of his time.

That time was the start of the high era of modern liberalism, a powerful and distinctive set of ideals that deeply influenced American public life in the decades following World War II. Most of those ideals can be characterized with the byword "integration." Postwar liberals preached economic integration, the weaving of the nation into a single, regulated market; governmental integration, the consolidation and development of Washington's administrative power, which was to guide an ever more complex society with help from scientific and policy experts; and racial integration, animated by a cosmopolitan ideal of tolerance supported by the most up-to-date understanding of the origin of human differences. Postwar liberals also tended to share another, often overlooked, integrative commitment: a dedication to integrating the self into society, guided by the tools and insights of social theory, political policy, and therapeutic practice. This task fell especially to the liberal social sciences, and it entered popular consciousness most powerfully through the "culture and personality school" of anthropology. Associated especially with Margaret Mead and Ruth Benedict, both students at Columbia of the German-Jewish émigré Franz Boas, the culture-and-personality school focused scientific attention on the individual self in relation to its cultural context.

Often described as the father of modern anthropology, Boas had sought to understand the complex phenomenon of human culture by attending to its presentation in particular communities, typically less technologically advanced societies such as the Inuit and North American Indians. Boasian scholars aimed to create a total picture of the societies they studied by exhaustively cataloguing their individual elements. These discrete features of a society—its dance forms, its tools, its sacred myths—together constituted a single cultural world. An underlying question of this method concerned how the many distinct elements of a culture were brought together to form a coherent pattern, how they achieved the unity known as "cultural integration." Influenced by Gestalt psychology (*Gestalt* is the German word for "form" or "figure"), the culture-and-personality school argued that the key organizing force of a culture was the individual personality, which was naturally driven to make symbolic configurations from disparate experiences. For the culture-and-personality school, "patterns of culture," to use a celebrated phrase of Ruth Benedict's, were formed as the self integrated its world into a meaningful design and then communicated the symbolic arrangement it had constructed to others. The mind's capacity to translate experience into symbolic order, and to communicate such intangible but essential meanings, was the bridge between culture and the individual self. One of the central implications of this argument was that the self reflects the culture in which it exists, forming a psychological microcosm informed by its social context—including, as the NAACP would argue in condemning Jim Crow, that part of the social context embodied in law.[8]

Kenneth Clark, who would become the most prominent Afro-American psychologist of his day, was cut from the cloth of this school of thought. Graduating from Howard University in 1931, he enrolled in graduate school at Columbia University at about the time Thurgood Marshall became director of the NAACP Legal Defense and Educational Fund. At Columbia, Clark's mentor was Otto Klineberg, a direct student of Franz Boas, and he took Ruth Benedict's *Patterns of Culture* as an important influence. Clark's own work was to chronicle the psychological effects of discrimination; and his experimental project that became known as "the doll studies" was so closely associated with the arguments over *Brown v. Board of Education* as to be virtually synonymous with the decision. Indeed, in the way those studies explained the interaction between culture and the self in the world of Jim Crow, they paralleled the very bridge between the self and the state that *Brown* hypothesized in its interpretation of the Fourteenth Amendment.

To take the measure of Clark's research as influenced by the culture-and-personality school and the various integrative impulses of modern liberalism, it is helpful to reflect on one of Clark's early presentations of his work. The setting was the Midcentury White House Conference on Children and Youth in 1950. The conference was not the first such meeting about children sponsored by the Oval Office. It was the fifth in a series begun in 1909 by Theodore Roosevelt, who had convened a group of scholars and policy-makers to consider the fate of children in poverty. In 1940, under President Franklin Roosevelt, the theme of the now regular White House Conference was changed. Its concern would no longer be children in poverty, but rather "Children in a Democracy," the place of children in a democratic state. "[We gather] here," announced the President in a speech opening the conference, "with a principal objective of considering the relationship between a successful democracy and the children who form an integral part of that democracy. We no longer set them apart from democracy as if they were a segregated group."[9] In 1948, President Truman created the Federal Interdepartmental Committee on Children and Youth to aid in the planning of the next meeting, which its members quickly decided was to be not just the latest gathering. Instead, they envisioned "truly a Midcentury Conference" that would consider American youth in light of all of the "outstanding advances in the last 50 years" in the social sciences, particularly "the developments in the field of human behavior and the relationship of people to each other and to their environment."

When the almost 6,000 conference delegates assembled in the National Guard Armory in Washington, D.C., they defined their subject not as poverty or democracy but "individual happiness and responsible citizenship"—which over the course of the conference became simply "the healthy personality." The organizers were interested in what psychologists today call social adjustment, the modification of the individual personality to meet the pressures of its environment. They also argued that responsible citizenship demanded a robust psyche. In all, it was a theme redolent of modern liberal social engineering. "What we desire in these days of strain and crisis," wrote the organizers in their post-conference report, "is that young people shall have both [happiness and civic responsibility], so that, among other things, they may produce a social order in which the chance for happiness will be greatly improved. . . . For it is the thesis of this [conference] that by putting to use what is currently known about conditions favoring or obstructing the healthy development of personality we can rear a generation of happy, responsible individuals who will be better able to 'take' modern life."[10]

Kenneth Clark was an active participant in the Midcentury White House Conference. Most important, he was assigned to draft a lengthy report on racial discrimination and youth. Titled "Effect of Prejudice and Discrimination on Personality Development," his paper relied heavily on innovative studies he had begun in 1939 together with his wife, Mamie Phipps Clark, who also received her doctorate from Columbia (the two had a lifelong intellectual partnership). The studies sought to determine the effect of racism on the self-image of Negro children aged five to seven by using a standard device of scholars of human personality: a projective test. In projective tests, a person is presented with an ambiguous stimulus, such as a group of inkblots on a page, and asked to respond to it, for instance by describing what the inkblots seem to depict. Because the stimulus has no objective meaning, the responses are necessarily subjective—they "project" one's internal emotions, attitudes, and perceptions onto the outside world. Projective tests aim to assess a personality and discover its hidden features (it might be meaningful, for instance, if a respondent consistently sees images of violence in abstract blots of ink). Moreover, such tests offer a window onto the symbolic patterns respondents have taken from their culture and assimilated. A projective test, that is, offers a view of the self as formed through its integration of the cultural forms in which it exists.

The tests the Clarks conducted involved two dolls. The dolls were identical, except in one feature: one was brown, the other white. Clark presented Negro children with the two toys and then asked a series of questions. The questions varied somewhat from study to study, but a typical course might go like this. First, Clark might ask the children to show him which was the "nice" doll. Next, he might ask them to point out the doll that looked "bad." He then asked to be shown the doll that looked "like a white child"; then, the doll that looked "like a colored child"—and finally, to be shown the doll that "looks like you." In a world free of racial prejudice, one would expect that Negro children would describe the white doll as nice or bad about 50 percent of the time. Instead, the children overwhelmingly described the white doll as nice, and upon hearing the final request, to show the doll that "looks like you," they would be thrown into a terrible state of psychological conflict, sometimes crying and becoming completely distraught. It was a horrifying thing to witness. Clark's conclusion, which he made clear in his report to the Midcentury Conference, has since become part of American common wisdom: segregation engenders low self-esteem among blacks—a feeling that moves children to believe they are "bad"—and it damages the personality in manifold ways. The Clarks' studies suggested that there was injury to the core of the black self resulting from the racial fissure in American life, as legally enforced and justified by the doctrine of separate but equal.

It was precisely the finding that Thurgood Marshall believed would gain the attention of American courts.

"Now, Mr. Clark," asked the NAACP's attorney Robert Carter, "you had occasion, did you not, to test the reactions of the infant plaintiffs involved in this case by the use of the methods that determine sensitivity to racial discriminations?" The setting for the question was the trial of *Briggs v. Elliott*, one of the four disputes that together became *Brown v. Board of Education*. The forum was a three-judge panel in federal court in Charleston, South Carolina, whose members were a study in contrasts, particularly Judges John Parker and J. Waties Waring. Parker was a judicial conservative whose nomination to the U.S. Supreme Court in 1930 had been blocked through the efforts of labor groups and of the NAACP (during a bid for governor in 1920, Parker seemed to oppose black participation in politics, calling it "a source of evil and danger to both races"). As for Waring, once a bulwark of southern establishment values, over the course of his judicial tenure he underwent such a change of heart as to become one of the legal heroes of the Civil Rights Movement. He would end his life in exile from the South, a pariah to his former kind.[11]

Briggs challenged a typical instance of southern segregation, in this case within District 22 in Clarendon County, and could have easily become another equalization suit. The report of an investigator for the NAACP was a litany of abuses, but it cited nothing that could not have been found throughout the South. The white schools of the district offered their students water from drinking fountains; in the black schools, there were "[o]pen galvanized buckets with dippers." The white schools had indoor flush toilets; the black schools had outhouses. The white schools provided bus transportation; the black schools, "located in isolated, unimproved areas," offered "no transportation whatever." The white schools had "a lunchroom with a paid attendant and other workers in charge"; the black schools had no lunchroom at all. The white schools were cleaned by janitors. In the black schools, "[t]hese chores were performed by the Negro teachers and students."[12] Such a system spoke rather as the whip did, if more softly: *Stay in your place, live in exile beneath us.* It was Carter's task, with Kenneth Clark's help, to show how that pernicious message had sunk into the deepest regions of the soul.

"Now, Mr. Clark," asked Carter, "you had occasion . . . to test the reactions of the infant plaintiffs . . . ?" The NAACP had asked Clark to conduct a series of doll studies, like those in his earlier work, on the black children of District 22.

"Yes, I did," Clark replied.

"Now, will you tell us when you made these tests and what you did?"

"I made these tests on Thursday and Friday of this past week at your request, and I presented it to children in the Scott's Branch Elementary school, concentrating particularly on the elementary group. I used these methods which I told you about—the Negro and White dolls—which were identical in every respect save skin color."

Clark looked at his notes. "May I read from these now," he asked.

Judge Waring: "You may refresh your recollection."

"Thank you. I presented these dolls to them and I asked them the following questions in the following order: 'Show me the doll that you like the best or that you'd like to play with,' 'Show me the doll that is the "nice" doll,' 'Show me the doll that looks "bad,"' and then the following questions also: 'Give me the doll that looks like a white child,' 'Give me the doll that looks like a colored child,' and 'Give me the doll that looks like you.'"

"'Like you?'" asked Carter.

"'Like you.' That was the final question," Clark explained, "and you can see why. I wanted to get the child's free expression of his opinions and feelings before I had him identified with one of these two dolls. I found that of the children between the ages of six and nine whom I tested, which were a total of sixteen in number, that ten of those children chose the white doll as their preference; the doll which they liked best. Ten of them also considered the white doll a 'nice' doll. And, I think you have to keep in mind that these two dolls are absolutely identical in every respect except skin color. Eleven of these sixteen children chose the brown doll as the doll which looked 'bad.' This is consistent with previous results which we have obtained testing over three hundred children, and we interpret it to mean that the Negro child accepts as early as six, seven or eight the negative stereotypes about his own group. And this result was confirmed in Clarendon County where we found eleven out of sixteen children picking the brown doll as looking 'bad.'"

"To show you that that was not due to some artificial or accidental set of circumstances," Clark continued, "the following results are important. Every single child, when asked to pick the doll that looked like the white child, made the correct choice. All sixteen of the sixteen [picked] that doll. Every single child, when asked to pick the doll that was like the colored child; every one of them picked the brown doll. My opinion is that a fundamental effect of segregation is basic confusion in the individuals and their concepts about themselves conflicting [within] their self images. That seemed to be supported by the results of these sixteen children, all of them knowing which of those dolls was white and which one was brown. Seven of them, when asked to pick the doll that was like themselves; seven of them picked the white doll. This must be seen as a concrete illustration of the degree to which the [pressures] which these children sensed against being brown forced them to evade reality—to escape the reality which seems too overburdening or too threatening to them."

"Well," asked Carter, "as a result of your tests, what conclusions have you reached, Mr. Clark, with respect to the infant plaintiffs involved in this case?"

"The conclusion which I was forced to reach," Clark replied, "was that these children in Clarendon County, like other human beings who are subjected to an obviously inferior status in the society in which they live, have been definitely harmed in the development of their personalities; that the signs of instability in the personalities are clear, and I think that every psychologist would accept and interpret these signs as such."

Other psychologists certainly did. In *Briggs*, *Brown v. Board of Education*, *Davis v. County School Board of Prince Edward County*, and the Delaware case of *Belton v. Gebhart*, the NAACP provided a parade of social scientists to testify on their behalf: Louisa Holt, M. Brewster Smith, Wilbur B. Brookover, Isidor Chein, and Hugh W. Speer among them. In *Briggs*, for instance, the court heard from David Krech, professor of psychology at the University of California–Berkeley. In his "very definite, and if I may say considered opinion," racial segregation in public schools—the fact that segregation was put in force by law—"is probably the single, most important factor to wreak harmful effect[s] on the emotional, physical and financial status of the Negro child." Except in rare cases, Krech explained, "a child who has for 10 or 12 years lived in a community where legal segregation is practiced . . . will probably never recover from whatever harmful effect racial prejudice and discrimination can wreak." To counter such testimony, attorneys for the defendant school board in Virginia produced some social scientists of their own: a child psychiatrist from Richmond, a clinical psychologist from Lynchburg, even the chair of the Columbia University Department of Psychology (a Virginia native). Naturally, they also cross-examined those of the NAACP, at times mockingly. In the *Davis* case, for example, the lead counsel for the Prince Edward County school board, a prominent utilities and corporations lawyer, was said by his co-counsel to have put on "a moronic face and the accent of a little darkey" while cross-examining Clark about a series of interviews he had held with teenage students from the area; and when examining Isidor Chein, his first line of questioning was aimed at establishing that he was a Jew from New York.

From the perspective of our own time, it is difficult to imagine that the deep sickness of mind represented in such behavior was not unknown among the leaders of American professional life—but such was the nature of the caste society that *Brown* helped destroy, especially in the South. In the same way, it is hard to conceive of federal judges either turning a deaf ear to the assertion that Jim Crow violated our basic civic principles or acquiescing to a system of white supremacy by failing to question the constitutionality of racial segregation. But such was the case as well. In *Briggs*, for instance, two of the three judges rejected the NAACP claim that racial segregation in public schools violated the Constitution—that the separation of the races by law was by definition opposed to our basic national values—and they did so categorically, even expressing a peculiar contempt for the notion that American courts (arbiters, after all, of constitutional law) might have had anything to say about the matter.

"We conclude," wrote Judge Parker for the majority, "that if equal facilities are offered, segregation of the races in the public schools as prescribed by the Constitution and laws of South Carolina is not of itself violative of the Fourteenth Amendment. We think that this conclusion is supported by overwhelming authority which we are not at liberty to disregard on the basis of theories advanced by a few educators and sociologists." Political tradition and doctrinal precedent, he correctly noted, were firmly on the side of Jim Crow. Even if the court "felt at liberty to disregard other authorities," he wrote, the Supreme Court had spoken. Indeed, he continued, "when seventeen states and the Congress of the United States have for more than three-quarters of a century required segregation of the races in the public schools, and when this has received the approval of leading appellate courts of the country including the unanimous approval of the Supreme Court of the United States at a time when that court included Chief Justice Taft and Justices Stone, Holmes and Brandeis"—all great jurists—it was "a late day to say that such segregation is violative of fundamental constitutional rights." To do so would require the "hardly reasonable" supposition that "legislative bodies over so wide a territory . . . and great judges of high courts" have either "knowingly defied the Constitution for so long a period or that they have acted in ignorance of the meaning of its provisions." Judges, wrote Parker, echoing the criticism of Justice Oliver Wendell Holmes that the Constitution does not enact the theories of Herbert Spencer, "have no more right to read their ideas of sociology into the Constitution than their ideas of economics," and if "conditions" had made clear that "segregation is no longer wise," then that was "a matter for the legislatures and not for the courts."

Judge Parker directed that the schools in District 22 be equalized in their facilities, and in doing so, he asserted, "[W]e are giving plaintiffs all the relief that they can reasonably ask."

If Judge Waring's blistering dissent sounds strikingly modern alongside Park's opinion, it is because it reflects what we have become—our vision of race, the self, the social role of courts, even our sense of time. "If a case of this magnitude can be turned aside," began Judge Waring, with the mere "admission that some buildings, blackboards, lighting fixtures and toilet facilities are unequal but that they may be remedied by the spending of a few dollars, then, indeed, people in the plight in which these plaintiffs are, have no adequate remedy or forum in which to air their wrongs. If this method of judicial evasion be adopted, these very infant plaintiffs now pupils in Clarendon County will probably be bringing suits for their children and grandchildren decades or rather generations hence in an effort to get for their descendants what are today denied to them. If they are entitled to any rights as American citizens, they are entitled to have these rights now and not in the future. And no excuse can be made to deny them these rights which are theirs under the Constitution and laws of America by use of the false doctrine and patter called 'separate but equal.'

"[T]he plaintiffs brought many witnesses, some of them of national reputation," Judge Waring continued sympathetically. From the testimony of social scientists like Clark, "it was clearly apparent, as it should be to any thoughtful person, irrespective of having such expert testimony, that segregation in education can never produce equality and that it is an evil that must be eradicated." "Segregation," he asserted, announcing the liberal civic principle at the heart of the NAACP's struggle, was "per se inequality." The "legal guideposts, expert testimony, common sense and reason point unerringly to the conclusion that the system of segregation in education adopted and practiced in the State of South Carolina must go"—indeed, there was no time to wait—"and must go now."[13]

When Judge Waring wrote this in 1951, his common sense was still uncommon. But it was prophetic.

.　　.　　.

The violence of history at times fertilizes the field for reason's harvest: When the first oral arguments in the school segregation cases were heard by the U.S. Supreme Court in December 1952, history had enriched the soil well for the transformation of constitutional doctrine. The Allied war against Nazi Germany was still a recent memory, and Allied propaganda had been directed not simply against the Nazi state, but also against the racial principles that stood behind it (the segregation of American armed forces notwithstanding). When *Brown* was argued, the nation was closer in time to that fight against the ideology of blood, soil, and the master race than it was to the 1963 March on Washington. More immediately, America's failure to live up to its egalitarian ideals was especially embarrassing during the Cold War. The lords of Soviet agitprop were delighted to use the official sanction of Jim Crow to portray America as a backwater of race hatred while extolling the cosmopolitan virtues of Communism. The rising independence movements in Africa and the Caribbean provided further impetus against the racial doctrine of separate but equal. Within ten years of the *Brown* decision, Sudan, Ghana, Zaire, Chad, Senegal, Nigeria, Sierra Leone, Jamaica, Trinidad, Kenya, and Malawi, among other nations, would gain independence. And the postwar American economic expansion did its part as well. A nation that relegated much of its population to poverty and ignorance was hardly a model of economic rationality. Jim Crow was like an anchor trailing an otherwise fleet ship.

Still, the advance of reason ultimately requires individuals prepared to yield to it. On the Supreme Court in 1954, five of the justices had been appointed by President Roosevelt (Hugo Black, Stanley Reed, Felix Frankfurter, William O. Douglas, and Robert Jackson) and four by President Truman (Chief Justice Fred Vinson and Justices Harold Burton, Tom Clark, and Sherman Minton). While some of them were sympathetic to the NAACP's underlying moral claims, the judicial sensibility is rightly restrained by obedience to the law, whose development proceeds according to its own strict rules; and as a matter of law, their support was by no means certain. Chief Justice Vinson, for instance, was loath to call segregation in public schools inequality per se, seeing this as a dangerous break with established precedent, and Justice Reed actively favored sustaining *Plessy*. Two thorny issues troubled the other justices. First, it was unclear what the framers of the Fourteenth Amendment had intended to say about the lawfulness of Jim Crow schools, in part because the public education system of the mid-nineteenth century was negligible in comparison with its role in the mid-twentieth (the Court ordered a special argument on this question, which proved inconclusive). Second, the justices were deeply worried about the kind of relief they could grant should they declare Jim Crow education unconstitutional. Just what would a ruling overturning the logic of *Plessy* require of the thousands of school boards throughout the South and across the nation? The matter struck potentially at the Court's self-interest as well: if the South chose to resist a command of such scope, the Court's institutional authority could be severely eroded.

Our country might look rather different today, and our national experience of the 1950s and 1960s would surely have been quite other than it was, had death not come to call on one of the nine men contemplating the Brown case. On September 8, 1953, Chief Justice Vinson died of a heart attack. In his place, President Eisenhower appointed Earl Warren, former governor of California. Eisenhower would later regret the choice—he was always lukewarm on civil rights and in his support of Afro-Americans—but Warren was to become known among scholars and the public as one of the greatest chief justices in American history. He had two skills that suited him to confront the monumental issue of Jim Crow facing the Court just as he assumed office. First, he had a knack for approaching constitutional interpretation as a way to validate and advance contemporary notions of what was moral and just, rather than as an exercise guided by a strict adherence to precedent and doctrinal niceties (conservatives would later fault Warren's approach as inappropriate to a democracy, which demands that broad decisions about justice be made by the people through their elected representatives, not by appointed judges). In matters of race, the Chief Justice's view of what was just was based on his belief, articulated within the secrecy of the Court's judicial conference, that traditional explanations of human difference were obsolete. Second, Earl Warren was a consummate politician, adept at navigating conflicting views and forging agreement, and mindful of the need that the Court speak with one voice in the *Brown* decision. After months of discussion, review, and argument, a consensus emerged both as to overturning the essential features of *Plessy* and how to do so. Chief Justice Warren persuaded Justice Jackson not to file a separate concurrence in the case, as he had planned, and he prevailed on Justice Reed not to file a lone dissent.

On May 17, 1954, the Court handed down its unanimous opinion. Before we examine its words, it is useful to consider the way that it reflected the temperaments and civic views of two of its central figures,

Earl Warren and Felix Frankfurter. The latter was the mentor of Nathan Margold, who had written the report suggesting a broad litigation strategy for the NAACP in the 1930s. As a man and a jurist, he was deeply concerned with the strength and coherence of American national identity, above and against the claims of the individual self. Born in Vienna in 1882, Frankfurter immigrated to New York's Lower East Side in 1894. After learning English as a teenager, he attended the City College of New York and Harvard Law School. He became assistant U.S. attorney for the Southern District of New York and thereafter pursued a long career of progressive public service, while also serving as a professor of law at Harvard. His civic views were those of the successful immigrant, infused with a deep spirit of national duty, patriotism, and cultural assimilation. An especially able legal draftsman, he often sought in his decisions for the Court to reconcile interests in a way that favored the concerns of groups over individual rights. He emphatically defended mandatory saluting of the American flag in an important case during World War II, for instance, and in another he upheld the suspension of a Jehovah's Witness from public school for refusing to recite the pledge of allegiance. Even more as a man than as a judge, he was a nationalist who held fast to the symbols of unified American identity. He was known to stride through the Supreme Court whistling "The Stars and Stripes Forever."

Chief Justice Warren's civic vision, while very different from Frankfurter's thought, was far from radical. As attorney general of California during World War II, for instance, he supported the removal of Japanese Americans to relocation camps, a lasting source of national shame. He was popular enough to be elected a governor during the height of a global war. Whereas Frankfurter was a Jewish immigrant, Warren was born in America, in 1891 (his father was a Norwegian immigrant who worked for the Southern Pacific Railroad). And while Frankfurter spent his early years in New York, Warren was raised in Bakersfield, at the time still a rough-and-tumble western town, and later attended the University of California–Berkeley and Boalt Hall School of Law. As Chief Justice, he was less a lawyer than a political man "for whom action was all"—fidelity in textual interpretation was hardly his paramount concern.[14] What did concern Chief Justice Warren during his years on the Court was the extension of individual rights and the use of his office to advance principles of social justice. The new era of "the Warren Court," now both celebrated and reviled for its judicial activism, is popularly known for decisions like *Miranda v. Arizona*, source of the "Miranda warning," and *Griswold v. Connecticut*, which established a "right to privacy" in sexual matters such as contraception (a doctrine that, many years later, would be extended in *Lawrence v. Texas*, whose significance for gays is not unlike that of *Brown* for blacks). In contrast to Justice Frankfurter, and in the liberal custom of his times, Chief Justice Warren was driven chiefly by a concern for maintaining the integrity of the boundaries of the individual self.

Drafted by Chief Justice Warren, with the assistance of one of his clerks, Earl Pollock, the opinion in *Brown v. Board of Education* integrated the disparate civic visions for which Warren and Frankfurter were known and put the full weight of the Court behind a symbolic change in American national identity. In a deliberately clear, straightforward style—the Chief Justice carefully enunciated each of his words when he read it aloud—the opinion carried the authority of every justice (even Jackson, still recovering from a massive heart attack, made a special appearance to sit with his colleagues the day it was announced). It was a day of high anticipation and drama: the Associated Press wired dispatches to newsrooms across the nation, providing updates of the Court's opinion even as it was being read. At 12:52, its wire read: "Chief Justice Warren today began reading the Supreme Court's decision in the public school segregation cases. The court's ruling could not be determined immediately." At 1:12, the wire announced that though the Court was denouncing segregation, Chief Justice Warren "had not read far enough into the court's opinion for newsmen to say that segregation was being struck down as unconstitutional."[15]

The opinion was in three parts. In the first, the Court considered the issue known as "original intent" first posed by Justice Frankfurter. How had the drafters intended the Fourteenth Amendment to speak to the question at hand? What was the scope of their understanding of "equal protection of the laws"? What light did the history of the amendment's creation shed on the question of Jim Crow education? The Court had heard a good deal of oral argument about the issue, but, in the end, the justices found the historical record inconclusive and decided that a review of the writing and passage of the amendment was "not enough to resolve the problem with which we are faced." If legal history provided the Court little guidance, there was another, more compelling consideration: the importance of public education to American civic life in the mid-twentieth century as compared with the mid-nineteenth. Public education, wrote the Court, had become the basis of "good citizenship" (by which the Court meant the notion of civic responsibility derived from Roman conceptions of virtue). It helped children "adjust normally" to their environment. And it played a central part in the inculcation and transmission of what it termed "cultural values" (the first use of the phrase in a published state or federal court decision). Asserting that "[e]ducation is perhaps the most important function of state and local governments," the Court argued that "such an opportunity, where the state has undertaken to provide it, is a right which must be made available to all on equal terms."

Could schools segregated by race provide education on equal terms? Could Jim Crow schooling form the foundation for normal, well-adjusted citizenship? In the third part of its opinion, the Court turned its attention to the individual personality, to the psychology of Afro-American children, and to the view of the self and its relation to legal harm at the heart of *Plessy*. Today, the Court's challenge might seem like what lawyers and legal scholars call an "easy case," simple to decide, but it was hardly so at the time. The Court began by noting that the hypothetical equality of "separate" institutions depended on more than elements that could be furnished through increased funding. "Intangible considerations" (such as those described in the Texas law school case of *Sweatt v. Painter* and in *McLaurin v. Oklahoma Regents*) were also relevant, and these included the psychological experience of education—intangibles, the Court noted, that "apply with added force to children in grade and high schools." And here, the Court ventured its only rhetorical, lyrical flourish in an otherwise deliberately prosaic opinion. Reflecting on those Afro-American children, the Court announced that "[t]o separate them from others of similar age and qualifications solely because of their race generates a feeling of inferiority as to their status in the community that may affect their hearts and minds in a way unlikely ever to be undone."

That harm to "hearts and minds," announced the Court, that damage to the Afro-American self, had a practical effect on the quality of education a school could provide—and it resulted not only from the fact of segregation, but from the existence of a law mandating it. Citing a finding of fact from the lower federal court in the Kansas case ("a court which," the *Brown* opinion noted, "nevertheless felt compelled to rule against the Negro plaintiffs"), the Court advanced the following logic: "Segregation of white and colored children in public schools has a detrimental effect upon the colored children. The impact is greater when it has the sanction of the law; for the policy of separating the races is usually interpreted as denoting the inferiority of the Negro group. A sense of inferiority affects the motivation of the child to learn. Segregation with the sanction of law, therefore, has a tendency to [retard] the educational and mental development of Negro children and to deprive them of some of the benefits they would receive in a racial[ly] integrated school system." Here, the Supreme Court returned to its own words. "Whatever may have been the extent of psychological knowledge at the time of *Plessy v. Ferguson*," it declared, "this finding is amply supported by modern authority. Any language in *Plessy v. Ferguson* contrary to this finding is rejected." The assertion carried a footnote, one of the most famous in American constitutional law: a reference to a series of studies by scholars white and black, including Isidor Chein, one of the psychologists who had served as an NAACP expert witness; the sociologist E. Franklin Frazier; and Gunnar Myrdal, whose study of southern Jim Crow, *An American Dilemma*, was a classic of its time. Its first reference, however, reads: "K. B. Clark, *Effect of Prejudice and Discrimination on Personality Development* (Midcentury White House Conference on Children and Youth, 1950)."

"We conclude," Chief Justice Warren announced, striking at the heart of the American caste system, "that in the field of public education the doctrine of 'separate but equal' has no place. Separate educational facilities"—and with this assertion the liberal revolution began—"are inherently unequal."

Later that afternoon, Thurgood Marshall was seen running through the halls of the Court, numb with happiness, with a white child on his shoulders.[16]

School desegregation would be a long, complex endeavor, not achieved by a simple proclamation in 1954—nor fully achieved today. A year after the *Brown* decision, the justices would order the lower federal courts to oversee the process by which individual school districts would admit students to public education "on a nondiscriminatory basis" (the order is known as *Brown II*). Most civil rights advocates found *Brown II* a disappointment. School districts were to integrate, the Court stated, but they were not obliged to do so immediately, but rather "with all deliberate speed"—language proposed by Justice Frankfurter. Among legal scholars, that phrase, and the way it envisioned the relation between constitutional rights and the passage of time, would become as famous as any in the original decision. A concession in part to Justice Reed—though he joined the Court, tears had rolled down his face as the Chief Justice read

the decision—the language of *Brown II* would enable the South to proceed slowly with the revolution it had been asked to undertake. In theory, deliberate speed allowed moderates time to cool down hotter heads.
But practically, it allowed segregationists to drag their feet, to display
the ideal that would become their motto in the years ahead: "massive
resistance."

That reaction was predictable. After all, *Brown* implied more than
the end of Jim Crow education. Its symbolic force challenged the vital
ideals of race and American civic life below the Mason-Dixon line. The
immediate result was an even more vigorous assertion of Jim Crow's
vision of racial caste. Ironically, in the near term, the decision strengthened the hand of white supremacy, and across the social spectrum.
Throughout the South, for instance, otherwise "respectable" men and
women organized groups such as the White Citizens' Council, known as
the "white-collar Klan," to maintain white racial dominance through
economic reprisals and social force (one leader described the council's
goal as being "to make it difficult, if not impossible, for any Negro who
advocates desegregation to find and hold a job, get credit, or renew a
mortgage"). The effort of many southern whites to cling to traditional
mores also enjoyed the acquiescence of the executive branch. Though
he deplored "extremists," President Eisenhower gave only lukewarm
public support to the Court's decision, and believed that the South
should be free to solve its problems in its own fashion and by its own
timetable.[17]

Brown's symbolic inclusion of Afro-Americans within American law
and civic life provoked terrible physical violence as well. No propaganda
of the deed was more galvanizing to the Civil Rights Movement than the
murder of a fourteen-year-old boy named Emmett Till. Sixteen months
after *Brown*, and less than three months after *Brown II*, Till's mother,
Mamie Bradley, sent her child from Chicago to Mississippi to visit rela-
tives near a town called Money. Waves of black refugees had traveled to
northern cities in the wake of World War II in search of a better life, but
they maintained strong family ties to the communities they left. Till was
a brash northern boy, and though he had been warned about southern
mores—"[i]f you have to get on your knees and bow when a white person goes past," his mother advised, "do it willingly"—he made a fatal
mistake: after buying some candy in a local store and meat market, he
said "Bye, Baby" to a pretty white woman (he may have also whistled at
her, though childhood polio had made Till a stutterer, and his mother
had taught him to whistle when the fits came on). Three days later, at

midnight, two men grabbed the boy from the cabin where he was staying with Mose Wright and killed him by the Tallahatchie River. The body was found in the water a few days later, the neck tied with barbed wire to a cotton gin fan, a bullet in the skull, the forehead bashed in, and an eye missing.

When Till's body was sent home to Chicago, his mother demanded an open-casket funeral. Pictures of the boy's mutilated corpse were published in the popular black magazine *Jet*. Even today, the images hardly fail to produce a gasp in those seeing them for the first time (I myself remember the experience, nearly twenty years ago, in the basement of Stanford University's main library). The reaction is partly one of horror: the body of the boy is at first unrecognizable as a human form. It also is one of awe at the strength of his mother, who was prepared to encounter that horror over and over again so that the world could see what Jim Crow had done to her son. Public anger boiled over when the two killers, Roy Bryant, the husband of the woman to whom Emmett Till had said his mischievous parting words, and J. W. Milam, were put on trial before an all-white jury. In a historic moment for southern justice, Mose Wright was asked to testify about what happened the night his nephew had been dragged from his cabin. For a black man to testify against a white person in Mississippi was nearly beyond imagining, but when asked if he knew who had taken Emmett away, the tall, sixty-four-year-old man raised his arm and, beneath the breeze of a rotating ceiling fan, pointed a single finger at each of the men in turn. "Thar he," Wright declared. Within the courtroom, there was no doubt that the two had killed—only whether killing a black boy made a white man guilty of a crime.

Bryant and Milam were quickly exonerated. Mose Wright moved immediately to Chicago. "What else could we do?" one of the two killers later explained to a journalist. "I'm no bully; I never hurt a nigger in my life. I like niggers in their place. . . . But I just decided it was time a few people got put on notice."

While *Brown* helped crystallize the caste vision of Jim Crow, opposition to the Court's opinion generated a reaction of its own, one that would help make the liberal ideals of *Brown* a reality. The civic vision of that reaction was based on the teachings and spirit of Christianity. In order to understand "the deep disillusion of the Negro," wrote the Reverend Martin Luther King, Jr., in his manifesto *Why We Can't Wait*, reflecting on the slowness of civil rights progress since *Brown*, "one must examine his contrasting emotions at the time of the decision and during the nine years that followed. One must understand the pendulum swing between the elation that arose when the edict was handed down and the despair that followed the failure to bring it to life." For King, much of that failure was the result of a misconception about the nature of time itself, a fallacy present throughout the history of American thought and culture. "I have just received a letter from a white brother in Texas," Reverend King explained of the attitude. "He writes: 'All Christians know that the colored people will receive equal rights eventually, but it is possible that you are in too great a religious hurry. . . . The teachings of Christ take time to come to earth.' Such an attitude stems," King declared, "from the strangely irrational notion that there is something in the very flow of time that will inevitably cure all ills. Actually, time itself is neutral; it can be used either destructively or constructively."

Drawing on the work of the theologian Reinhold Niebuhr as well as the philosophy and methods of Mahatma Gandhi, King helped develop a social movement, centered firmly in the black church, that redeemed worldly time with an activist vision that hearkened back to the antebellum evangelical revival. As a prisoner in a Birmingham jail, King wrote the following in 1963:

> For years now I have heard the word "Wait!" . . . Perhaps it is easy for those who have never felt the stinging darts of segregation to say, "Wait." But when you have seen vicious mobs lynch your mothers and fathers at will and drown your sisters and brothers at whim; when you have seen hate-filled policemen curse, kick, and even kill your black brothers and sisters; when you see the vast majority of your twenty million Negro brothers smothering in an airtight cage of poverty in the midst of an affluent society; when you suddenly find your tongue twisted and your speech stammering as you seek to explain to your six-year-old daughter why she can't go to the public amusement park that has just been advertised on television, and see tears welling up in her eyes when she is told that Funtown is closed to colored children, and see ominous clouds of inferiority beginning to form in her little mental sky, and see her beginning to distort her personality by developing an unconscious bitterness toward white people; when you have to concoct an answer for a five-year-old son who is asking, "Daddy, why do white people treat colored people so mean?"; when you take a cross-country drive and find it necessary to sleep night after night in the uncomfortable corners of your automobile because no motel will

accept you; when you are humiliated day in and day out by nagging signs reading "white" and "colored"; when your first name becomes "nigger," your middle name becomes "boy" (however old you are) and your last name becomes "John," and your wife and mother are never given the respected title "Mrs."; when you are harried by day and haunted by night by the fact that you are a Negro, living constantly at tiptoe stance, never quite knowing what to expect next, and are plagued with inner fears and outer resentments; when you are forever fighting a degenerating sense of "nobodiness"—then you will understand why we find it difficult to wait.[18]

As a young preacher in his early twenties, King first refused to wait in 1955 in Montgomery, Alabama, with Rosa Parks's iconic self-assertion: from then on, he asserted, the blacks of that city would either sit in the bus where they pleased, or they would not ride at all.

Like Thurgood Marshall, King was dedicated to the principles of law. The ideal of legality stood at the center of his life: the law of the Constitution brought into being through the healing spirit of egalitarian Christianity. In leading the Civil Rights Movement, a fight for black inclusion throughout civic life—in education, in voting, in economic opportunity—King replaced Marshall as the embodiment of black American legal aspiration. The lawyer gave way to the preacher, the man of Christ, who applied a religious jurisprudence of civic life, based on a story of a child's miraculous birth, to make liberal legal ideals a reality. But it would not be the only path taken by Afro-Americans through with waiting.

12

To Die for the People

▲

In 1964, Huey P. Newton, cofounder of the Black Panther Party, once described as "the living embodiment of black power," assaulted a young tough named Odell Lee with a steak knife after a minor dispute of honor at an Oakland, California, party.[1] After representing himself at trial, he was convicted and sentenced to six months in county jail. After serving his time, Newton was required to report regularly to a probation officer. He described the officer as "really a pretty nice guy, intelligent and fair"—impressive, as Newton was hardly one to compliment representatives of the criminal justice system.[2] Still, probation was not easy for him, and on October 27, 1967, when his probation was to end and his parole to begin, it was time to celebrate. He planned to spend the night with his girlfriend, LaVerne Williams. But in the meantime, on that watershed day in the postwar history of black trials, he had some business to take care of.

Newton spent the afternoon at a forum on the "black liberation movement" at San Francisco State College criticizing black students for their racism. Over the course of 1967, the year of riots in Newark and Detroit, Afro-American students across the country had espoused increasingly radical political views, and many had come to embrace or fellow-travel in the militant world of racial nationalism. These positions were anathema to liberals like Thurgood Marshall, who had taken his oath of office as a justice of the Supreme Court just twenty days before. They were also abhorrent to Huey Newton. Newton was a coalition builder who actively sought alliances with white leftists—an effort for which he was roundly condemned. "Everywhere I went in 1967," he later reported, "I was vehemently attacked by Black students for this position." In the eyes of students, he said, "all white people were devils; they wanted nothing to do with them." The afternoon Newton spent at San Francisco State was no exception, and he left reflecting that "many of the students who were supposedly learning how to analyze and understand phenomena" were in fact just like the allegorical prisoners in "Plato's cave": with their backs to the entrance, they take for reality the shadows projected on the wall by the sun, without bothering to turn around. "[F]ar from preparing them to deal with reality," he thought, "college kept their intellects in chains." He left feeling more strongly than ever that the Black Panther Party "would have to develop a program to implement Point 5 in our program"—to create, that is, "a true education for our people."[3]

Newton continued to discuss the troubling racial attitudes he encountered at San Francisco State with his family that evening over a "righteous dinner of mustard greens and corn bread" (it was the last time he would eat with them for thirty-three months). He then set out on foot for his girlfriend's house, thinking as he walked "about some of the things I might do now that I no longer had to report to my probation officer." When Newton arrived, he found that Williams was sick and in no condition for an evening out. Not wanting to spoil the occasion, she insisted that Newton take her Volkswagen and celebrate on his own. "She knew how much it meant to me that probation was over," he recalled later. And so at about ten o'clock, he drove "to visit a few of my favorite places." He began at a bar called Bosn's Locker, where he drank a Cuba libre. From there, he went to a church social and at about two in the morning—it was now October 28—drove to San Pablo Street, where some friends were throwing a party. He stayed until it ended at four o'clock and then left with a friend, Gene McKinney. The two headed to Seventh Street in West Oakland, a center of the social scene. The area was noted for its authentic barbecue, and Newton and McKinney wanted "to get righteous soul food."[4]

As Newton turned onto Seventh to look for a parking space, he noticed the red light of a police car in his rearview mirror. The officer inside radioed headquarters to announce that he was stopping a "known

Panther vehicle."[5] Newton pulled to the side of the road. After a minute had passed, a young white cop named John Frey approached his window. The twenty-three-year-old Frey was notorious in the Oakland force, known for racial prejudice and a special hostility toward the Black Panthers. "Well, well, well, what do we have here?" said the officer. "The great, *great* Huey P. Newton." Another police car arrived, and Officer Frey asked Newton to step out of his car. The second officer on the scene, Herbert Heanes, asked McKinney to do the same. As Newton entered the early-morning air, he picked up a legal textbook he kept between the bucket seats (he had been studying law at San Francisco Law School). "I thought it was my criminal evidence book," he would remember, "which covers laws dealing with reasonable cause for arrest and the search and seizure laws. If necessary I intended to read the law to this policeman, as I had done so many times in the past. However, I had mistakenly picked up my criminal law book, which looks exactly like the other one."[6]

The officer told Newton to lean against the car. Newton put both his hands on his criminal law text and leaned against the roof of the Volkswagen as he was frisked. Officer Frey then took Newton's left arm, and began leading him toward the police car. Newton began to open his book, saying, "You have no reasonable cause to arrest me." According to Newton, the officer's reply was a snarl: "You can take that book and shove it up your ass, nigger." As Newton would later describe the event in his autobiography, *Revolutionary Suicide*, Officer Frey then hit him with a left, straight-arm blow to the face, which sent him reeling to the ground. What happened next would be the subject of controversy for years. In the next few moments, Newton would be shot in the abdomen ("My stomach seemed to explode, as if someone had poured a pot of boiling soup all over me," he recalled); Officer Heanes, who had been interviewing Gene McKinney, would take shots in his arm, knee, and chest; and Officer John Frey would die, shot in the leg, chest, and stomach.[7] Newton was soon apprehended while being treated for his injury at Kaiser Hospital, five miles away—handcuffed to his hospital gurney. Soon, he would be on trial for his life, in a legal case that would put black power and its distinctive vision of law on trial as well.

Huey P. Newton was born in 1942 in Monroe, Louisiana. He was named for former Louisiana governor Huey P. Long. His mother, Armelia, was a dark-skinned woman from Louisiana with an infectious sense of humor and a positive attitude that would buoy the spirit of her youngest son throughout his roughest years. His father, Walter, was a light-skinned man from Alabama (on the first page of his autobiography, Newton would describe his father's father as "a white rapist"). Walter was tremendously disciplined, worked several jobs in addition to serving as a preacher, and garnered Huey's deep respect. "Walter Newton is rightly proud of his role as family protector," Newton would write in 1973. "To this day, my mother has never left her home to earn money."[8] In 1945, the family moved to Oakland, joining a wave of blacks migrating west in search of work and a life away from the racial neuroses of the South. California was indeed an improvement in many respects. It had a better history of racial tolerance, even considering its tensions with Asians and Asian Americans and the violation of Japanese-American civil liberties in World War II. Socially and culturally, it was a liberal state, certainly more so than those below the Mason-Dixon line. In only twenty years, the Bay Area would give birth to the national student movement and become a center of bohemia. Still, life for blacks in Oakland was often as difficult as, if not more so than, the life they had left behind, and these difficulties were typical of the experience of blacks in the urban North and West.

The black ghetto held out many challenges to its residents. Poverty and unemployment were serious problems, especially for men (women could more easily find work, as domestics). Violence and crime among blacks, too, was a constant menace. But most troubling to residents of places like East Oakland was the behavior of the white police who patrolled their neighborhoods. Often recruited from among whites who had also escaped the southern trap of sharecropper poverty, the Oakland police had gained a reputation for their brutality and for their assumption that all blacks were criminals. Poverty was degrading; violent crime was a terrible thing; but to know that the police were inclined to view you as a thief because of the color of your skin, and to shoot first and ask questions later—these were matters of symbolic as well as practical importance. In the minds of blacks of the Bay Area, the most visible representatives of the law were a symbol of their own civic marginality.

The weight of that symbolic burden fell particularly on the dispossessed masses of unemployed black men; without even a marginal place rightly their own, they breathed hopelessness and alienation. At the time, they were called the "brothers on the block." Huey Newton grew up among these men and would always be drawn to them, even after he was catapulted to stardom. He knew the streets and called them home. But through force of will, Newton also educated himself. He was a brother on the block, but with a difference, and in this way his life linked those of two of his older brothers. Melvin Newton, to whom Huey remained close throughout his life, was a serious student, an intellectual model, who would go on to teach sociology at Merritt College in Oakland. On the other hand, there was his eldest brother, Walter, to whom Huey was "given" as a toddler in a ritual that probably derived from an old African practice (in it, Walter had led Huey on horseback around the family house, thereby assuming a special responsibility for his care). A street hustler, Walter was known as "Sonny Man," and spent his early years in and out of jail. Among other lessons, Sonny Man taught young Huey how to fight (his advice: look your opponent in the eye and keep advancing).

The young Huey Newton was a bit of both Melvin and Sonny Man. Like Walter, he was known as a tough brawler, and he dabbled in petty criminality, stealing, burglary, gambling. But even as a boy, he was drawn to the poetry and ideas about which Melvin often spoke. Exercising the relentless self-discipline that would characterize his entire life (the self-discipline required of a political revolutionary), he taught himself to read and then devoted himself to mastering the English language. Always ambitious, he began his studies with Plato's *Republic*, the great Socratic dialogue, sitting for days with a dictionary in hand, reading the text over and over until he understood every word. After Newton graduated from high school in 1959, he continued to move in the world of ideas and in the street—and in both, his interest grew in the subject at the heart of the *Republic*: the nature of law. At Merritt College, he studied philosophy and criminal justice. He took his studies in earnest, at least when the ideas interested him; but when class ended, he would return to the brothers on the block, carrying on with petty crime. At times he would come to lectures drunk, shoeless, or sopping wet from the rain.

Newton was gregarious and had many friends and acquaintances at Merritt, but one would exert a most profound influence on his life, the young Bobby Seale. The two had much in common. Like Newton, Seale could relate to the brothers on the block. He was also deeply concerned about the poverty and social conditions of the black ghetto. At the same time, Seale stood in some awe of Newton's charisma and intelligence and the two spent much of their time together discussing black history and politics. They also joined an early black nationalist group at Merritt, but quickly became dissatisfied with it, bolting to form their own organization, one more attuned to their distinctive vision of the needs of black

America. That group was to become the Black Panther Party. In later years, Seale would credit Newton for establishing the party this way: "Brother Huey P. Newton put the Black Panther Party in motion. . . . It is impossible to talk about the Black Panther Party without first talking about Huey P. Newton, because brother Huey put it all into motion. We sometimes talk about 'the genius of Huey P. Newton.'"9

The Black Panther Party was a political organization for the brothers on the block, aimed at uniting residents of the black ghetto to advance their interests. The party was especially concerned with stemming police brutality. One of its main strategies, which would yield controversy as well as symbolism, to say nothing of results, was clearly announced in the full name of the original group: the Black Panther Party for Self Defense. To make the Oakland police more accountable, and raise the political awareness of blacks generally, the Panthers would openly carry guns. (At the time, there was no law in California against carrying unconcealed weapons.) It was a tactic of which John Brown would have approved.

Their first work was to police the police. Organized into small units, groups of Panthers would drive through Oakland, keeping watch. If they encountered a police officer who had stopped a black resident or was preparing to arrest him, the Panthers would step out of their vehicle and, with their shotguns held to their chests, observe the proceedings. It was not a tactic that endeared them to law enforcement. Nor did Newton's public lectures. "I always carried my law books in my car," Newton explained. "Sometimes, when a policeman was harassing a citizen, I would stand off a little and read the relevant portions of the penal code in a loud voice to all within hearing distance. In doing this, we were helping to educate those gathered to observe these incidents. . . . Nobody had ever given them any support or assistance when the police harassed them, but here we were, proud Black men armed with guns and a knowledge of the law." The animus of the Black Panthers against the Oakland police was embodied in an epithet they lodged in the popular American lexicon: pig, which the party newspaper defined as "an ill-natured beast who has no respect for law and order, a foul traducer who is usually found masquerading as a victim of an unprovoked attack."10

Although Seale was party chairman, it was Huey Newton who served as spokesman and chief ideologist: his official title was Minister of Defense. Newton's facility for abstraction ("abstract and theoretical ideas interest me most," he once asserted), in particular, allowed him to develop in quick order a systematic agenda and conceptual framework to guide the party's work.[11] That agenda was embodied in the ten-point Black Panther "party platform." The platform is a curious document, a mixture of rhetoric and demands at once radical and liberal, some impossibly divisive and others that would have been embraced by some of the leftist thinkers of the New Deal. It includes demands for black self-determination through a United Nations–supervised plebiscite; full employment ("the federal government is responsible and obligated to give every man employment or a guaranteed income"); and "an end to the robbery by the white man of our Black Community," for "the overdue debt of forty acres and two mules." It calls for blacks to be given "decent housing, fit shelter for human beings," as well as an "education that teaches us our true history." Black men were also to be exempt from military service. And, naturally, there were several demands about the operation of the law, including one for the "immediate end to POLICE BRUTALITY and MURDER of black people" (the only words capitalized in the document), and one for the release of "all black people" from federal, state, county, and city prisons and jails. In addition, the trials of blacks facing criminal charges were to be heard by exclusively black juries. The document concludes with an extended quotation from the first two paragraphs of the Declaration of Independence.[12]

In addition to the ten-point party program, as practical as it was unrealistic, Newton poured forth essays, lectures, and interviews in which he elaborated his political philosophy. He was especially taken with Marxism-Leninism, and his turn toward socialism put Newton in conflict with many black political organizations and a substantial body of black popular thought in his day (Communists viewed the Panthers as an inevitable outgrowth of American exploitation). In particular, Newton was resolutely opposed to what today we often call "identity politics," with its search for an authentic black identity, often in a mythological African past, and its racial separatism. He derided such positions as "porkchop nationalism" and decried their proponents as "black racists."[13] Instead, he believed it imperative that blacks pursue "liberation" by making common cause with white left-wing groups.

That liberation would come about, according to Newton, through the process of historical change that Marxists call the dialectic, a principle at the heart of Newton's thought. In this view, which Marx adapted from Hegel, every historical phenomenon generates within itself its own contradiction, or "negation," and in doing so produces a third term that at once negates and incorporates the two previous terms into a more advanced historical phenomenon, in an upward motion of social, politi-

cal, and spiritual progress. Engels and then Stalin extended this fundamental dynamic to the natural world, seeing it at work even in the
motion of atomic particles. The "struggle of mutually exclusive opposing tendencies within everything that exists," Newton believed, "explains
the observable fact that all things have motion and are in a constant state
of transformation";[14] this fact, that "matter is constantly in transformation in a dialectical manner," formed "[t]he essence of the ideology of
the Black Panther Party."[15] In political terms, Newton saw the United
States as the highest stage of development of an aggressively imperialist
capitalism that kept Afro-Americans and other racial minorities in subjugation, both at home and abroad; black "so-called citizens" in America, once endowed with class consciousness and organized by the party,
would become the absolute antithesis, or negation, of American power,
and through their struggle help bring about political liberation throughout the world. They would help usher in a global political system that
Newton called "revolutionary intercommunalism."[16]

Significantly, to form a part of this vanguard, according to Newton,
to know the laws of motion and work to advance them—to be, that is, a
revolutionary—put one in a unique metaphysical position: a special relation to death. Newton was deeply preoccupied with the meaning of the
death of black men, a concern evident in the titles of his two books, *Revolutionary Suicide* and *To Die for the People*. He developed that concern, as
was his tendency, into a systematic analysis, one that drew on Émile
Durkheim's sociological classic *Suicide*, to classify black death into two
types. The first was "reactionary suicide," the death of a person who has
been ground down by the oppressive social demands of "the Establishment," who "takes his own life in response to social conditions that overwhelm him and condemn him to helplessness." This form of suicide
was symbolic of the widespread "spiritual death" that was to be "found
everywhere today in the Black community."[17]

According to Newton, the black revolutionary was to rise above this
culture of reactionary death by putting his life at the service of "the
people." Merging his life with that of his community, he advanced black
interests and moved the dialectic of history forward by committing himself to the inevitability of a violent death; citing the anarchist writings of
Bakunin, Newton stressed that "the first lesson a revolutionary must
learn is that he is a doomed man" and that unless he understands his fate,
"he does not grasp the essential meaning of his life." Newton understood revolutionary suicide as a feat of tremendous self-discipline. It also
required a man to be buoyed by a spirit of the future. "The concept of

revolutionary suicide," he wrote, "is not defeatist or fatalistic. On the contrary, it conveys an awareness of reality in combination with the possibility of hope—reality because the revolutionary must always be prepared to face death, and hope because it symbolizes a resolute determination to bring about change. Above all it demands that the revolutionary see his death and his life as one piece." Turning to the work of Chairman Mao, Newton asserted the fundamental principle of his existential commitment, that "death comes to all of us, but it varies in its significance: to die for the reactionary is lighter than a feather; to die for the revolution is heavier than Mount Tai."[18]

"By surrendering my life to the revolution," Newton announced in an epigraph to his autobiography, "I found eternal life. Revolutionary suicide."[19]

Newton's murder charge launched the Black Panthers into action. Their first job was to find a lawyer. This proved extremely controversial, for here as elsewhere in their advocacy for the brothers on the block, the Panthers' ideological rigor led them to shun the path of least resistance and walk directly into a quarrel with other Afro-American militants over a "problem" Bobby Seale described as "a bit of black racism." Newton's family and the Black Panther Party decided that their lawyer was to be Charles Garry. One of the most prominent radical lawyers of his day, Garry was of Armenian descent. "Our argument," Seale explained, "was that we couldn't judge the man by the color of his skin. . . . We said that if you had cancer or another bad disease, you would want the best medical technician that you could find. This was our argument, but they didn't understand it."[20]

Charles Garry stood in a long line of white attorneys devoted to defending controversial political figures against criminal charges. Often taking Clarence Darrow as their model, they include the likes of the late William Kunstler, who most famously defended the Chicago Seven on conspiracy charges stemming from the 1968 Democratic National Convention, and Leonard Weinglass, the former attorney of onetime Black Panther Mumia Abu-Jamal. These men spend their professional lives in the midst of what scholars call "political trials."[21]

The term is a slippery but important one. Most broadly, political trials are legal cases that involve high-profile defendants involved in political life, individuals whose prominence increases the risk of procedural unfairness, tilted either for or against their interests. A more robust view takes them as legal prosecutions driven by a desire to imprison dissidents and intimidate their supporters. The United States has an unfortunate history of such prosecutions, particularly against socialists and anarchists in the early twentieth century, and they still serve quite effectively to suppress dissent in many parts of the developing world. Finally, political trials have been defined, especially in the 1960s and 1970s, as legal prosecutions against politically active individuals for crimes that are not in themselves political acts. Political activists sentenced to prison for robbing a bank to finance their political activities, for instance, have often characterized themselves as "political prisoners," though they were convicted of a serious crime that would incur prosecution regardless of the defendant's ideology.

This final sense of political trials had a deep, some might say insidious, effect on racial conflict in Huey Newton's time. For in the eyes of the Black Panther Party and other Afro-American militants, the United States was governed by a political and economic structure that had reduced the mass of black Americans to degradation and despair (the "black bourgeoisie" was allowed to exist simply to dampen the momentum for mass revolt). If black degradation was the consequence of a "system" of political oppression, then all black criminality could be understood as being, to some degree, political. Even a common mugging of a white man by a black man, for instance, could be described as a small act of revolt against three hundred years of racial inequality and its handmaid, the law. Crime was the political tool of a class without access to the traditional political sphere. The crime of which Huey Newton stood accused—murdering a police officer—was by such logic the ultimate gesture of this sort.

For many lawyers, defending a political prisoner involved more than simply attempting to secure their client's acquittal. Indeed, it was not uncommon for the defendant's guilt to have been perfectly clear. In such cases, defending the interests of one's client meant questioning the assumptions that had made his acts criminal in the eyes of the law—a questioning carried out both inside the courtroom, before judge and jury, and outside, in the court of public opinion that radical organizations were seeking to influence. The Black Panthers were certain that Huey Newton would be executed for killing Officer Frey; and they concentrated on using his trial, as Newton would have wanted, as an instrument of "public education."

Garry's preparation was consistent with this general approach. "Very frankly," he wrote later, "I didn't spend any time with Huey discussing the facts of the case." Instead, he "had to do a tremendous amount of studying on black history and attitudes, and Huey was a good teacher." Seemingly indifferent to what actually happened that early morning in late October, he applied himself instead to the work of the Algerian radical Franz Fanon. Rather than developing alternative theories of the crime, he pored over the recent Kerner Commission Report published in the wake of the ghetto riots of 1967, which asserted that the United States was still infected with racist attitudes despite the successes of the Civil Rights Movement. "Until three or four days before he took the witness stand in July 1968," Garry mused of his high-profile murder client, "I did not even go into his story of the incident . . . I wasn't particularly interested. I had come to the conclusion that the only way Newton could be defended was to take him in the context of his world and see the facts from that viewpoint."[22]

Garry put these views into practice most famously in the jury-selection stage of the trial. During voir dire, the firebrand assiduously questioned prospective jurors about their racial attitudes, as well as about experiences in their lives that might indicate their views on black radicalism, the police, and government authority. Garry's innovative line of questioning is the direct precursor of the jury-selection methods used in the O. J. Simpson case of the 1990s. "Let me hear in your own words," Garry asked, "how you feel about black people generally and what your relationships with them have been." "Do you equate shabbiness with black people?" "Have you ever made a statement to anyone that negroes should be able to help themselves just like anybody else?" "Have you heard of the words black power?" "Are you willing to accept the fact that America has been a racist society?" Garry's hope was to assemble a panel of men and women who would be sympathetic to his client or, at the very least, not prejudiced against him. In the end, the jury was made up of eleven whites and one black, who was chosen as foreman. It remained to be seen what they would make of a politically militant black man who very likely had killed a police officer.

With typical intellectual integrity, Newton held the man prosecuting him, District Attorney Lowell Jensen, in real, if grudging admiration. He saw him as a worthy opponent. And Jensen did mount a strong case. His eyewitnesses, including a black bus driver, all offered powerful evidence that Newton had shot Officer Frey—perhaps even in cold blood—and then, after being shot himself, forced an innocent bystander at gunpoint to drive him and McKinney to Kaiser Hospital. Garry's defense team did its best to discredit Jensen's witnesses (under astute cross-examination virtually any witness can be called into some question). But its larger effort to raise reasonable doubt in the jury about Newton's guilt depended on an insinuation with a strong symbolic charge: that Newton had fired his gun in self-defense against Frey's unprovoked attack or that he had lost consciousness after being shot in the stomach and fired his weapon unintentionally, without fully understanding his actions. Garry tried to portray Newton as a victim, even a figure of manly virtue.

The widely publicized vision of Huey Newton defending himself righteously against police aggression, or else acting without full awareness, dazed by his brutal attack, drew substantial funds to the party for its leader's support. It also served precisely its aims of "public education." "Free Huey Now!" became a loud echo of the founding demand of the Black Panther Party, stated in its ten-point program, that all black men, whatever their crime and regardless of their guilt or innocence, should be released from prison immediately.

In his closing arguments, Garry claimed the trial hinged not on the specific, disputed facts of the case, but rather on the matter of Huey Newton the man and the principles for which he stood. "As I have sat in this courtroom like you have, at first picking the jury, asking you questions that probably infuriated you," stated Garry, "I hope that it got you to thinking about the things that are going on in my beloved America and your beloved America. . . . I hope that you remember the things that we asked you in this *voir dire*." Huey Newton, stated Garry, "doesn't ask very much for himself." He was, in Garry's opinion, "a selfless man," a man who "is not interested in himself as a person; he is a devoted man; he is a rare man." Placing his client's actions in a biblical frame, Garry quoted Matthew 10:34: "Think not that I come to send peace on earth: I came not to send peace, but a sword." The passage, he argued, taught an important lesson about race in American civic life:

> What is Huey Newton saying, what is Christ saying? Christ wasn't saying get out the sword and destroy people. He was saying that the twelve disciples in order to be able to carry out their mandate and their responsibilities would also at a time have to resort to the sword for self-defense. Huey Newton is saying to the black community and the black ghetto there has got to be times when you will have to defend yourself by political means and any other means for your life, for your survival.

Had Newton murdered Officer Frey? Garry's implicit answer: was not Christ crucified?

To this religious analogy, Garry added one from recent history. "You know we fought a great war against fascism," he asserted, "which had as its cradle the destruction of the freedom of the human being. We fought a great war because one nation practiced genocide on six million Jews." And what of America? "Fifty million black people throughout this world since history has been able to document, have been destroyed, eliminated." Suggesting the consequences of that history were reaching their crisis today in the black ghetto, where a struggle of historic importance was taking place, he argued that blacks were fighting for nothing less than "the right of survivalship"—in response to which "[t]he white community is sitting smug and saying, 'Let's have more police, let's have more guns, let's arm ourselves against the blacks.'" Huey Newton was part of this world-historical fight for survival against an older, corrupt vision of law. "My client and his party are not for destruction," Garry pleaded. "They want to build. They want a better America for black people. They want the police out of their neighborhoods. They want them out of their streets."

"White American, listen, white American, listen!" Garry concluded his peroration on the meaning of his client's revolutionary life: "The answer is not to put Huey Newton in the gas chamber, it is not the answer to put Huey Newton and his organization into jail. The answer is not that. The answer is not more police. The answer is to wipe out the ghetto, the conditions of the ghetto, so that black brothers and sisters . . . can walk down the streets in dignity."[23] It was a statement remarkable for the directness of its political appeal. "The whole ten-point platform and program and the Party's true ideology and philosophy really came out during Huey's trial," Bobby Seale reflected, "although much of the press didn't want to print it. . . . Charles Garry is the man who really brought all that out. . . . A lot of judges in the future are going to try to cut it off, but they can't separate our ideology and our philosophy from ourselves, when they trump charges up on us and try to railroad us to prisons and jails."[24]

If Garry's plea for his client was stirring, the jury was nonetheless not persuaded of Newton's innocence—but nor were they convinced that Newton had killed Officer Frey in cold blood. After four days of deliberation, they handed down a verdict that seems to have been something of a compromise. While they found Newton not guilty of shooting Officer Heanes, they also found that he had shot Officer Frey;

however, they found him guilty not of murder, but of the lesser charge of manslaughter. Newton had killed Frey, as the defense contended, only after being provoked. The lesser degree of homicide would save Newton from execution, though it carried a potential sentence of two to fifteen years.

"Manslaughter, not murder. *That* was a surprise," wrote Newton. "The verdict caused a lot of dissatisfaction in the Black community. Some people were particularly angry at David Harper, the jury foreman, who, to them, had sold out in typical Uncle Tom fashion." To "counteract this opinion," Newton sent out a message to his followers asserting that "Brother Harper and other members of the jury who believed in my innocence" had done what they believed was for the best. Newton wrote that he wanted to "ask the Black community sincerely and Brother Harper's son to forgive not only him, but also the other people who believed in my innocence, and who were compromising because they did not know what they were doing. I believe that they thought they were doing the best thing in my interest, and the best thing in the interest of the Black community, under the racist circumstances wherein which they had to operate." Above all, Newton counseled restraint: no violence. He asked the Black Panthers to keep the streets calm. "The community responded to my request," he wrote, "and stayed cool. Any spontaneous and unorganized outburst would have caused great suffering."[25]

Huey Newton also surely knew, as he made his way into the depths of California's criminal justice system, first to the Alameda County Jail, then to the Vacaville Medical Facility, and eventually to the California Men's Colony, East Facility, in San Luis Obispo—known to prisoners as "the penal colony"—that his legal case was, in fact, just beginning.

It might fairly be said that Newton achieved his greatest triumph through imprisonment. His incarceration offered a new opportunity, greater than any he had known before, to demonstrate his tremendous physical self-discipline in the name of his ideological principles. If belief is a means of transforming reality, through his convictions Newton transformed imprisonment into a daily act of public consciousness raising—and into his own "revolutionary suicide."

Enduring the institutional regime of prison was a badge of high status within the black radical movement of the late 1960s and 1970s. Among early civil rights leaders—who had been dedicated to black collective improvement and advancing individual liberty by supporting respectable individuals seeking bourgeois privileges—imprisonment for a crime other than civil disobedience was a thing to be avoided, if not a mark of shame. Many of the militants prized by Newton's circle were probably not innocent of the serious criminal activity of which they had been convicted. And if they were, they were surely not innocent of a life of criminality. But the worldview they forged during their incarceration was valorized as a particularly insightful view of political life and placed at the center of black militant thought.

The most celebrated prisoners in this rising ideological movement were a group that had become politically active in California's Soledad Prison, becoming widely known as the "Soledad Brothers." Their spokesman was George Jackson, whose book *Soledad Brother* became a popular leftist treatise, published with a glowing introduction by Jean Genet and widely cited by prominent writers. It was Jackson who attracted the political and, later, romantic attentions of the era's foremost female black militant, Angela Davis. (She herself would stand trial in 1972 for her alleged part in a hostage takeover designed to free the Soledad Brothers. The failed attempt, undertaken by Jackson's brother, Jonathan—who, in the process, would blow the head off a Marin County judge with a shotgun—was denounced by the Black Panther Party.) Jackson's writings presented prison as the crystallization of American racism, at once its most extreme and its most representative manifestation. And, he argued, it was in the crucible of the criminal justice system that black inmates forged both their political awareness and their sense of themselves as revolutionary agents of history. Prison turned men into what Newton called, using the rhetoric of dialectical materialism, "the negation of the negation"—the antithesis of the racist, capitalist power structure that had created them and that they in turn would destroy, thereby transforming society and advancing history to its third term.

"Would you like to know a subhuman," George Jackson wrote to Angela Davis in 1970. "I certainly hope you have time. I'm not a very nice person. I'll confess out front, I've been forced to adopt a set of responses, reflexes, attitudes that have made me more kin to the cat than anything else, the big black one."[26] The terms of his revolutionary life, Jackson wrote his lawyer that same year, were set in his mind. "I *want* my food and drink from the people's stash," he claimed. "I *want* to hide, run, and look over my shoulder. The only woman that I could ever accept is one who would be willing to live out of a flight bag, sleep in a coal car. . . ." For white radicals as much as black, this revolutionary racial vision was not simply a phenomenon of individuals, but rather a harbinger of the collective future. "We have known for a long time now," wrote Jean Genet, "that the black man is, from the start, natively, the guilty man. . . . But already Huey Newton, Bobby Seale, the members of the Black Panther party, George Jackson, and others have stopped lamenting their fate. . . . They are creating, each according to his means, a revolutionary consciousness."[27]

Newton tried to hone that revolutionary consciousness through acts large and small. Most important, he drew on his experience of solitary confinement during his first extended prison stay in 1964, for the assault on Odell Lee. After he had helped organize a prison strike, he had been placed in "the hole." A fetid, dank space into which light came only when guards served the meager rations that would be eliminated through the slimy opening in the center of the floor, the hole was also known as "the soul-breaker." Many men quickly approached insanity within its silence. But Newton was determined to conquer prison life, and inside the hole he developed a series of mental and physical exercises, presaging his later serious interest in Buddhism, to help him endure. Much of the time he lay flat with his back slightly arched, breathing slowly and deliberately, at first emptying his mind and later, with practice, learning to call forth positive memories, running them through his mind like a video loop. Prison guards were awed by his equanimity, and Newton drew strength from their reaction as a signal that he had won his battle with the system. Most inmates could endure solitary confinement for two or three days. Newton was confined for a month.[28] He was twenty-two years old.

At the Men's Colony, Newton's experience was light compared with what he had survived in the soul-breaker. He was put for months on "lock-up," forced to remain in his cell except for meals, and bore it with relative ease—it "was bearable, really more than that." His mind, he wrote, "was active; there were many things to think about, and I filled the days working out ideas I had begun to develop back in Oakland City College."[29] Again the guards marveled and again he celebrated the triumph. Once released from lock-up, he continued his political work, smuggling out a series of essays that appeared in various radical publications and maintaining contacts with radicals both within and outside the California penal system. At one point, so many came to see him that he spent each day from 9 a.m. to 4 p.m. in the visitors' gallery. Even for those who had never before seen him or read his work, he had become a cause célèbre (after his release from prison, many followers would express deep disappointment on first hearing him talk—Newton's high, nasal voice and scholarly, if not pedantic, speech did not fit the romantic ideal of the black militant).

In the meantime, his lawyers were appealing his conviction on a number of grounds, both technical and substantive. Garry's brief would claim that the trial jury had been selected improperly and was "illegally tainted with racism," that the judge had "contributed to the highly charged atmosphere and made many prejudicial rulings," that the publicity surrounding the trial had made a fair proceeding impossible, and that the prosecution had suppressed material evidence. Most fruitfully, it also claimed that the jury had been improperly instructed, the judge having neglected to advise jurors that they were entitled to choose between judgments of involuntary and voluntary manslaughter.[30] Though based on a technical distinction, the claim in fact went to the heart of how Newton's case was perceived by the radical left. Had Newton killed Officer Frey voluntarily, or rather in an act of self-defense conditioned by years of white racism? In the difference hung the whole legal theory of black militancy—its notion of black power, of black self-determination, and of long-standing black civic subjugation by American law enforcement.

After months of wending through the legal process, the Court found that technical argument compelling—not on ideological grounds, naturally, but as a matter of proper, liberal legal procedure. Newton's conviction was overturned and a new trial ordered on the question of manslaughter. There would in fact be two retrials. In the first, Newton's defense challenged the credibility of the witnesses in the initial proceeding. Could the black bus driver truly have seen Newton commit the murder if, according to the transit authority's own route schedule, the bus could not have been on Seventh Street at the time? How could Newton have been the perpetrator of the crime if the witness indicated that the man who killed Officer Frey was wearing a tan jacket and a black shirt, not Newton's black jacket and light shirt? Could Newton really have whipped a hidden P-38 from his jacket pocket, as Frey's assailant was seen to have done, when such a pistol was far too large for the shallow pocket of Newton's coat? The effort to expose the witnesses' uncertainty paid off. A mistrial was declared in the first trial, when the jury deadlocked, and when a second retrial went the same way, the State of California, its witnesses seemingly confused and discredited, grudgingly dropped its case against Newton.

On his release on August 5, 1970, Huey Newton was greeted on the steps of the San Francisco courthouse by an adoring throng of radicals, both black and white. Strong and muscular from his concerted prison exercise regime, he climbed onto the back of a Volkswagen and, in the heat of the day, took off his shirt and addressed the crowd. Thus began his life as a leading symbol of black militancy and a feared enemy of the American mainstream. One of his first official announcements as a free man was that the Black Panther Party would offer a troop of its disciplined members as volunteers in the North Vietnamese army. His next major public appearance was in Philadelphia, where the party, now a broad, national group, was holding a Revolutionary People's Constitutional Convention, in which representatives of all "oppressed communities" had gathered "for the solemn purpose of formulating a new *constitution for a new world.*"[31] Under Newton's leadership, the Panthers, whose original ten-point platform concluded with a long citation from the Declaration of Independence, once again sought to express the principles of liberation in a document of law.

For all its fanfare and revolutionary solidarity, the Black Panther Party would not long endure after Newton's release. It enjoyed some real, practical success, both in raising consciousness and improving the daily lives of blacks in the ghetto. For instance, to its lasting fame, the party established a "survival" program giving free breakfasts to black children, and it sponsored a project to have blacks tested for sickle-cell anemia. But the group that was galvanized by opposition to established law and ready for collective revolutionary suicide was also led by those strengths toward a fractious demise.

The Federal Bureau of Investigation, through a series of undercover operations, managed to breed paranoia and suspicion among party members and to instigate infighting among the leadership—not that they needed much encouragement. As differences grew, top figures were regularly purged from the ranks. Among those expelled were Eldridge Cleaver, the famous minister of information and author of *Soul on Ice*; much of the leadership of the East Coast branch of the party, many of whom had been put on trial in New York in 1969 for conspiracy to bomb public buildings and railroads; and Stokely Carmichael, former leader of the Student Nonviolent Coordinating Committee and originator of the phrase "black power" (Newton himself had inducted Carmichael into the party with the charge to "establish revolutionary law, order, and justice" east of the Mississippi).

Such volatility is typical of militant groups. More ominously, the Panthers were overtaken by the street criminality and violence with which they had been associated from the start, especially in California. In their first major public act, after all, they had inaugurated their "pick up the gun" pose by entering the California statehouse brandishing rifles. But it was also the natural consequence of the Panthers' practical effort to make a vanguard of the brothers on the block, the black "lumpen," as Newton called them, who more often shared the Panthers' methods than they did their ideology. The Panthers never transcended the criminal culture of the streets where they worked and whose most desperate residents they sought to help. Operating expenses seem to have come at least partly from petty crime and the sale of drugs. Food for the breakfast program was procured in part by intimidating store owners. At least one associate, accused of being a police informant, was killed for her apostasy, possibly on Newton's direct order. They would continue to trip over the line between gangsterism and revolution. Such was the paradox of their mission to transform the lawless into the guardians of a new law. It remains unclear whether that mission was not only doomed from the start but also counterproductive for the majority of blacks—not least by valorizing the experience of marginality and opposition—or whether, in the end, it advanced the cause of black citizenship by encouraging America to live up to its liberal civic ideals. As the nation strove to contain threats of organized violence, Panther radicalism, it seems, ironically strengthened American liberalism.

As for Newton, he would never reconcile the contradiction embodied by his brothers Melvin and Sonny Man. He remained the young burglar who had taught himself to read by studying Plato's *Republic*. He would earn a doctorate at the University of California–Santa Cruz in the History of Consciousness (a leading interdisciplinary academic program long home to radical intellectual luminaries such as Norman O. Brown, where today Angela Davis holds an endowed chair). At the same time, he would pursue a path that could lead only to psychological and emotional collapse. After his release from prison, Newton was taken up by not only white and black radicals, but also by the radical chic of New York and Hollywood, men and women who showed him life in a very fast lane. He had never demonstrated a special talent for sustained intimacy and had long expressed a principled hostility to marriage, but his iconic notoriety, and particularly the aura of the former inmate, presented him with many sexual opportunities, in which he freely indulged. He also became involved with drugs, despite the party's official condemnation of drug use.

Cocaine would ultimately prove his downfall. In the 1970s, the white powder stirred the erratic behavior and delusions of grandeur to which he was already inclined. After changing his title from Minister of Defense to Servant of the People, for instance, he came to call himself the Supreme Servant—and, finally, simply "The Servant." In the 1980s, crack cocaine unraveled him fully: he became paranoid, dissipated, constantly high. His closest friends expected he would die on the street. In late August of 1989, early one morning in Oakland, Newton was shot in the head by a young dealer named Tyrone Robinson, or "Double R," the kind of brother on the block the Panthers once sought to organize. As Double R pistol-whipped the dying Panther with a .45, Newton cried out his last, true words, "You can kill my body, but you can't kill my soul. My soul will live forever!"[32]

For the future of black citizenship, for the full inclusion of Afro-Americans within a liberal ideal of American civic identity, the value of that promise was not without ambiguity.

PART FIVE

After Caste,

1991–2004

Passage

The history of Afro-American citizenship—and American notions of civic belonging—has reached a critical divide. There is no better way to understand its significance than considering the divide that exists within black life itself. On one hand, the United States today has the largest Afro-American middle class in its history, and black men and women have assumed prominent roles in the circles of political power—they have entered, that is, the heart of the law. From a historical perspective, careers like those of Vernon Jordan, Colin Powell, Condoleezza Rice, and Clarence Thomas, and their complete acceptance in the most prominent roles of the national elite, signals a true revolution in America. Caste, the white republic, a world of white purity and black pollution, is dead. It is a simple matter, as well, to offer statistical evidence of extraordinary black professional achievement. In 1940, there were only 1,000 black attorneys, whereas in 1990, there were 27,000; in 1940, there were 300 black engineers, while in 1990, there were over 59,000; in 1940, there were about 2,600 black college teachers, and in 1990, over 37,000.[1] Similarly, though social scientists and policy-makers may argue about just how to calculate the economic condition of the "black middle class," its size and whether or not it is "rising" or "falling" and, if so, how quickly, no one with eyes to see can dispute the vast historical increase of Afro-Americans in the ranks of mainstream economic life—including its highest levels, with business titans like Kenneth Chenault, chief executive officer of American Express, Richard Parsons of AOL Time Warner, Stanley O'Neal of Merrill Lynch, and Franklin Raines of Fannie Mae. At the same time, there exists another world of black America, a separate "nation," as a recent public television documentary called it: that of the black urban underclass. The cycle of multigenerational poverty and family breakdown in our inner cities that has persisted despite the Great Society and later efforts to address it—it is this point to which the "next Reconstruction," whatever shape it takes, will have to be directed. The destitution of the ghetto affects far more than those who live there. The criminality its conditions breed has tended to stigmatize all blacks with an association with violence and lawlessness—caste is dead, but black legal exile is not—a phenomenon that has substantially hindered their full assimilation into mainstream civic life, despite their collective social and economic accomplishments.

The implications of this divide for black citizenship were reflected in the cultural complexities of the murder case of O. J. Simpson. For the most salient feature of Simpson's life was not the mere extent of his personal wealth, nor the fact of his having so notably failed as a celebrity to link himself with black social concerns or even social circles, but rather that he was an Afro-American man who had achieved success from humble beginnings only to be subject at last to an effort to place him outside the law, to brand him a criminal. In this, his life seemed to play out a primal nightmare for the black middle class. The readiness of many black Americans to view Simpson's prosecution as a frame-up by the Los Angeles police sprang from their own experience of being suspected of criminal behavior, despite their financial success and lawfulness, and being denied enjoyment of public goods and private services free from suspicion. The anecdotes have become part of the fabric of our popular culture: the black professional asked for multiple forms of identification when writing a check; the black executive unable to hail a taxicab in New York; the black college student who sees a white woman clutch her purse as he walks down the street; or, most of all, the black man or woman driving a high-status car stopped for the "crime" of Driving While Black. In an age when the criminality of the black underclass stigmatizes all black Americans, the force of the desire for Simpson's acquittal sprang from a fervent, desperate hope to see an end to black legal exile in the wake of the Civil Rights Movement.

The two cases in this chapter each reflect aspects of the character of black trials in this peculiar moment of our history. The first is the legal drama of the hearings in Clarence Thomas's nomination to the U.S. Supreme Court in 1991. The Hill-Thomas hearings would not only signal the end of a civic culture of caste in the United States, but also indicate the shape of the debates over Afro-American citizenship that are taking place within the now-dominant liberal tradition. Moreover, they suggest how the rhetoric of caste persists after the practical death of caste as a social force: in a post-caste era, the language of caste is used as a weapon of critique, primarily by liberals, those left of center, to advance their positions on race and civic life. (In this period, there is a distinction between liberals as a political group and the liberal tradition of political thought and jurisprudence examined throughout this book.) The second case is that of Mumia Abu-Jamal. He and Justice Thomas share many personal and intellectual similarities: they are of roughly similar age, both were deeply touched by the militancy of the Black Panther Party (and by cultural trends that led each of them to name one of their sons Jamal), and each adheres to a vision of what he calls "natural law" (though of radically different kinds). Abu-Jamal is currently imprisoned in Pennsylvania for murdering a police officer, and has become both celebrated and notorious for his writings on the experience of death row. Whether he is guilty or not, Abu-Jamal's case has become a focal point for the debate over the most significant barrier to Afro-American civic progress today: the mass incarceration of black men. Ironically, this widespread form of civic death is the product, contrary to the views of many of Abu-Jamal's supporters, not of the caste principles against which liberals long fought, but rather of tensions and limitations within the liberal tradition that supplanted it. Black trials of our own era are struggles for black citizenship within this liberal tradition, and over its meaning, that seek to harness the energy of a civic rhetoric whose time has passed.

1 3

Confirmation

▲

The Russell Senate Office Building in Washington is an unassuming, even inconspicuous-looking structure, at least from the outside. The white-marble and limestone edifice sits on Constitution Avenue, between First and Delaware, just across the street from the Capitol, and its architects were wary of drawing attention away from the great, white dome of Congress. The Caucus Room inside, however, is another matter. The achievement of John Carrère and Thomas Hastings, both trained at the École des Beaux-Arts in Paris, it is the oldest Senate assembly room outside the Capitol itself, and the space unabashedly boasts its importance. Even the approach to the room is imposing. A visitor stands in the three-story rotunda just inside the southwest entrance, strides up one of the beautiful marble stairways encircled by gleaming columns, and then passes through a pair of dark, elegant wooden doors. The room itself is a masterpiece of Beaux Arts design: finely proportioned, eclectic, richly decorated. Over seventy feet long and fifty feet wide, it is surrounded by white Corinthian columns and pilasters and garlanded with intricate molding, and features an elaborate coffered ceiling. Above the red, patterned carpet hangs a series of crystal chandeliers, with globes depicting symbols of early American civic life and government (these include the Phrygian hat, or "liberty cap," the headdress that slaves in ancient Rome were granted upon their release from bondage, which served in the eighteenth century as an icon of revolutionary freedom in France and the United States).

This space, which so elegantly represents the ideals and aspirations of the American nation, has been the stage for some of the most dramatic Senate investigations of the twentieth century. The inquiry into the Teapot Dome scandal of President Warren G. Harding took place here in 1923–24; so did the investigation of American organized crime in the early 1950s; and the Army-McCarthy hearings; and Watergate; and Iran-Contra. And it was here that the most prominent black trial of the post–Civil Rights period—the era after caste—would take place as well, broadcast live, on television, across the country.

It began shortly after ten o'clock on Friday, October 11, 1991, the Caucus Room crowded with spectators and reporters. The battle that would take place over the next three days was unprecedented in American history. It involved a dispute between two prominent Afro-American lawyers—one of whom would shortly be elevated to the acme of American legal life—who presented baldly contradictory testimony, each supported in their stories by many successful fellow black professionals. The battle would lead to spectacular accusations and counteraccusations laced with the bitterness of former intimates, and would take place within a unique linguistic house of mirrors, an elaborate web of politically coded rhetoric. But most important for the history of black trials, the event would see a collision of two contrasting positions about the place of blacks in American civic life—and this clash was *within* the liberal tradition itself, between two different ways of interpreting it. This battle would symbolically mark the death of caste jurisprudence in the United States even as it highlighted the persistence of the rhetoric of caste in liberal social commentary.[1]

Senator Joseph Biden called the meeting to order. "Let me inform the Capitol Hill Police," he announced, "that if there is not absolute order and decorum in here, we will recess the hearing and those who engage in any outburst at all will be asked to leave the committee room." Three extraordinary days of hearings to determine Judge Clarence Thomas's suitability to serve on the United States Supreme Court—and to consider the charges of sexual harassment made against him by a law professor, Anita Hill—were about to begin.[2]

On June 27, 1991, Justice Thurgood Marshall sent a curt message to President George H. W. Bush. "The strenuous demands of Court work and its related duties required or expected of a Justice," he wrote, "appear at this time to be incompatible with my advancing age and medical condition." An icon of American liberalism—the man who had litigated *Brown v. Board of Education* and helped bring about a revolution in American law—had decided to leave the stage. Justice Marshall had hoped to relinquish his office during a Democratic administration that would replace him with a jurist sympathetic to his views, especially those on race and civil rights. But by 1991, it had become clear that failing health would force his hand. And so Justice Marshall reluctantly announced his resignation not to a Democrat who admired the Warren court, but rather to a president whose party fundamentally opposed the judicial principles for which he had long fought. Marshall left the Court in bitterness and died eighteen months later. Had the matter been entirely his to decide, President Bush might well have nominated someone other than Clarence Thomas to fill the seat. The President was something of a moderate, a compromiser. But the right wing of the Republican Party, which had played a vital role in his election, had been demanding a Supreme Court justice to represent its interests on the bench. The President's earlier nomination of Judge David Souter, former attorney general of New Hampshire, left that debt unpaid (Justice Souter would consistently disappoint the right in his voting record and written opinions). Presented with the opportunity, President Bush would have to make good, and when Justice Marshall stepped down, Judge Thomas was at the top of the list presented by the Christian right. He was a logical choice. In addition to native ambition, intelligence, and religiosity—a firm Catholic, Thomas also worshiped for a time in a charismatic Episcopal church—he had two great virtues that, until recently, rarely existed in a single person: he was an intellectual conservative, and he was black.

Conservative black thinkers or, as the legal scholar Stephen Carter calls them, black dissenters, are a rare breed. Afro-Americans have long formed one of the most devoted Democratic constituencies, and the allegiance is hardly surprising. After all, Republicans opposed the basic civil rights legislation of the post–World War II era—laws that aimed at giving minority groups not preferential treatment but simply freedom from invidious discrimination—and the Republican Party has a recent history of attracting racial extremists, such as Klansman and Louisiana gubernatorial candidate David Duke. Contemporary Republican political platforms also typically oppose affirmative action or racial preference policies, especially in college and university admissions, which most blacks believe remain necessary to ensure their collective social and economic progress. To be a black conservative thus implies more than an intellectual leap, away from the basic political faith of one's fathers and ethnic peers; it also carries the risk of being publicly branded as a race traitor, an Uncle Tom, a charge that few, understandably, are willing to endure. One prominent black conservative, Thomas Sowell, has described the attendant marginality: a black conservative, he has said, is "perhaps not considered as bizarre as being a transvestite, but it is certainly considered more strange than being a vegetarian or a birdwatcher."[3]

Strange to some, perhaps, black conservatism also is a sign of the many substantial, positive changes that have come to black America in the wake of the Civil Rights Movement. For one, the dismantling of Jim Crow laws helped blacks to enter the ranks of the middle and professional classes. Statistics hint at the revolution. In 1940, about 5 percent of black men and 6 percent of black women held middle-class, white-collar jobs. By 1990, those numbers had jumped to 32 and nearly 60 percent, respectively. Or consider education. In 1960, about 37 percent of blacks between the ages of twenty-five and twenty-nine had received four years of high-school education—by 1995, that figure had jumped to 86.5 percent (for whites, it was 87.4 precent). In 1960, only 7.2 percent of black Americans over twenty-five had attended college—by 1995, that figure had climbed to 37.5 percent (compared with 49 percent of whites).[4] This profound economic and social change has helped produce a black population with an increasing range of individual interests and, in turn, a slowly growing diversity of political views. Economic success, that is, has begun to expand the ideological affiliations of Afro-Americans as a group (to a degree even greater than that represented by the poles of men such as W. E. B. DuBois and Marcus Garvey). And with increasing numbers of Afro-Americans receiving first-rate graduate educations and becoming leaders in intellectual life, there has emerged a set of independent-minded black thinkers who, for a host of reasons—honest intellectual inquiry, professional expedience, a contrarian temperament—have come to identify themselves with schools of thought and with a political party seen as anathema by most Afro-Americans.

Black conservatism is one part, though a symbolically important one, of the broader intellectual and political movement of libertarianism and, to a lesser degree, neoconservatism. In domestic politics, beginning in the mid-1960s, these movements sought to dismantle the social democratic consensus of the postwar years, particularly the faith its exponents placed in government regulation and the ability of technocrats to guide social and economic life. Drawing on the libertarian tradition of Adam Smith, they challenged that consensus, attacking liberal policy through a powerful set of practical and normative criticisms based on the inviolability of individual economic freedom, the sanctity of private property, a skepticism toward government intrusiveness, and a faith in the efficacy of free trade to achieve the greatest good for the greatest number. (In these policies, neoconservatives shared the faith of their conservative forebears in limited government but, in a mood of high optimism, associated conservatism explicitly with capitalist markets and an overarching concern for material prosperity, which ran contrary to many branches of the conservative political tradition, notably that of evangelicals, with whom neoconservatives are otherwise allied on moral and cultural matters.) These movements began to influence domestic policy beginning in the Reagan and first Bush administrations, and today they represent a major ideological influence on American government.

Thomas's conservatism has diverse intellectual roots. In part, they are religious—though it is notable that in his public writings his Christian commitments do not seem to figure significantly into his views on race. In his skepticism of affirmative action, more potently, he has been informed by the writings of economist Thomas Sowell, now a senior fellow at the Hoover Institution in Stanford, California. Sowell has argued that the consequences of affirmative action in education and employment in the United States, as elsewhere in the world, have been disastrous for the nation as a whole and for the very minorities such policies have been intended to help. The benefits of affirmative action, Sowell argues, typically extend disproportionately to the most economically fortunate members of minority groups, rather than to the truly disadvantaged, and the programs cause counterproductive resentment against blacks as beneficiaries, especially among whites and Asians. More significantly, he asserts, whatever the justifications for affirmative action policies—whether as a redress for past discrimination or an effort to secure a racial "balance" in mainstream and elite institutions—empirical data indicate that they not only fail to help, but actually harm blacks. In college education, in particular, they contribute to the spectacularly high percentage of black students who fail to graduate. In his 1990 work *Preferential Policies*, for instance, Sowell indicates that at the time over 70 percent of black students at both the University of California at Berkeley and San Jose State University had dropped out before graduation.

The reasons behind this failure rate are not difficult to see. In 1983, for instance, a plethora of colleges and universities in the United States boasted student bodies whose median combined score on the verbal and mathematics portions of the Scholastic Aptitude Test was over 1,200. In that same year, there were fewer than six hundred black students in the country with a score of 1,200 or above. For elite colleges to achieve representation of black students in their student bodies at all close to the percentage of Afro-Americans in the general population, they are required to select students who have test scores often well below their own median. In 1986, for instance, at Berkeley, black students had a median SAT score of 952, whereas the university average was 1181 (the median for Asian-Americans was 1,254). A great many of these students would have fallen well within the median SAT score range of well-regarded colleges but—as is suggested by their SAT scores, a good predictor of college achievement—they do less well and often drop out of the elite institutions for which, on the basis of their scores, they are mismatched. Sowell argues that this "process of mismatching" grows worse in "second-tier institutions," which "find that the minority students who meet their normal standards of admission have been siphoned off and so must take minority students whose qualifications are more appropriate for [even] lower-ranked institutions." Thus, for Sowell, as an empirical matter, policies meant to improve the lives of black Americans as a whole perhaps have saddled them with a tragically high level of college attrition, a phenomenon whose economic and psychological consequences are borne by those individual blacks who are the subject of a well-intended but misconceived policy experiment.

Thomas's conservatism, as it relates to race in particular and public policy in general, also derives from his commitment to a jurisprudence of "natural law." An ancient and diverse line of thought, the natural law tradition asserts that there are certain transcendent principles—whether born of logic, the revealed will of God, or empirical observation—that should constrain the scope of human lawmaking and, at times, may constitute the true law by which citizens are bound. Natural law thinking has been developed most fully by Catholic theologians drawing on the work of Saint Thomas Aquinas, but a great many founders of the Revolutionary generation subscribed to some form of natural law belief, via the seventeenth-century writings of Thomas Hobbes and John Locke. In the realm of American constitutional interpretation, natural law finds its first full judicial expression in the late-eighteenth-century case of *Calder v. Bull*, where Justice Samuel Chase argued that there were certain unwritten ideals, existing beyond the Constitution itself, that constrained legislative policy. Natural law has since become associated in legal scholarship with the tradition of "substantive due process"—whose exponents argue that the guarantee by the Fifth and Fourteenth amendments that a person's "liberty" shall not be taken without "due process of law" imports into the Constitution a broad set of unwritten principles of natural right—and with the view, held by Justice Thomas, that the interpretation of the Constitution should be guided by the principles of "self-evident" truth announced in the Declaration of Independence.

In contemporary legal and political life, natural law philosophy tends to be associated with social conservatism, particularly in the realm of women's rights, for natural law thinkers generally oppose abortion. But what makes at least one branch of natural law especially interesting today is the link it forges between economic development and civil rights. In the economic realm, many natural law proponents are known for their strong belief in the sanctity of individual and corporate property and their hostility to governmental restrictions on its use—that is, for their embrace of laissez-faire capitalism and its individualist bias. An underlying principle of this position is the belief that the highest benefits for society as a whole will be achieved by allowing the uninhibited, free flow of goods and capital and the broadest possible liberty to individual economic actors. Natural law thinkers bring this same analysis of individual rights and collective welfare to questions of race and citizenship. They maintain a strong, principled commitment to individual over group rights and an antagonism toward racial preferences, which they view as illegitimate restrictions of individual liberty. But they also believe that such individualist values are the best means by which to achieve progress for racial minorities as a whole. The civil rights vision of many natural law thinkers tends to be much like their economic vision: one in which, ideally, individual actors operate in a marketplace free from regulation. It is a vision of race and civic life in which, if left alone rather than "assisted" through programs of social engineering, blacks would, one by one, like so many Horatio Algers, raise themselves up by their bootstraps.

Nominating a black conservative to take Justice Marshall's place on the Supreme Court was a stroke of political genius. Republicans calculated that, much as liberals might disagree with his legal views, Thomas's color would shield him from attack. Failure to confirm Thomas would risk eliminating entirely the "black seat" on the Court. For whites of any party, this would have been a grave matter, but for Democrats, it would be political suicide. Republicans also calculated that nominating Thomas would divide Afro-American political leaders, many of whom would find it difficult to oppose any black candidate, no matter his or her political views (and, as expected, while the NAACP announced its opposition to Thomas, the National Urban League and the Southern Christian Leadership Conference came out in his favor). Had it not been for Anita Hill, the strategy probably would have gone down in Republican political history as an unalloyed success; indeed, before her accusations surfaced, the *New York Times* reported that Thomas's confirmation seemed all but "inevitable." But Hill's challenge—an accusation of sexual harassment—struck with exceptional force, and Republicans shared responsibility for that as well, precisely because of the care they took in guiding Thomas through his confirmation.

For the Republicans had learned from past mistakes. When liberals at the time spoke the name Clarence Thomas, the one to be heard next was usually Robert Bork. Thomas was in many respects just as judicially conservative as Judge Bork, and the Bush administration was keen to avoid a repeat of the fiasco before the Judiciary Committee that followed Bork's nomination to the Supreme Court by President Ronald Reagan in 1987. In those hearings, the spirited, aggressive judge had engaged his liberal opponents in tense debate about the substantive merits of his views on constitutional adjudication. Even in his opening statement to the Committee, Judge Bork stated forthrightly that the hearings centrally involved fundamental questions of "philosophy." This approach made Bork appear to be an extremist, outside the mainstream of American law, and it failed miserably. He lost his confirmation by a vote of 58 to 42. Exultant over their success, liberals began to use the candidate's last name as a verb. Republicans decided that with Thomas—who, like Bork, had a strong adversarial streak—they would take a very different tack. President Bush's nominee would be presented to the Judiciary Committee not so much as a legal thinker but rather as a particular type of man; instead of forthrightly asserting Thomas's judicial views, the Republicans would focus attention on his admirable personal history. This approach, known in the Bush administration as the "Pin Point strategy," after the small, impoverished town in which Thomas was born, would transform Thomas's story into an unassailable proxy for his legal ideas, fusing his character and his jurisprudence.

When the strategy became apparent in the Caucus Room on September 10, before a national audience, it seemed unbeatable. The fourteen senators on the Judiciary Committee, led by Joseph Biden, had been prepared for a clash of political titans. Among those on the committee were Senator Edward Kennedy of Massachusetts and Senator Strom Thurmond of South Carolina, icons respectively of the left and right ends of the political spectrum of the Senate. Senator Thurmond had argued strongly in Judge Bork's favor, and Senator Biden and Senator Kennedy had both spoken vociferously, and devastatingly, against him ("[i]n Robert Bork's America," declared Kennedy, "there is no room at the inn for blacks and no place in the Constitution for women, and in our America there should be no seat on the Supreme Court for Robert Bork").[5] But rather than seeing a direct ideological confrontation, the senators found themselves serenaded by an inspirational story—the narrative of a man who worked his way out of poverty to reach great professional success. Thomas did not attack; from the start, he dodged and weaved.

Clarence Thomas is a large, athletic man, very dark-skinned, with a booming baritone and great charisma, but he opened his testimony modestly, with a tone of self-effacement. "Mr. Chairman, Senator Thurmond, members of the committee," he began, "I am humbled and honored to have been nominated by President Bush to be an Associate Justice of the Supreme Court of the United States. I would like to thank the committee, especially you, Chairman Biden, for your extraordinary fairness throughout this process, and I would like to thank each of you and so many of your colleagues here in the Senate for taking the time to visit with me. . . . I hope these hearings will help to show more clearly who this person Clarence Thomas is and what really makes me tick." "My earliest memories," explained Thomas, "are those of Pin Point, Georgia, a life far removed in space and time from this room, this day and this moment. As kids, we caught minnows in the creeks, fiddler crabs in the marshes, we played with pluffers, and skipped shells across the water. It was a world so vastly different from all this." That world, he elaborated, was no little idyll, however; it was one of real adversity and a noble struggle against it. "In 1955, my brother and I went to live with my mother in Savannah," he continued:

> We lived in a one room tenement. We shared a kitchen with other tenants and we had a common bathroom in the backyard which was unworkable and unusable. It was hard, but it was all we had and all there was. Our mother only earned twenty dollars every two weeks as a maid, not enough to take care of us. So

she arranged for us to live with our grandparents later, in 1955. Imagine, if you will, two little boys with all their belongings in two grocery bags.

Imagine, also, Thomas asked, a world restricted not only by poverty, but also by race—and imagine a man who overcame those barriers through his religious training and the strong work ethic he learned through the example of his grandfather. "I attended segregated parochial schools and later attended a seminary near Savannah," Thomas emphasized.

> The nuns gave us hope and belief in ourselves when society didn't. . . . I can still hear my grandfather, "Y'all goin' have mo' of a chance than me"—and he was right. He felt that if others sacrificed and created opportunities for us we had an obligation to work hard, to be decent citizens, to be fair and good people— and he was right.

Turning to Senator Biden, Thomas continued: "You see, Mr. Chairman, my grandparents grew up and lived their lives in an era of blatant segregation and overt discrimination. Their sense of fairness was molded in a crucible of unfairness. I watched as my grandfather was called 'boy.' I watched as my grandmother suffered the indignity of being denied the use of a bathroom. But through it all they remained fair, decent, good people. Fair in spite of the terrible contradictions in our country."[6]

From such humble beginnings, Thomas rose, by dint of self-discipline and initiative: beginning, first, to train for the Catholic priesthood, he chose not to take robes and went instead to Holy Cross College in Massachusetts, and then Yale Law School, a training ground for American political leadership. Working for the Reagan administration, he became chair of the Equal Employment Opportunity Commission, before being appointed to the bench of the D.C. Circuit Court of Appeals. It was a narrative, to invoke the work of Booker T. Washington, "up from slavery." Thomas was living proof that the progress of individuals, given their full liberty, will be limited only by the scope of their talents and ambitions. "If confirmed by the Senate," he concluded, "I pledge that I will preserve and protect our Constitution and carry with me the values of my heritage: fairness, integrity, open-mindedness, honesty, and hard work." It was an extraordinary performance—and it was meaningful as much for what it left unsaid as for what it stated explicitly.

As liberal critics would later note, Thomas's personal narrative was

silent about the ways in which his steady march up the professional lad-
der had been aided at critical moments by his race, by the very racial
preferences he and other black conservatives resolutely opposed. Holy
Cross and Yale Law School both seem to have granted Thomas admission under a form of affirmative action. His first job after leaving Yale
was a direct result of Senator Danforth's active recruitment of black
employees for his office. Even his nomination to the Court itself depended
on his race. Thomas was only too well aware of that history; indeed,
throughout his years as a student and a young legal professional, he felt
that affirmative action programs had imposed a mark of inferiority on
him: whites, he believed (and not without reason), would view him as
having achieved his success not by virtue of hard work or native ability
alone, but also, if not mainly, because he was black. No matter what its
justification, liberals thought Thomas's silence symptomatic of the problems of the conservative interpretation of the liberal tradition, especially
its emphasis on individual initiative rather than social justice. According
to that interpretation, the Civil Rights Movement had demolished explicit
legal barriers to black achievement, and fair play was, if not the reality,
at least the clear ideal of civic life. In this new era, when only explicit
racial discrimination would meet with stern enforcement, Afro-Americans
could achieve success if they worked hard under the discipline that the
marketplace imposes on all persons, regardless of color. To the extent that
Afro-Americans were prevented from achieving high standards, Thomas's
life narrative suggested, they were held back not so much by racism as by
their own diminished expectations of themselves, to which panaceas like
affirmative action ultimately contributed.

The conservative vision of race and civic life was in fact consistent
with the individualist rhetoric of much of the early Civil Rights Movement, but Thomas's espousal of it made him anathema in most liberal
circles of the early 1990s. In those years, many liberals had come to
believe that the most significant force behind racial inequality was not an
open and direct racism, but rather a largely invisible process of racial
subordination. Specifically, in the liberal view, which sees discrimination
less as an assault on individuals than as a "structural" pathology, laws
that are race-neutral—or "color blind," to recall Justice Harlan's dissent
in *Plessy*—serve in fact to calcify existing racial hierarchies, the residue of
two centuries of inequality that was far from cleansed by a mere half
century of legal remedy. Strict individualist principles raise the same
criticism embodied in Anatole France's comment on the criminal laws of
the nineteenth century: "The majestic equality of the law," he asserted,

"forbid[s] rich and poor alike to sleep under the bridges, to beg in the streets, and to steal their bread."[7] Structural inequality, say liberals, requires structural, race-conscious solutions. In concealing the extent to which he had been helped in his own life by just such preferment policies, Judge Thomas also seemed, by implication, to be denying the existence of the hidden, structural discrimination that prevented most other blacks from assimilating fully into American civic life and making further social and economic progress. The failure to confront such a salient feature of his personal experience, moreover, suggested the deficiencies of his jurisprudence. Senator Biden and other Democrats on the Judiciary Committee sought to bring out what they saw as those deficiencies in questioning Thomas about issues of natural law and its judicial implications, but Thomas was either studiously vague or placatory in his answers, and he continually avoided being pinned down. His confirmation seemed assured.

But the Pin Point strategy was to be hoist on its own petard. As the hearings came to a close, it would be suggested that Judge Thomas had a secret history of his own—a history of discrimination perpetrated out of sight—and the fusion of individual character and conservative jurisprudence that Republicans sought to achieve was to reveal, in the eyes of liberals, a fatal deceit.

The woman responsible for revealing that secret history was, in outward respects, not unlike Thomas himself; in fact, the two had much more in common with each other than with most members of the political factions that supported them. For while she would later become a liberal heroine, Anita Faye Hill, like Thomas, was something of a black conservative. Born to a family of Oklahoma farmers in 1956, Hill was the youngest of thirteen children, and her poor, rural upbringing was strictly religious (her family was Baptist). Like Thomas, the dark-skinned Hill was taught the values of strong self-discipline and hard work, and also like Thomas, she excelled in school, ultimately receiving a law degree from Yale. A supporter of Ronald Reagan, her first job after graduation was in the Equal Employment Opportunity Commission, where she worked directly under Thomas, who was carrying out the agenda of their political party in regard to civil rights, which was to put an end to policies that smacked of liberal social engineering. After leaving government, Hill took a teaching position at Oral Roberts University, a conservative, evangelical institution, and later rose to become a professor of commercial law at the University of Oklahoma.

But if Hill and Thomas shared certain outward similarities, and had held to a common political ideology, they were strikingly different personalities, especially when it came to matters of the heart and, more explosively, issues of sex. For her part, Anita Hill had throughout her life continued to forge the deep personal relationships she had learned to develop within her large family. Her classmates and colleagues remember the warmth and the support she gave others, even while pursuing a promising career. Hill would return from vacations at her family's home with a suitcase full of vegetables from her mother's garden. In keeping with the values of her youth, she was prim, and reserved in intimate matters. Thomas, on the other hand, had been a boy whose father had abandoned his mother, leaving him to feel isolated and victimized through much of his life. His mighty struggle to raise himself up in the world also seemed to demand that he distance himself from his immediate family. "She is so dependent [on public assistance]," Thomas asserted about his sister Emma Mae Martin in a 1980 interview, "she gets mad when the mailman is late with her welfare check. . . . What's worse is that now her kids feel entitled to the check too. They have no motivation for doing better or getting out of that situation."[8] Anyone who has had contact with welfare dependency knows the potential for truth in such a characterization, but, far more important, it reveals a certain callousness on Thomas's part. (In this, Thomas rather resembles Charlie Hexam, the ambitious scholar who spent his childhood in poverty beside the Thames in Charles Dickens's *Our Mutual Friend.*)

Thomas also seems to have had a taste for pornography. It is, one hastens to add, no slander to say so. Though its expression is very much restricted in polite society, interest in pornography is entirely legal, and as a billion-dollar industry, would seem to draw the majority of American males at some point in their lives. Moreover, Thomas came of age during the sexual revolution, a transformation in American values that, for a time, caused even hard-core pornography to be perceived as a vehicle for liberation. (Huey Newton, for instance, was early associated with a Bay Area group known as the Sexual Freedom League.) This having been said, by all accounts, Thomas's interest in pornography seems to have been extreme even by the standards of the time. He apparently favored depictions of black men and women with inordinately large sexual organs (now-notorious figures such as Long Dong Silver and Bad Mama Jama), and even his male colleagues from New Haven found his tastes in cinema embarrassing. Moreover, consistent with these tastes, in at least some of his relations with women, Thomas seems to have taken pleasure in verbal coercion; he enjoyed, that is, a woman's discomfort in his sexual talk, rather as he enjoyed, one is tempted to add, the ideological discomfort of liberals when he spoke as a black conservative.

The complexity of that sexual dynamic can be glimpsed in what Hill would describe before the committee as "one of the oddest episodes I remember." Hill and Thomas were alone together in his office and the EEOC chair was drinking a can of Coca-Cola. What happened next would be repeated in ribald conversations across the country for weeks. Thomas, claimed Hill, "got up from the table, which we were working at, went over to his desk to get the Coke, looked at the can and asked, 'Who has put pubic hair on my Coke?'"[9] While Hill cited the incident as bizarre, it is—perhaps—a subtle indication of Thomas's tense relation to issues of race, sex, politics, and civic belonging. Hair is a central feature of Afro-American identity and the tightness of its coils is sometimes jokingly compared by blacks to the hair of the human pubis. The subtext of the aggressive if joking question "Who has put pubic hair on my Coke?" asked between two dark-skinned Afro-Americans in the office of the chair of the EEOC, one might conclude, was that black men, reduced to their sexual functions in the perverse white psychological universe of Jim Crow, were now at the heart of American power—and that one ribald, assertive black man in particular was now in a high office of American government. Thomas was, one might say, asking Hill to acknowledge the sentiment and affirm their common origins, in what Orlando Patterson calls a "down-home" style of courting, or, and at the same time, trying simply to make Hill squirm.[10]

Anita Hill claimed that while she was an attorney working under Thomas in the EEOC, she was frequently made party to a wide range of such aggressive, sexually charged comments. As she would assert in her testimony before the Senate Judiciary Committee, Thomas repeatedly goaded her to become physically involved with him ("You're going to be dating me," he would declare). In the inner office of the EEOC, he would make comments "on what I was wearing in terms of whether it made me more or less sexually attractive." Sometimes, Hill claimed, Thomas "would call me into his office for reports on education issues and projects or he might suggest that because of the time pressures of his schedule, we go to lunch to a government cafeteria":

> After a brief discussion of work, he would turn the conversation to a discussion of sexual matters. His conversations were very vivid.

He spoke about acts that he had seen in pornographic films involving such matters as women having sex with animals, and films showing group sex or rape scenes. He talked about pornographic materials depicting individuals with large penises, or large breasts, involved in various sex acts.

On several occasions Thomas told me graphically of his own sexual prowess. Because I was extremely uncomfortable talking about sex with him at all, and particularly in such a graphic way, I told him that I did not want to talk about these subjects. I would also try to change the subject to education matters, or to nonsexual personal matters, such as his background or his beliefs. My efforts to change the subject were rarely successful.

In most other circumstances, Thomas's behavior would have been simply as Hill described it, "very ugly . . . very dirty . . . disgusting"; but on the part of a supervisor toward a young employee, fresh out of law school, it was far more significant.[11] It was a form of sexual discrimination; it used the theme of sexuality to create an untenable, "hostile" work environment for an employee based on her sex. By her own account, the behavior struck Hill hard and, later, she would attribute a hospital stay of five days for a stomach illness to the resulting stress. As chair of the EEOC, Thomas was ironically guilty himself of the very principles he was sworn to uphold. It also was, arguably, a form of behavior Hill might have done more to nip in the bud and avoid. But she was in a difficult spot: Thomas was a mentor, and, especially in the legal world, powerful mentors can make or break a person's career. If she shared responsibility by allowing Thomas's conversations to continue, she could reasonably be excused as a recent law school graduate concerned about her professional future and as a prim, embarrassed woman from a strict Baptist family—two elements of her character and background that indeed may have added to Thomas's enjoyment of the situation.

Hill was a private person, but Thomas's behavior so troubled her that she confided in friends, who provided what consolation they could—and, more fatefully, would remember what had happened to Hill years later, when Judge Thomas appeared on television with President Bush, who presented him as the "most qualified" man to fill Justice Marshall's seat on the Supreme Court. After Hill disclosed her story to the Judiciary Committee, in whose confidence she hoped that it would remain sealed, it was revealed publicly, against her will, by a reporter for

National Public Radio. When the story broke, the friends in whom Hill had trusted were willing to testify on her behalf, not only to save the honor of an old friend and colleague, now accused of lying, but also to assist the coalition of liberal organizations that had seized onto Hill's story as onto a life raft. The possibility that Judge Thomas had made the comments Hill claimed he did was an important weapon for his critics in two related ways. First, it undermined the goal of the Pin Point strategy to portray Thomas as a man worthy of serving as the highest symbolic representative of American law; it suggested that Thomas himself was constitutionally incapable of adhering to certain basic social and legal norms, much less upholding the Constitution. The charge not only made Thomas seem a moral and religious hypocrite; it placed him, as an individual, outside the law itself. Moreover, implicitly, the form of behavior in which Thomas engaged seemed to give the lie to the very structure of Thomas's jurisprudential thought and his vision of American civic identity.

For sex discrimination operates by and large in secret. Outside of explicit declarations of discriminatory policies or preferences, sex discrimination typically occurs through a set of unquestioned assumptions that operate in realms closed to public view and accountability. Sex discrimination—and, more specifically, sexual harassment—is thus notorious in the law for producing stories of the "he-said-she-said" variety, an impasse of conflicting testimony in which the victims, typically women, have a difficult time gaining credence. But such discrimination is no less systematic for being private and directed at only one person—one need only contemplate Hill's experience reenacted thousands of times each year, in countless workplaces across the country, to conceive of it as not individual but structural. The liberal view of racial discrimination, significantly, conceives of it as a secret, too, an akin covert structure. Racial discrimination is viewed not so much as a matter of discrete acts of explicit prejudice as one of "institutional racism," in which the application of otherwise neutral, individualist principles (such as a disproportionate reliance on standardized test scores in university admissions) results in disparities in education and employment that disfavor certain racial minorities. The discrimination Hill experienced occurred in private; to understand it as part of a broad pattern of male social oppression requires a leap of imagination whereby the unseen and personal is made visible and social. An analogous effort to make the hidden injury plain forms the heart of the liberal critique of conservative policies on race. In the context of the Pin Point strategy, in which Thomas's life story was bound up with his jurisprudential commitments, his previously hidden life had shattering personal and political consequences.

The three days that followed Hill's accusations signaled a profound change in the national drama of race and civic belonging. For this was no spectacle of Afro-Americans as victims moving whites to sympathy and guilt; nor of Afro-Americans struggling heroically in the face of oppression and the obstacles of racism; the hearings involved black Americans advantaged in every way yet dishonored by all-too-universal human foibles, men and women with no more or less courage, baseness, and self-knowledge than one would expect of any American, regardless of race. They also featured a cast of high-level Afro-American professionals. The nation stood riveted while blacks who had graduated from the top colleges and law schools of America and who worked for some of its most prestigious offices in government, finance, and the bar were taken in deadly earnest by the Judiciary Committee of the United States Senate. And these professionals spanned the spectrum from traditional liberals such as Anita Hill's counsel Charles Ogletree and her liberal supporters such as Kimberley Crenshaw through establishment brokers for Goldman Sachs to right-wing conservatives such as Thomas himself and some of those supporters who testified on his behalf.

In this way, the ritual drama in the Caucus Room helped enact a definitive, nationally televised end to the civic tradition of caste, wherein the individual is captive to the group. For all the pain visited upon their participants, the hearings consistently revealed the realities of black professional achievement, Afro-American political diversity—as well as the growth of deep, intimate relations between blacks and whites in mainstream American life. Thomas himself was married to a white woman descended from a scion of American mainstream conservatism, and he was prominently depicted with her lending support (this in a nation where hinting at racial amalgamation once could lead to bloody riots). Similarly, the hearings made clear that Hill's friendships were fundamentally interracial. Some of her strongest supporters were whites, especially middle-class white women. And far from lacking power, Hill's accusations—the assertions of personal pain visited on a single black professional woman—almost scuttled a major political initiative of a conservative administration.

Ironically, few features of the hearings demonstrated more compellingly the death of caste thinking than the absence of Christian rhetorical appeals and the calculated use of the caste language of purity and pollution, appropriated with varying degrees of earnestness, cynicism, and irony, on both sides of the political divide. For amid disagreement about the status of Afro-Americans *within* the liberal tradition—a debate over not the rightness of black inclusion in American civic life, but rather how best to achieve it—the traditional yoking of Christianity to liberalism as a critical vision of racial inclusion lost its force and relevance. And so in one of the most charged civic events involving Afro-Americans since the Civil Rights Movement, almost no reference was made to the tradition of religious political thought central to the black struggle for full citizenship for most of American history (even with two highly religious participants in the civic drama). Instead, each side in the hearings tried to portray the other as being maliciously motivated by principles of caste. "I think," Thomas stated, in words characteristic of much public reaction as well, "that it is disgusting. I think that this hearing should never occur in America. This is a case in which this sleaze, this dirt, was searched for by staffers or members of this committee . . . and displayed on prime time over our entire nation. How would any member of this committee or any person in this room or any person in this country like sleaze said about him or her in this fashion or this dirt dredged up . . . ?" Trashing the hearings as "a disgrace," Thomas offered the phrase by which the proceedings indeed would be indelibly remembered. From his standpoint, "as a black American," Thomas stated, "as far as I'm concerned, [the hearings were] a high-tech lynching for uppity blacks who in any way deign to think for themselves, to do for themselves, to have different ideas, and it is a message that, unless you kowtow to an old order, this will happen to you, you will be lynched, destroyed, caricatured by a committee of the U. S. Senate, rather than hung from a tree."[12]

This characterization was echoed in the testimony of one of Thomas's former employees at EEOC, Nancy Fitch. A professor of African-American studies at Temple University in Philadelphia, Fitch was a strong Thomas supporter—"besides being a person of great moral character, I found him to be a most intelligent man"—and when asked to explain Thomas's allusion to lynching, she reinforced the comparison:

> I have a student who is working on lynching right now, so I have been thinking about this. Lynching was something that was done to intimidate people, that was done to control them, as well as kill them. And I think, if I understand what the Judge was saying, was that this was an attempt to do that to him; that the process . . . was patently unfair, that it was a way to neutralize and control and intimidate not just him, but possibly through

him, any person that was considered, as he put it, uppity. When black soldiers came back from World War I, they felt that they had proved themselves to the country and to their fellow citizens; and wore their uniforms down south and that was a sure way to get yourself lynched, because they were wrapped, so to speak, in the American flag. That was to tell these people that they were not Americans. I see a connection and understood what he meant by that.[13]

At the same time, black intellectuals supporting Hill deployed a rhetoric born of the fight against slavery and caste—but, significantly, lacking any Christian referent—for their own modern political ends, particularly through vitriolic characterizations of Thomas himself (the kind of ostracism typically faced by black conservatives taken to an extreme). For example, in an essay titled "Collard Greens, Clarence Thomas, and the High-Tech Rape of Anita Hill," a professor of African-American studies at the University of Michigan asserted that Thomas was a "nouveau pork chopper," and that she "could hear the echo of Linda Brent's complaint in *Incidents in the Life of a Slave Girl* as Anita Hill alleged the indignities of the sexual harassment she had suffered. . . ." Another critic asserted that "when Clarence Thomas invoked his right of protection from a twentieth-century, high-tech lynching, he obscured the effort to determine if he was a twentieth-century, high-tech overseer." Still another characterized the hearings as "the gang rape of Anita Hill and the assault upon all women of African descent." In the same vein, another described Thomas as "the noble, loyal and faithful Uncle Tom," who, during the hearings, "evolved into Sambo, that colorful, comic minstrel character who can remember nothing without his master's help."[14]

The characterizations were not only unfair, but grotesquely cruel. But it ultimately was precisely the lack of fairness and measure, the rhetorical duel of racial and sexual humiliation, that made the hearings so significant in the history of black civic belonging. The hyperbolic calumny of accusation and counteraccusation sprang from a world whose ideological convergences were far greater than its differences. In that world, opponents could no longer effectively employ religious appeals as a basis for civic vision, and they sought the poetry and passion provided by religious rhetoric in language used to fight an ideological enemy, caste, that had already died. The hearings also turned two black American antagonists into figures of sympathetic identification for every American of whatever color or political orientation. At one point, Thomas's wife revealed she had found the nominee on the floor of their home, wrapped in a fetal position. Over the course of the hearings, he told the committee, he had "died a thousand deaths." He was experiencing a newly invented collective rite of passage that would result in a new justice on the Supreme Court—and a new culture of race and citizenship in the United States.[15]

The Senate confirmed the nomination of Clarence Thomas on Wednesday, October 16, by the narrow margin of 52 to 48. Judge Thomas chose not to watch the vote on television. When it occurred, he was in the bathtub. His wife came to tell him the news. He shrugged. The White House quickly staged an unofficial swearing-in on October 18, and he was officially sworn to his office in a private, unannounced ceremony on October 23.

In his years on the Court, Justice Thomas has made good on President Bush's debt to the Republican right, advancing through his vote and written opinions conservative principles in matters of the separation of church and state (Thomas would relax the restrictions developed by the Warren Court), in women's rights (he dissented in *Planned Parenthood v. Casey*, in which the Court refused to overturn *Roe v. Wade*), in economics (he lent support in various cases to strong protections of private property), and in state's rights.

But it is on matters of race, especially, that Thomas's legal views have been most important, less for contributing to a majority, which has been rare, but rather for being expressed by a black man in the preeminent chamber of American legal life. In the most crucial instance, in 2003, Justice Thomas vigorously dissented from the Court's majority opinion in *Grutter v. Bollinger*, which upheld the affirmative action policies of the University of Michigan School of Law. In that case, Justice Sandra Day O'Connor wrote that racial preferences were justified to achieve the law school's compelling state interest in achieving racial "diversity," though she predicted that, in twenty-five years, American society would likely change to such a degree that such programs would no longer be needed. Joined by Justice Antonin Scalia, Justice Thomas began his opinion by citing a speech Frederick Douglass gave to a group of abolitionists, advancing a principle "lost on today's majority." Regarding black Americans, claimed Douglass,

> there is always more that is benevolent, I perceive, than just, manifested towards us. What I ask for the negro is not benevolence, not pity, not sympathy, but simply *justice*. The American

people have always been anxious to know what they shall do with us. . . . I have had but one answer from the beginning. Do nothing with us! Your doing with us has already played the mischief with us. Do nothing with us! If the apples will not remain on the tree of their own strength, if they are worm-eaten at the core, if they are early ripe and disposed to fall, let them fall! . . . And if the negro cannot stand on his own legs, let him fall also. All I ask is, give him a chance to stand on his own legs! Let him alone! . . . [Y]our interference is doing him positive injury.

It was an injury, Thomas asserted, that violated "the principle of equality embodied in the Declaration of Independence and the Equal Protection Clause"—and of which he could speak in strong, personal tones. "I must contest the notion that the Law School's discrimination benefits those admitted as a result of it," he wrote. "The Law School tantalizes unprepared students with the promise of a University of Michigan degree and all of the opportunities that it offers. These overmatched students take the bait, only to find that they cannot succeed in the cauldron of competition. And this mismatch crisis is not restricted to elite institutions." In support of the proposition, Justice Thomas cited the 1994 work of Thomas Sowell, *Race and Culture*: "Even if most minority students are able to meet the normal standards at the 'average' range of colleges and universities, the systematic mismatching of minority students begun at the top can mean that such students are generally overmatched throughout all levels of higher education." Moreover, asserted Thomas, the programs stamped minorities with a "badge of inferiority," causing their actual qualifications to be questioned for the rest of their lives. "This problem of stigma does not depend on determinacy as to whether those stigmatized are actually the 'beneficiaries' of racial discrimination," he noted. "When blacks take positions in the highest places of government, industry, or academia, it is an open question today whether their skin color played a part in their advancement. The question itself is the stigma."[16]

Justice Thomas had felt that stigma throughout his professional career; and in the wake of his nomination hearings, what he wanted back, more than anything else, was his good name.[17]

1 4

Statistics and Citizenship

▲

In a desolate corner of rural Pennsylvania, about fifteen miles from the West Virginia border in the town of Waynesburg, lies a prison known as SCI Greene, the State Correctional Institute of Greene County. One of the most modern, secure prison facilities in the nation, intended as a model for other states, it stands low to the ground, concealing within its concrete walls an intricate network of cells and passageways, all kept under strict surveillance. Cameras, microphones, loudspeakers—everything about SCI Greene speaks immobility and control. Opened in 1993, SCI houses about 2,000 of the state's most dangerous criminals, including the majority of men on Pennsylvania's death row. The condemned prisoners spend twenty-three hours a day in cells about the size of an average American bathroom. Weather permitting, they are allowed one hour of fresh air in the prison yard, and less regular access to the prison library. Depending on one's view of crime and punishment, the life of inmates at SCI Greene may be fitting and just; in some respects the control the institution exerts may be preferred to the conditions in some less secure facilities. By any measure, however, it is physically and spiritually brutal.[1]

Almost none of the nearly 230 men on death row in Pennsylvania are famous. From February 1995 to November 2001, Governor Tom

Ridge signed 220 execution warrants (16 of the condemned were His-
panics, 67 were white, 1 was Asian, and 136 were black), the names
mostly forgotten by all but their families and those of the victims they
killed. But SCI Greene also is home to the world's most renowned death
row prisoner, an international symbol of the American practice of legal
execution. His correspondence is addressed to AM8335, but at birth he
was given the Christian name Wesley. To his fellow inmates, he is known
as Mu, and to those on the outside, he is known by the name he adopted
later in life, Mumia Abu-Jamal—or, to his supporters, simply Mumia.
He has been a prisoner of the State of Pennsylvania since 1983, after he
was convicted and sentenced to die for murdering a young Philadelphia
police officer, shot at close range in the back and, then, directly in the
head. His supporters make various claims on his behalf. Some, like the
black scholar-activist Cornel West, maintain that he has been "unjustly
imprisoned for a crime he did not commit."[2] Others, like the author
E. L. Doctorow, argue that his trial so egregiously violated the norms of
American constitutional law and international human rights that it is
impossible to draw conclusions about his guilt or innocence from the
facts presented there. His supporters demand that Mumia be exonerated
or, at the very least, granted a new trial.

Those who oppose such demands, naturally, tell a different story.
They describe Abu-Jamal as a cold-blooded cop killer, a man capable of
standing over a wounded officer of the law, Daniel Faulkner, and shooting him again just in the eye. They characterize him as a villain whose
revolutionary political commitments, nurtured first within the Black Panther Party, in fact made a virtue of killing police. For them, Abu-Jamal's
support is composed of tendentious intellectual radicals who would per-
vert the truth in the name of criticizing the institutions of government;
duped innocents, well-intentioned but naïve observers; impressionable
young people, especially white college students feeling the guilt of their
privileges; and ill-informed Europeans, especially the French, always
eager to accuse the United States of some imagined injustice. Abu-Jamal
has had protests mounted on his behalf throughout the world and across
the United States, while supporters of his conviction, less organized and
more poorly funded, have been a visible presence during the most significant moments in his twenty-year legal odyssey, especially in
Philadelphia. Where Abu-Jamal's supporters chant "Free Mumia!"
those opposed answer "Fry Mumia." And, even among those without
retributive motives, there is a widespread feeling in the City of Brotherly
Love that even if Jamal's trial was not a paragon of proper procedure, its

shortcomings were largely the result of the defendant's own outrageous conduct. One way or another, they argue, Abu-Jamal is guilty of murder, and the will of the people should be carried out by putting him to death.

Whatever the truth, Mumia Abu-Jamal's case touches far more than the life of an individual (Abu-Jamal himself is fond of the African proverb "I am we"). It has become, rather, a platform for the debate of issues with much larger civic significance. In particular, the "Free Mumia!" movement is fueled by legitimate anger at a cultural and legal fact of which Abu-Jamal is but a symbol: a vastly disproportionate number of America's prison population is made up of Afro-American men. Despite the guilt of most of these men (and in his probable guilt, Abu-Jamal is representative of the group), this imbalance is the most formidable barrier in our day to the development of full Afro-American citizenship—it represents a mass banishment of Afro-Americans from the civic community of law. The demands Abu-Jamal's supporters make for an end to the death penalty and fundamental reform of the criminal justice system are thus part of a broader desire to bring Afro-Americans more fully within the circle of American civic life. Fittingly, the theme of legal and civic exile infuses Abu-Jamal's writings, particularly *Live from Death Row*, a collection of essays about prison life, and his collection of religious meditations, *Death Blossoms*, printed by the publishing house of the Bruderhof New Testament Community. These works appeared during the 1990s, when Abu-Jamal filed his most important appeals and his fame was at its height, and their blend of law and religion is fully within the American tradition of discussion of race and citizenship. But to understand their significance and the place of Abu-Jamal's case in the history of Afro-American civic belonging, it is first necessary to return to the 1970s, to Abu-Jamal's youthful political experience in the Black Panthers and, later, with the "family" of a strange, cult-like group of utopian activists known as MOVE.

Every society, in every age, has its mainstream and its margin. The mainstream is home to the conventional and powerful, the conservators of a community. The margin is home to the unconventional and avant-garde, the creative, destabilizing forces that keep a society from stultifying. The subversions of this latter group may be subtle, easily incorporated into the mainstream, for its benefit, but there are also sometimes within the margin those men and women whom we might label radical visionaries—uncompromising extremists of various shades who set themselves squarely against the community, condemning mainstream values as fundamentally corrupt. A very few of these individuals have been geniuses, people who have made some of the great contributions to social and moral thought. William Blake in eighteenth-century England comes to mind, as does the historical Jesus. Most of these radicals, however, whatever their genuinely creative impulses, have been mere eccentrics or cranks. America's disunited society of the 1970s was strewn with them, false prophets of hope and redemption who gathered around them devoted, yearning followings of the lost. One born with the mystical name of Leaphart—Vincent Leaphart—would come to be judged by contemporaries, depending on their sympathies, as a carpenter-seer, a mystical folk thinker, a radical naturalist, or a dangerous sociopath.

In the bohemian hurly-burly of West Philadelphia of the late 1960s and the 1970s, Leaphart was known as "the dog man." The appellation was appropriate, most obviously because the handyman devoted himself to caring for strays around town, but also because the system of thought and style of life he would develop resembled, in some respects, that of the ancient Cynics—*cynic* being the Greek word for "doglike"—who believed that humans should look to the example of the lower animals, and become rugged, free, and indifferent to social custom and human law. The best known cynic, Diogenes of Sinope, gave away all his possessions, practiced various forms of strict physical discipline, and utterly rejected the temptations of mainstream society (it was said when Alexander the Great asked whether he might render the philosopher some service, Diogenes, who was resting on the ground, asked that the young king stand aside, because he was blocking the light from the sun). Though lacking formal education, Leaphart had his own strong, independent worldview, which he worked to clarify through conversations with the students and university-educated whites who lived in the ethnically mixed neighborhood of Powelton Village. He became especially close to a young white student of social work named Donald Glassey, who was drawn to Leaphart's distinctive ideas, at once heady and earthy, about God, justice, and nature, as well as to his readiness to put those ideas into practice. According to Glassey, the tall, dark black man, his hair knitted into dreadlocks, was, more than anyone he had met, "precisely in tune with his beliefs." Glassey encouraged him to collect his oral reflections and proverbs into a book, and with the social worker's help, Leaphart eventually produced *The Guidelines*.

Apparently lost to history, but said to have run anywhere from 300 to 1,000 typewritten pages, *The Guidelines* would come to serve as the bible of the community that coalesced around Leaphart in the 1970s.

Leaphart called the group the Christian Movement for Life (his ideas were inspired, in part, by an obscure Protestant sect known as the Kingdom of Yahweh—America, land of religious schism) and later simply MOVE. Not an acronym, MOVE is, rather, Leaphart's monosyllabic exhortation to emulate nature by leading an active life. For it was the worship of nature, or a distinctive idea of it, that formed the core of Leaphart's spirituality. In tribute to "Mother Nature" or "Mama," Leaphart would soon take a new name, John Life, which he would later change to John Africa in recognition of the fact that human life was said to have originated on the African continent. Other members of the MOVE "family," generally poor, untethered men and women who found solace in his words and vision, changed their surnames to Africa as well. Reaching about fifty strong—black and white, though mostly black—they lived under one roof on Osage Avenue in West Philadelphia, where they sought to act in accord with their guiding philosophical principle, the all-encompassing basis of *The Guidelines:* natural law.

In its philosophical structure, their notion of natural law was not so different from the one that constitutional thinkers such as Justice Clarence Thomas would espouse, particularly in the belief that written laws should be subordinate to or constrained by higher moral principles. But in their commitment to natural law, MOVE looked to far more extreme and all-encompassing elements of the Western religious and political tradition, calling on humans to live fully outside the artificial codes of civilization. They left their hair "the way nature intended," uncombed and uncut, and shunned many modern hygienic practices, including washing with soap (preferring an herbal mixture that included garlic). They buried their garbage in their backyard, and allowed all animals, including rats, to roam free on their property. They tried to eat only raw food, to overcome the unhealthy "addiction" to the cooked and processed nourishment of advanced civilization, which they called "distortion." They shunned tobacco, drugs, and alcohol, and they kept fit by running their dogs, washing cars, and engaging in arduous calisthenics, at times jogging for miles with backpacks full of phone books or bricks. Though it is likely that few complied, MOVE women were asked to lick their newborns clean and eat their umbilical cords. Like William Lloyd Garrison, the group flatly rejected electoral politics, but they saw protest as essential to the observance of their religious beliefs and utopian ideals (their first public demonstration was directed against the local zoo).

But the perfect, as Voltaire once remarked, is the enemy of the good. In their embrace of a rugged autonomy—the life of natural law—

MOVE members were called on to reject the human law around them and the community that law helped define. The same radical jurisprudence that galvanized family life within their Osage Avenue home, that is, encouraged contempt for the civic order beyond. "We believe in natural law, the government of self," announces the group's manifesto:

> Man-made laws are not really laws, because they don't apply equally to everyone and they contain exceptions and loopholes. Man-made laws are constantly being amended or appealed. Natural law stays the same and always has. Man's laws require police, sheriffs, armies, and courts to enforce them, and lawyers to explain them. True law is self-explanatory and self-enforcing. In the undisturbed jungles, oceans and deserts of the world, there are no courtrooms or jails. The animals and plants don't need them. No living being has to consult a law book to be able to know if they have to cough, sneeze, or urinate. Natural law says that when you see something getting too close to your eye, you will blink, whether you are a German shepherd or a Supreme Court Justice.[3]

Unsurprisingly, MOVE soon became a bane to its neighbors. Their radical naturalism was situated in the heart of one of the most dense of American urban centers (Leaphart rejected suggestions that they move to a farm). Troubles began when their largely black neighborhood started to complain about MOVE's sanitation practices—they may have been devoted to an ideal of natural purity and clean living, but their home was a breeding ground for vermin. Later, locals would be disturbed by the group's habit of haranguing passersby from their porch, blasting from megaphones their foul-mouthed diatribes against modern civilization.

MOVE also soon adopted the violent means typical of radicals at the time. The turn to militancy seems to have been partly the result of John Africa's own love of power. According to Glassey, who grew increasingly disenchanted with MOVE, Leaphart became intoxicated with his authority and came to view it as appropriate, indeed imperative, that at times his will be done through intimidation and force. No longer simply an amiable, eccentric patriarch, he had evolved into something a good deal more sinister—a cult leader. But the transformation of the group's spirit, it must be said, was itself an outgrowth of its commitment to natural law. As anyone who has spent time in the wilderness knows, nature can be merciless and cruel in its indifference to human will and its quickness to destroy those who defy it. Among the principles Leaphart transcribed from the book of nature into *The Guidelines* was the principle of self-defense. "All living things instinctively defend themselves," the manifesto announces. "This is a God-given right of all life. If a man goes into a bear's cave, he violates and threatens the bear's place of security. The bear will defend his home by instinctively fighting off the man and eliminating him. The bear is not wrong, because self-defense is right."[4] The group began to stockpile weapons. Donald Glassey would enter the Federal Witness Protection Program after helping federal authorities investigate the illegal cache.

John Africa and MOVE had reason to fear for their security. Philadelphia police were hardly well disposed toward a group that explicitly denounced law and agitated against the existence of the state. And ironically, Mayor Frank Rizzo's police department would itself become known as one of the most "lawless" in the country, engaging in a pattern of brutality and racial discrimination that, in time, would bring down upon it the hand of the federal Department of Justice. In 1985 MOVE effectively came to an end—shamefully, violently—when, after an extended siege of its headquarters on Osage Avenue, city authorities dropped an explosive device into the building in the hope of driving its members outside, into custody. The building caught fire, and the conflagration quickly spread, possibly because MOVE members had poured gasoline on the roof, trying to prevent just such a siege by creating a threat of mass annihilation. If true, the scheme worked all too well. The blaze killed seven people, the flames engulfing a city block and, ultimately, destroying the entire neighborhood. John Africa was killed in the chaos. His body was discovered in the ruins, mysteriously severed from its head. The incident was to the anarchist elements of the nation's radical left what the federal siege of the Branch Davidian compound in Waco, Texas, in 1993 would be to the radical right and to religious separatists across the political spectrum (Abu-Jamal has written favorably of the Branch Davidians and bitterly of the tragic result of the siege).[5] Abu-Jamal was not in the MOVE compound when it exploded that day in 1985. By then, he was already on death row. But had he not been convicted of killing Officer Daniel Faulkner, he might have perished, too.

He was born Wesley Cook to what he later described as "petit bourgeois" parents in 1954, less than a month after the Supreme Court's *Brown v. Board of Education* decision (making him a rough contemporary of Clarence Thomas, another deeply religious, highly intelligent black radical).[6] His father died when he was only ten, and he was raised lovingly by an extended family. From a young age he was passionately spiritual, returning home from Bible study to excitedly teach other children what he had learned. In time, he would contact local religious leaders of various faiths, exploring whether he should convert to Judaism, Catholicism, or Islam. Otherwise, it was a childhood that Abu-Jamal himself calls "unremarkable"—at least, until he came into contact with the Black Panther Party. He joined when he was just a teenager, before he had even graduated from high school. The decision was the result of an unanticipated, violent favor. One afternoon in 1968, Cook and four black friends attended a Philadelphia rally for the presidential candidate and implacable segregationist George Wallace. During the speech, they raised their fists in the air and chanted black power slogans. As the five were leaving the stadium, Cook was seized by some members of the crowd, thrown to the ground, and beaten. When he cried for help, a police officer approached and took the opportunity to kick him for good measure. "I have been thankful to that faceless cop ever since," Abu-Jamal wrote later, "for he kicked me straight into the Black Panther Party."[7]

Cook was a dedicated, ambitious recruit, and he rose quickly within the ranks of the Philadelphia BPP, which despite revolutionary rhetoric focused its attention more squarely on social activism and breakfast programs than on the armed militancy that distinguished the group's New York and Oakland chapters. He soon became the chapter's minister for communication, beginning a career as a radical journalist in a frigid, makeshift office, covering chapter activities for the national Panther newspaper. And radical he was. The Philadelphia Panthers may have been more social activists than violent revolutionaries, but they were still Panthers, and Cook espoused their militant rhetoric (he once even served as a bodyguard for Huey Newton). He has written admiringly that the group "established bona fide, shonuff diplomatic relations with progressive and revolutionary states and movements across the globe— the People's Republic of China, North Korea, Congo-Brazzaville, the African National Congress, the Palestinian Liberation Organization, Cuba, and the like."[8] After briefly attending Goddard College in Vermont, a school known for its tradition of alternative thinking, he began work as a radical radio journalist, using his deep, mellifluous voice to rail against injustice (at times upsetting his editors and program directors, who felt that the young reporter increasingly lacked professional objectivity).

This radical sensibility—his driving concern for the relation among society, justice, and law—fostered a natural sympathy with MOVE, whose members he first encountered when they were protesting a speech by the Reverend Jesse Jackson. By that time, Cook had married his first wife and, after the birth of a son, Jamal—a name that had become popular among black parents of the day—changed his own name, adopting a Swahili one, Mumia, given to him in a high school language class. He also changed Cook to Abu-Jamal, or "father of Jamal." For Mumia, it should be said, MOVE did not inspire love at first sight. They seemed bizarre and out of touch. More viscerally, he now "distrusted organizations" after the Panthers, "to whom I had loaned my life," descended into "an internecine, bicoastal, and bloody feud." But by temperament, Abu-Jamal was receptive to claims of truth from the margins—a vestige perhaps of the Christianity in which he was raised—and he soon became impressed by the passion and ethical commitment of MOVE members, and by their radical vision for a just society of true law. "Who cares about a bunch of dirty, unwashed niggas who don't comb their hair?" Abu-Jamal recalls Reverend Jackson's saying ("I did," was Abu-Jamal's reply). As an investigative journalist, he would cover MOVE sympathetically, and soon he began to identity with its beliefs, until he was virtually one of them. He grew his hair in long dreadlocks, in the MOVE style. People took notice. Among some officers of the Philadelphia police, he became known as "Mumia Africa." Once, he recalls, a police officer looking at him from a squad car pointed his finger as though it were a gun, pretended to shoot, and smiled.[9]

The early 1980s were difficult times for Abu-Jamal. He was in his late twenties, his marriage had begun to unravel, and so had his young journalistic career. Whether to supplement his income or simply to survive, he began to drive a taxicab on the night shift. And, fatefully, at about 4 a.m. on December 9, 1981, he was sitting in his cab in a parking lot in downtown Philadelphia, near Locust and Thirteenth streets. There, his free life ended.

What Abu-Jamal was doing parked in the lot is unclear. He may simply have been waiting for a fare from a nearby nightclub. Similarly, what happened next is the subject of great dispute. All accounts agree, however, that shortly before four, Abu-Jamal looked up to see his younger brother, William, across the parking lot, on Locust Street, standing beside his Volkswagen Beetle. He also saw that something was amiss. William Cook idolized his older brother, who had always been more successful and directed (when Wesley changed his name to Mumia, William asked to be called Wesley). What Abu-Jamal saw across the parking lot was his adoring younger brother in an altercation with the police. Moments before, William Cook had been stopped by Officer Faulkner, a proud, by-the-book cop in his mid-twenties. For reasons that are unclear, Officer Faulkner moved to arrest Cook, turning him around, arms behind his back. Cook then jerked, striking Officer Faulkner in the face, whereupon Faulkner tried to subdue him with a flashlight or blackjack. Abu-Jamal witnessed the drama unfold from his taxicab—in which he kept a gun for protection. He raced through the lot and across the street. A witness saw him running with his hand raised in the air.

A few seconds later, he was lying on the ground, barely conscious, with bullet wounds to his leg and chest—and Officer Faulkner was dead, shot in the back before a fatal bullet, fired at close range, entered his skull directly above the eye. Examiners first said the bullet in Faulkner's brain was from a .44-caliber pistol; later, they revised the identification, asserting that it came from a .38, the caliber of Abu-Jamal's gun, which was lying beside him. When police reinforcements arrived moments afterward, they found Mumia's brother leaning against a nearby wall. His first words were "I ain't got nothing to do with it."[10] Later, writing from prison, Abu-Jamal would describe what happened next. "On December 9, 1981, the police attempted to execute me in the street," he wrote, reconstructing the trauma in words that invoke love and pain, time and family, death and the passing of black generations. "Time seems slower, easier, less oppressive":

> I feel strangely light. I look down and see a man slumped on the curb, his head resting on his chest, his face downcast. "Damn! That's me!" A jolt of recognition ripples through me.
>
> A cop walks up to the man and kicks him in the face. I feel it, but don't feel it. Three cops join the dance, kicking, blackjacking the bloody, handcuffed fallen form. Two grab each arm, pull the man up, and ram him headfirst into a steel utility pole. He falls.
>
> "Daddy?"
>
> "Yes, Babygirl?"
>
> "Why are those men beating you like that?"

"It's okay, Babygirl, I'm okay."

"But why, Daddy? Why did they shoot you and why are they hitting and kicking you, Abu?"

"They've been wanting to do this for a long time, Babygirl, but don't worry, Daddy's fine—see? I don't even feel it!"

The chubby-cheeked child's face softly melts into the features of a broad-nosed, bald, gold-toothed, and frizzled old man, his dark brown skin leathery and nicely wrinkled.

"Boy, you all right?"

"Yeah, Dad, I'm okay."

"I love you, boy."

"And I love you, Daddy."

The "I love you" echoes like feedback, booming like a thousand voices, and faces join the calming cacophony: wife, mother, children, old faces from down south, older faces from—Africa? Faces, loving, warm, and dark, rushing, racing, roaring past. Consciousness returns to find me cuffed, my breath sweet with the heavy metallic taste of blood, in darkness.

I lie on the paddy wagon floor and am informed by the anonymous crackle on the radio that I am en route to the police administration building a few blocks away.

I feel no pain—just the omnipresent pressure that makes every bloody breath a labor.

I recall my father's old face with wonder at its clarity, considering his death twenty years before.

I am en route to the Police Administration Building, presumably on the way to die.[11]

It was, said District Attorney Joseph McGill, "the strongest homicide case I ever tried."[12] But it in fact became one of the most contentious. It was no ordinary murder case, nor even a typical killing of a police officer. For in his defense, Abu-Jamal wished to do more than avoid imprisonment or save his life. Consistent with MOVE principles, he also wished to turn the trial into a political drama, specifically to transform it into a debate about the fundamental nature of law and the rules to which he should be subject. He was motivated, it is important to emphasize, not so much to discredit the considerable evidence of his having committed the murder (he has yet to offer his own account of what took place). Instead, Abu-Jamal saw his trial as a jurisprudential battle, a clash between the law of revolutionaries, with their transcendent concern for social rather than individual justice, and the state's demand for "law and order," and he used his case to dramatize the difference. Both John Africa and a number of other MOVE members who had gone on trial in Philadelphia in recent years had attempted to do the same (nine were convicted of killing a police officer in 1978).

Abu-Jamal could not have had a judge less tolerant of his aims: Albert Sabo, former undersheriff and past member of the Fraternal Order of Police. Small, acerbic, and seemingly without empathy for defendants, he was known to some as the "King of Death Row," sending over a dozen men there during his tenure. Sabo's overriding judicial concern was for expeditiousness, to keep trials moving along, a defendant's personal doubts about receiving due process notwithstanding. From the choosing of jurors through his sentencing, Abu-Jamal would wrangle with Judge Sabo in a tone that could not have endeared himself to either judge or jury. "I need a microphone at the table," he demanded in a typical exchange. "I don't have one," responded the judge. "You get one," ordered the accused. Abu-Jamal's stated intent was not to be unreasonably antagonistic, nor was his hostility caused by simple hot-headedness. Instead, it was a calculated performance of disobedience on the part of a committed revolutionary legal radical.[13]

Chief among Abu-Jamal's objections to the trial he would be forced to undergo involved the representation he received from Anthony Jackson, his court-appointed counsel. Jackson, who was black, was not inexperienced. He had worked previously in the District Attorney's Office and had completed a stint with the Philadelphia public defender. Now, he was setting up his own practice. Coming to the case during a transition in his career, before he had even established a physical location for his new office, Jackson had little time to prepare for trial. But Abu-Jamal was not concerned with Jackson's résumé, his race, or even his lack of preparation. His objection was to the fact that Jackson was a lawyer at all. Abu-Jamal wished to be represented by John Africa and, if not by him directly, then to have Vincent Leaphart at the defense table as an "advisor" during trial. According to Abu-Jamal, Jackson was a "legal-trained lawyer," educated in the laws and procedures of the "system," and thus beholden to its aims; he wanted counsel versed in a higher law.[14]

The law of Pennsylvania permits only members of the bar to act as counsel to criminal defendants. The rule is a wise and reasonable one: criminal law, the law of evidence, and courtroom procedure are all technical, complex matters. State governments have a compelling interest in ensuring that defendants not undermine their own defense by choosing unqualified representation. Apart from straining the efficiency of justice (with irrelevant objections, blundering points, and so on) such counsel threaten to undermine the interests of the state (by creating grounds for mistrial) and the accused (by providing incomplete defense). The monopoly of lawyers in representing defendants before courts, that is, is in the public interest. And while no law of Pennsylvania expressly prohibited Judge Sabo from allowing John Africa to sit with Abu-Jamal while he conducted his own defense, the judge made a reasonable choice in barring Leaphart from a potentially active role in the proceedings. It would have been rather unusual for a judge to have ruled otherwise, particularly given John Africa's record of disruptive courtroom behavior. Sabo was willing to have John Africa sit in the gallery and meet with Abu-Jamal during breaks or in jail while the court was not in session. But Abu-Jamal viewed the denial of his request as a negation of the fundamental legal principles by which he lived.

The jury witnessed the dispute in its full heat. "Mr. Jamal," exclaimed an exasperated Judge Sabo, "it is quite evident to this court that you are intentionally disrupting the orderly procedure of this court. I have warned you time and time again that if you continue with that attitude that I would have to remove you as counsel in this case." The response was forthright and crystal clear: "Judge, your warnings to me are absolutely meaningless . . . I need counsel of my choice, someone I have faith in, someone I have respect for; not someone paid by the same pocket that pays the D.A., not a court-appointed lawyer, not a member of the ABA, not an officer of this court. . . ." "Your Honor," inserted McGill, "so the record could be clear I believe Mr. Jamal is speaking about a Mr. John Africa . . . who is not a member of the Bar of the Commonwealth of Pennsylvania"—"not a bar of any court," asserted the judge—"As a result of this, Your Honor is not only obligated under the law to prevent a non-attorney to represent the defendant even though the defendant wants that . . . [to] protect the defendant against himself. So it is clear that Your Honor, in accordance with the law of this Commonwealth, is acting appropriately. That I believe would be a response to what Mr. Jamal is attempting to do." "That may be a response," Jamal asserted, "but it is not true. This man"—turning to Jackson—"has gone to law school, right, but he cannot guarantee me my freedom. . . . John Africa can do that." "No, nobody can," McGill asserted. Judge Sabo warned that if Abu-Jamal continued, he would be forced to remove him from the court and have Jackson continue to defend him in his absence.[15]

Reading the transcript of the trial that took place from June 17 to July 3, 1982, it would be difficult to see how the jury could not have found Abu-Jamal guilty, no matter what one's position on the merits of his case or issues of contemporary racial inequality. The prosecution presented a rich factual record, including the testimony of two witnesses to the crime and others who saw its immediate aftermath. The witnesses themselves were hardly pillars of society—they ranged from a night-shift cab driver to a prostitute—predictable denizens of the rough downtown of Philadelphia at four o'clock in the morning. But in one way or another, they confirmed Abu-Jamal as the killer. Neither did Abu-Jamal himself, nor for that matter his admiring brother William, offer an explanation as to how he came to be found shot, slumped next to a dead police officer. "I was standing on the corner and I noticed the lights on top of the police car . . . ," explained Cynthia White, a local prostitute.

> The policeman got out of the car and walked—started walking over towards the Volkswagen. The driver of the Volkswagen got out of the car. A few words passed. They both walked between the police car and the Volkswagen up to the sidewalk. A few more words passed again between them. The driver of the Volkswagen then struck the police officer with a closed fist to his cheek, and the police turned the driver of the Volkswagen around in a position to handcuff him. . . . I looked across the street in the parking lot and I noticed [Abu-Jamal] was running out of the parking lot and he was practically on the curb when he shot two times at the police officer. It was the back. The police officer turned around and staggered and seemed like he was grabbing for something. Then he fell. Then [Abu-Jamal] came over and he came on top of the police officer and shot some more times. After that he went over and he slouched down and he sat on the curb.[16]

A hospital security guard testified that after Abu-Jamal was brought in for treatment, as he lay bleeding, he shouted, "I shot the mother-fucker and I hope he dies!" Much of that evidence would be contested in various ways by the defense, on appeal and before the bar of public opinion, but at this point in the state's case, the facts seemed clear indeed. The jury began deliberating shortly before noon on Friday, July 2; by half past two, they sent a note to Judge Sabo, asking for more explanation as to the difference between murder and manslaughter; at about a quarter after five o'clock, they found Abu-Jamal guilty of murder in the first degree. The next day, they met to determine his sentence.

The prosecution had asked for death. Abu-Jamal, asserted McGill, had killed a police officer, which the law of Pennsylvania counted as an "aggravating" factor that could properly influence a jury's sentencing decision. Police officers, after all, were symbols of the law itself, the guardians of community life. Earlier in the trial, McGill had made clear to the jury—in a legally questionable move—that Abu-Jamal was a former Black Panther. "The fact of the matter is simply this," explained McGill. "It's all called law and order. That is why that is so important, that aggravating circumstance. Law and order. And, ladies and gentlemen, this is what this trial is all about more than any other trial I have ever seen." McGill's paramount interest, like Abu-Jamal's, was ultimately jurisprudential. "[A]re we going to live in a society with law and order," he asked rhetorically, "and are we going to enforce the laws consistent with the intention of law and order, or are we going to decide our own rules and then act accordingly? That's really what we are talking about." And, significantly, that vision of law and order, violated by the dreadlocked Abu-Jamal, had a symbolic marker of its own. "Daniel Faulkner on December the 9th, 1981, in very plain view was wearing his officer's uniform," McGill continued, and Daniel Faulkner, "ladies and gentlemen, actually wore his hat, you may not think—he wore his hat when he got out of his car. This hat"—McGill gestured with his hand—"right here." When Jamal shot Officer Faulkner, McGill explained, "[f]rom head to toe that man was a police officer," and "once we have the opportunity presented that anybody can kill a cop and it doesn't matter, you may as well forget about law and order—just throw it right out."[17]

But Abu-Jamal believed himself to be living under a decidedly different legal order, as he made sure to tell the jury members, in a statement made shortly before they were to decide his sentence. "Today's decision comes as no surprise," Abu-Jamal exclaimed. "[I]n fact, many will remember that I said this would happen last week when John Africa predicted and prophesied this jury decision."

> I want everyone to know it came after a legal trained lawyer was imposed upon me against my will. A legal trained lawyer whose interests were clearly not my own. . . . To quote John Africa, "When a lawyer chooses to follow the conditions of the court, he compromises his obligation to his client." . . . Who does he truly represent or work for? To again quote John Africa, "When you judges hang a person, put a person in an electric chair, gas a person, shoot a person to death for a crime you all didn't see that person commit, you ain't solving the problem of crime or the so-called criminal or the victim. You've caused a burden for the mother that is now without a son, the wife that is now without a husband, the daughter that is now without a father and society for putting faith in this goddamning procedure, for it is the system that is guilty of the crimes of all that is criminal, all crimes are committed within the system not without, because the influence of that ignorant black boy you judges gassed to death, poor white boy you judges shot to death, unaware Puerto Rican boy, girl, adult you judges electrocuted to death came straight from you judges, your bosses, their crimes. In short, this system." A quotation by John Africa. . . . I am innocent despite what you twelve people think and the truth shall set me free. . . . This decision today proves neither my guilt nor my innocence. It proves merely that the system is finished. Babylon is falling! Long live MOVE! Long live John Africa!

After deliberating for a little over three hours, the twelve jurors sentenced Mumia Abu-Jamal to die.[18]

The physical separation of criminals from the communities in which they once lived is, whatever the material conditions of imprisonment, a relegation to a world of spiritual degradation; and by imposing on them a variety of social and political disabilities, criminal imprisonment exiles men and women from civic life. It lowers their status in the eyes of the law, and makes them but semicitizens, both formally and in cultural terms. The execution of a prisoner, in addition to being an act of brutality regulated and legitimized by the state, is the extreme and irreducible instance of this symbolic process. In the years since he was condemned to die, Mumia Abu-Jamal has become an icon for civic death because of his proximity to death itself.

The number of people living under a death sentence in the United States has, with minor variations from year to year, been steeply increasing for the past half-century. In 1955, there were 125 people on death row; by 1960, that number had almost doubled, to 212; by 1970, it had nearly tripled, to 631. Beginning in the 1980s, the numbers rose even more rapidly. In 1980, there were 692 men and women condemned to die; in 1985, there were 1,575; by 1990, there were 2,346; and by the year 2000, there were 3,601.[19] The majority of death row inmates is not black, but the representation of Afro-Americans is shockingly disproportionate to their presence in the general population. In 2000, there were about 35.5 million blacks and about 211 million whites in the United States. On death row, there were 1,541 blacks and 1,989 whites. Statistics for the general prison population tell a similar story. In 1990, for every 100,000 white residents, 106 were in jail; for every 100,000 black residents, there were 569. By 1998, for every 100,000 whites, 145 were incarcerated; for every 100,000 blacks, 733. By 2003, over 1.9 million black men were either currently in prison or had been at some point in their lives—16.6 percent of the total Afro-American male population. Mumia Abu-Jamal's fame as a death row inmate grew within this particular legal and cultural context.

It is often erroneously claimed by liberals that this imbalance results from the social agenda of political conservatives. In fact, it is the unfortunate product of a confluence of conservative and liberal reform impulses—including, ironically, a desire to reduce racial discrimination in the criminal justice system. Among the innovations that grew from liberal initiatives, the most important concerned the process of criminal sentencing. Specifically, beginning in the 1970s, policy-makers at the state and federal levels sought to devise ways to ensure that offenders who had committed the same crime and had similar criminal histories would be given the same basic punishment, regardless of their race. Judges and juries would no longer be granted wide freedom to impose whatever penalty they believed most appropriate to the crime, tailoring their sentences to the individual offenders' circumstances—a freedom believed to have opened the door to discrimination. Instead, they would be required to determine punishment on the basis of a formula, calculating penalties based on a set of predetermined relevant features of a crime. The type of crime (a robbery, murder, kidnapping), whether it was committed with a weapon and what type, whether the weapon was hidden or concealed, whether a person was injured and with what degree of severity, whether the crime was committed to fund further criminal activity, whether it was committed alone or in concert with others, whether it was the perpetrator's first or fifteenth offense—all were to be taken into account within a rigid, race-neutral guideline structure.

Had it been the only revolution in American criminal justice at the time, it is unlikely that the sentencing guideline movement would on its own have produced the great racial disparity in American prisons. But it took place in conjunction with two other new trends in crime control. The first was the rising call to "get tough on crime," used to great effect in state and national electoral politics by liberals and conservatives alike. Its supporters advocated increasingly lengthy mandatory prison terms within a retributive regime of criminal punishment, intended no longer to "reform" or "correct," but rather to incapacitate, removing perpetrators for extended periods of time from the general population. The second, related transformation was the social and political initiative known as the War on Drugs. While the civic good of preventing the use of addictive drugs in the United States is clear (like the gin taken by the English poor in the nineteenth century, heroin, cocaine, and other illicit drugs have visited disproportionate devastation on poor and minority communities), as the criminal justice scholar Michael Tonry has argued, another consequence of the War on Drugs of the 1980s and 1990s was also plain. All but the most oblivious political leaders knew that blacks would bear an exceptional burden as targets in that war, and that the conflict in American cities would result in vast numbers of black men convicted of serious crimes. Taken together, these two trends would dramatically swell the number of Afro-Americans languishing in prison.[20]

It is an irony, though not an accident, that during these years when the United States was putting "an entire generation of black men in jail," racial discrimination in sentencing dramatically declined; it is now either negligible or so indirect as to be nearly impossible to isolate by the most sophisticated statistical methods. A substantial study of sentencing in Pennsylvania during the mid-1980s (about the time Abu-Jamal went on trial), for instance, found among convicted felons of different racial groups almost perfect parity in sentencing rates and term lengths. Similarly, the most important recent studies of the death penalty indicate that when racial discrimination in sentencing exists, it does not relate to the race of the perpetrator, but rather is influenced by the race of the victim: an offender of whatever race is more likely to receive the death penalty when his victim is white—a statistic indicating, in turn, that murder of and by Afro-Americans is, in fact, less vigorously prosecuted, as most murderers and victims are of the same race. We thus live in a society with little racial discrimination in criminal sentencing, yet which nevertheless holds Afro-Americans prisoner in numbers that far outstrip their presence in the general population. Our liberal ideals and policies, so far from a world of caste, exist side by side with and may even contribute to vastly disproportionate rates of black incarceration. This is one of the fundamental conundrums of black civic belonging in our era.

Whatever social factors predispose black males to criminality and conviction—including, prominently, the perverse social and economic effects of the War on Drugs—in the meanwhile, this mass incarceration affects more than those living behind bars: it affects the civic life of black Americans as a whole. Most immediately, imprisonment visits often-unbearable harm on the families of imprisoned men. It not only subtracts one breadwinner from the family unit, but also saddles (usually poor) families with less obvious financial burdens, including the cost of traveling to and from a correctional facility for visits. This is to say nothing of the social stigma, which is by no means confined to the family members of the incarcerated. From the world of multigenerational poverty to the black middle class, the entire black population continues to suffer from a cultural association with lawlessness and criminality in the eyes of mainstream America, at precisely the time when its formal social and economic opportunity is greater than it has ever been in U.S. history. It is a disastrous civic development that when many Americans encounter a black man on the street, they may fear he has spent time in prison, or is more likely to be a criminal than a college graduate—a fear that, statistically, is entirely supportable.

After his conviction and imprisonment, Abu-Jamal was transferred to SCI Greene—a place he describes as the "valley of the shadow of death," where "humans are transformed into nonpersons, numbered beings cribbed into boxes of unlife, where the very soul is under destructive onslaught." Since that time, he has mounted a series of legal appeals, with a succession of attorneys, including the death penalty specialist Daniel Williams, and Leonard Weinglass, a radical attorney in the tradition of Charles Garry and William Kunstler. As a matter of law, Abu-Jamal's appeals have rested, especially, on his claim that Judge Sabo was biased against him during his trial and in the course of his various requests for postconviction relief. For the most part, these claims have come to nothing. In 1998, the Pennsylvania Supreme Court flatly rejected all the new evidence Abu-Jamal's attorneys attempted to submit, as well as their efforts to call into question the state's testimony in Abu-Jamal's original trial. And as for Judge Sabo, the court found that "for the most part, [he] displayed much patience with appellant's diatribes" and that, "simply stated, [the] appellant's own disruptive behavior cannot be used to demonstrate that the judge bore hostility towards him."[21] (Notably, Abu-Jamal later fired Williams and Weinglass after Williams published *Executing Justice*, a book suggesting Abu-Jamal is guilty; the two had also refused to present the claim, made by Abu-Jamal's current lawyers, that Officer Faulkner was killed by a professional hit man because he tried to stop payoffs made to local police in exchange for turning a blind eye to prostitution, gambling, and drugs in Philadelphia's Center City. Williams and Weinglass believed that the signed confession by the hit man stretched beyond credibility.) In 2001, a federal district judge confirmed Abu-Jamal's conviction while overturning his death sentence on narrow, technical grounds, and called on Pennsylvania to grant him a new sentencing proceeding or sentence him directly to life in prison. The decision is in the process of appeal.[22]

Abu-Jamal and his supporters have been more successful in their appeals to the court of national and world public opinion. The symbol of a variety of liberal and radical causes, he has advocated not simply for his own release, but also against the death penalty, current standards of criminal punishment, and various manifestations of racial inequality. Indeed, throughout the 1990s, when Abu-Jamal made his most tactically important and potentially fruitful postconviction legal appeals, his case became a focal point in a broader effort by widely disparate groups to reenergize leftist political activism—tying their organizational life to the continuing possibility of his death. And his cause is championed not by radicals alone. Amnesty International has written a report questioning the legality of his trial under standards of international human rights. A wide assortment of liberal writers, artists, intellectuals, and celebrities have agitated on his behalf or written favorably about him and questioned the legitimacy of his imprisonment. His supporters include not only Noam Chomsky but also William Styron; not only bell hooks but also Ed Asner, Joyce Carol Oates, Bishop Desmond Tutu, Grace Paley, Harry Belafonte, Barbara Kingsolver, and scholars such as Cornel West. Protests have been staged on his behalf throughout the world. He even has been made an honorary citizen of Paris (the previous man to receive the honor was Pablo Picasso).

Perhaps the greatest inspiration for the attention and sympathy he has received has been Abu-Jamal's moving writings about his own life on death row, the ultimate civic exile. His essays suggest a mind deepened under the strain of imprisonment, one that has developed an increasingly complex vision of the relation among death, law, and race in the United States. Those writings also expose the psychological and spiritual degradation to which all prisoners are subject. In SCI Greene, for instance, prisoners—no matter, it should be said, what their race—are separated from their visitors by a Plexiglas wall and, most dehumanizing, barred from physical contact with their own family members. "The ultimate effect of noncontact visits is to weaken, and finally to sever, family ties," Abu-Jamal has written.

> Through this policy and practice the state skillfully and intentionally denies those it condemns a fundamental element and expression of humanity—that of touch and physical contact—and thereby slowly erodes family ties already made tenuous by the distance between home and prison. Thus prisoners are as isolated psychologically as they are temporally and spatially. By state action, they become "dead" to those who know and love them, and therefore dead to themselves. For who are people, but for their relations and relationships. . . . To such men and women, the actual execution is a *fait accompli*, a formality already accomplished in spirit, where the state concludes its premeditated drama by putting the "dead" to death a second time.

Whatever the justice of putting these men in prison, the number of them who are black places a burden on the black community that most blacks, especially men, feel at some point in their lives.[23]

In this respect, it is not surprising that Abu-Jamal the writer also remains, in the end, a man whose social and political concerns are entwined with a spiritual vision, and whose prison writings have turned increasingly to the religious questions at the center of his youth (though, significantly, his supporters seem largely to disregard the religious aspects of his writing). His most recent work, *Faith of Our Fathers*, is "an examination of the spiritual life of African and African-American people." For all his radicalism, Abu-Jamal's case issues directly from the mainstream of our civic experience, in its dimensions of both tragedy and aspiration. In his cell, he sits between two worlds, that of the living and that of the dead, straddling the divide that characterizes black American civic life at this decidedly liberal moment in American history.

Coda

▲

Since the birth of a slaveholding society in North America in the late seventeenth century, blacks have resisted their legal and civic exile and sought a greater measure of inclusion in American civic life. They have worked, individually and collectively, to advance claims of citizenship. The history of black trials has registered the vicissitudes of this effort because, as rituals of civic belonging, they have provided central occasions in which it has taken place. This history, it bears emphasis, has been important for all minority groups, racial or otherwise. The black struggle for citizenship has not merely served as a model, a paradigm case, for others seeking greater civic inclusion: it has established the legal and cultural terms of that search itself. The black experience forged our contemporary understanding of the Fourteenth Amendment and its guarantees, the meaning of equal protection, and it set the pattern for minority claims of civic capacity and recognition in cultural life, how a group becomes a people of law. In this, the history of black citizenship reflects the core of American civic identity—it is a mirror of what our nation has been and may become.

Today, black America stands at a critical, transitional moment in its civic history—and America, therefore, stands at a critical moment, too. The source of this difficult position, when we have begun to see the real possibility of achieving full Afro-American citizenship, lies in part in the fracture of black social and economic life, its division into two nations, one visibly successful or with a foothold in the American mainstream, the other caught in a cycle of poverty and violence and, in consequence, almost as much outsiders to our society as were antebellum southern slaves, the latter stigmatizing the former and impeding their civic assimilation. But the source of black America's peculiar status lies, as importantly, in the character of our civic and political rhetoric—it is a problem of language and ideas.

The Civil Rights Movement ferried the United States to a new political shore, where our memory and past experience no longer guide us adequately forward, and which we have yet to fully comprehend. It is a curious place. Ours is a new world whose essential civic fact, seen from a historical perspective, is the consensus which exists that the liberal tradition, in its universalism, constitutes the aspiration of our national identity; only the most extreme and marginal members of our society hold to the principles of white Anglo-Saxon supremacy that most Americans held for centuries. Debate, often heated, exists within the liberal tradition, particularly regarding the legitimacy of using race-conscious remedies to redress racial inequality, but in the long light of history it is agreement rather than dissension that stands out most powerfully. At the same time, our public discourse exhibits the remarkable persistence of language traditionally used to attack principles of racial caste in the wake of the robust presence of caste ideology in American life; and, despite the substantial influence of Christian conservatives in electoral politics and political debate, especially around issues of abortion and public morality, Christianity no longer speaks with particular force or uniqueness to matters of race and civic life, certainly paling in comparison with its role throughout the nineteenth and early twentieth centuries.

In this last respect, ironically, the culture of liberal civic inclusion— and the effort to achieve full black citizenship—faces one of its greatest challenges. For, as political philosophers have frequently noted, in itself, the liberal commitment to a civic identity free from racial or ethnic associations provides a thin basis for individual loyalty and enthusiasm. Liberalism instead has been most powerful and compelling when it has been a revolutionary, critical force, or when it has been yoked to other, transcendent positive ideals. Bereft of its traditional enemies and untethered from the emotional force of religion, the liberal vision of racial civic inclusion threatens to lose the will it needs to overcome the forces of civic exile that remain.

The principal way in which we might recover that force is to clarify our ideals and become ever more conscious of how we put them into practice, and the best way to clarify our ideals is to touch our past, specifically the black American legal past. As Latinos strive to overcome the civic stigma they accrue from the widespread presence of "illegal aliens" within our borders; gays end their status as what Justice Sandra Day O'Connor once described as "strangers to the law"; Arab-Americans contemplate their civic position in the face of the suspicions engendered by September 11, 2001, and the war on terrorism; prisoners seek to overcome their social death and civic banishment; Americans with disabilities achieve a civil rights bill with their own name; and as a host of other minority groups make their own, distinctive civic claims heard, it is well to recall and learn from the history of a people whose ancestors arrived in our country long before those of most Americans, but who, until very recently, were a people apart. Their history can help us craft a new civic language in which we might navigate our way forward, and thereby strengthen the cultural foundations of the liberal rule of law for an inclusive society. It has been a goal of this book to contribute to that common effort.

Notes

PREFACE

1. See, for example, Michael Walzer, *What It Means to Be an American: Essays on the American Experience* (New York: Marsilio, 1996).
2. E. P. Thompson, "The Crime of Anonymity," in P. Linebaugh et al., *Albion's Fatal Tree: Crime and Society in Eighteenth-Century England* (New York: Pantheon, 1975), 255–344.

INTRODUCTION: RITUALS OF CITIZENSHIP

1. Some prominent examples include Kenneth L. Karst, *Belonging to America: Equal Citizenship and the Constitution* (New Haven: Yale University Press, 1989); James H. Kettner, *The Development of American Citizenship, 1608–1780* (Chapel Hill: University of North Carolina Press, 1980); Will Kymlicka, *Multicultural Citizenship: A Liberal Theory of Minority Rights* (Oxford: Clarendon Press, 1995); David A. Hollinger, *Postethnic America: Beyond Multiculturalism* (New York: Basic Books, 1995); Martha Minow, *Making All the Difference: Inclusion, Exclusion, and American Law* (Ithaca: Cornell University Press, 1990); Judith N. Shklar, *American Citizenship: The Question for Inclusion* (Cambridge: Harvard University Press, 1991); and Rogers M. Smith, *Civic Ideals: Conflicting Visions of Citizenship in U.S. History* (New Haven: Yale University Press, 1997).
2. For an example, which also indicates the convergence of public and scholarly debate, see Charles Taylor et al., *Multiculturalism: Examining the Politics of Recognition*, ed. and with an intro. by Amy Gutmann (Princeton: Princeton University Press, 1992), especially 12–13.
3. For an early discussion, see T. H. Marshall, *Citizenship and Social Class and Other Essays* (Cambridge: Cambridge University Press, 1950).
4. See Kymlicka, *Multicultural Citizenship*. For a variety of ways the law affects the possibilities of community solidarity in a pluralistic society, see Jill Norgren and Serena Nanda, *American Cultural Pluralism and the Law*, 2nd ed. (Westport, Conn.: Greenwood Press, 1996).
5. For a recent account, see Howard W. French, "Insular Japan Needs, but Resists, Immigration," *New York Times*, July 24, 2003.
6. William E. B. Du Bois, *The Souls of Black Folk*, in *Three Negro Classics*, with an intro. by John Hope Franklin (New York: Avon Books, 1965), 215.

7. Smith, *Civic Ideals*. See also Rogers M. Smith, *Stories of Peoplehood: The Politics and Morals of Political Membership* (New York: Cambridge University Press, 2003).

8. The "assimilationist era" of U.S. Indian policy can be divided into two periods, an initial "idealistic" phase, in which reformers attempted to assimilate native peoples into Euro-American life and values, and a second period, in which whites became more skeptical about the possibilities of assimilation and reflected that skepticism in their political advocacy. See Frederick E. Hoxie, *A Final Promise: The Campaign to Assimilate the Indians, 1880–1920* (Lincoln: University of Nebraska Press, 1984). On the tragic history of federal Indian policy, see also Francis Paul Prucha, *The Great Father: The United States Government and the American Indians*, vol. 2 (Lincoln: University of Nebraska Press, 1984), 609–758.

9. Academic scholars disagree on how precisely to define the concept of caste. The disagreements include the degree to which one of the three grounding principles of caste societies—structural hierarchy, psychological repulsion, and hereditary labor specialization—predominates. On caste, see Celestin Bougle, *Essays on the Caste System* (Cambridge: Cambridge University Press, 1971 [1927]); Louis Dumont, *Homo Hierarchicus: An Essay on the Caste System*, trans. Mark Sainsbury (Chicago: University of Chicago Press, 1970); Edmund Leach, *Aspects of Caste in South India, Ceylon, and North-west Pakistan* (Cambridge: Cambridge University Press, 1960); and Gerald Berreman, "Caste as a Structural Principle," in Anthony deReuck and Julie Knight, eds., *Caste and Race* (London: Churchill, 1968). For a brief introduction, see Charles Lindholm, "Caste, Caste Societies," in Thomas Barfield, ed., *The Dictionary of Anthropology* (Oxford, Engl.: Blackwell Publishers, 1997), 50–51.

10. Yalkut 951, par. "Vayomer," 1.

11. Jon-Christian Suggs, *Whispered Consolations: Law and Narrative in African American Life* (Ann Arbor: University of Michigan Press, 2000).

12. The anthropological literature on ritual is vast. For its foundation, see Émile Durkheim, *The Elementary Forms of Religious Life*, trans. Karen E. Fields (New York: Free Press, 1995 [1912]). See also J. S. La Fontaine, ed., *The Interpretation of Ritual: Essays in Honour of A. I. Richards* (London: Tavistock Publications, 1972). For a brief introduction, see Andrew S. Buckser, "Ritual," in Barfield, ed. *Dictionary of Anthropology*, 410–12.

13. Robert Westbrook, "Fighting for the American Family: Private Interests and Political Obligations in World War II," in Richard Wightman Fox and T. J. Jackson Lears, eds., *The Power of Culture: Critical Essays in American History* (Chicago: University of Chicago Press, 1993), 194–221.

14. A related legal academic literature on "popular constitutionalism" is just beginning to emerge. See, for instance, the work of James Pope on popular constitutionalism and the labor movement, "The Thirteenth Amendment versus the Commerce Clause: Labor and the Shaping of American Constitutional Law, 1921–1957," *Columbia Law Review* 102 (2002): 1–122; "Labor's Constitution of Freedom," *Yale Law Journal* 106 (1997): 941–1031; and Larry Kramer, *The People Themselves: Popular Constitutionalism and Judicial Review* (Oxford: Oxford University Press, 2004). For a study that has influenced my analysis by drawing parallels

between jurisprudence and individual biography, see Philip Bobbitt, *Constitutional Fate: Theory of the Constitution* (New York: Oxford University Press, 1982).

15. For a classic, albeit critical, account, see Louis Hartz, *The Liberal Tradition in America* (New York: Harcourt Brace, 1955). For a discussion of Hartz and the liberal tradition, see Smith, *Civic Ideals*, passim. On liberalism, see also John Zvesper, "Liberalism," in David Miller, ed., *The Blackwell Encyclopedia of Political Thought* (Cambridge, Mass. and Oxford: Blackwell, 1991), 285–89, and sources recommended there.

16. For an introduction to racial theories, see Thomas F. Gossett, *Race: The History of an Idea in America* (New York: Oxford University Press, 1997 [1963]). For two classic discussions of caste in the American South in the twentieth century, see John Dollard, *Caste and Class in a Southern Town* (New Haven: Yale University Press, 1938); and Gunnar Myrdal, *An American Dilemma: The Negro Problem and American Democracy* (New York: Harper & Row, 1962 [1944]). On white perceptions of Afro-Americans, see also George M. Fredrickson, *The Black Image in the White Mind: The Debate on Afro-American Character and Destiny, 1817–1914* (New York: Harper & Row, 1971); and Winthrop Jordan, *White Over Black: American Attitudes Toward the Negro, 1550–1812* (New York: Norton, 1977).

17. For a systematic statement of the proslavery Christian position, see Thornton Stringfellow, "A Brief Examination of Scripture Testimony on the Institution of Slavery," in Drew Gilpin Faust, ed., *The Ideology of Slavery: Pro-Slavery Thought in the Antebellum South, 1830–1860* (Baton Rouge: Louisiana State University Press, 1981): 136–67.

18. On the transformation of American Christianity in the nineteenth century on which modern Christian social reform rests, see Nathan O. Hatch, *The Democratization of American Christianity* (New Haven: Yale University Press, 1989). See also Jon Butler, *Awash in a Sea of Faith: Christianizing the American People* (Cambridge: Harvard University Press, 1990). For a discussion of individual denominations, see Timothy L. Smith, *Revivalism and Social Reform in Mid-Nineteenth-Century America* (New York: Abingdon Press, 1957).

19. Clifford Geertz, *The Interpretation of Cultures* (New York: Basic Books, 1973), 5.

PART ONE: COLONIAL VISIONS, 1619–1773

The Birth of Black Trials

1. For an indispensable recent discussion, see Ira Berlin, *Many Thousands Gone: The First Two Centuries of Slavery in North America* (Cambridge: Belknap Press of Harvard University Press, 1998). On American slavery, see also Peter Kolchin, *American Slavery 1619–1877* (New York: Hill & Wang, 1993), which contains a valuable bibliographic essay. Demographic statistics throughout this volume, unless otherwise noted, can be found in Charles M. Christian, *Black Saga: The African American Experience* (Boston: Houghton Mifflin, 1995); and Randall M. Miller and John David Smith, eds., *Dictionary of Afro-American Slavery* (Westport, Conn.: Praeger, 1997).

2. Berlin, *Many Thousands Gone*, 369–71.
3. On these "first impressions," see Winthrop D. Jordan, *White Over Black: American Attitudes Toward the Negro, 1550–1812* (New York: Norton, 1977), 3–43.
4. Like the case of Anthony Johnson or "Antonio a Negro" that follows, the example is much discussed. See, for example, Edmund S. Morgan, *American Slavery, American Freedom: The Ordeal of Virginia* (New York: Norton, 1975), 333.
5. Berlin, *Many Thousands Gone*, 43.
6. See J. Douglas Deal, *Race and Class in Colonial Virginia: Indians, Englishmen, and Africans on the Eastern Shore of Virginia During the Seventeenth Century* (New York: Garland, 1993), 217–50; and T. H. Breen and Stephen Innes, *"Myne Owne Ground": Race and Freedom on Virginia's Eastern Shore, 1640–1676* (New York: Oxford University Press, 1980). On slave culture in the eighteenth century, see also Philip D. Morgan, *Slave Counterpoint: Black Culture in the Eighteenth-Century Chesapeake and Lowcountry* (Chapel Hill: Published for the Omohundro Institute of Early American History and Culture by the University of North Carolina Press, 1998).
7. See Orlando Patterson, *Slavery and Social Death: A Comparative Study* (Cambridge: Harvard University Press, 1982).
8. M. I. Finley, ed., *Slavery in Classical Antiquity: Views and Controversies* (Cambridge, Engl.: W. Heffer & Sons, 1960).
9. For a discussion of this transformation, see Berlin, *Many Thousands Gone*, 93–194. See also Richard S. Dunn, *Sugar and Slaves: The Rise of the Planter Class in the English West Indies, 1624–1712* (Durham: University of North Carolina Press, 1972); and Richard B. Sheridan, *Sugar and Slavery: An Economic History of the British West Indies, 1623–1775* (Baltimore: Johns Hopkins University Press, 1973). Useful essays also can be found in *The Encyclopedia of the North American Colonies*, ed. Jacob Ernest Cooke et al. (New York: Scribner, 1993); see especially entries on "The Slave Trade," 45–66; "Slavery," 83–101; and "Free Blacks," 185–93.
10. For an early discussion, see Edmund S. Morgan, *American Slavery—American Freedom*.
11. Berlin, *Many Thousands Gone*, 369–71. On slavery in the North in these years, see Lorenzo Johnston Greene, *The Negro in Colonial New England* (New York: Atheneum, 1968).

CHAPTER I: LET US MAKE A TRYAL

1. Cotton Mather, *Tremenda. The Dreadful Sound with Which the Wicked Are to Be Thunderstruck* (Boston: B. Green, 1721), 23. There have been few previous discussions of Joseph Hanno, and none that have examined documents beyond Mather's sermon and the brief mention of Hanno's case in the *Boston News-letter* and the records of the Massachusetts House of Representatives, cited below. While the case has been thought important, almost nothing specific about its legal and factual details seems to exist in print. For instance, no studies have examined original court documents related to the murder, considered who Joseph Hanno or Nanny Negro were, or noted the medical context of the case. The starting point for any discussion is Richard Slotkin's "Narratives of Negro Crime in New England,

1675–1800," *American Quarterly* 25 (1973): 3–31, which argues that "Cotton Mather's sermon on the execution of Joseph Hanno, a black wife-murderer, sets the pattern for Puritan narratives and sermons on Negro crime" (10). Hanno's trial plays an equally central symbolic role in Lawrence W. Towner, "'A Fondness for Freedom': Servant Protest in Puritan Society," *William and Mary Quarterly* 14 (1962), 201–19. The case is not discussed in Daniel A. Cohen's excellent study, *Pillars of Salt, Monuments of Grace: New England Crime Literature and the Origins of American Popular Culture, 1674–1860* (New York: Oxford University Press, 1993). On race and law in colonial America, see A. Leon Higginbotham, Jr., *In the Matter of Color: Race and the American Legal Process: The Colonial Period* (Oxford: Oxford University Press, 1978).

2. *Journals of the House of Representatives of Massachusetts, 1718–1720* (Boston: Massachusetts Historical Society, 1921), 286 [November 15, 1720]; Cotton Mather, *Tremenda*, cover.

3. Mather, *Tremenda*, 35; Cotton Mather, *Diary of Cotton Mather*, vol. 2, *1709–1724* (New York: Frederick Ungar Publishing Co., 1957), 620 [May 25, 1721]; Mather, *Tremenda*, cover.

4. John Daniels, *In Freedom's Birthplace* (New York: Arno Press and the New York Times, 1969 [1914]), 17. For a discussion of black patterns of settlement in Boston that includes references to the early eighteenth century, see George A. Levesque, *Black Boston: African American Life and Culture in Urban America, 1750–1860* (New York: Garland, 1994). *Report of the Record Commissioners of the City of Boston* 28 (Boston: Rockwell & Churchill, 1898), 28:13; *Report* (Boston, 1884), 11:210 (some spellings have been altered here to standardize variant spellings that exist in the volume). Lorenzo Johnston Greene, *The Negro in Colonial New England* (New York: Atheneum, 1968), 80–81, 84–85.

5. *Boston News-letter*, May 22–29, 1721, 2(1).

6. In 1676, the English Privy Council ordered Massachusetts Governor John Leverett to assist the Royal African Company in sending a ship on a "navigation" the governor claimed had not been undertaken by Massachusetts seamen in forty years. *Calendar of State Papers: Colonial Series, America and West Indies*, 42 vols. (London: H.M.S.O., 1860–1953), 4:274 (#662). *Calendar of State Papers*, 5:529 (#1360). See also Elizabeth Donnan, ed., *Documents Illustrative of the History of the Slave Trade to America*, 3:14–15. On the Muslim role in the slave trade at the time of Hanno's sale, see Pierre Verin, *The History of Civilisation in North Madagascar*, trans. David Smith (Rotterdam: A. A. Balkema, 1986), 104–6.

7. See generally Berlin, *Many Thousands Gone*; Greene, *Negro in Colonial New England*; Edgar J. McManus, *Black Bondage in the North* (Syracuse: Syracuse University Press, 1973); William D. Piersen, *Black Yankees: The Development of an Afro-American Subculture in Eighteenth-Century New England* (Amherst: University of Massachusetts Press, 1988); and Lawrence William Towner, *A Good Master Well Served: Masters and Servants in Colonial Massachusetts, 1620–1750* (New York: Garland, 1998). On slavery and Christian conversion, see Marcus W. Jernegan, "Slavery and Conversion in the American Colonies," *American Historical Review* 21 (1916): 504–27; Bernard Rosenthal, "Puritan Conscience and New England Slavery,"

New England Quarterly 46(1) (1973): 62–81; and Robert C. Twombly and Robert H. Moore, "Black Puritan: The Negro in Seventeenth-Century Massachusetts," *William and Mary Quarterly* 24(2) (1967): 224–42.

8. *Boston News-letter*, May 22–29, 1721, 2(1). Mather, *Tremenda*, 33. Hanno's fondness for scriptural citation may have been influenced by his Madagascar roots: Malagasy speakers are known for their proverbial expressions.

9. See Helen Turncliff Catterall, *Judicial Cases Concerning American Slavery and the Negro*, 4:463–64 (citing I Acts of Prov. 606), noting that "they are not charged with training, watchings and other services required of her majesty's subjects."

10. *Reports of the Record Commissioners*, 11:233; *Reports*, 13:8, 42, 69; *Report of the Record Commissioners*, vol. 24 (Boston, 1894). The Nanny Negro indicated here is listed as being "of Mr. William Harriss." It is unclear whether she is Joseph Hanno's wife. Her name may have been a designation of her work status; it also might have been derived from the Nanny family of Valentine Hill and Elbow Alley. See Justin Winsor, *The Memorial History of Boston, 1630–1880* (Boston: Ticknor & Co., 1881), 2:xii–xiii.

11. On Pollard's home, see *Report of the Records Commissioners* (Boston, 1883), 8:52–53. On the geography of Boston, see Annie Haven Thwing, *The Crooked & Narrow Streets of the Town of Boston, 1630–1822* (Boston: Marshall Jones Co., 1920). Superior Court of Judicature, Suffolk County Court Files, Massachusetts State Archives, reel 72, #15186. Although Gee's name has been largely torn from the coroner's form, a comparison of what remains of his preserved signature indicates his identity. See Winsor, *Memorial History of Boston*, 2:vii.

12. See Edmund S. Morgan, *The Puritan Family: Religion and Domestic Relations in Seventeenth-Century New England*, new ed. (New York: Harper & Row, 1966).

13. *Journals of the House of Representatives*, 286–87.

14. Rules of civil law in Massachusetts, however, as well as its actual system of courts, were derived from a jurisprudential mixture that included English local law and custom, the royal common law, and improvised practice influenced by the special problems posed by colonial life. See generally George Lee Haskins, *Law and Authority in Early Massachusetts: A Study in Tradition and Design* (New York: Macmillan, 1960); and Lawrence M. Friedman, *A History of American Law*, 2nd ed. (New York: Simon & Schuster, 1985), 33–93.

15. On Mather, see Ralph and Louise Boas, *Cotton Mather: Keeper of the Puritan Conscience* (Hamden, Conn.: Archon Books, 1964); David Levin, *Cotton Mather: The Young Life of the Lord's Remembrancer, 1663–1703* (Cambridge: Harvard University Press, 1978); Kenneth Silverman, *The Life and Times of Cotton Mather* (Cambridge: Harper & Row, 1970); and Robert Middlekauf, *The Mathers: Three Generations of Puritan Intellectuals, 1596–1728* (London: Oxford University Press, 1971). On Puritanism, see Edmund S. Morgan, *Visible Saints: The History of a Puritan Idea* (New York: New York University Press, 1963); and Perry Miller, *The New England Mind: The Seventeenth Century* (Cambridge: Belknap Press of Harvard University Press, 1982 [1939]). For Mather and slavery, see also Daniel K. Richter, "'It Is God Who Has Caused Them to Be Servants': Cotton Mather and Afro-American Slavery in New England," *Bulletin of the Congregational Library* 30(3) (1979), 4–17.

16. Mather's role in the witch trials is generally misunderstood, particularly his assessment of spectral evidence. For a treatment of the trials by a legal historian, see Peter Charles Hoffer, *The Devil's Disciples: Makers of the Salem Witchcraft Trials* (Baltimore: Johns Hopkins University Press, 1996).

17. See Silverman, *Life and Times of Cotton Mather,* 308–10, 381–89; Mather, *Diary,* 2:617 [May 10, 1721] and 2:621 [May 28, 1721].

18. *Reports of the Record Commissioners,* 13:81; Mather, *Diary,* 2:621 [May 28, 1721]. Upon learning of the descending pox, Mather anxiously sought to "humble myself exceedingly, and ly in the Dust, [lest] the least Vanity of mine upon seeing my poor prediction accomplished, should provoke the holy One to do some grievous Thing unto me."

19. Cotton Mather, *The Negro Christianized. An Essay to Excite and Assist that Good Work, the Instruction of Negro-Servants in Christianity* (Boston: B. Green, 1706), 23,2.

20. Mather, *Negro Christianized,* 2,36.

21. Mather, *Diary,* 1:579 [December 13, 1706]. Mather, *Negro Christianized,* 26–27.

22. Mather, *Negro Christianized,* 39.

23. Ola Elizabeth Winslow, *Samuel Sewall of Boston* (New York: Macmillan, 1964), 141.

24. See Greene, *Negro in Colonial New England,* 179–86; and McManus, *Law and Liberty,* 129–30; see, e.g., Superior Court of Judicature, Suffolk County Court Files, #13953, #14224. On black use of courts in the colonies of this period, see generally Berlin, *Many Thousands Gone.*

25. On Adam Saffin's black trial, popularly known by the name of Samuel Sewall's pamphlet, see Lawrence W. Towner, "The Sewall-Saffin Dialogue on Slavery," *William and Mary Quarterly* 21 (1964), 40–52. See also Albert J. Von Frank, "John Saffin: Slavery and Racism in Colonial Massachusetts," *Early American Literature* 29 (3) (1994): 254–72; and Sidney Kaplan, "'The Selling of Joseph': Samuel Sewall and the Iniquity of Slavery," in *American Studies in Black and White: Selected Essays,* ed. Allan D. Austin (Amherst: University of Massachusetts Press, 1991), 3–17. For text of *The Selling of Joseph* and surrounding documents, see Abner C. Goodell, "John Saffin and his Slave Adam," *Publications of the Colonial Society of Massachusetts* 1 (March 1895): 85–112; Samuel Sewall, *The Selling of Joseph: A Memorial,* ed. Sidney Kaplan (Amherst: University of Massachusetts Press, 1969); and George W. Williams, *History of the Negro Race in America from 1619 to 1880,* 2 vols. (New York, 1883), 1: 214–17. For Sewall's further thoughts on whether slavery "be in it self Unlawful, and especially contrary to the great Law of CHRISTIANITY," see Josephine K. Piercy, *Studies in Literary Types in Seventeenth Century America (1607–1710)* (New Haven: Yale University Press, 1939), 342–47. Adam Saffin and Joseph Hanno worked on a road crew of twenty-five persons constituted on August 9, 1715 (Saffin worked for six days, Hanno for five). *Reports of the Record Commissioners,* 11:232–33.

26. On Massachusetts court procedures, see Haskins, *Law and Authority in Early Massachusetts*; Bradley Chapin, *Criminal Justice in Colonial America, 1606–1660* (Athens: University of Georgia Press, 1983); David T. Konig, *Law and Society in Puritan Massachusetts: Essex County, 1629–1692* (Chapel Hill: University of North Carolina Press, 1979); Edgar J. McManus, *Law and Liberty in Early New England:*

Criminal Justice and Due Process, 1620–1692 (Amherst: University of Massachusetts Press, 1993), which contains a useful bibliography; William E. Nelson, *Americanization of the Common Law: The Impact of Legal Change on Massachusetts Society, 1760–1830* (Cambridge: Harvard University Press, 1975); Samuel Walker, *Popular Justice: A History of American Criminal Justice* (New York: Oxford University Press, 1980); and John M. Murrin, "Magistrates, Sinners, and a Precarious Liberty: Trial by Jury in Seventeenth-Century New England," in David D. Hall et al., eds., *Saints & Revolutionaries: Essays on Early American History* (New York: Norton, 1984). Proceedings against Hanno were initiated by grand jury indictment, probably based on Pollard's coroner's report.

27. Superior Court of Judicature, Suffolk County Court Files, #14687.
28. Mather, *Diary*, 2:618 [May 12, 1721]. On execution interviews and sermons, see Cohen, *Pillars of Salt*; Ronald A. Bosco, "Lectures at the Pillory: The Early American Execution Sermons," *American Quarterly* 30(3) (1978): 156–76; Karen Halttunen, "Early American Murder Narratives: The Birth of Horror," in Richard Wightman Fox and T. J. Jackson Lears, eds., *The Power of Culture: Critical Essays in American History* (Chicago: University of Chicago Press, 1993), 67–101; Lawrence W. Towner, "True Confessions and Dying Warnings in Colonial New England," *Publications of the Colonial Society of Massachusetts* 59 (Boston: Colonial Society of Massachusetts, 1982); and Daniel E. Williams, "'Behold a Tragic Scene Strangely Changes into a Theater of Mercy'": The Structure and Significance of Criminal Conversion Narratives in Early New England," *American Quarterly* 38(5) (1986): 827–47.
29. For Mather's interview with Hanno, see *Tremenda*, 31–40.
30. Job 15:20 and 28. Mather, *Tremenda*, 1.
31. Mather, *Tremenda*, 13,12,16.
32. Mather, *Diary*, 2:623 [May 31, 1721].
33. *Boston News-letter* of May 22–29, 1721, 2(1).
34. *Boston News-letter* of May 22–29, 1721, 2(1).
35. *Reports of the Record Commissioners*, 13:82–83.
36. On Mather, smallpox, and theories of disease, including a discussion of Mather's theory of the "*Nishmath-Chajim*," see Richard H. Shryock, "Cotton Mather: First Significant Figure in American Medicine," *Proceedings of the American Antiquarian Society* 63 (Worcester: American Antiquarian Society, 1953): 37–274; see also Margot Minardi, "The Boston Inoculation Controversy of 1721–1722: An Incident in the History of Race," *William and Mary Quarterly* 61(1) (2004), 47–67.
37. Mather, *Diary*, 2:620–21 [May 26, 1721].

CHAPTER 2: THIS VILLAINOUS CONSPIRACY

1. The essential primary source on the New York Conspiracy is Daniel Horsmanden's *Journal of the Proceedings in the Detection of the Conspiracy Formed by Some White People in Conjunction with Negro and Other Slaves for Burning the City of New-York in America and Murdering the Inhabitants* (New York: James Parker, 1744), which is readily available in a modern edition. See Daniel Horsmanden, *The New*

York Conspiracy, ed. and with an intro. by Thomas J. Davis (Boston: Beacon Press, 1973). Also essential is the *Calendar of Historical Manuscripts in the Office of the Secretary of State, Albany, N.Y.*, 2 vols. (Albany, 1866); the *Documentary History of New York*, 4 vols. (Albany, 1849–51); and *Documents Relative to the Colonial History of New York*, 15 vols. (Albany, 1856–87). See also the late-nineteenth-century discussion in J. T. Headley, *Pen and Pencil Sketches of the Great Riots* (New York: E. B. Treat, 1882), 15–45. Documentary material on the proceedings in the New York State Archives has been substantially damaged by fire. A helpful discussion of source material can be found in T. J. Davis, *A Rumor of Revolt: The "Great Negro Plot" in Colonial New York* (Amherst: University of Massachusetts Press, 1985), which, with Peter Hoffer, *The Great New York Conspiracy: Slavery, Crime, and Colonial Law* (Lawrence: University Press of Kansas, 2003), provide the most complete secondary accounts. A shorter account also appears in Edwin G. Burrows and Mike Wallace, *Gotham: A History of New York City to 1898* (New York: Oxford University Press, 1999), 159–66. Other important secondary material includes Julius Goebel, Jr. and T. Raymond Naughton, *Law Enforcement in Colonial New York: A Study in Criminal Procedure, 1664–1776* (New York: Commonwealth Fund, 1944); Thomas J. Davis, "Slavery in Colonial New York City" (Ph.D. dissertation, Columbia University, 1974); Vivienne L. Kruger, "Born to Run: The Slave Family in Early New York, 1626 to 1827" (Ph.D. dissertation, Columbia University, 1985); and Edgar J. McManus, *A History of Negro Slavery in New York* (Syracuse: Syracuse University Press, 1966). The discovery of the Negro Burial Ground in New York has sparked a good deal of discussion and debate; two accounts include Cheryl J. LaRoche and Michael L. Blakey, "Seizing Intellectual Power: The Dialogue at the New York African Burial Ground," in *Historical Archaeology* 31(3) (1997): 84–106; and Michele H. Bogart, "Public Space and Public Memory in New York's City Hall Park," *Journal of Urban History* 25(2) (1999): 226–57.

2. Horsmanden, *New York Conspiracy*, 65.
3. Horsmanden, *New York Conspiracy*, 165.
4. Headley, *Great Riots*, 37.
5. Horsmanden, *New York Conspiracy*, 276.
6. McManus, *History of Negro Slavery*, 11.
7. Ernst van den Boogaart, "The Servant Migration in New Netherland, 1624–1664," in P. E. Emer, ed., *Colonialism and Migration: Indentured Labour Before and After Slavery* (Dordrecht: Martinus Nijhoff Publishers, 1986), 55–75, 69.
8. Thomas J. Davis, "New York's Long Black Line: A Note on the Growing Slave Population, 1626–1790," *Afro-Americans in New York Life and History* 2(1) (January 1978): 41–59, 44, 47.
9. On the 1712 revolt, see Kenneth Scott, "The Slave Insurrection in New York in 1712," *New York Historical Society Quarterly* 45 (1961): 42–74, 57, 66, 63; Burrows and Wallace, *Gotham*, 148–49.
10. Scott, "Slave Insurrection," 72.
11. Horsmanden, *New York Conspiracy*, 16.
12. Horsmanden, *New York Conspiracy*, 17.
13. Horsmanden, *New York Conspiracy*, 27.

14. Horsmanden, *New York Conspiracy*, 27.
15. Horsmanden, *New York Conspiracy*, 29.
16. Horsmanden, *New York Conspiracy*, 41.
17. Horsmanden, *New York Conspiracy*, 42.
18. Horsmanden, *New York Conspiracy*, 67.
19. Horsmanden, *New York Conspiracy*, 83–84.
20. Horsmanden, *New York Conspiracy*, 467–74.
21. Horsmanden, *New York Conspiracy*, 106–9.
22. Horsmanden, *New York Conspiracy*, 110–11.

CHAPTER 3: AIR TOO PURE

1. The Steuart manuscripts consulted are housed in the National Library of Scotland, the Liverpool Record Office, and the Historical Society of Pennsylvania, though microfilm copies also are available for on-site use at the Library of Virginia, in Richmond, and the John D. Rockefeller, Jr. Library of the Colonial Williamsburg Foundation. Steuart's family name was and is frequently misspelled; its proper spelling is Steuart. The only published article based fully on the Steuart papers was written by one of Steuart's descendants, who donated them to the National Library of Scotland; see A. F. Steuart, "Letters from Virginia, 1774–1781," *Magazine of History* 3(3) (March 1906): 151–61, and *Magazine of History* 3(4) (April 1906): 211–18. Given the notoriety of *Somerset's Case* and Steuart's assiduous preservation of his letters, the general lack of material about the litigation in the Steuart manuscripts is noteworthy. It seems possible that extensive references to the dispute have been systematically excised. It also is possible that Steuart or a descendant set aside manuscript materials relating to *Somerset's Case* and that these either were inadvertently destroyed or have yet to be found. No further documents could be obtained through correspondence with Steuart family descendants. Lord Mansfield's papers were destroyed in the Gordon riots of 1780. Other papers concerning the litigation may still await discovery in the collections of the "West India Planters and Merchants" who took over the management of the case but who have yet to be identified. Charles Steuart to James Murray (June 15, 1772), "[Stuart-Murray Letters]," *Proceedings of the Massachusetts Historical Society*, 63 (October 1909–June 1910): 449–57, 451. For the text of *Somerset's Case*, see *Somerset v. Stewart* [*Somerset's Case*], 98 *English Reports* 499, 1 *Lofft* 1 (KB 1772). A modern copy, with arguments of counsel, can be found as "The Case of James Sommersett, a Negro, on a Habeas Corpus, King's-Bench: 12 George III. A. D. 1771–72," in W. Cobbett, T. B. Howell, et al., eds., *State Trials*, 34 vols. (London: T. C. Hansard, 1809–28), 20:1–82. The return to the writ of habeas corpus can be found in the Public Record Office, K.B./16/17. For a discussion of the inadequacies of various reports of *Somerset's Case*, see David Brion Davis, *The Problem of Slavery in the Age of Revolution, 1770–1823* (Ithaca: Cornell University Press, 1975), 476–77. For primary materials relating to the case, see Paul Finkelman, ed., *Slavery, Race, and the American Legal System, 1700–1872*, series 1, vol. 1, *Southern Slaves in Free State Courts* (Finkelman's collection of pri-

mary materials on the history of Afro-Americans and the law is an indispensable resource). Extensive documentation of the lives of James Somerset and Charles Steuart, including a portrait of Steuart, as well as some discussion of the secondary literature, can be found in Mark S. Weiner, "New Biographical Evidence on *Somerset's Case*," *Slavery & Abolition* 23(1) (April 2002): 120–36. For recent scholarship on *Somerset's Case*, see Patricia Bradley, *Slavery, Propaganda, and the American Revolution* (Jackson: University of Mississippi Press, 1999); Robert M. Cover, *Justice Accused: Anti-Slavery and the Judicial Process* (New Haven: Yale University Press, 1975); Davis, *Problem of Slavery*; William M. Wiecek, *The Sources of Anti-Slavery Constitutionalism in America, 1760–1848* (Ithaca: Cornell University Press, 1977); William R. Cotter, "The *Somerset* Case and the Abolition of Slavery in England," *History* 79 (255) (February 1994): 31–56; Jerome Nadelhaft, "The Somerset Case and Slavery: Myth, Reality, and Repercussions," *Journal of Negro History* 51 (1) (January 1966): 193–208; and James Oldham, "New Light on Mansfield and Slavery," *Journal of British Studies* 27 (1) (January 1988): 45–68. For a history and discussion of the case, including descriptions of its counsel, see F. O. Shyllon, *Black Slaves in Britain* (London: Oxford University Press, 1974), which also contains a bibliographic discussion. An essential contemporary source is Prince Hoare, *Memoirs of Granville Sharp, Esq.* (London: Henry Colburn, 1820). For useful studies of blacks in eighteenth-century England, see Gretchen Holbrook Gerzina, *Black London: Life Before Emancipation* (New Brunswick, N.J.: Rutgers University Press, 1995); James Walvin, *Black and White: The Negro in English Society, 1555–1945* (London: Allen Lane, Penguin Press, 1973); and Paul Edwards and James Walvin, *Black Personalities in the Era of the Slave Trade* (Baton Rouge: Louisiana State University Press, 1983). On Scotland and Britain, see Linda Colley, *Britons: Forging the Nation, 1707–1837* (New Haven: Yale University Press, 1992).

2. Olaudah Equiano, *The Interesting Narrative of the Life of Olaudah Equiano, or Gustavus Vassa, the African*, in Henry Louis Gates, ed., *The Classic Slave Narratives* (New York: New American Library, 1987), 32–33.

3. Peter Kolchin, *American Slavery 1619–1877* (New York: Hill & Wang, 1993), 22.

4. Robert McColley, "Virginia, Slavery in," in Randall M. Miller and John David Smith, eds., *Dictionary of Afro-American Slavery* (Westport, Conn.: Praeger, 1997), 779–787, 780, 782.

5. James Steuart, "Narrative Concerning the Late Chas. Steuart Esq. by His Brother Mr. James Steuart" (1797), *Charles Steuart Papers, 1758–1798* (Microfilm Collection, John D. Rockefeller, Jr. Library of the Colonial Williamsburg Foundation [hereafter *Steuart Papers*], originals in the National Library of Scotland), reel 6, 262. See also *Gentleman's Magazine* (May 1798): 442–44.

6. Letter of Charles Steuart to Benjamin [Massiah] (July 5, 1751), *Charles Steuart Letterbooks* (Microfilm Collection, John D. Rockefeller, Jr. Library of the Colonial Williamsburg Foundation [hereafter *Steuart Letterbooks*], originals in the Historical Society of Pennsylvania). Steuart was referring to either the War of Jenkins' Ear or King George's War.

7. Letter of Charles Steuart to Anthony [Fahie] (August 21, 1751), *Steuart Letterbooks*.

8. *Virginia Gazette* (January 10, 1752): 4. In another *Virginia Gazette* entry, Steuart is listed as one of the Norfolk citizens to whom a particular set of runaways should be returned if found, *Virginia Gazette* (March 12, 1752): 3; letter of Charles Steuart to Thomas Ogilvie (July 22(?) [illegible], (1752), *Steuart Letterbooks*.

9. Letter of Coffin to Steuart (August 7, 1769), *Steuart Papers*.

10. On Granville Sharp, see Hoare, *Memoirs of Granville Sharp*; E. C. P. Lascelles, *Granville Sharp and the Freedom of Slaves in England* (London: Oxford University Press, 1928); and Charles Stuart [no relation to Charles Steuart], *A Memoir of Granville Sharp, To Which Is Added Sharp's Law of Passive Obedience and an Extract from His Law of Retribution* (New York: American Anti-Slavery Society, 1836). An admiring portrait also can be found in Charles Sumner, "Position and Duties of the Merchant, Illustrated by the Life of Granville Sharp," in *The Works of Charles Sumner* (Boston: Lee & Shepard, 1871), 3:480–519.

11. Granville Sharp, "An Account of the Occasion Which Compelled Granville Sharp to Study Law, and Undertake the Defence of Negroe Slaves in England," *Granville Sharp Manuscripts*, New-York Historical Society.

12. Granville Sharp, *A Representation of the Injustice and Dangerous Tendency of Tolerating Slavery in England* (London, 1769), 4.

13. Hoare, *Memoirs of Granville Sharp*, 37; Sharp, *Representation*, 38, 29.

14. Hoare, *Memoirs of Granville Sharp*, 7.

15. Hoare, *Memoirs of Granville Sharp*, 75–77. The opinion referenced can be found in John Rushworth, *Historical Collections. The Second Part* (London: 1680), 468. Contemporary news accounts of the case relied upon here include *London Evening Post*, February 8–11, 1772 and June 23–25, 1772; *Gazetteer and New Daily Advertiser*, February 8, 1772, May 13, 1772, May 22, 1772, June 23, 1772; *General Evening Post* (London), February 8, 1772, May 14, 1772, May 22, 1772, June 23, 1772, and June 25–27, 1772; *Gentleman's Magazine* (June 1772), 293–294; and *Scots Magazine* 34 (June 1772), 297–299.

16. *Somerset's Case*, Howell, *State Trials*, 24.

17. *Somerset's Case*, Howell, *State Trials*, 69; Hoare, *Memoirs of Granville Sharp*, 86.

18. *Somerset's Case*, *State Trials*, 79.

19. *State Trials*, 74.

20. *State Trials*, 80–82.

21. *Public Advertiser* (London), June 27, 1772.

22. Hoare, *Memoirs of Granville Sharp*, 91.

23. Letter of John Riddell to Charles Steuart, (July 10, 1772), *Steuart Papers*, reel 2, pt. 1, 192.

24. Letter of Steuart to James Parker (October 23, 1773), *Parker Family Papers* (Microfilm Collection, John D. Rockefeller, Jr. Library of Colonial Williamsburg Foundation; originals in the Liverpool Records Office).

PART TWO: WHITE REPUBLIC, 1776–1849

National Identity on Trial

1. A prominent discussion of the transformation in moral sensibility that fed the antislavery movement can be found in Thomas Bender, ed., *The Antislavery Debate: Capitalism and Abolitionism as a Problem in Historical Interpretation* (Berkeley: University of California Press, 1992).

2. For one analysis of the relation between Revolutionary propaganda and slavery, see Patricia Bradley, *Slavery, Propaganda, and the American Revolution* (Jackson: University Press of Mississippi, 1998). But see John Philip Reid, *The Concept of Liberty in the Age of the American Revolution* (Chicago: University of Chicago Press, 1988), which minimizes the conceptual significance of colonists' rhetorical use of the word "slavery" in their agitation against England. On antislavery sentiment, see Roger Bruns, ed., *Am I Not a Man and a Brother: The Antislavery Crusade of Revolutionary America, 1688–1788* (New York: Chelsea House, 1976).

3. See Arthur Zilversmit, *The First Emancipation: The Abolition of Slavery in the North* (Chicago: University of Chicago Press, 1967).

4. For a view of the Constitutional Convention that advances a modern version of the analysis of William Lloyd Garrison, see Paul Finkelman, *An Imperfect Union: Slavery, Federalism, and Comity* (Chapel Hill: University of North Carolina Press, 1981); and "Slavery and the Constitutional Convention: Making a Covenant with Death," in Richard Beeman, Stephen Botein, and Edward C. Carter II, eds., *Beyond Confederation: Origins of the Constitution and American National Identity* (Chapel Hill: University of North Carolina Press, 1987), 188–225.

5. See Nathan O. Hatch, *The Democratization of American Christianity* (New Haven: Yale University Press, 1989); Mark A. Noll et al., *Evangelicalism* (New York: Oxford University Press, 1994); and Timothy L. Smith, *Revivalism and Social Reform in Mid-Nineteenth Century America* (New York: Abingdon Press, 1957).

CHAPTER 4: I SHOULD NOT TURN HER OUT

1. Primary source materials on the case of Prudence Crandall include Andrew Thompson Judson, *Andrew T. Judson's Remarks to the Jury on the Trial of the Case, State v. P. Crandall* (Hartford, Conn.: John Russell, 1833), *Report of the Trial of Miss Prudence Crandall* (Brooklyn, Conn.: Unionist Press, 1833), *A Statement of Facts, Respecting the School for Colored Females* (Brooklyn, Conn.: 1833); Samuel J. May, *The Right of Colored People to Education, Vindicated* (Brooklyn, Conn.: Advertiser Press, 1833); and [A Member of the Bar], *Report of the Arguments of Counsel in the Case of Prudence Crandall vs. State of Connecticut* (Boston: Garrison & Knapp, 1834)—all in Paul Finkelman, ed., *Abolitionists in Northern Courts: The Pamphlet Literature*, series 3 (New York: Garland, 1988). Contemporary or near-contemporary secondary materials consulted here include Wendell Philips Garrison, *William Lloyd Garrison, 1805–1879: The Story of His Life as Told by His Children* (New York: Century Co., 1885–1889), 1:315–347; William Jay, *An Inquiry into the Character and Tendency of the American Colonization and American Anti-Slavery Societies* (New

York: Leavitt, Lord & Co., 1835); John C. Kimball, *Connecticut's Canterbury Tale* (Hartford, Conn.: Plimpton Press, 1888); Ellen D. Larned, *History of Windham County, Connecticut* (Worcester, 1874–1880); Samuel J. May, *Some Recollections of Our Anti-Slavery Conflict* (Boston: Fields, Osgood, 1869); George B. Thayer, *Pedal and Path: Across the Continent Awheel and Afoot* (Hartford: Hartford Evening Post Association, 1887); and C. G. Woodson, *The Education of the Negro Prior to 1861* (New York: Arno Press, 1968). The story of Prudence Crandall has inspired the following accounts: Edmund Fuller, *Prudence Crandall: An Incident of Racism in Nineteenth-Century Connecticut* (Middletown, Conn.: Wesleyan University Press, 1971); Philip S. Foner and Josephine F. Pacheco, *Three Who Dared: Prudence Crandall, Margaret Douglass, Myrtilla Miner—Champions of Antebellum Black Education* (Westport, Conn: Greenwood Press, 1984); and, most important, Susan Strane, *A Whole-Souled Woman: Prudence Crandall and the Education of Black Women* (New York: Norton, 1990). The Prudence Crandall Museum in Canterbury merits a visit. On Garrison, see George M. Fredrickson, ed., *William Lloyd Garrison* (Englewood Cliffs, N.J.: Prentice-Hall, 1968).

2. Thayer, *Pedal and Path*, 213.
3. Quoted in Strane, *Whole-Souled Woman*, 9.
4. *Congressional Record* 2 (February 7, 1874), 1314.
5. Larned, *History of Windham County*, 491.
6. Garrison, *William Lloyd Garrison*, 1:315–16.
7. Larned, *History of Windham County*, 492.
8. Quoted in Strane, *Whole-Souled Woman*, 72.
9. Quoted in Fuller, *Prudence Crandall*, 37–38.
10. Quoted in Strane, *Whole-Souled Woman*, 74.
11. CPI conversion by Economic History Services, www.eh.net (January 1, 2004).
12. May, *Some Recollections*, 53–55.
13. *Report of the Trial of Miss Prudence Crandall*, 3.
14. *Report of the Trial of Miss Prudence Crandall*, 3.
15. *Report of the Trial of Miss Prudence Crandall*, 4.
16. *Report of the Trial of Miss Prudence Crandall*, 5.
17. *Report of the Trial of Miss Prudence Crandall*, 7; for Ellsworth's arguments, quoted here and in pages following, see 7–14.
18. *Report of the Trial of Miss Prudence Crandall*, 20.
19. Judson, *Andrew T. Judson's Remarks*, 3, 12, 21–23.
20. Judson, *Andrew T. Judson's Remarks*, 25.
21. May, *Some Recollections*, 71.

CHAPTER 5: ALL WE WANT IS MAKE US FREE

1. Primary material about the case of the *Amistad* Africans has been drawn from John W. Barber, "A History of the Amistad Captives," a contemporary source reprinted in *Journal of the New Haven Colony Historical Society* 26(2) (Spring 1990): 32–64, and the wealth of items in Paul Finkelman, ed., *The African Slave Trade and American Courts: The Pamphlet Literature*, series 5, vol. 1 (New York: Garland, 1988),

which contains essential source material about the *Jeune Eugénie*, accounts of the *Amistad* trial and of the captive Africans, and the arguments of Roger S. Baldwin and John Quincy Adams. For the main secondary account of the *Amistad* case, see Howard Jones, *Mutiny on the* Amistad: *The Saga of a Slave Revolt and Its Impact on American Abolition, Law, and Diplomacy* (New York: Oxford University Press, 1987). On the case of the *Antelope*, see John T. Noonan, Jr., *The* Antelope: *The Ordeal of the Recaptured Africans in the Administrations of James Monroe and John Quincy Adams* (Berkeley: University of California Press, 1977). On Adams, see also William Lee Miller, *Arguing About Slavery: John Quincy Adams and the Great Battle in the United States Congress* (New York: Vintage, 1998).

2. Barber, "History of the Amistad Captives," 36.
3. Quoted in Jones, *Mutiny on the* Amistad, 107.
4. Quoted in Jones, *Mutiny on the* Amistad, 122.
5. Barber, "History of the Amistad Captives," 52.
6. Barber, "History of the Amistad Captives," 56–63.
7. Joseph Story, *A Discourse Pronounced upon the Inauguration of the Author as Dane Professor of Law in Harvard University* (Boston: Hillard, Gray, Little, & Wilkins, 1829), 21.
8. Story, *Discourse*, 42, 43
9. *U.S. v. The La Jeune Eugénie*, 26 F. Cas. 832 (1821), 840, 845, 846.
10. *The Antelope*, 10 Wheat (23 U.S.) 66 (1825), 120, 115.
11. Baldwin, *Argument of R. S. Baldwin*, 14–15.
12. Baldwin, *Argument of R. S. Baldwin*, 23–27.
13. Baldwin, *Argument of R. S. Baldwin*, 27–28.
14. Quoted in Jones, *Mutiny on the* Amistad, 182.
15. Adams, *Argument of John Quincy Adams*, 6.
16. Adams, *Argument of John Quincy Adams*, 8–9.
17. Adams, *Argument of John Quincy Adams*, 38–40, 43.
18. Adams, *Argument of John Quincy Adams*, 71.
19. Adams, *Argument of John Quincy Adams*, 86.
20. Adams, *Argument of John Quincy Adams*, 89.
21. Adams, *Argument of John Quincy Adams*, 135.
22. *U.S. v. The Libellants and Claimants of the Schooner Amistad*, 40 U.S. 518 (1841), 593, 596.
23. Quoted in Jones, *Mutiny on the* Amistad, 203.

CHAPTER 6: CHRISTIAN WITNESS

1. The Supreme Court decision can be found as *Jones v. Van Zandt*, 5 How. (46 U.S.) 1847. Original case files and materials are available through the National Archives–Great Lakes Region, in the records of the U.S. Circuit Court, Southern District of Ohio, Western Division, Cincinnati, General Records, Records (Journals), 1808–1868, vol. R, and General Records, Journals (Order Books), 1807–1911, vols. F–G, Record Group 21. See also *Jones v. Van Zandt, U.S. Supreme Court Records and Briefs*, pt. 1, December 1845 to December 1846, vol. 1, reel 10. For

published reports of the district and circuit court proceedings, see *Jones v. Vanzandt*, 2 McClean 596, 1 West. Law J. 2, 2 O.F.D. 220, 13 Fed. Cas. 1040 (1842); *Jones v. Vanzandt*, 2 McClean 611, 1 West. Law J. 56, 13 Fed. Cas. 1047 (1842); *Jones v. Vanzandt's Administrator*, 4 McClean 599, 2 O.F.D. 652, 13 Fed. Cas. 1054 (1849); *Jones v. Vanzandt's Administrator*, 4 McClean 604, 2 O.F.D. 656, 13 Fed. Cas. 1056 (1849); and *Jones v. Van Zandt*, 5 McClean 214 (1851), 3 O.F.D. 12, 13 Fed. Cas. 1057 (1851) (citations that follow are to the reports in *Federal Cases*, the most usable source). Material on Van Sandt and Hamilton County can be found in *History of Cincinnati and Hamilton County, Ohio* (Cincinnati: S. B. Nelson & Co., 1894); Henry A. Ford and Kate B. Ford, *History of Hamilton County, Ohio* (Cleveland: L. A. Williams & Co., 1881); Charles W. Hoffman, *Oak Hill. Historical Sketch* (Norwood, Ohio: Stanley M. Landon & Co., 1896), 18–22; Henry Howe, *Historical Collections of Ohio* (Cincinnati: Derby, Bradley & Co., 1848), 205–37; J. T. Trowbridge, *The Ferry-boy and the Financier* (Boston: Walker, Wise, 1864), 295–300; and Henry Wilson, *History of the Rise and Fall of the Slave Power in America*, 3d ed. (Boston: James R. Osgood & Company, 1875), 1:475–77. The Van Sandt family, whose name is properly spelled as indicated here, has a strong sense of transatlantic identity, and one of their members, Harry Van Sandt, has been helpful in providing information about his ancestor. See Harry Van Sandt, with Bart and Irene Van Sandt, "John Van Sandt, 1791–1847," manuscript in possession of the author; Mary C. Francis, "A Sketch of John Van Sandt," *Bixby's Bazoo* (September 1893), transcript in possession of the author, courtesy of Harry Van Sandt. See also Bill James Cook, "John Vanzandt—A Man Among Men," manuscript in possession of the author. On the case, its background and significance, see William M. Wiecek, "Slavery and Abolition Before the United States Supreme Court, 1820–1860," *Journal of American History* 65 (June 1978): 34–59; and Leo Alilunas, "Fugitive Slave Cases in Ohio Prior to 1850," *Ohio Archaeological and Historical Quarterly*, 49 (1940): 160–84. Samuel Chase's argument is reprinted in Paul Finkelman, ed., *Fugitive Slaves and American Courts: The Pamphlet Literature* (New York: Garland, 1988), 341–449. On Chase, see John Niven, *Salmon P. Chase: A Biography* (New York: Oxford University Press, 1995); and see Harold M. Hyman, *The Reconstruction Justice of Salmon P. Chase: In Re: Turner and Texas v. White* (Lawrence: University Press of Kansas, 1997); John Niven et al., eds., *The Salmon P. Chase Papers*, vol. 1 (Kent, Ohio: Kent State University Press, 1993); and "A Symposium on Salmon P. Chase and the Chase Court: Perspectives in Law and History," *Northern Kentucky Law Review* 21(1) (Fall 1993). On Seward, see Earl Conrad, *Mr. Seward for the Defense* (New York: Rinehart, 1956); for his argument in *Jones v. Van Zandt*, see Finkelman, ed., *Fugitive Slaves and American Courts*, 451–486; on his innovative argument in the black trial of William Freeman, not examined here, see Paul Harris, *Black Rage Confronts the Law* (New York: New York University Press, 1997). On McLean, see Francis P. Weisenburger, *The Life of John McLean: A Politician on the United States Supreme Court* (Columbus: Ohio State University Press, 1937). On *Prigg v. Pennsylvania*, see *Argument of Mr. Hambly*, in Finkelman, *Fugitive Slaves and American Courts*, 121–56; Paul Finkelman, "*Prigg v. Pennsylvania* and Northern State Courts: Anti-Slavery Use of a Pro-Slavery

Decision," *Civil War History* 25 (March 1979): 5–35, and "*Prigg v. Pennsylvania*: Understanding Justice Story's Proslavery Nationalism," *Journal of Supreme Court History* 2 (1997): 51–64; William R. Leslie, "The Pennsylvania Fugitive Slave Act of 1836," *Journal of Southern History* 18 (November 1952): 429–45; and Joseph Nogee, "The Prigg Case and Fugitive Slavery, 1842–1850," *Journal of Negro History* 39(3) (July 1954): 185–205. For accounts of two other important fugitive cases, see Gary Collison, *Shadrach Minkins: From Fugitive Slave to Citizen* (Cambridge: Harvard University Press, 1997); and Albert J. Von Frank, *The Trials of Anthony Burns: Freedom and Slavery in Emerson's Boston* (Cambridge: Harvard University Press, 1998).

2. Quoted in Francis, "A Sketch."

3. Cook, "John Vanzandt," 1–2.

4. Cook, "John Vanzandt," 2.

5. *History of Cincinnati*, 454; see also Hoffman, *Oak Hill*, 18–22.

6. Harriet Beecher Stowe, *Uncle Tom's Cabin*, ed. and with an intro. by Jean Fagan Yellin (New York: Oxford University Press, 1998 [1852]), 197–98.

7. Quoted in Hoffman, *Oak Hill*, 21.

8. Hoffman, *Oak Hill*, 19.

9. *Jones v. Vanzandt*, 13 Fed. Cas. 1041.

10. *Jones v. Van Zandt*, U.S. Circuit Court, Southern District of Ohio, Western Division, Cincinnati. General Records, Records (Journals), 1808–1868, vol. R., Record Group 21, National Archives-Great Lakes Region, 670.

11. *Jones v. Vanzandt*, 13 Fed. Cas. 1041.

12. CPI conversion performed by Economic History Services, www.eh.net (January 9, 2004).

13. *Argument of Mr. Hambly*, 10.

14. Hoffman, *Oak Hill*, 21.

15. *Jones v. Vanzandt*, 13 Fed. Cas. 1041.

16. Wilson, *History of the Rise and Fall of the Slave Power*, 1:476.

17. *Jones v. Vanzandt*, 13 Fed. Cas. 1043–45.

18. *Jones v. Vanzandt*, 13 Fed. Cas. 1048.

19. *Jones v. Van Zandt*, 5 How. (46 U. S.) 215, 223.

20. Chase, "*An Argument for the Defendant*," in Finkelman, ed., *Fugitive Slaves*, 6–7.

21. Chase, "*An Argument for the Defendant*," in Finkelman, ed., *Fugitive Slaves*, 5.

22. Seward, [Argument in *Jones v. Van Zandt*], 40.

23. *Jones v. Van Zandt*, 5 How., 231.

24. Salmon P. Chase to Charles Sumner (April 24, 1847), in *Salmon Chase Papers*, 149.

PART THREE: NEW AMERICANS, 1850–1896

CHAPTER 7: THE LAW OF BLOOD

1. Henry David Thoreau, "The Last Days of John Brown," in Louis Ruchames, *John Brown: The Making of a Revolutionary* (New York: Grosset & Dunlap, 1969 [1959]), 277.

2. The transcript of the Brown trial can be found in *The Life, Trial, and Execution of*

Captain John Brown (New York: Robert M. De Witt, 1859; Miami: Mnemosyne Publishing Co., 1969). Brown's letters and writings can be found in Ruchames, *John Brown*. The work of Benjamin Quarles, *Allies for Freedom* (New York: Oxford University Press, 1974) and, especially, *Blacks on John Brown* (Urbana: Board of Trustees of the University of Illinois, 1972), contains contemporary material on Brown and black responses to his raid, and now is available in a single volume from De Capo Press. For contemporary responses, see also Richard Warch and Jonathan F. Fanton, eds. *John Brown* (Englewood Cliffs, N.J.: Prentice-Hall, 1973). The Bible read while Brown was awaiting execution is housed in the Harpers Ferry National Historic Park, and a transcript of marked verses is available from the institution. The best biography is Stephen B. Oates, *To Purge This Land with Blood: A Biography of John Brown*, 2nd ed. (Amherst: University of Massachusetts Press, 1984 [1970]), which follows in an illustrious history of biographical studies, beginning with the contemporary James Redpath, *The Public Life of Capt. John Brown* (Boston: Thayer & Eldridge, 1860); others include W. E. Burghardt Du Bois, *John Brown* (New York: International Publishers, 1962 [1909]); Richard J. Hinton, *John Brown and His Men* (New York: Arno Press, 1968 [1894]); Oswald Garrison Villard, *John Brown, 1800–1859: A Biography Fifty Years After* (Boston: Houghton Mifflin, 1911). Two recent studies have been especially helpful on Brown: Jeffrey Rossbach, *Ambivalent Conspirators: John Brown, the Secret Six, and a Theory of Slave Violence* (Philadelphia: University of Pennsylvania Press, 1982); and John Stauffer, *The Black Hearts of Men: Radical Abolitionists and the Transformation of Race* (Cambridge: Harvard University Press, 2002). See also the collection of essays in Paul Finkelman, ed., *His Soul Goes Marching On: Responses to John Brown and the Harpers Ferry Raid* (Charlottesville: University Press of Virginia, 1995). For a discussion of the Brown case and issues of interpretation, see Robert A. Ferguson, "Story and Transcription in the Trial of John Brown," *Yale Journal of Law and the Humanities* 6(37) (1994): 37–73. On *Dred Scott*, see Don E. Fehrenbacher, *The Dred Scott Case: Its Significance in American Law and Politics* (New York: Oxford University Press, 1978).

3. Du Bois, *John Brown*, 20.
4. John Brown to Henry L. Stearns (July 15, 1857), in Ruchames, *John Brown*, 43–49.
5. Oates, *To Purge This Land with Blood*, 23–24.
6. Edward Brown, remarks on John Brown, in Ruchames, *John Brown*, 187–89.
7. John Brown to Frederick Douglass (January 9, 1854), in Ruchames, *John Brown*, 92–93.
8. John Brown, "Sambo's Mistakes," in Ruchames, *John Brown*, 69–72.
9. John Brown, "Words of Advice," in Ruchames, *John Brown*, 84.
10. Hebrews 9:22.
11. John Brown to Thomas Wentworth Higginson (February 12, 1858), in Ruchames, *John Brown*, 118–19.
12. *Daily Times* (New York) (March 9, 1857), quoted in Finkelman, *Dred Scott v. Sandford: A Brief History with Documents* (Boston: Bedford Books, 1997), 146.
13. *Journal of Commerce* (New York) (March 12, 1857), quoted in Finkelman, *Dred Scott v. Sandford*, 139–41.

14. *Life, Trial, and Execution*, 51.
15. *Life, Trial, and Execution*, 45–47.
16. *Life, Trial, and Execution*, 55.
17. *Life, Trial, and Execution*, 66, 70.
18. *Life, Trial, and Execution*, 73–74.
19. *Life, Trial, and Execution*, 53.
20. Herman Melville, "The Portent," *Collected Poems of Herman Melville*, ed. Howard P. Vincent (New York: Hendricks House, 1947). *Life, Trial, and Execution*, 93.
21. *Life, Trial, and Execution*, 94–95.
22. Quarles, *Blacks on John Brown*, 62.
23. Wendell Phillips, "The Lesson of the Hour," in Warch and Fanton, eds., *John Brown*, 107.
24. *Life, Trial, and Execution*, 100–101; Oates, *To Purge This Land with Blood*, 349–52.

CHAPTER 8: ORIGINAL PURITY

1. *Report of the Joint Select Committee to Inquire into the Condition of Affairs in the Late Insurrectionary States*, vols. 1–5 (Washington, D.C.: Government Printing Office, 1872), 3:379, 365.
2. The best source to understand Ku Klux Klan activity and the federal prosecutions is the *Report of the Joint Select Committee* and the report on *Conditions of the South* by the 43d Cong., 2nd Sess. (Washington, D.C.: Government Printing Office, 1875). For black accounts of South Carolina during slavery and Reconstruction, see also George P. Rawick, ed., *The American Slave: A Composite Autobiography*, vols. 2, 3 [South Carolina Narratives] (Westport, Conn.: Greenwood Press, 1972 [1941]). The best academic treatment of the federal prosecutions is Lou Falkner Williams, *The Great South Carolina Ku Klux Klan Trials, 1871–1872* (Athens: University of Georgia Press, 1996). See also Everette Swinney, *Suppressing the Ku Klux Klan: The Enforcement of the Reconstruction Amendments* (New York: Garland, 1987); and Allen W. Trelease, *White Terror: The Ku Klux Klan Conspiracy and Southern Reconstruction* (Westport, Conn.: Greenwood Press, 1971). Accounts of Reconstruction focusing on doctrinal questions include Stephen P. Halbrook, *Freedmen, the Fourteenth Amendment, and the Right to Bear Arms, 1866–1876* (Westport, Conn: Praeger, 1998); and Robert J. Kaczorowski, *The Nationalization of Civil Rights: Constitutional Theory and Practice in a Racist Society, 1866–1883* (New York: Garland, 1987). See also the treatment of freedmen and the vote in Robert M. Goldman, *Reconstruction and Black Suffrage: Losing the Vote in Reese and Cruikshank* (Lawrence: University Press of Kansas, 2001), which discusses the dramatic black trial of the Cruikshank case. On South Carolina during Reconstruction, see Thomas Holt, *Black over White: Negro Political Leadership in South Carolina During Reconstruction* (Urbana: University of Illinois Press, 1977); and Joel Williamson, *After Slavery: The Negro in South Carolina During Reconstruction, 1861–1877* (Chapel Hill: University of North Carolina Press, 1965). On blacks and race relations generally in the postbellum South, see Lawrence J. Friedman, *The White Savage: Racial Fantasies in the Postbellum South* (Englewood Cliffs, N.J.: Prentice-

Hall, 1970); Leon F. Litwack, *Been in the Storm So Long: The Aftermath of Slavery* (New York: Vintage, 1979); Joel Williamson, *The Crucible of Race: Black-White Relations in the American South Since Emancipation* (New York: Oxford University Press, 1984) and *A Rage for Order: Black-White Relations in the American South Since Emancipation* (New York: Oxford University Press, 1986); and Forrest G. Wood, *Black Scare: The Racist Response to Emancipation and Reconstruction* (Berkeley: University of California Press, 1968). On Reconstruction, see Eric Foner, *Reconstruction: America's Unfinished Revolution, 1863–1877* (New York: Harper & Row, 1988); and W. E. B. Du Bois, *Black Reconstruction in America, 1860–1880*, with an intro. by David Levering Lewis (New York: Atheneum, 1992 [1935]).

3. Testimony of Clem Bowden, *Report of the Joint Select Committee*, 3:379–86.

4. Testimony of William M. Champion, July 6, 1871, *Report of the Joint Select Committee*, 3:365–73.

5. "Ritual, Constitution, and By-Laws of the National Council, U.L. of A.," *Report of the Joint Select Committee*, 4:949–60.

6. [Ku Klux Klan Obligation, Constitution, and By-Laws], *Report of the Joint Select Committee*, 5:1686–87.

7. Testimony of Alberry Bonner, July 7, 1871, *Report of the Joint Select Committee*, 3:440–46.

8. Testimony of Harriet Hernandes, July 10, 1871, *Report of the Joint Select Committee*, 3:585–91.

9. Testimony of Caleb Jenkins, July 12, 1871, *Report of the Joint Select Committee*, 4:696–98.

10. Testimony of Dick Wilson, December 13, 1871 [Twelfth Day's Proceedings], *Report of the Joint Select Committee*, 5:1746–52.

11. Testimony of Lewis Merrill, July 26, 1871, *Report of the Joint Select Committee*, 5:1463–87, 1470, 1482. For Merrill's report, see "Report of Major Merrill," *Report of the Joint Select Committee*, 5:1599–1606.

12. Testimony of Lewis Merrill, 1482; Lewis Merrill, "Report of Major Merrill," *Report of the Joint Select Committee*, 5:1602–6.

13. Merrill, "Report of Major Merrill," *Report of the Joint Select Committee*, 5:1602.

14. Quoted in Williams, *Great South Carolina Ku Klux Klan Trials*, 52–53.

15. *Report of the Joint Select Committee*, 5:1715.

16. Testimony of Ed McCrorey, Rawick, ed., *American Slave*, vol. 3 [South Carolina Narratives], 148.

17. Daniel Corbin, [opening statement], December 11, 1871 [Tenth Day's Proceedings], *Report of the Joint Select Committee*, 5:1678–79.

18. Testimony of Lieutenant Godfrey, December 12, 1871 [Eleventh Day's Proceedings], *Report of the Joint Select Committee*, 5:1679–80.

19. Testimony of Albertus Hope, December 12, 1871 [Eleventh Day's Proceedings], *Report of the Joint Select Committee*, 5:1680–85.

20. Testimony of Kirkland L. Gunn, December 12, 1871 [Eleventh Day's Proceedings], *Report of the Joint Select Committee*, 5:1689–1692.

21. Testimony of Gadsden Steel, December 12, 1871, Evening Session [Eleventh Day's Proceedings], *Report of the Joint Select Committee*, 5:1718–20; Testimony of

Rosy Williams, December 12, 1871, Evening Session [Eleventh Day's Proceedings], *Report of the Joint Select Committee*, 5:1720–23.

22. Testimony of Andy Timons, December 12, 1871, Evening Session, *Report of the Joint Select Committee*, 5:1712–17; Testimony of John Caldwell, December 12, 1871, Evening Session [Eleventh Day's Proceedings], *Report of the Joint Select Committee*, 5:1724–32.

23. "Argument of Hon. D. H. Chamberlain," December 16, 1871 [Fifteenth Day's Proceedings], *Report of the Joint Select Committee*, 5:1799–1810.

24. "Argument of Hon. Henry Stanbery," December 16, 1871, *Report of the Joint Select Committee*, 5:1810–19.

25. "Argument of Hon. D. T. Corbin," December 18, 1871 [Sixteenth Day's Proceedings], *Report of the Joint Select Committee*, 5:1826–36.

26. "Judge Bond's Charge to the Jury in United States vs. Mitchell," December 18, 1871, *Report of the Joint Select Committee*, 5:1837–38.

27. Personal conversation with Walter B. Mason, Jr. (descendant of Minerva Bowden), July 13, 2002.

CHAPTER 9: IN THE NATURE OF THINGS

1. Files of individual suits that composed *The Civil Rights Cases* are available through the regional National Archives in their respective circuits, with the exception of *U.S. v. Ryan*, the files of which appear to have been lost. See *U.S. v. Hamilton*, Criminal Case #2692, Middle District of Tennessee, Circuit Court (Nashville), Box 36, Record Group 21, National Archives-Southeast Region; *U.S. v. Nichols*, #821, Law and Equity Case Files, Circuit Court, Western District, Central Division of Missouri, Record Group 21, National Archives–Central Plains Region; *U.S. v. Singleton*, A-501 [case file and docket sheet], National Archives–Northeast Region; *U.S. v. Stanley*, #1568, Law and Equity Case Files, Circuit Court, District of Kansas, First Division, Record Group 21, National Archives–Central Plains Region. See also *Robinson v. Memphis and Charleston Rail Road Company*, Law Case 2611, Western District of Tennessee, Circuit Court (Memphis), Box 29, Record Group 21, National Archives–Southeast Region, which ultimately was not decided with the remaining cases. For the Supreme Court decision, see *The Civil Rights Cases*, 109 U.S. 3 (1883), and the transcripts of records in *Supreme Court Records and Briefs*. For newspaper accounts from which the account of *Singleton* and *Ryan* is drawn, see *New York Times*, June 7, 1876; September 9, 1879; September 21, 1879; November 17, 1879; November 25, 1879; December 10, 1879; January 15, 1880; January 24, 1883; October 16, 1883; October 18, 1883; October 24, 1883; November 8, 1883; November 9, 1883; November 18, 1883; December 10, 1883; December 31, 1883; and *San Francisco Chronicle*, January 4, 1876; January 5, 1876 ; January 9, 1876; January 12, 1876; January 16, 1876; January 17, 1876; January 19, 1876; January 20, 1876; February 29, 1876. For another telling of *Singleton*, see Alan F. Westin, "The Case of the Prejudiced Doorkeeper," in John A. Garraty, ed., *Quarrels That Have Shaped the Constitution* (New York: Harper & Row, 1987 [1964]), 139–56. On the Brotherhood of Liberty's jurisprudence, see [The Brotherhood of Liberty], *Justice and Jurisprudence:*

An Inquiry Concerning the Constitutional Limitations of the Thirteenth, Fourteenth, and Fifteenth Amendments (New York: Negro Universities Press, 1969 [1889]). For a reading of *Justice and Jurisprudence*, see Jon-Christian Suggs, *Whispered Consolations: Law and Narrative in African American Life* (Ann Arbor: University of Michigan Press, 2000). On the Brotherhood, see Elaine Freeman, "Harvey Johnson and Everett Waring: A Study of Leadership in the Baltimore Negro Community, 1880–1900" (M.A. thesis, George Washington University, 1968); and J. Clay Smith, Jr., *Emancipation: The Making of the Black Lawyer, 1844–1944* (Philadelphia: University of Pennsylvania Press, 1993). For its own account of the Navassa case, see W. M. Alexander, *The Brotherhood of Liberty; or, Our Day in Court* (Baltimore: J. F. Weishamsel, 1891). On the Brotherhood and legal change in Maryland, the work of Henry Jared McGuinn also deserves special mention. See Henry Jared McGuinn, "The Courts and the Changing Status of Negroes in Maryland" (Ph.D. dissertation, Columbia University, 1940) [collection of the following articles by McGuinn: "The Courts and Equality of Property Rights," *Quarterly Journal* 8(3) (July 1919): 11–22; "The Courts and the Occupational Status of Negroes in Maryland," *Social Forces* 18(2) (December 1939): 256–68; "Equal Protection of the Law and Fair Trials in Maryland," *Journal of Negro History* 24(2) (April 1939): 143–66; "The Courts and Equality of Educational Opportunity," *Journal of Negro Education* (April 1939): 150–63]. McGuinn seems to have had an original account of the Brotherhood by one of the organization's founders, which since his death appears to be lost; it would be a meaningful contribution to the literature on the topic were an enterprising researcher to find it. For the *Plessy* decision, see *Plessy v. Ferguson*, 163 U.S. 537 (1896). On *Plessy*, see Charles A. Lofgren, *The Plessy Case: A Legal-Historical Interpretation* (New York: Oxford University Press, 1987). Some primary documents related to the case can be found in Otto H. Olsen, *The Thin Disguise: Turning Point in Negro History* (New York: Humanities Press, 1967); and Brook Thomas, *Plessy v. Ferguson: A Brief History with Documents* (Boston: Bedford Books, 1997). For Tourgée's full brief, as well as those of other counsel in the case, see Philip B. Kurland and Gerhard Casper, eds., *Landmark Briefs and Arguments of the Supreme Court of the United States: Constitutional Law*, vol. 13 (Arlington: University Publications of America, 1975). On Tourgée, see Theodore Gross, *Albion W. Tourgée* (New York: Twayne Publishers, 1963). For his Reconstruction memoir, see Albion W. Tourgée, *Bricks Without Straw*, ed. Otto H. Olsen (Baton Rouge: Louisiana State University Press, 1969). Justice Bradley's writings can be found in Joseph P. Bradley, *Miscellaneous Writings*, ed. Charles Bradley (Newark, N.J.: L. J. Hardham, 1901). On Justice Bradley, see Allison Dunham and Philip B. Kurland, *Mr. Justice* (Chicago: University of Chicago Press, 1956); Dennis H. Pope, "Personality and Judicial Performance: A Psychobiography of Justice Joseph P. Bradley" (Ph.D. dissertation: Rutgers University, 1988); and Ruth Ann Whiteside, "Justice Joseph Bradley and the Reconstruction Amendments" (Ph.D. dissertation: Rice University, 1981). On Sumner, see David Donald, *Charles Sumner and the Rights of Man* (New York: Alfred A. Knopf, 1970); see also Bertram Wyatt-Brown, "The Civil Rights Act of 1875," *Western Political Quarterly* 18(4) (December 1965): 763–75; and Ronald B. Jager, "Charles Sumner, the Constitution, and the Civil Rights Act of 1875," *New England*

Quarterly 42(3) (September 1969): 350–72. On Sumner's jurisprudence and advocacy for the future Civil Rights Act, see Charles Sumner, "Reply to Mr. Morrill," *The Works of Charles Sumner,* vol. 14 (Boston: Lee & Shepard, 1883); "Powers to Prohibit Inequality, Caste, and Oligarchy of the Skin," in *Charles Sumner: His Complete Works,* intro. George Frisbie Hoar (Boston: Lee & Shepard, 1900), 17:34–52; "The Question of Caste," 133–183; "Equal Before the Law Protected by National Statute" [Speeches in Senate on Supplementary Civil Rights Bill], in *Charles Sumner: His Complete Works,* 19:204–321; and "The Supplementary Civil-Rights Bill Again: Immediate Action Urged," in *Charles Sumner: His Complete Works,* 20:286–314. For Sumner's admiration of Granville Sharp, see Charles Sumner, "Position and Duties of the Merchant, Illustrated by the Life of Granville Sharp," in *The Works of Charles Sumner,* 3:481–519. On the Fourteenth Amendment, see William E. Nelson, *The Fourteenth Amendment: From Political Principle to Judicial Doctrine* (Cambridge: Harvard University Press, 1988).

2. *New York Times,* November 25, 1879, p. 8, col. 3.
3. *San Francisco Chronicle,* January 4, 1876, p. 4, col. 6; January 5, 1876, p. 4, col. 6.
4. *San Francisco Chronicle,* January 4, 1876, p. 3, col. 5; January 9, 1876, p. 5, col. 1.
5. *San Francisco Chronicle,* January 7, 1876, p. 1, col. 1; January 9, 1876, p. 4, col. 1.
6. *San Francisco Chronicle,* January 12, 1876, p. 4, col. 2; January 19, 1876, p. 3, col. 6.
7. *San Francisco Chronicle,* January 19, 1876, p. 3, col. 7.
8. *San Francisco Chronicle,* June 20, 1876, p. 1, col. 2.
9. *San Francisco Chronicle,* February 29, 1876, p. 2, col. 8.
10. *San Francisco Chronicle,* January 17, 1876, p. 3, col. 4.
11. Sumner, "Position and Duties of the Merchant."
12. Charles Sumner, "Speech of Hon. C. Sumner" ["The Crime Against Kansas"], *Congressional Globe,* Senate, 34th Cong., 1st Sess., May 19–20, 1856, 529–44, 543.
13. Charles Sumner, [Reply to Mr. Morrill], in *The Works of Charles Sumner,* 14:424; "Powers of Congress to Prohibit Inequality, Caste, and Oligarchy of the Skin," in *Charles Sumner: His Complete Works,* 17:37–38.
14. Sumner, [Reply to Mr. Morrill], in *Charles Sumner: His Complete Works,* 19:266–67.
15. David Donald, *Charles Sumner,* 586–87.
16. *New York Times,* October 18, 1883, p. 1, col. 7.
17. [Brotherhood of Liberty], *Justice and Jurisprudence,* 42, 13.
18. [Brotherhood of Liberty], *Justice and Jurisprudence,* 32, 30–31.
19. [Brotherhood of Liberty], *Justice and Jurisprudence,* 250, 237, 240, 342.
20. Birth record of Homere Patris Plessy, March 17, 1863, Orleans Parish Vital Records Office, The Louisiana State Archives, Baton Rouge, Louisiana; Certificate of Marriage of Homer Plessy and Louise Bordenave, July 14, 1888, Archdiocese Archives, Archdiocese of New Orleans, New Orleans, Louisiana.
21. For an important study of common carrier suits, see Kenneth Mack, "Law, Society, and the Making of the Jim Crow South: Travel and Segregation on Tennessee Railroads, 1875–1905," *Law and Social Inquiry* 24(377) (1999): 317–29.
22. *Hall v. DeCuir,* 95 U.S. 485 (1877), 503.
23. Kurlind, *Landmark Briefs,* 39, 41; Tourgée, "Brief for Homer A. Plessy," in Olsen, ed., *Thin Disguise,* 102–3, 90.

24. Henry Billings Brown, "Memoranda for Biographical Sketch," in Charles A. Kent, ed. *Memoir of Henry Billings Brown* (New York: Duffield & Co., 1915), 1–33, 1.

25. Tourgée, "Brief for Homer A. Plessy," 90; *Plessy v. Ferguson*, 163 U.S., 544, 552; *Plessy v. Ferguson*, 163 U.S. 557–559 (Harlan, J., dissenting).

26. Suggs, *Whispered Consolations*, 15.

27. William E. B. Du Bois, *The Souls of Black Folk*, in *Three Negro Classics*, with an intro. by John Hope Franklin (New York: Avon Books, 1965), 215.

PART FOUR: UPLIFT THE RACE, 1903–1970

Overcoming Jim Crow

1. William E. B. Du Bois, *The Souls of Black Folk*, in *Three Negro Classics*, with an intro. by John Hope Franklin (New York: Avon Books, 1965), 239.

CHAPTER 10: BLACK, WHITE, AND RED

1. The best and most innovative contemporary work on the Scottsboro case is James Goodman, *Stories of Scottsboro* (New York: Vintage, 1994). For an excellent albeit more straightforward account, see Dan T. Carter, *Scottsboro: A Tragedy of the American South* (Baton Rouge: Louisiana State University Press, 1969). Unless otherwise noted, my account is drawn from these two sources. For discussion contemporary to the case, see Arthur Garfield Hays, *Trial by Prejudice* (New York: Covici Friede Publishers, 1933). Much useful material can be found in Clarence Norris and Sybil D. Washington, *The Last of the Scottsboro Boys: An Autobiography* (New York: Putnam, 1979); and Kwando Mbiassi Kinshasa, *The Man from Scottsboro: Clarence Norris and the Infamous 1931 Alabama Rape Trial, in His Own Words* (Jefferson, N.C.: McFarland & Co., 1997). The "Famous Trials" online collection of documents compiled by Doug Linder, cited below, contains useful materials readily available. For a discussion of the symbolic foundations of lynching, see Orlando Patterson, "Feast of Blood: 'Race,' Religion, and Human Sacrifice in the Postbellum South," in *Rituals of Blood: Consequences of Slavery in Two American Centuries* (Washington, D.C.: Civitas/Counterpoint, 1998), 169–232. See also Trudier Harris, *Exorcising Blackness: Historical and Literary Lynching and Burning Rituals* (Bloomington: Indiana University Press, 1984). For three recent studies of the history of lynching, see W. Fitzhugh Brundage, *Lynching in the New South: Georgia and Virginia, 1880–1930* (Urbana: University of Illinois Press, 1993); Philip Dray, *At the Hands of Persons Unknown: The Lynching of Black America* (New York: Random House, 2002); and James H. Madison, *A Lynching in the Heartland: Race and Memory in America* (New York: Palgrave, 2001). See also Mark Curriden and Leroy Phillips, Jr., *Contempt of Court: The Turn-of-the-Century Lynching that Launched 100 Years of Federalism* (New York: Faber & Faber, 1999). For a historic discussion, see the work of Ida B. Wells-Barnett, e.g., *On Lynchings: Southern Horrors, A Red Record, Mob Rule in New Orleans* (New York: Arno Press and the New York Times, 1969). See also Paul Finkelman, ed., *Lynching, Racial Violence, and Law*, vol. 9 of *Race, Law, and American History 1700–1990: The African-American Experience* (New York: Garland, 1992).

2. Clarence Norris in Kinshasa, *The Man from Scottsboro*, 34.

3. For a discussion of the nature and function of honor in the pre–Civil War South, see Bertram Wyatt-Brown, *Southern Honor: Ethics and Behavior in the Old South* (Oxford: Oxford University Press, 1982).

4. Carter, *Scottsboro*, 18, 22.

5. Norris in Kinshasa, *Man from Scottsboro*, 24.

6. *Weems v. State*, 225 Ala. 524 (1932), 531; Carter, *Scottsboro*, 39–40; *Daily Worker*, April 10, 1931.

7. Quoted in Mark Naison, *Communists in Harlem During the Depression* (Urbana: University of Illinois Press, 1983), 47–49.

8. *New York Times*, March 28, 1933.

9. *New York Times*, March 31, 1933.

10. "Judge Horton's Warning to Potential Lynchers," available at www.law.umkc.edu/faculty/projects/FTrials/scottsboro/SB_tri33tml.html.

11. Carter, *Scottsboro*, 265; "Judge Horton's Decision Overturning Patterson's Conviction," available at www.law.umkc.edu/faculty/projects/FTrials/scottsboro/SB_tri33.tml.

12. Quoted in Carter, *Scottsboro*, 275.

13. *New York Times*, November 24, 1933.

14. *New York Times*, November 26, 1933.

15. Carter, *Scottsboro*, 275, 319; Goodman, *Stories of Scottsboro*, 243; *New York Times*, November 24, 1933; November 26, 1933.

16. *New York Times*, April 2, 1935.

CHAPTER 11: HEARTS AND MINDS

1. Scholarship about *Brown v. Board of Education* is vast. The place to begin is Richard Kluger, *Simple Justice: The History of* Brown v. Board of Education *and Black America's Struggle for Equality* (New York: Vintage, 1975). A useful collection of primary materials is Mark Whitman, ed., *Removing a Badge of Slavery: The Record of* Brown v. Board of Education (Princeton: Markus Weiner Publishers, 1993). On liberal social science and the *Brown* decision, see Daryl Michael Scott, *Contempt and Pity: Social Policy and the Image of the Damaged Black Psyche, 1880–1996* (Chapel Hill, N.C.: University of North Carolina Press, 1997). For Myrdal's study, see Gunnar Myrdal, *An American Dilemma: The Negro Problem and Modern Democracy*, 2 vols. (New Brunswick, N.J.: Transaction Publishers, 1996). For a critique, see Herbert Aptheker, *The Negro People in America: A Critique of Gunnar Myrdal's "An American Dilemma"* (New York: International Publishers, 1946); and Ralph Ellison, *"An American Dilemma: A Review,"* in John F. Callahan, ed., *The Collected Essays of Ralph Ellison* (New York: Modern Library, 1995), 328–40. On Clark, see also *American Psychologist* 57(1) (January 2002). On Justice Thurgood Marshall, see Howard Ball, *A Defiant Life: Thurgood Marshall and the Persistence of Racism in America* (New York: Crown, 1998); Michael D. Davis and Hunter R. Clark, *Thurgood Marshall: Warrior at the Bar, Rebel on the Bench* (New York: Birch Lane Press, 1992); Mark V. Tushnet, *Making Civil Rights Law: Thurgood*

Marshall and the Supreme Court, 1936–1961 (New York: Oxford University Press, 1994); Mark V. Tushnet, ed., *Thurgood Marshall: His Speeches, Writings, Arguments, Opinions, and Reminiscences* (Chicago: Lawrence Hill Books, 2001); and, notably, Juan Williams, *Thurgood Marshall: American Revolutionary* (New York: Times Books, 1998). On the case of Emmett Till, see Stephen J. Whitfield, *A Death in the Delta: The Story of Emmett Till* (Baltimore: Johns Hopkins University Press, 1988).

2. Kluger, *Simple Justice*, 710; Juan Williams, *Eyes on the Prize: America's Civil Rights Years, 1954–1965* (New York: Penguin, 1987), 38; Williams, *Thurgood Marshall*, 228; Kluger, *Simple Justice*, 708; Owen Fiss, *The Troubled Beginnings of the Modern State, 1888–1910* (New York: Macmillan, 1993), 395.

3. Personal communication, Charles Jones, April 20, 2004.

4. Kluger, *Simple Justice*, 132.

5. Kluger, *Simple Justice*, 133, 136.

6. Quoted in Geena Rae McNeil, *Groundwork: Charles Hamilton Houston and the Struggle for Civil Rights* (Philadelphia: University of Pennyslvania Press, 1983), 84.

7. Williams, *Eyes on the Prize*, 20.

8. On the culture-and-personality school, see Philip K. Bock, *Continuities in Psychological Anthropology: A Historical Introduction* (San Francisco: W. H. Freeman & Co., 1980), 60–61. For a critical analysis and historical contextualization of one of its leading exponents, see Christopher Shannon, "A World Made Safe for Differences: Ruth Benedict's *The Chrysanthemum and the Sword*," *American Quarterly* 47 (4) (December 1995): 659–80.

9. Franklin Delano Roosevelt, "Address by the President of the United States," in United States Department of Labor, *Conference on Children in a Democracy: Papers and Discussions at the Initial Session Held in Washington, D.C., April 26, 1939* (Children's Bureau Publication No. 265) (Washington, D.C.: Government Printing Office, 1939), 2–5, 2. For proceedings of the 1940 conference, see United States Department of Labor, *Proceedings of the White House Conference on Children in a Democracy, Washington, D.C., January 18–20, 1940* (Children's Bureau Publication No. 2660) (Washington, D.C.: Government Printing Office, 1940).

10. Roosevelt, "Address by the President of the United States," xviii.

11. Testimony of Kenneth Clark, in Whitman, ed., *Removing a Badge of Slavery*, 49–52; quoted in Kluger, *Simple Justice*, 142.

12. Kluger, *Simple Justice*, 332.

13. *Briggs v. Elliott*, 98 F. Supp. 529 (1951), 548 (Waring, J., dissenting).

14. Anthony Lewis, "Earl Warren," in *Justices of the United States Supreme Court, 1789–1978: Their Lives and Major Opinions*, eds. Leon Friedman and Fred L. Israel (New York: Chelsea House Publishers, 1980), 5:2721–2800, 2727.

15. Kluger, *Simple Justice*, 702, 704.

16. *Brown v. Board of Education*, 347 U.S. 483 (1954); Williams, *Thurgood Marshall*, 227.

17. Quoted in Williams, *Eyes on the Prize*, 39.

18. Martin Luther King, Jr., *Why We Can't Wait* (New York: Harper & Row, 1964), 6,19,83.

CHAPTER 12: TO DIE FOR THE PEOPLE

1. "Black Lawyers," in Philip S. Foner, ed., *The Black Panthers Speak* (New York: Da Capo Press, 1995), 15. For Huey Newton's writing and thought, see Huey P. Newton, *Revolutionary Suicide* (New York: Harcourt Brace Jovanovich, 1973); Toni Morrison, ed., *To Die for the People: The Writings of Huey P. Newton* (New York: Writers & Readers Publishing, 1999); and Erik H. Erikson and Huey P. Newton, *In Search of Common Ground* (New York: Norton, 1973). Foner's edited collection contains primary material from the Panthers, and Bobby Seale, *Seize the Time: The Story of the Black Panther Party and Huey P. Newton* (Baltimore: Black Classic Press, 1991 [1970]), provides an account of Newton and the Black Panther Party by its cofounder. Contemporary writings from black militants discussed here also include George Jackson, *Soledad Brother: The Prison Letters of George Jackson* (New York: Bantam Books, 1970); and Eldridge Cleaver, *Soul on Ice* (New York: Dell, 1992 [1968]). On the life of Huey Newton, see Hugh Pearson, *In the Shadow of the Panther: Huey Newton and the Price of Black Power in America* (Cambridge, Mass.: Perseus Publishing, 1996). For some of the arguments used in Newton's case, see Ann Fagan Ginger, ed., *Minimizing Racism in Jury Trials: The Voir Dire Conducted by Charles R. Garry in* People of California v. Huey P. Newton (Berkeley, Calif.: National Lawyers Guild, [c. 1969]). A scholarly account of black militant activism can be found in Clayborne Carson, *In Struggle: SNCC and the Black Awakening of the 1960s* (Cambridge: Harvard University Press, 1981). On the New York Panthers and issues of militant self-image, see Murray Kempton, *The Briar Patch: The Trial of the Panther 21* (New York: Da Capo Press, 1997). On Angela Davis, whose own legal battles were as important as Newton's for the history of black trials, see Angela Davis, *Angela Davis: An Autobiography* (New York: International Publishers, 1974, 1988); see also Bettina Aptheker, *The Morning Breaks: The Trial of Angela Davis*, 2nd ed. (Ithaca: Cornell University Press, 1997).
2. Newton, *Revolutionary Suicide*, 171.
3. Newton, *Revolutionary Suicide*, 173.
4. Newton, *Revolutionary Suicide*, 173–74.
5. Foner, ed., *Black Panthers Speak*, xxxii.
6. Newton, *Revolutionary Suicide*, 175.
7. Newton, *Revolutionary Suicide*, 176.
8. Newton, *Revolutionary Suicide*, 11–13.
9. Seale, *Seize the Time*, 13.
10. Newton, *Revolutionary Suicide*, 121; Foner, ed., *Black Panthers Speak*, 14.
11. Newton, *Revolutionary Suicide*, 172.
12. Foner, ed., *Black Panthers Speak*, 2–4
13. Newton, "To the Black Movement," in *To Die for the People*, 92.
14. Erikson and Newton, *In Search of Common Ground*, 25.
15. Newton, "He Won't Bleed Me: A Revolutionary Analysis of Sweet Sweetback's Baadasssss Song," in *To Die for the People*, 138.
16. For a general statement, see Newton, "Speech Delivered at Boston College, November 18, 1970," in *To Die for the People*, 20–38.

17. Newton, *Revolutionary Suicide*, 4.
18. Newton, *Revolutionary Suicide*, 5–7.
19. Newton, *Revolutionary Suicide*, ix.
20. Seale, *Seize the Time*, 205.
21. See Michal R. Belknap, ed., *American Political Trials* (Westport, Conn: Greenwood Press, 1994); Ron Christenson, *Political Trials: Gordian Knots in the Law* (New Brunswick, N.J.: Transaction Press, 1986); Ron Christenson, ed., *Political Trials in History: From Antiquity to the Present* (New Brunswick, N.J.: Transaction Press, 1991); and Otto Kirchheimer, *Political Justice: The Use of Legal Procedure for Political Ends* (Princeton: Princeton University Press, 1961).
22. Charles R. Garry, "Attacking Racism in Court Before Trial," in Ginger, ed., *Minimizing Racism in Jury Trials*, xv.
23. For the closing argument, see Charles R. Garry, "Closing Argument to the Jury," in Ginger, ed., *Minimizing Racism in Jury Trials*, 199–204.
24. Seale, *Seize the Time*, 244.
25. Newton, *Revolutionary Suicide*, 242–45.
26. Jackson, *Soledad Brother*, 215.
27. Jackson, *Soledad Brother*, 169–70, 8.
28. Newton, *Revolutionary Suicide*, 100–103.
29. Newton, *Revolutionary Suicide*, 254.
30. See Fay Stender, "Appellate Brief on Jury Selection," in Ginger, ed., *Minimizing Racism in Jury Trials*, 205–41.
31. Newton, "Resolutions and Declarations: December 5, 1970," in *To Die for the People*, 39, 43.
32. Newton, "Executive Mandate #2: June 29, 1967," in *To Die For the People*, 10; Pearson, *In the Shadow of the Panther*, 315.

PART FIVE: AFTER CASTE, 1991–2004

Passage

1. For these and other indications of black socioeconomic development, see Stephen Thernstrom and Abigail Thernstrom, *America in Black and White: One Nation, Indivisible* (New York: Simon & Schuster, 1997), 183–202.

CHAPTER 13: CONFIRMATION

1. A transcript of the Hill-Thomas hearings is found in Anita Miller, ed., *The Complete Transcripts of the Clarence Thomas–Anita Hill Hearings* (Chicago: Academy Chicago Publishers, 1994). Daily coverage and thoughtful analysis was published serially in the *New York Times*. The most thorough secondary treatment of the hearings and the life of Clarence Thomas is Jane Meyer and Jill Abramson, *Strange Justice: The Selling of Clarence Thomas* (Boston: Houghton Mifflin, 1994). For black contemporary commentary, see Robert Chrisman and Robert L. Allen, eds., *Court of Appeal: The Black Community Speaks out on the Racial and Sexual Poli-*

tics of Clarence Thomas vs. Anita Hill (New York: Ballantine, 1992). See also Toni Morrison, ed., *Race-ing Justice, En-gendering Power: Essays on Anita Hill, Clarence Thomas, and the Construction of Social Reality* (New York: Pantheon, 1992); and Geneva Smitherman, *African American Women Speak Out on Anita Hill–Clarence Thomas* (Detroit: Wayne State University Press, 1995). For academic analysis, see also Jane Flax, *The American Dream in Black and White: The Clarence Thomas Hearings* (Ithaca: Cornell University Press, 1998); and Sandra L. Ragan et al., eds., *The Language of Lynching: Gender, Politics, and Power in the Hill-Thomas Hearings* (Urbana: University of Illinois Press, 1996). On Justice Thomas's legal thought, see Scott Douglas Gerber, *First Principles: The Jurisprudence of Clarence Thomas* (New York: New York University Press, 1999). For works by other "black dissenters," see Stephen L. Carter, *Reflections of an Affirmative Action Baby* (New York: Basic Books, 1991); Shelby Steele, *A Dream Deferred: The Second Betrayal of Black Freedom in America* (New York: HarperCollins, 1998); and Thomas Sowell, *Preferential Policies: An International Perspective* (New York: Quill, 1990). For one criticism, see Ronald Suresh Roberts, *Clarence Thomas and the Tough Love Crowd: Counterfeit Heroes and Unhappy Truths* (New York: New York University Press, 1995). My own analysis is largely in agreement with that provided by Orlando Patterson in "Race, Gender, and Liberal Fallacies," in Chrisman and Allen, eds., *Court of Appeal*, 165–169.

2. Miller, ed., *Complete Transcripts*, 9.
3. Carter, *Reflections*, 154.
4. Thernstrom and Thernstrom, *America in Black and White*, 185, 191–92.
5. *New York Times*, September 16, 1987.
6. For Thomas's statement and excerpts from the following Senate session, see *New York Times*, September 11, 1991.
7. Anatole France, *Le Lys Rouge* (The Red Lily), trans. Winfred Stephens (New York: Dodd, Mead and Company, 1995), 191.
8. Juan Williams, "Black Conservatives," *Washington Post*, December 16, 1980. See Neil A. Lewis, "Thomas's Journey on Path of Self-Help," *New York Times*, July 7, 1991.
9. "Testimony of Anita F. Hill," in Miller, ed., *Complete Transcripts*, 24.
10. Patterson, "Race, Gender, and Liberal Fallacies," 163.
11. "Testimony of Anita F. Hill," 23, 35.
12. "Further Testimony of Hon. Clarence Thomas," in Miller, ed., *Complete Transcripts*, 117–18.
13. "Testimony of Nancy E. Fitch," in Miller, ed., *Complete Transcripts*, 336.
14. Melba Joyce Boyd, "Collard Greens, Clarence Thomas, and the High-Tech Rape of Anita Hill," in Chrisman and Allen, eds., *Court of Appeal*, 45, 43; Henry Vance David, "The High-Tech Lynching and the High-Tech Overseer: Thoughts from the Anita Hill/Clarence Thomas Affair," in *Court of Appeal*, 59; Barbara Ransby, "The Gang Rape of Anita Hill and the Assault Upon All Women of African Descent," *Court of Appeal*, 169–75; Llenda Jackson-Leslie, "Tom, Buck, and Sambo, or How Clarence Thomas Got to the Supreme Court," *Court of Appeal*, 106.

15. "Further Testimony of Hon. Clarence Thomas," in Miller, ed., *Complete Transcripts*, 206.

16. *Grutter v. Bollinger*, 123 S. Ct. 2325 (2003), 2350–2365 (Thomas, J., dissenting).

17. "Further Testimony of Hon. Clarence Thomas," 206, 213.

CHAPTER 14: STATISTICS AND CITIZENSHIP

1. Important writings by Mumia Abu-Jamal can be found in his *Death Blossoms: Reflections from a Prisoner of Conscience* (Farmington, Pa.: Plough Publishing House, 1997); *Faith of Our Fathers: An Examination of the Spiritual Life of African and African-American People* (Trenton, N.J.: African World Press, 2004); and *Live from Death Row* (New York: Avon Books, 1995, 1996). The transcript of Abu-Jamal's trial and records of his case are accessible in PDF format, made available by Abu-Jamal's opponents: www.justice4danielfaulkner.com. The most complete discussion of the case is Daniel R. Williams, *Executing Justice: An Inside Account of the Case of Mumia Abu-Jamal* (New York: St. Martin's, 2001). The analysis by Amnesty International can be found in Amnesty International, *The Case of Mumia Abu-Jamal: A Life in the Balance* (New York: Seven Stories Press, 2000). For a discussion of the case in the mid-1990s, see Stuart Taylor, Jr., "Guilty and Framed," *The American Lawyer* (December 1995), 75–84. Some writings by Abu-Jamal's supporters that indicate the confluence of social and political phenomena that factor into his case are collected in S. E. Anderson and Tony Medina, eds., *In Defense of Mumia* (New York: Writers & Readers Publishing, 1996). A short, highly sympathetic biography is Terry Bisson, *On a Move: The Story of Mumia Abu-Jamal* (Farmington, Penn.: Litmus Books, 2000). MOVE material is housed at Temple University, Urban Archives Collection, Paley Library. The book *25 Years on the MOVE* (Philadelphia: MOVE, 1996) clearly lays out the group's principles. Discussion of MOVE ideology can be found in J. M. Floyd-Thomas, "The Burning of Rebellious Thoughts: MOVE as Revolutionary Black Humanism," *Black Scholar* 32(1) (2002): 11–21; and Jeffrey Nelson and Gina Kaye Maddox, "A Rhetorical Study of the MOVE Diatribe in Contemporary America," *Pennsylvania Speech Communication Annual* 52 (1996): 59–72. An examination of the tragic confrontation with Philadelphia authorities, which also discusses aspects of the group itself, is John Anderson and Hilary Hevenor, *Burning Down the House: MOVE and the Tragedy of Philadelphia* (New York: Norton, 1987); a further discussion can be found in Hizkias Assefa and Paul Wahrhaftig, *Extremist Groups and Conflict Resolution: The MOVE Crisis in Philadelphia* (New York: Praeger, 1988). A helpful overview of race and the criminal justice system, with extensive bibliographic references, is Samuel Walker et al., eds., *The Color of Justice: Race, Ethnicity, and Crime in America*, 2nd ed. (Belmont, Calif.: Wadsworth/Thomson Learning, 2000). And see generally Randall Kennedy, *Race, Crime, and the Law* (New York: Pantheon, 1997). On the sentencing guideline movement, see Kate Stith and Jose Cabranes, *Fear of Judging: Sentencing Guidelines in the Federal Courts* (Chicago: University of Chicago Press, 1998). On disparities in incarceration rates, see David Cole, *No Equal Justice: Race and Crime in the American Criminal*

Justice System (New York: New Press, 1999); Marc Mauer, *Race to Incarcerate: The Sentencing Project* (New York: New Press, 1999); and Michael Tonry, *Malign Neglect—Race, Crime, and Punishment in America* (New York: Oxford University Press, 1995). On some of the unexpected consequences of contemporary policy, see Marc Mauer and Meda Chesney-Lind, eds., *Invisible Punishment: The Collateral Consequences of Mass Imprisonment* (New York: New Press, 2002), especially Donald Braman, "Families and Incarceration," 117–35. The distressing statistics on race and imprisonment can be readily accessed through the Web page of the Bureau of Justice Statistics of the U.S. Department of Justice: www.ojp.usdoj.gov/bjs.

2. Cornel West, "Foreword," in Mumia Abu-Jamal, *Death Blossoms*, xii.

3. "MOVE: Belief & Practice," in *25 Years on the MOVE*, 68.

4. "Move: Belief & Practice," 68. MOVE describes the *Guidelines* as "the *most powerful statement in existence*, as the clarity, the analytical ability of the author is unequaled, unparalleled in any of the writings of man, past or present." See "MOVE is a Philadelphia based organization founded by John Africa," undated letter (41 typewritten pages), Urban Archives, Temple University, 1.

5. See Abu-Jamal, "Deadly Déjà Vu," in *Live from Death Row*, 118–120.

6. Abu-Jamal, "Philly Daze: An Impressionistic Memoir," in *Live from Death Row*, 152.

7. Abu-Jamal, "Philly Daze," 151.

8. Abu-Jamal, "Philly Daze," 153.

9. Abu-Jamal, "Philly Daze," 152–153.

10. Quoted in Taylor, "Guilty and Framed," 176.

11. Abu-Jamal, "Philly Daze," 163–165.

12. Buzz Bissinger, "The Famous and the Dead," *Vanity Fair* (August 1999), 66–78.

13. *Pennsylvania v. Mumia Abu-Jamal* (Court of Common Pleas, First Judicial District of Pennsylvania), June 17, 1982, 1.44.

14. *Pennsylvania v. Mumia Abu-Jamal*, "Sentencing Hearing," July 3, 1982, 10; see also June 17, 1982, 1.50–1.60.

15. *Pennsylvania v. Mumia Abu-Jamal*, June 17, 1982, 1.73–1.75.

16. Cynthia White, *Pennsylvania v. Mumia Abu-Jamal*, June 22, 1982, 165–166; June 21, 1982, 92–94.

17. Joseph McGill, Summation to Jury, *Pennsylvania v. Mumia Abu-Jamal*, July 3, 1982, 62–64.

18. Mumia Abu-Jamal, Statement to Jury, *Pennyslvania v. Mumia Abu-Jamal*, July 3, 1982, 10–16.

19. The single exception to this trend is the period from 1972–73, when the number of death row inmates dropped from 334 to 134.

20. See Tonry, *Malign Neglect*, passim.

21. Abu-Jamal, "Preface," in *Live from Death Row*, xv; Abu-Jamal, "Human Waste Camps," in *Live from Death Row*, 73; *Commonwealth v. Abu-Jamal*, 553 Pa. 485, 720 A.2d 79 (Pa. 1998), 90.

22. *Abu-Jamal v. Horn*, No. 99-5089, U.S. Dist. Ct. (E.D. Pa.) (2001) (Yohn, J.).

23. Abu-Jamal, "Teetering on the Brink between Life and Death," in *Live From Death Row*, 10–11.

Index

A NOTE ABOUT THE AUTHOR

Mark S. Weiner was born and raised in Los Angeles. After graduating from Stanford University, he received a Ph.D. in American Studies and a law degree from Yale. He now teaches constitutional law, legal history, and legal ethics at Rutgers School of Law in Newark, New Jersey.

A NOTE ON THE TYPE

This book was set in Janson, a typeface long thought to have been made by the Dutchman Anton Janson, who was a practicing type-founder in Leipzig during the years 1668–1687. However, it has been conclusively demonstrated that these types are actually the work of Nicholas Kis (1650–1702), a Hungarian, who most probably learned his trade from the Dutch typefounder Dirk Voskens. The type is an excellent example of the influential and sturdy Dutch types that prevailed in England up to the time William Caslon (1692–1766) developed his own incomparable designs from them.

Composed by NK Graphics,
Keene, New Hampshire

Printed and bound by Berryville Graphics,
Berryville, Virginia

Designed by Soonyoung Kwon